CULTURE

MATTERS

CULTURE
MATTERS

How Values Shape
Human Progress

LAWRENCE E. HARRISON
SAMUEL P. HUNTINGTON

Editors

BASIC
BOOKS

A Member of the Perseus Books Group

Carolina Guerrero / 2003

Published by Basic Books,
A Member of the Perseus Books Group

Library of Congress Cataloging-in-Publication Data
Culture matters : how values shape human progress / Lawrence E. Harrison and
Samuel P. Huntington, editors.
    p. cm.
  Includes bibliographical references and index.
  ISBN 0-465-03175-7 (cloth)
  ISBN 0-465-03176-5 (paper)
1. Social values.   2. Culture.   I. Harrison, Lawrence E.   II. Huntington, Samuel P.

HM681.C85   2000
306—dc21
                                                                          00-0229

Designed by Jeff Williams

MV   02 03 04 05   13 12 11 10 9 8 7 6 5

In memory of Edward Banfield,
who illuminated the path for so many of us

CONTENTS

TABLE AND
ILLUSTRATIONS

ACKNOWLEDGMENTS

This book appears under the sponsorship of Harvard University's Academy for International and Area Studies, which organized the symposium on which it is based. The project has also benefited from the support of Harvard's Weatherhead Center for International Affairs and its director, Jorge Domínguez.

We wish to express our gratitude to the Monitor Company, the Carthage Foundation, the John Templeton Foundation, the Sidney A. Swensrud Foundation, John Tanton of the U.S., Inc., Foundation, Richard Wittrup, and Max Thelen for the financial support that made the project possible.

We are particularly indebted to Michael Fairbanks of the Monitor Company's Country Competitiveness Practice, with whom we worked from the outset on the design of the symposium that led to this book. That the symposium ran so smoothly was largely the result of Beth Hastie's dedication, energy, and efficiency. We are also grateful to Patrick McVay for his help with the financial management aspects of the symposium, and to Carol Edwards and Thomas Murphy for their administrative assistance.

We wish to thank the moderators of the symposium's eight panels: Jorge Domínguez, Christopher DeMuth, Harriet Babbitt, Howard Gardner, Roderick MacFarquhar, Phyliss Pomerantz, Richard Lamm, and Robert Klitgaard, all of whom not only added to the richness of the symposium but also succeeded in keeping it on schedule. We also wish to thank Stephen Thernstrom for his participation on the shortest possible notice.

We are particularly indebted to our editor at Basic Books, Tim Bartlett, for his unflagging interest and support, and his wise counsel. The book has been the beneficiary of the skillful and sure hand of copy editors Donald Halstead and Chrisona Schmidt.

Finally, Lawrence Harrison wishes to acknowledge the encouragement and help he received at the outset from William Ratliff of the Hoover Institution.

Lawrence E. Harrison
Samuel P. Huntington

foreword

CULTURES COUNT

SAMUEL P. HUNTINGTON

In the early 1990s, I happened to come across economic data on Ghana and South Korea in the early 1960s, and I was astonished to see how similar their economies were then. These two countries had roughly comparable levels of per capita GNP; similar divisions of their economy among primary products, manufacturing, and services; and overwhelmingly primary product exports, with South Korea producing a few manufactured goods. Also, they were receiving comparable levels of economic aid. Thirty years later, South Korea had become an industrial giant with the fourteenth largest economy in the world, multinational corporations, major exports of automobiles, electronic equipment, and other sophisticated manufactures, and a per capita income approximating that of Greece. Moreover, it was on its way to the consolidation of democratic institutions. No such changes had occurred in Ghana, whose per capita GNP was now about one-fifteenth that of South Korea's. How could this extraordinary difference in development be explained? Undoubtedly, many factors played a role, but it seemed to me that culture had to be a large part of the explanation. South Koreans valued thrift, investment, hard work, education, organization, and discipline. Ghanaians had different values. In short, cultures count.

Other scholars were arriving at the same conclusions in the early 1990s. This development was part of a major renewal of interest in culture among social scientists. In the 1940s and 1950s, much attention was paid to culture as a crucial element in understanding societies, analyzing differences among them, and explaining their economic and political development. Among the scholars involved were Margaret Mead, Ruth Benedict, David McClelland, Edward Banfield, Alex Inkeles, Gabriel Almond, Sidney Verba, Lucian Pye, and Seymour Martin Lipset. In the wake of the rich literature these scholars produced, work on culture in the academic community declined dramatically in the 1960s and 1970s. Then, in the 1980s, interest in culture as an explanatory variable began to revive. The most prominent and most controversial early contribution to this revival was written by a former USAID official, Lawrence Harrison, and was published by the Harvard Center for International Affairs in 1985. Entitled *Underdevelopment Is a State of Mind—The Latin American Case,* Harrison's book used parallel case studies to demonstrate that in most Latin American countries, culture had been a primary obstacle to development. Harrison's analysis generated a storm of protest from economists, experts on Latin America, and intellectuals in Latin America. In the following years, however, people in all these groups began to see elements of validity in his argument.

Increasingly social scientists turned to cultural factors to explain modernization, political democratization, military strategy, the behavior of ethnic groups, and the alignments and antagonisms among countries. Most of the scholars represented in this book played major roles in the renaissance of culture. Their success was signaled by the emergence of a countermovement that pooh-poohed cultural interpretations, symbolically and visibly manifested in a highly skeptical December 1996 critique in the *Economist* of recent works by Francis Fukuyama, Lawrence Harrison, Robert Kaplan, Seymour Martin Lipset, Robert Putnam, Thomas Sowell, and myself. In the scholarly world, the battle has thus been joined by those who see culture as a major, but not the only, influence on social, political, and economic behavior and those who adhere to universal explanations, such as devotees of material self-interest among economists, of "rational choice" among political scientists, and of neorealism among scholars of international relations. Indeed, the reader will find some of these views expressed in this book, which by design includes dissent from the thesis captured in the title.

Perhaps the wisest words on the place of culture in human affairs are those of Daniel Patrick Moynihan: "The central conservative truth is that it is culture, not politics, that determines the success of a society. The central liberal truth is that politics can change a culture and save it from itself." To explore the truth of Moynihan's two truths, the Harvard Academy for International and Area Studies organized, under the direction of Lawrence Harrison, the project of which this book is the principal but not the only product. To what extent do cultural factors shape economic and political development? If they do, how can cultural obstacles to economic and political development be removed or changed so as to facilitate progress?

To wrestle with these questions effectively, it is first necessary to define our terms. By the term "human progress" in the subtitle of this book we mean movement toward economic development and material well-being, social-economic equity, and political democracy. The term "culture," of course, has had multiple meanings in different disciplines and different contexts. It is often used to refer to the intellectual, musical, artistic, and literary products of a society, its "high culture." Anthropologists, perhaps most notably Clifford Geertz, have emphasized culture as "thick description" and used it to refer to the entire way of life of a society: its values, practices, symbols, institutions, and human relationships. In this book, however, we are interested in how culture affects societal development; if culture includes everything, it explains nothing. Hence we define culture in purely subjective terms as the values, attitudes, beliefs, orientations, and underlying assumptions prevalent among people in a society.

This book explores how culture in this subjective sense affects the extent to which and the ways in which societies achieve or fail to achieve progress in economic development and political democratization. Most of the papers thus focus on culture as an independent or explanatory variable. If cultural factors do affect human progress and at times obstruct it, however, we are also interested in culture as a dependent variable, that is, Moynihan's second truth: How can political or other action change or remove cultural obstacles to progress? Economic development, we know, changes cultures, but that truth does not help us if our goal is to remove cultural obstacles to economic development. Societies also may change their culture in response to major trauma. Their disastrous experiences in World War II changed Germany and Japan from the two most militaristic countries in the world to two of the most pacifist. Similarly, Mariano Grondona has suggested that Argentina was making progress toward economic reform, economic stability, and political democracy in the mid-1990s in part as a result of its disastrous experiences with a brutal military dictatorship, military defeat, and super-hyperinflation.

The key issue thus is whether political leadership can substitute for disaster in stimulating cultural change. That political leadership can accomplish this in some circumstances is exemplified in Singapore. As the chapter by Seymour Martin Lipset and Gabriel Salman Lenz in this book emphasizes, levels of corruption among countries tend to vary along cultural lines. Among the most corrupt are Indonesia, Russia, and several Latin American and African societies. Corruption is lowest in the Protestant societies of northern Europe and of British settlement. Confucian countries fall mostly in the middle. Yet one Confucian society—Singapore—ranks with Denmark, Sweden, Finland, and New Zealand as one of the least corrupt countries in the world. The explanation of this anomaly is clearly Lee Kwan Yew, who was determined to make Singapore as uncorrupt as possible and succeeded. Here "politics did change a culture and save it from itself." The issue, however, is how uncorrupt Singapore will remain after Lee Kwan Yew is no longer there. Can politics "save" a society from itself permanently? How political and social action can make cultures more favorable to progress is the central question that we hope to explore in follow-up studies.

The Cultural Values and Human Progress project and this book are overwhelmingly the product of the ideas, energy, and commitment of Lawrence Harrison. He conceived the project, identified the topics to be covered, recruited the panelists, edited their products, and raised the funds that made it all possible. The Harvard Academy for International and Area Studies was delighted to join in and sponsor this effort because it relates directly to the interests of the Academy. Since its start in 1986, the Academy has provided substantial two-year fellowships to young social scientists who combine excellence in their discipline with expertise in the language, culture, sociology, institutions, and politics of a major non-Western country or region. Alumni of the Academy now teach in leading universities and colleges throughout the country. The work of the Academy is supervised by a committee of senior Harvard scholars who are first-rank experts in particular foreign areas. Three years ago, the Academy undertook to build upon the this foreign area expertise and to expand its work from the study of individual societies and cultures to include the study of the similarities, the differences, and the interaction among the world's principal cultures and civilizations. A conference in 1997 explored the perspectives of the elites of the major countries and regions on trends in world politics and the characteristics of a desirable world order. This book is a second, comparable study of how different cultures affect economic and political development.

In a 1992 study of the relationship between culture and development, Robert Klitgaard posed the question: "If culture is important and people have studied culture for a century or more, why don't we have well-developed theories, practical guidelines, close professional links between those who study culture and those who make and manage development policy?" The central purpose of this book and the further work we hope to undertake is to develop the theories, elaborate the guidelines, and foster the links between scholars and practitioners that will foster the cultural conditions that enhance human progress.

introduction

WHY CULTURE
MATTERS

LAWRENCE E. HARRISON

It is now almost half a century since the world turned its attention from rebuilding the countries devastated by World War II to ending the poverty, ignorance, and injustice in which most of the people of Africa, Asia, and Latin America lived. Optimism abounded in the wake of the stunning success of the Marshall Plan in Western Europe and Japan's ascent from the ashes of defeat. Development was viewed as inevitable, particularly as the colonial yoke disappeared. Walt Rostow's highly influential 1960 book, *The Stages of Economic Growth*, suggested that human progress was driven by a dialectic that could be accelerated.

And indeed the colonial yoke did substantially disappear. The Philippines became independent in 1946, India and Pakistan in 1947. The British and French post-Ottoman mandates in the Middle East vanished soon after the war. The decolonization process in Southeast Asia, Africa, and the Caribbean was substantially completed by the end of the 1960s.

The Alliance for Progress, John F. Kennedy's answer to the Cuban Revolution, captured the prevailing optimism. It would duplicate the Marshall Plan's success. Latin America would be well on its way to irreversible prosperity and democracy within ten years.

But as we enter a new century, optimism has been displaced by frustration and pessimism. A few countries—Spain, Portugal, South Korea, Taiwan, and

Singapore, as well as former British colony Hong Kong—have followed Rostow's trajectory into the First World. But the vast majority of countries still lag far behind, and conditions for many people in these countries are not materially improved over what they were a half century ago. Of the roughly 6 billion people who inhabit the world today, fewer than 1 billion are found in the advanced democracies. More than 4 billion live in what the World Bank classifies as "low income" or "lower middle income" countries.

The quality of life in those countries is dismaying, particularly after a half century of development assistance:[1]

- Half or more of the adult population of twenty-three countries, mostly in Africa, are illiterate. Non-African countries include Afghanistan, Bangladesh, Nepal, Pakistan, and even one in the Western Hemisphere—Haiti.

- Half or more of women are illiterate in thirty-five countries, including those just listed and Algeria, Egypt, Guatemala, India, Laos, Morocco, Nigeria, and Saudi Arabia.

- Life expectancy is below sixty years in forty-five countries, most in Africa but also Afghanistan, Cambodia, Haiti, Laos, and Papua New Guinea. Life expectancy is less than fifty years in eighteen countries, all in Africa. And life expectancy in Sierra Leone is just thirty-seven years.

- Children under five die at rates in excess of 100 per 1,000 in at least thirty-five countries, most again in Africa. Non-African countries include Bangladesh, Bolivia, Haiti, Laos, Nepal, Pakistan, and Yemen.

- The population growth rate in the poorest countries is 2.1 percent annually, three times the rate in the high-income countries. The population growth rate in some Islamic countries is astonishingly high: 5 percent in Oman, 4.9 percent in the United Arab Emirates, 4.8 percent in Jordan, 3.4 percent in Saudi Arabia and Turkmenistan.

The most inequitable income distribution patterns among countries supplying such data to the World Bank (not all countries do) are found in the poorer countries, particularly in Latin America and Africa. The most affluent 10 percent of Brazil's population accounts for almost 48 percent of income; Kenya, South Africa, and Zimbabwe are only a fraction of a point behind.

The top 10 percent in Chile, Colombia, Guatemala, and Paraguay claims about 46 percent of income; in Guinea-Bissau, Senegal, and Sierra Leone about 43 percent. For purposes of comparison, the top 10 percent in the United States, where income distribution is among the most inequitable of the advanced democracies, accounts for 28.5 percent of the total.

Democratic institutions are commonly weak or nonexistent in Africa and the Islamic countries of the Middle East and the rest of Asia. Democracy has prospered in Latin America in the past fifteen years, but the democratic experiments are fragile, as recent events in Peru, Paraguay, Ecuador, Venezuela, Colombia, and Mexico underscore. And there remains a weighty question: Why after more than 150 years of independence has Latin America, an extension of the West, failed to consolidate democratic institutions?

In sum, the world at the end of the twentieth century is far poorer, far more unjust, and far more authoritarian than most people at mid-century expected it would be.

Poverty also lingers in the United States, decades after the heady years of the Great Society and the War on Poverty. Hispanics, with 30 percent below the poverty line, have displaced blacks as the poorest large minority, and on some Indian reservations the unemployment rate is above 70 percent. Impressive progress has been recorded for blacks, and particularly black women, but 27 percent of blacks still live below the poverty line—at a time when the U.S. economy has experienced almost a decade of sustained growth and low unemployment.

The optimism of those who fought the war on poverty at home and abroad has been replaced by fatigue and even pessimism.

EXPLAINING THE FAILURE:
COLONIALISM, DEPENDENCY, RACISM

As it became apparent that the problems of underdevelopment were more intractable than the development experts had predicted, two explanations with Marxist-Leninist roots came to dominate the universities and politics of the poor countries and the universities of the rich countries: colonialism and dependency. Lenin had identified imperialism as a late and inevitable stage of capitalism that reflected what he viewed as the inability of increasingly monopolistic capitalist countries to find domestic markets for their products and capital.

For those former colonies, possessions, or mandate countries that had recently gained independence from Britain and France, by far the most prominent colonial powers, but also from the Netherlands, Portugal, the United States, and Japan, imperialism was a reality that left a profound imprint on the national psyche and presented a ready explanation for underdevelopment. This was above all true in Africa, where national boundaries had often been arbitrarily drawn without reference to homogeneity of culture or tribal coherence.

For those countries in what would come to be called the "Third World" that had been independent for a century or more, as in Latin America, imperialism took the shape of "dependency"—the theory that the poor countries of "the periphery" were bilked by the rich capitalist countries of "the center," who depressed world market prices of basic commodities and inflated the prices of manufactured goods, and whose multinational corporations earned excessive profits at the expense of the poor countries.

Neither colonialism nor dependency has much credibility today. For many, including some Africans, the statute of limitations on colonialism as an explanation for underdevelopment lapsed long ago. Moreover, four former colonies, two British (Hong Kong and Singapore) and two Japanese (South Korea and Taiwan), have vaulted into the First World. Dependency is rarely mentioned today, not even in American universities where it was, not many years ago, a conventional wisdom that brooked no dissent. There are several reasons, among others, the collapse of communism in Eastern Europe; the transformation of communism in China into conventional, increasingly free-market authoritarianism; the collapse of the Cuban economy after Russia halted massive Soviet subventions; the success of the East Asian "dragons" in the world market; the decisive defeat of the Sandinistas in the 1990 Nicaraguan elections; Mexico's initiative to join Canada and the United States in NAFTA. (For an apt discussion of dependency theory, see David Landes's chapter in this volume.)

And so an explanatory vacuum has emerged in the last decade of the century. Over the years, the development assistance institutions have promoted an assortment of solutions, including land reform, community development, planning, focus on the poorest, basic human needs, appropriate technology, women in development, privatization, decentralization, and now "sustainable development." One 1970s innovation, by the way, introduced anthropologists in development institutions to adapt projects to existing cultural realities. All of these initiatives, not to mention the emphasis on free market economics and political pluralism, have been useful, in varying degrees. But individually and cumulatively, they have failed to produce widespread rapid growth, democracy, and social justice in the Third World.

At mid-century, underachievement by black Americans was easy to understand. It was an obvious consequence of the denial of opportunity—in education, in the workplace, in the polling booth—to the minority that had never been invited into the melting pot, the minority for whom the Bill of Rights really didn't apply. In many respects, a racial revolution has occurred in the past fifty years, not only in terms of breaking down barriers to opportunity but also in sweeping changes in attitudes about race on the part of whites. The revolution has brought a mass movement of blacks into the middle class, the substantial closing of the black-white education gap, major black inroads in politics, and increasingly frequent intermarriage. But a racial gap remains in advanced education, income, and wealth, and, with 27 percent of blacks below the poverty line and a majority of black children being born to single mothers, the problems of the ghetto are still very much with us.

The racism/discrimination explanation of black underachievement is no longer viable fifty years later, although some racism and discrimination continue to exist. This conclusion is underscored by Hispanic underachievement, which is now a greater problem. Thirty percent of Hispanics are below the poverty line, and the Hispanic high school dropout rate is also about 30 percent, more than twice the black dropout rate. Hispanic immigrants have been discriminated against, but surely less than blacks and probably no more so than Chinese and Japanese immigrants, whose education, income, and wealth substantially exceed national averages. We note in passing the significantly higher poverty rate—almost 50 percent—and high school dropout rate—about 70 percent—in Latin America.[2]

THE CULTURAL PARADIGM:
THE HARVARD ACADEMY SYMPOSIUM

If colonialism and dependency are unsatisfactory explanations for poverty and authoritarianism overseas (and racism and discrimination are unsatisfactory explanations for minority underachievement at home), and if there are too many exceptions (e.g., tropical Singapore, Hong Kong, Barbados, and Costa Rica; see discussion below) to geographic/climatological explanations, how else can the unsatisfactory progress of humankind toward prosperity and political pluralism during the past half century be explained?

A growing number of scholars, journalists, politicians, and development practitioners are focusing on the role of cultural values and attitudes as facilitators of, or obstacles to, progress. They are the intellectual heirs of Alexis de Tocqueville, who concluded that what made the American political system work was a culture congenial to democracy; Max Weber, who explained the rise of capitalism as essentially a cultural phenomenon rooted in religion; and Edward Banfield, who illuminated the cultural roots of poverty and authoritarianism in southern Italy, a case with universal applications.

Cultural studies and emphasis on culture in the social sciences were in the mainstream in the 1940s and 1950s. Interest then dropped off. But a renaissance in cultural studies has taken place during the past fifteen years that is moving toward the articulation of a new culture-centered paradigm of development, of human progress.

In the summer of 1998, the Harvard Academy for International and Area Studies decided to explore the link between culture and political, economic, and social development, chiefly with respect to poor countries but also mindful of the problems of underachieving minorities in the United States. We were fortunate enough to interest a very large proportion of the scholars who are responsible for the renaissance in cultural studies as well as others of contrasting views. The symposium, Cultural Values and Human Progress, took place at the American Academy of Arts and Sciences in Cambridge, Massachusetts, 23–25 April 1999, with the participation of a distinguished audience.

SYMPOSIUM STRUCTURE AND PARTICIPANTS

The symposium was structured in eight panels, four on each of the first two days, followed by a half-day wrap-up.

The first panel, moderated by Jorge Domínguez of Harvard, addressed the relationship between political development and culture. Ronald Inglehart, who coordinates the World Values Survey, argued that there is a powerful link between cultural values and the political—and economic—performance of nations. Francis Fukuyama discussed the key role that social capital plays in promoting democratic institutions. And Seymour Martin Lipset traced the connection between culture and corruption.

Christopher DeMuth, president of the American Enterprise Institute, moderated the first of two panels on culture and economic development. David Landes elaborated on his conclusion in *The Wealth and Poverty of Nations* that "culture makes all the difference."[3] Michael Porter acknowledged that culture influences economic development and competitiveness but stressed that globalization includes cultural transmission that will tend to homogenize culture and make it easier for countries to overcome cultural and geographic disadvantages. Jeffrey Sachs argued that culture is an insignificant factor by comparison with geography and climate.

In the second panel on culture and economic development, moderated by deputy administrator of the U.S. Agency for International Development Harriet Babbitt, Mariano Grondona presented his typology of development-prone and development-resistant cultures, which derives chiefly from his appreciation of how the resistant factors have impeded Argentina's progress. Carlos Alberto Montaner explained how that same Latin American culture influences the behavior of elite groups to the detriment of the broader society. And Daniel Etounga-Manguelle discussed the cultural obstacles to Africa's development and competitiveness.

The last panel on the first day, moderated by Howard Gardner of Harvard, brought together three anthropologists: one (Robert Edgerton) who believes that some cultures do better for people than others; one (Richard Shweder) who identifies himself as a cultural pluralist, tolerant and respectful of all cultures; and one (Thomas Weisner) who focuses on the transmission of culture, particularly in childhood.

Harvard's Roderick MacFarquhar moderated the panel on the Asian crisis, which included economist Dwight Perkins, political scientist Lucian Pye, and sinologist Tu Wei-ming. There were some parallels in the presentations of Perkins and Pye, both emphasizing the need for change from the traditionally particularistic personal relationships that have dominated the East Asian economies, and the prominent role of government leadership in the private sector. Tu contrasted the Western and Confucian approaches to development.

Barbara Crossette of the *New York Times* opened the panel on gender and culture, moderated by the World Bank's Phyliss Pomerantz, by addressing the conflict between cultural relativism and the U.N. Declaration on Human Rights. Her conclusions were in sharp contrast with those of Richard Shweder. Mala Htun discussed changes in gender relationships in Latin America and the cultural and other obstacles to their effectuation. Rubie Watson spoke of the cultural forces that shape the subordinated condition of women in China. In passing, we express regret that she chose not to have her presentation included in this volume.

Former Colorado governor Richard Lamm moderated the panel on culture and American minorities. It was opened by Orlando Patterson, who, in stressing the link between culture and the problems of minorities, analyzed the impact of slavery and Jim Crow on the institution of marriage and related those experiences to the high incidence of single black mothers today. Richard Estrada was unable to attend the symposium because of a last-minute health problem.* Stephen Thernstrom of Harvard substituted for him with a presentation on population trends. Nathan Glazer addressed, among other issues, the political and emotional problems evoked by cultural analyses of the varying performance of ethnic groups.

The final panel, moderated by the RAND Corporation's Robert Klitgaard, was dedicated to a description of some of the initiatives already under way to promote positive values and attitudes. I referred to the growing literature that links underdevelopment to culture, much of it by Third World authors,

---

*We were saddened to learn that Richard Estrada died on 29 October 1999 at age forty-nine.

and also described several homegrown initiatives in Latin America whose objective is cultural change. Stace Lindsay and Michael Fairbanks described the approach of the Monitor Company, a consulting company located in Cambridge, Massachusetts, to "changing the mind of a nation."

Each panel was followed by a lively discussion that culminated in a debate in the closing session of the pros and cons of promoting cultural change. No consensus was reached, nor was one expected, given the controversial nature of the culture issue and the diverse orientations of the participants. But most of the panelists believe that cultural values and attitudes are an important and neglected factor in human progress. Moreover, even among the skeptics, there was recognition of the need for improved understanding of several questions that are discussed at the end of this introduction.

MAJOR ISSUES

The presentations and discussions gravitated around five major issues, which I address in this section and on which I offer my own views:

- the link between values and progress
- the universality of values and Western "cultural imperialism"
- geography and culture
- the relationship between culture and institutions
- cultural change

The Link Between Values and Progress

Skepticism about the link between cultural values and human progress is found particularly in two disciplines: economics and anthropology. For many economists, it is axiomatic that appropriate economic policy effectively implemented will produce the same results without reference to culture. The problem here is the case of multicultural countries in which some ethnic groups do better than others, although all operate with the same economic signals. Examples are the Chinese minorities in Thailand, Malaysia, Indonesia, the Philippines, and the United States; the Japanese minorities in Brazil and the United States; the Basques in Spain and Latin America;[4] and the Jews wherever they have migrated.

Federal Reserve Board chairman Alan Greenspan was among the economic traditionalists on this issue—until he pondered the post-Soviet experience of Russia. He started with the assumption that humans are natural capitalists and that communism's collapse "would automatically establish a free-market entrepreneurial system." He assumed that capitalism was "human nature." But he has concluded, in the wake of the Russian economic disaster, that it was "not nature at all, but culture."[5]

Greenspan's words constitute a powerful endorsement for David Landes's analysis and conclusions in *The Wealth and Poverty of Nations*, not to mention the long chain of insight into the importance of culture and its link to progress going back at least to Tocqueville. But the fact remains that most economists are uncomfortable dealing with culture, particularly since it presents definitional problems, is difficult to quantify, and operates in a highly complex context with psychological, institutional, political, geographic, and other factors.

It is with these problems in mind that I invite the reader's attention to Mariano Grondona's chapter in this book. It presents a typology of development-prone and development-resistant cultures. Although Grondona evolved his typology with Argentina and Latin America principally in mind, I believe that its relevance is far broader. Carlos Alberto Montaner's chapter is comparably important: it explains how a development-resistant culture shapes the behavior of elite groups.

The chief problem for many anthropologists, and other social scientists influenced by them, is the tradition of cultural relativism that has dominated the discipline in this century and rejects the evaluation of another society's values and practices.

This is one of the factors in play in Nathan Glazer's highly qualified, reluctant approach to the role of culture in explaining the wide range of achievement among ethnic groups in the United States (Chapter 16). Among the most compelling arguments for confronting culture is that of Glazer's panel colleague Orlando Patterson, for whom culture is a central factor in explaining the problems of Afro-Americans (Chapter 15).

The very title of this book may pose problems for those who are loath to make value judgments about other cultures. Many believe that culture is, by definition, harmonious and adaptive and that conflict and suffering are the consequence of external intrusions. Yet some anthropologists see culture very differently, prominently among them panelist Robert Edgerton, who says, with particular relevance to the symposium

> Humans in various societies, whether urban or folk, are capable of empathy, kindness, even love, and they can sometimes achieve astounding mastery of the challenges posed by their environments. But they are also capable of maintaining beliefs, values, and social institutions that result in senseless cruelty, needless suffering, and monumental folly in their relations among themselves as well as with other societies and the physical environment in which they live.[6]

The Universality of Values and Western "Cultural Imperialism"

The idea of "progress" is suspect for those who are committed to cultural relativism, for whom each culture defines its own goals and ethics, which cannot be evaluated against the goals and ethics of another culture. Some anthropologists view progress as an idea the West is trying to impose on other cultures. At the extreme, cultural relativists and cultural pluralists may argue that Westerners have no right to criticize institutions such as female genital mutilation, suttee (the Hindu practice of widows joining their dead husbands on the funeral pyre, whether they want to or not), or even slavery.

But after a half century of the communications revolution, progress in the Western sense has become a virtually universal aspiration. The idea of progress—of a longer, healthier, less burdensome, more fulfilling life—is not confined to the West; it is also explicit in Confucianism and in the creeds of a number of non-Western, non-Confucian high-achieving minorities—India's Sikhs, for example. I am not speaking of progress as defined by the affluent consumer society, although an end to poverty is clearly one of the universal goals, and that inevitably means higher levels of consumption. The universal aspirational model is much broader and is suggested by several clauses in the U.N. Universal Declaration of Human Rights:

> Everyone has the right to life, liberty and the security of person. . . . human be-
> ings shall enjoy freedom of speech and belief. . . . All are equal before the law
> and are entitled without any discrimination to equal protection. . . . Everyone
> has the right to take part in the government of his country, directly or through
> freely chosen representatives. . . . Everyone has the right to a standard of living
> adequate for the health and well-being of himself and of his family, including
> food, clothing, housing and medical care and necessary social services.
> . . . Everyone has the right to education.

I note in passing that, in 1947, the Executive Board of the American Anthropological Association decided not to endorse the declaration on the grounds that it was an ethnocentric document. Their position notwithstanding, I believe that the vast majority of the planet's people would agree with the following assertions:

Life is better than death.
Health is better than sickness.
Liberty is better than slavery.
Prosperity is better than poverty.

Education is better than ignorance.
Justice is better than injustice.

Richard Shweder, who agrees with the American Anthropological Association Executive Board's decision, viewed the symposium (if I may crib from the title of his chapter) as a "First World conceit" promoted by "the new evangelists." The presence of three panelists from the Third World, Daniel Etounga-Manguelle, Mariano Grondona, and Carlos Alberto Montaner, who believe that traditional cultural values are at the root of the poverty, authoritarianism, and injustice of, respectively, Africa and Latin America, constituted a direct challenge to his views. Shweder dismisses them in an endnote to his chapter as not truly representative of their societies, as "cosmopolitan intellectuals" for whom "travel plans now matter more than ancestry," who "look up to the United States for intellectual and moral guidance and material aid."

The responses of Etounga-Manguelle, Grondona, and Montaner to the Shweder endnote are included in a section following Shweder's chapter, along with a further comment by him. The exchange leaves one wondering whether some anthropologists may not be engaging in a kind of anthropological imperialism that would encase cultures in permafrost. Shweder may recognize that risk when he says, "I would define a 'genuine' culture, a culture deserving of appreciation, as a way of life that is defensible in the face of criticism from abroad." (Presumably criticism from *within* should be all the more compelling.) If there are cultures "deserving of appreciation," then presumably there are cultures *undeserving* of appreciation, suggesting that Shweder may in fact agree with Robert Edgerton's views.

Richard Shweder may thus not be as much of a "heretic at a revival meeting" as he professes.

Geography and Culture

In his chapter, Jeffrey Sachs emphasizes geography and climate as decisive factors in explaining economic growth. His views evoke Jared Diamond's recent book, *Guns, Germs, and Steel,* which concludes that "the striking differences between the long-term histories of peoples of the different continents have been due not to innate differences in the people themselves but to differences in their environments."[7]

It is clear that geography, including resource endowment, and climate are major factors in explaining the wealth and poverty of nations. Almost all the advanced democracies are in the temperate zones, and the large majority of the poor countries are in the tropical zone. But the exceptions are noteworthy: Russia occupies the same latitudes as highly prosperous and democratic northern Europe and Canada. (We might add that the northern European countries and Canada account for most of Transparency International's ten least corrupt countries in the world, whereas Russia appears among the ten most corrupt, reminding us of Alan Greenspan's comment.) Singapore, Hong Kong, and half of Taiwan are in the tropics. Their success, which recapitulates that of Japan, suggests that Confucianism trumps geography, as does the success of South Korea; the Chinese minorities in tropical Thailand, Indonesia, Malaysia, and the Philippines; and the Japanese minorities in tropical Peru and Brazil.

Geography cannot adequately explain the striking contrasts between the north and the south in Italy; comparable contrasts among Guatemala, Honduras, El Salvador, and Nicaragua on the one hand and Costa Rica on the other; the despair of Haiti, once the richest slave-sugar colony in the Caribbean, and the democratic prosperity of former slave-sugar colony Barbados. And we might note that the three temperate-zone countries in Latin America—Argentina, Uruguay, and Chile—still do not enjoy First World prosperity, and all three experienced military dictatorships in the 1970s and 1980s.

In his concluding chapter, Jared Diamond takes note of the potential power of culture:

> Cultural factors and influences . . . loom large . . . human cultural traits vary greatly around the world. Some of that cultural variation is no doubt a product of environmental variation. . . . but an important question concerns the possible significance of local cultural factors unrelated to the environment. A minor cultural factor may arise for trivial, temporary local reasons, become fixed, and then predispose a society toward more important cultural choices. . . . their significance constitutes an important unanswered question.[8]

The Relationship Between Culture and Institutions

To repeat, culture is not an independent variable. It is influenced by numerous other factors, for example, geography and climate, politics, the vagaries of history. With respect to the relationship between culture and institutions, Daniel Etounga-Manguelle says, "Culture is the mother; institutions are the children." This is particularly true in the long run. In the short run, institutional modifications, often impelled by politics, can influence culture consistent with Daniel Patrick Moynihan's sage observation. Such was to some extent the case when Italy chose to decentralize public policy and administration in the 1970s, a case that has been chronicled by Robert Putnam in *Making Democracy Work.*⁹ Although Putnam's central conclusion is that culture is at the root of the vast differences between the North and South in Italy, he also notes that decentralization has promoted a degree of trust, moderation, and compromise in the South, the same area whose social pathology was so memorably analyzed as a cultural phenomenon by Edward Banfield in *The Moral Basis of a Backward Society.*

The relationship between institutions and culture is touched on repeatedly in Douglass North's work in ways suggesting that North, whose focus is on institutions rather than culture, might agree with Etounga-Manguelle's observation. In *Institutions, Institutional Change, and Economic Performance*, North identifies "informal constraints" on institutional evolution as coming "from socially transmitted information [that is] a part of the heritage we call culture . . . [which is] a language-based conceptual framework for encoding and interpreting the information that the senses are presenting to the brain."¹⁰ North subsequently explains the divergent evolution of the former colonies of Britain and Spain in the New World in the following terms:

> In the former, an institutional framework has evolved that permits the complex impersonal exchange necessary to political stability and to capture the potential economic gains of modern technology. In the latter, personalistic relationships are still key to much of the political and economic exchange. They are a consequence of an evolving institutional framework that produces neither political stability nor consistent realization of the potential of modern technology.¹¹

In his comments following the panel on culture and political development, which he moderated, Jorge Domínguez questioned the power of culture, since all the countries in Latin America except Cuba have become democracies in the past fifteen years. The relevance of Douglass North's observation is apparent in the fragility of the democratic experiments in Latin America today. In Colombia, a democratic government faces a grave threat from an anachronistic left-wing revolutionary force. Economic chaos threatens to topple democratic institutions in neighboring Ecuador. Peru's president often behaves as if he were a traditional *caudillo*. Argentina's recent president, Carlos Saúl Menem, repeatedly dropped hints about his interest in a third term, in contravention of the country's constitution. And the recently elected president of Venezuela, a former military officer who attempted two coups d'état, has left observers in doubt about his respect for democratic norms.

Following a visit I made to Guatemala in December 1999 to lecture on the relationship between culture and democracy, the Guatemalan sociologist

Bernardo Arévalo made an apt observation: "We have the hardware of democracy but the software of authoritarianism."[12]

A question I posed earlier is evoked by the North comment: Why did it take more than 150 years for Latin America to have come around to democracy, particularly given the fact that Latin America is an offshoot of the West? A similar question might be posed about Spain and Portugal, at least until the past few decades.

Cultural Change

A consensus existed among all panelists and members of the participatory audience that cultural values change, albeit slowly in most cases. (Attitudes change more rapidly—the shift in Spain from authoritarian to democratic attitudes about governance is a case in point.) One of the most controversial issues debated at the symposium, an issue that dominated the wrap-up session, was the extent to which cultural change should be integrated into the conceptualizing, strategizing, planning, and programming of political and economic development. The issue becomes highly controversial when the initiative for such changes comes from the West, as was the case with this symposium.

Anthropologists have been working in development institutions like the World Bank and USAID for more than two decades. But in almost all cases, their efforts have been aimed at informing decisionmakers about the cultural realities that would have to be reflected in the design of policies and programs and in their execution. Few interventions were designed to promote cultural change, and indeed the whole idea of promoting cultural change has been taboo.

A similar taboo has existed in the United States with respect to cultural explanations for ethnic group underachievement. The issue in the domestic setting was joined by Richard Lamm, moderator of the panel on culture and American minorities, when he posed the following question: "Approximately half of the Hispanic high school students in Colorado and most of the other states in the west are dropping out. To what extent could or should the state of Colorado be looking at cultural factors?"

Had Richard Estrada been able to participate in the symposium, he almost surely would have expressed similar concerns. He was a member of the U.S. Commission on Immigration Reform, chaired by Barbara Jordan, which recommended significant reductions in immigration. Estrada had been particularly concerned that the heavy immigrant flow from Latin America impedes the working of the melting pot.

Nathan Glazer points out that one of the reasons for the aversion to confronting culture is that it touches the highly sensitive nerves of national, ethnic, and personal self-esteem by communicating the idea that some cultures are better than others, at least in the sense that they do more to promote human well-being. Glazer implies that the risks of pursuing cultural explanations, at least in the United States, may be greater than the gains, particularly since the melting pot tends to attenuate the initial differences. But Richard Lamm's question must give him pause.

The Lamm-Glazer debate highlights the question of where the symposium leads—how it should be followed up. If some cultural values *are* fundamental obstacles to progress—if they help explain the intractability of the problems of poverty and injustice in a good part of the Third World—then there is no alternative to the promotion of cultural change. It need not, indeed should not, be viewed as a Western imposition. Daniel Etounga-Manguelle, Mariano Grondona, and Carlos Alberto Montaner are not the only Africans and Latin Americans who have come to the conclusion that culture matters. Indeed, there are many people from different walks of life, at least in Latin America, who have concluded that cultural change is indispensable and are taking steps to promote such change—in the schools, in the churches, in the workplace, in politics. They want to understand better what it is in their culture that stands in the way of their aspirations for a more just, prosperous, fulfilling, and dignified life—and what they can do to promote change.

Orlando Patterson wrote in *The Ordeal of Integration* that "culture must contain the answers as we search for an explanation of the skill gap, the competence gap, the wage gap, as well as the pathological social sink into which several million African Americans have fallen."[13] Both in that book and its sequel, *Rituals of Blood: Consequences of Slavery in Two American Centuries*, he points to the slavery experience as the root of the cultural problem:

> Slavery, in which Afro-Americans spent two-thirds of their existence in this country was . . . a viciously exploitative institution that severely handicapped Afro-Americans, especially in the way it eroded vital social institutions such as the family and marital relations, in the way it excluded Afro-Americans from the dominant social organizations and, in the process, denied them the chance to learn patterns of behavior fundamental for survival in the emerging industrial society.[14]

Can the United States afford to ignore culture as it attempts to find solutions for black and Hispanic underachievement?

A further issue that arose during the wrap-up session was the extent to which there are cultural universals—values that work, or don't work, in whatever geographic, political, or ethnic setting. Several of the participants argued against a "black box" or "laundry list" approach to cultural change, preferring what might be termed an "ethnographic approach"—one that looks at individual cultures with limited reference to experience elsewhere. I believe that there are value patterns that cross geographic boundaries with comparable consequences in very different settings. An example is the work ethic/education/merit/frugality values common to Western Europe, North America, Australia and New Zealand, and East Asia.

But it was clear that we need to know much more about several major issues if we are to have, in Robert Klitgaard's words, "well-developed theories, practical guidelines, and close professional links between those who study culture and those who make and manage development policy."

INTEGRATING VALUE AND ATTITUDE CHANGE INTO DEVELOPMENT: A THEORETICAL AND APPLIED RESEARCH PROGRAM

Human progress since World War II has been disappointing, even disheartening, except among East Asians, Iberians, and Afro-Americans. A principal reason for the shortfall is, I believe, the failure of governments and development institutions to take into account the power of culture to thwart or facilitate progress. It is, for example, the cultural contrast between Western Europe and Latin America that I believe chiefly explains the success of the Marshall Plan and the failure of the Alliance for Progress.

Culture *is* difficult to deal with both politically and emotionally. It is also difficult to deal with intellectually because there are problems of definition and measurement and because cause-and-effect relationships between culture and other variables like policies, institutions, and economic development run in both directions.

A substantial consensus emerged in the symposium that a comprehensive theoretical and applied research program should be undertaken with the goal of integrating value and attitude change into development policies, planning, and programming in Third World countries and in anti-poverty programs in the United States. The end product of the research would be value- and attitude-change guidelines, including practical initiatives, for the promotion of progressive values and attitudes.

The research agenda comprises six basic elements:

1. A value/attitude typology: The objectives are (1) to identify the values and attitudes that promote progress, including an assessment

of the priority that attaches to each, and those that impede it; and (2) to establish which values/attitudes positively and negatively influence evolution of democratic political institutions, economic development, and social justice; and to rank them.

2. Relationship between culture and development: The objectives are (1) to develop an operationally useful understanding of the forces/actors that can precipitate development in the face of values and attitudes that are not congenial to development; (2) to trace the impact on traditional values and attitudes when development occurs as a consequence of these forces/actors; and (3) to address the question of whether democratic institutions can be consolidated and economic development and social justice sustained if traditional values and attitudes do not change significantly.

3. Relationships among values/attitudes, policies, and institutions: The objectives are (1) to assess the extent to which policies and institutions reflect values and attitudes, as Tocqueville and Daniel Etounga-Manguelle argue; (2) to understand better what is likely to happen when values and attitudes are not congenial with policies and institutions; and (3) to establish to what degree policies and institutions can change values and attitudes.

4. Cultural transmission: The objective is to gain an understanding of the chief factors in value/attitude transmission, for example, child rearing practices, schools, churches, the media, peers, the workplace, and "social remittances" from immigrants back to native countries. We need to know (1) which of these factors are today most powerful generally as well as in different geographic and cultural areas of the world; (2) how each can contribute to progressive value and attitude change; and (3) what role government might play with respect to value and attitude change.

5. Value/attitude measurement: The objective is to expand the reach of the international system for measuring value and attitude change, integrating it with the results of research task 1 above. This would include (1) identifying existing instruments for measuring values and attitudes (e.g., the World Values Survey) and (2) tailoring these instruments to support value- and attitude-change initiatives.

6. Assessing cultural change initiatives already under way: At least in Latin America, a number of homegrown cultural change initiatives are already under way, for example, the Human Development Institute in Peru, which promotes "the ten commandments of development" in school systems in several Latin American countries.

Other initiatives, for example, property-titling programs, may have important cultural change consequences, although that is not their objective. Such initiatives need to be evaluated and the results converted into guidelines for governments and development institutions.

The role of cultural values and attitudes as obstacles to or facilitators of progress has been largely ignored by governments and aid agencies. Integrating value and attitude change into development policies, planning, and programming is, I believe, a promising way to assure that, in the next fifty years, the world does not relive the poverty and injustice that most poor countries, and underachieving ethnic groups, have been mired in during the past half century.

part one

CULTURE AND
ECONOMIC DEVELOPMENT

1

Culture Makes Almost All the Difference

DAVID LANDES

Max Weber was right. If we learn anything from the history of economic development, it is that culture makes almost all the difference. Witness the enterprise of expatriate minorities—the Chinese in East and Southeast Asia, Indians in East Africa, Lebanese in West Africa, Jews and Calvinists throughout much of Europe, and on and on. Yet culture, in the sense of the inner values and attitudes that guide a population, frightens scholars. It has a sulfuric odor of race and inheritance, an air of immutability. In thoughtful moments, economists and other social scientists recognize that this is not true, and indeed they salute examples of cultural change for the better while deploring changes for the worse. But applauding or deploring implies the passivity of the viewer—an inability to use knowledge to shape people and things. The technician would rather change interest and exchange rates, free up trade, alter political institutions, manage. Besides, criticisms of culture cut close to the ego and injure identity and self-esteem. Coming from outsiders, such animadversions, however tactful and indirect, stink of condescension. Benevolent improvers have learned to steer clear.

But if culture does so much, why does it not work consistently? Economists are not alone in asking why some people—the Chinese, say—have long been so unproductive at home yet so enterprising away. If culture matters, why didn't it change China? (We should note that with policies that now encourage rather than suppress economic development, the imbalance between Chinese performance at home and abroad is disappearing, as China sustains the phenomenal growth rates that propelled the Confucian "dragons" from the Third World to the First.)

An economist friend, a master of political-economic therapies, solves the earlier, perhaps now obsolete paradox by denying any connection with culture. Culture, he says, does not permit him to predict outcomes. I disagree. One could have foreseen the postwar economic success of Japan and Germany by taking account of culture. The same with South Korea versus Turkey, Indonesia versus Nigeria.

On the other hand, culture does not stand alone. Economic analysis cherishes the illusion that one good reason should be enough, but the determinants of complex processes are invariably plural and interrelated. Monocausal explanations will not work. The same values thwarted by "bad government" at home can find opportunity elsewhere, as in the case of China. Hence the special success of emigrant enterprise. The ancient Greeks, as usual, had a word for it: These *metics*, alien residents, were the leaven of societies that sneered at money and crafts (hence the pejorative sense of the Greek-rooted word "banausic"—of an artisan, dull, pedestrian). So strangers found and sold the goods and made the money.

Because culture and economic performance are linked, changes in one will work back on the other. In Thailand, all good young men used to spend years undergoing a religious apprenticeship in Buddhist monasteries. This period of ripening was good for the spirit and soul; it also suited the somnolent pace of traditional economic activity and employment. That was then. Today, Thailand moves faster; commerce thrives; business calls. As a result, young men spiritualize for a few weeks—time enough to learn some prayers and rituals and get back to the real, material world. Time, which everyone knows is money, has changed in relative value. One could not have imposed this change, short of revolution. The Thais have voluntarily adjusted their priorities. (It should be noted in passing that the Chinese minority led the charge.)

The Thai story illustrates culture's response to economic growth and opportunity. The reverse is also possible—culture may shift against enterprise. We have the Russian case, where seventy-five years of anti-market, anti-profit schooling and insider privilege have planted and frozen anti-entrepreneurial attitudes. Even after the regime has fallen, people fear the uncertainties of the market and yearn for the safe tedium of state employment. Or they yearn for equality in poverty, a common feature of peasant cultures around the world. As the Russian joke has it, peasant Ivan is jealous of neighbor Boris because Boris has a goat. A fairy comes along and offers

Ivan a single wish. What does he wish for? That Boris's goat should drop dead. Fortunately, not all Russians think that way. The collapse of Marxist prohibitions and inhibitions has led to a rush of business activity, the best of it linked to inside deals, some of it criminal, much of it the work of non-Russian minorities (Armenians, Georgians, etc.). The leaven is there, and often that suffices: the initiative of an enterprising, different few. In the meantime, old habits remain, corruption and crime are rampant, culture war rages— elections hang on these issues, and the outcome is not certain.

DEPENDENCY THEORY, ARGENTINA, AND FERNANDO HENRIQUE CARDOSO'S METAMORPHOSIS

Dependency theory was a comforting alternative to cultural explanations of underdevelopment. Latin American scholars and outside sympathizers explained the failure of Latin American development, all the worse by contrast with North America, as the consequence of the misdeeds of stronger, richer nations. Note that the dependency vulnerability implies a state of inferiority in which one does not control one's fate; one does as others dictate. Needless to say, these others exploit their superiority to transfer product from the dependent economies, much as the earlier colonial rulers did. The pump of empire becomes the pump of capitalist imperialism.

Yet to co-opt independent sovereign nations requires lending and investment; simple pillage is not an option. So with Argentina, which saved little and drew increasingly on foreign capital. (The chief architect of dependency theory was Raúl Prebisch, an Argentine economist.) Some economists contend that foreign capital hurts growth; others, that it helps, but less than domestic investment. Much obviously depends on the uses. In the meantime, no one is prepared to refuse outside money on grounds of efficiency. The politicians want it and are willing to let the dependency theorists wring their hands.

Argentina had some very rich people, yet "for reasons that have never been clear . . . has always been capital-dependent and thereby beholding [sic] to loaner [lender] nations, in ways that seriously compromise the country's ability to run its own affairs."[1] The British built Argentina's railroads—less than 1,000 kilometers in 1871, over 12,000 kilometers two decades later— but built them to British purposes. But how does one build such a network without fostering internal markets? And if not, whose fault is it? What does that say about the spirit of native enterprise? Most Argentines were not asking such questions. It is always easy to blame the Other. The result: a xenophobic anti-imperialism and self-defeating sense of wrong.

In the nineteenth century, a distinguished Argentine, Juan Bautista Alberdi, worried about the spirit of native enterprise. In 1852, he wrote, in words that anticipated what Max Weber would write fifty years later,

> Respect the altar of every belief. Spanish America, limited to Catholicism to the exclusion of any other religion, resembles a solitary and silent convent of nuns. . . . To exclude different religions in South America is to exclude the English, the Germans, the Swiss, the North Americans, which is to say the very people this continent most needs. To bring them without their religion is to bring them without the agent that makes them what they are.[2]

Some have attributed Argentina's low rate of savings to rapid population growth and high rates of immigration—to which I would add bad habits of conspicuous consumption. In any event, foreign capital flows depended as much on supply conditions abroad as on Argentine opportunities. During World War I, the British needed money and had to liquidate foreign assets. Although remaining Argentina's biggest creditor, they no longer played the growth-promoting role of earlier decades. The United States picked up some of the slack, but here too politics and the business cycle called the tune, so that Argentina found itself in intermittent but repeated difficulty both for the amount and the terms of foreign investment and credit. All of this promoted conflict with creditors, which led in turn to reactive isolationism—restrictive measures that only aggravated the economic stringency and dependency. When Argentine economists and politicians denounced these circumstances and the misdeeds, real and imagined, of outside interests, they only compounded the problem. To be sure, cocoon economics—the logical prescription of the *dependencistas*—helped shelter Argentina and other Latin American economies from the worst effects of the Great Depression. Such is the nature of cocoons. But it also cut them off from competition, stimuli, and opportunities for growth.

Dependencista arguments flourished in Latin America. They traveled well, resonating after World War II with the economic plight and political awareness of newly liberated colonies. Cynics might say that dependency doctrines have been Latin America's most successful export. But they have been bad for effort and morale. By fostering a morbid propensity to find fault with everyone but oneself, they promote economic impotence. *Even if they were true, it would have been better to stow them.*

And indeed, that is what Latin America appears to have done. Today, all countries in the Western Hemisphere, including Cuba, welcome foreign investment. Argentina has been a leader in the transformation. The statism that dependency theory counseled has been dismantled in a welter of privatizations. Mexico, once the home of some of the most strident *dependencistas*, has developed a broad national consensus, symbolized by NAFTA, that its interests are best served by economic intimacy with the United States and Canada. The lamb has leapt into the mouth of the lion and appears to have benefited from the encounter.

For years, Fernando Henrique Cardoso was a leading figure of the Latin American dependency school. In the 1960s and 1970s, the sociologist Cardoso wrote or edited some twenty books on the subject. Some of them became the standard texts that shaped a generation of students. Perhaps the best known was *Dependency and Development in Latin America*. In its English version, it ended with a turgid, less-than-stirring credo:

> The effective battle . . . is between technocratic elitism and a vision of the formative process of a mass industrial society which can offer what is popular as specifically national and which succeeds in transforming the demand for a more developed economy and for a democratic society into a state that expresses the vitality of truly popular forces, capable of seeking socialist forms for the social organization of the future.[3]

Then, in 1993, Cardoso became Brazil's minister of finance. He found a country wallowing in an annual inflation rate of 7,000 percent. The government had become so addicted to this monetary narcotic and Brazilians so ingenious in their personal countermeasures (taxis used meters that could be adjusted to the price index, and perhaps to the client) that serious economists were ready to make light of this volatility on the pretext that certainty of inflation was a form of stability.

This may have been true of those Brazilians able to take precautions; but inflation played havoc with Brazil's international credit, and the country needed to borrow. It also needed to trade and work with other countries, especially those rich, capitalist nations that were marked as the enemy. So Cardoso began to see things differently, to the point where observers praised him as a pragmatist. Gone now were the anti-colonialist passions; gone the hostility to foreign links, with their implicit dependency. Brazil has no choice, says Cardoso. If it is not prepared to be part of the global economy, it has "no way of competing. . . . It is not an imposition from outside. It's a necessity for us."[4]

To each time its virtues. Two years later, Cardoso was elected president, in large part because he had given Brazil its first strong currency in many years.

JAPAN'S MEIJI RESTORATION—
COUNTERPOISE TO DEPENDENCY THEORY

Bernard Lewis once observed that "when people realize that things are going wrong, there are two questions they can ask. One is, 'What did we do wrong?' and the other is 'Who did this to us?' The latter leads to conspiracy theories and paranoia. The first question leads to another line of thinking: 'How do we put it right?'"[5] In the second half of the twentieth century, Latin America chose conspiracy theories and paranoia. In the second half of the nineteenth century, Japan asked itself, "How do we put it right?"

Japan had a revolution in 1867–1868. The feudal shogunate was overthrown—really it collapsed—and control of the state returned to the emperor in Kyoto. So ended a quarter millennium of Tokugawa rule. But the Japanese call this overturn a restoration rather than a revolution because they prefer to see it as a return to normalcy. Also, revolutions are for China. The Chinese have dynasties—Japan has one royal family, going back to the beginning.

The symbols of national unity were already present; the ideals of national pride, already defined. This saved a lot of turmoil. Revolutions, like civil wars, can be devastating to order and national efficacy. The Meiji Restoration had its dissensions and dissents, often violent. The final years of the old, the first of the new, were stained with the blood of assassinations, of peasant uprisings, of reactionary rebellion. Even so, the transition in Japan was far smoother than the French and Russian varieties of political overturn, for two reasons: the new regime held the moral high ground, and even the disaffected and affronted feared to give arms and opportunity to the enemy outside. Foreign imperialists were lurking to pounce, and internal divisions would have invited intervention. Consider the story of imperialism elsewhere: Local quarrels and intrigue had fairly invited the European powers into India and would soon subordinate China.

In a society that had never admitted the stranger, the very presence of westerners invited trouble. More than once, Japanese bullyboys challenged and assaulted these impudent foreigners, the better to show them who was boss. Who was boss? In the face of Western demands for retribution and indemnities, the Japanese authorities could only temporize and, by waffling, discredit themselves in the eyes of foreigner and patriot alike.

The pretensions of the outsiders were the heart of the matter. "Honor the emperor; expel the barbarians!" went the pithy slogan. The leaders of the move for change, lords of the great fiefs of the Far South and West, once enemies, now united against the shogunate. They won; and they lost. That was another paradox of this revolution-restoration. The leaders thought they were going back to the days of yore. Instead, they found themselves caught up in tomorrow, in a wave of modernization, because that was the only way to defeat the barbarians. You westerners have the guns. All right, one day we'll have them too.

The Japanese went about modernization with characteristic intensity and system. They were ready for it—by virtue of a tradition (recollection) of effective government, by their high levels of literacy, by their tight family structure, by their work ethic and self-discipline, by their sense of national identity and inherent superiority.

That was the heart of it: The Japanese knew they were superior, and because they knew it, they were able to recognize the superiorities of others. Building on earlier moves under Tokugawa, they hired foreign experts and technicians while sending Japanese agents abroad to bring back eyewitness accounts of European and American ways. This body of intelligence laid the basis for choices, reflecting careful and supple consideration of comparative merit. Thus the first military model was the French army; but after the defeat of France by Prussia in 1870–1871, the Japanese decided that Germany had more to offer. A similar shift took place from French to German legal codes and practice.

No opportunity for learning was lost. In October 1871, a high-level Japanese delegation that included Okubo Toshimichi traveled to the United States and Europe, visiting factories and forges, shipyards and armories, railways and canals. They returned in September 1873, almost two years later, laden with the spoils of learning and "on fire with enthusiasm" for reform.[6]

This direct experience by the Japanese leadership made all the difference. Riding on an English train, Okubo confided ruefully that, before leaving Japan, he had thought his work done: the imperial authority restored, feudalism replaced by central government. Now he understood that the big tasks lay ahead. Japan did not compare with "the more progressive powers of the world." England especially offered a lesson in self-development. Once a small, insular nation—like Japan—England had systematically pursued a policy of self-aggrandizement. The Navigation Acts were crucial in raising the national merchant marine to a position of international dominance. Not until Britain had achieved industrial leadership did it abandon protection for laissez-faire. (Not a bad analysis. Adam Smith would have agreed.)

To be sure, Japan would not have the tariff and commercial autonomy that seventeenth-century England had enjoyed. Here, however, the German example made sense. Germany, like Japan, had only recently come through a difficult unification. Also, Germany, like Japan, had started from a position of economic inferiority, and look how far it had come. Okubo was much impressed by the German people he met. He found them thrifty, hardworking, "unpretentious"—like Japanese commoners, one imagines. And he found their leaders to be realists and pragmatists: Focus, they said, on building national power. They were the mercantilists of the nineteenth century. Okubo came back and gave a German orientation to the Japanese bureaucracy.

First came those tasks ordinary to government: a postal service, a new time standard, public education (for boys and then for girls as well), universal military service. General schooling diffused knowledge; that is what schools are for. But it also instilled discipline, obedience, punctuality, and a worshipful respect for the emperor. This was the key to the development of a we/they national identity transcending the parochial loyalties nurtured by the feudal shogunate. The army and navy completed the job. Beneath the sameness of the uniform and the discipline, universal military service wiped out distinctions of class and place. It nurtured nationalist pride and democratized the violent virtues of manhood—an end to the samurai monopoly of arms.

Meanwhile, state and society went about the business of business: how to make things by machine, how to do more without machines, how to move goods, how to compete with foreign producers. Not easy. European industrial producers had taken a century. Japan was in a hurry.

To begin with, the country built on those branches of industry already familiar—silk and cotton manufacture in particular but also the processing of food staples immune to foreign imitation: sake, miso, soy sauce. From 1877 to 1900—the first generation of industrialization—food accounted for 40 percent of growth, textiles 35 percent. In short, the Japanese pursued comparative advantage rather than the will-o'-the-wisp of heavy industry. Much of this was small-scale: cotton mills of 2,000 spindles (as against 10,000 and up in Western Europe); wooden waterwheels that were generations behind European technology; coal mines whose tortuous seams and hand-drawn baskets made the infamous British pits of an earlier time look like a promenade.

The economists' usual explanation for this inversion of the late-follower model (late is great and up-to-date) is want of capital: meager personal resources, no investment banks. In fact, some Japanese merchants had accumulated large fortunes, and the state was ready to build and subsidize plants. As it did. But the long haul to parity needed not so much money as people—people of imagination and initiative, people who understood economies of scale, who knew not only production methods and machinery but also organization and what we now call software. The capital would follow and grow.

The Japanese determined to go beyond consumer goods. If they were to have a modern economy, they had to master the heavy work: to build machines and engines, ships and locomotives, railroads and ports and shipyards. The government played a critical role here, financing reconnaissance abroad, bringing in foreign experts, building installations, and subsidizing commercial ventures. But more important were the talent and determination of Japanese patriots, ready to change careers in the national cause, and the quality of Japanese workers, especially artisans, with skills honed and attitudes shaped by close teamwork and supervision in craft shops.

Japan moved into the second industrial revolution with an alacrity that belied its inexperience. The traditional account of Japan's successful and rapid industrialization rings with praise, somewhat mitigated by distaste for the somber and intense nationalist accompaniment—the ruthless drive that gave the development process meaning and urgency. This was the first non-Western country to industrialize, and it remains today an example to other late bloomers. Other countries sent young people abroad to learn the new ways and lost them; Japanese expatriates came back home. Other countries imported foreign technicians to teach their own people; the Japanese largely taught themselves. Other countries imported foreign equipment and did their best to use it; the Japanese modified it, made it better, made it themselves. Other countries may, for their own historical reasons, dislike the Japanese (how many Latin Americans like gringos?), but they do envy and admire them.

The explanation lay partly in an intense sense of group responsibility: an indolent, self-indulgent worker would be hurting not only himself but the rest of the family. And the nation—don't forget the nation. Most Japanese peasants and workers did not feel this way to begin with—under Tokugawa, they scarcely had a notion of nation. That was a primary task of the new imperial state: to imbue its subjects with a sense of higher duty to the emperor and country and to link this patriotism to work. A large share of schooltime was devoted to the study of ethics; in a country without regular religious instruction and ceremony, school was the temple of virtue and morality. As a 1930 textbook put it: "The easiest way to practice one's patriotism [is to] discipline oneself in daily life, help keep good order in one's family, and fully discharge one's responsibility on the job."[7] Also to save and not waste.

Here was a Japanese version of Weber's Protestant ethic. Along with government initiatives and a collective commitment to modernization, this work ethic made possible the so-called Japanese economic miracle. Any serious understanding of Japanese performance must build on this phenomenon of culturally determined human capital.

ON WEBER

Max Weber, who began as a historian of the ancient world but grew into a wonder of diversified social science, published in 1904–1905 one of the most influential and provocative essays ever written: "The Protestant Ethic and the Spirit of Capitalism." His thesis: that Protestantism—more specifically its Calvinist branches—promoted the rise of modern capitalism; that is, the industrial capitalism he knew from his native Germany. Protestantism did this, he said, not by easing or abolishing those aspects of the Roman faith that had deterred or hindered free economic activity (the prohibition of usury, for example) nor by encouraging, let alone inventing, the pursuit of wealth, but by defining and sanctioning an ethic of everyday behavior that conduced to economic success.

Calvinistic Protestantism, said Weber, did this initially by affirming the doctrine of predestination: One could not gain salvation by faith or deeds; that question had been decided for everyone from the beginning of time, and nothing could alter one's fate.

Such a belief could easily have encouraged a fatalistic attitude. If behavior and faith make no difference, why not live it up? Why be good? Because, according to Calvinism, goodness was a plausible sign of election. Anyone could be chosen, but it was only reasonable to suppose that most of the chosen would show by their character and ways the quality of their souls and the nature of their destiny. This implicit reassurance was a powerful incentive to proper thoughts and behavior. And while hard belief in predestination did not last more than a generation or two (it is not the kind of dogma that has lasting appeal), it was eventually converted into a secular code of behavior: hard work, honesty, seriousness, the thrifty use of money and time.

All of these values help business and capital accumulation, but Weber stressed that the good Calvinist did not aim at riches. (He might easily believe, however, that honest riches are a sign of divine favor.) Europe did not have to wait for the Protestant Reformation to find people who wanted to be rich. Weber's point is that Protestantism produced a new kind of businessman, one who aimed to live and work a certain way. It was the *way* that mattered, and riches were at best a by-product. It was only much later that the Protestant ethic degenerated into a set of maxims for material success and smug, smarmy sermons on the virtues of wealth.

The Weber thesis gave rise to all manner of rebuttal. The same kind of controversy has swirled around the derivative thesis of the sociologist Robert K. Merton, who argued that there was a direct link between Protestantism and the rise of modern science. Indeed, it is fair to say that most historians today would look upon the Weber thesis as implausible and unacceptable: It had its moment and it is gone.

I do not agree. Not on the empirical level, where records show that Protestant merchants and manufacturers played a leading role in trade, banking, and industry. Nor on the theoretical. The heart of the matter lay indeed in the making of a new man—rational, ordered, diligent, productive. These virtues, while not new, were hardly commonplace. Protestantism generalized them among its adherents, who judged one another by conformity to these standards.

Two special characteristics of the Protestants reflect and confirm this link. The first was stress on instruction and literacy, for girls as well as boys. This was a by-product of Bible reading. Good Protestants were expected to read the Holy Scriptures for themselves. (By way of contrast, Catholics were catechized but did not have to read, and they were explicitly discouraged from reading the Bible.) The result: greater literacy from generation to generation. *Literate mothers matter.*

The second was the importance accorded to time. Here we have what the sociologist would call "unobtrusive evidence": the making and buying of clocks and watches. Even in Catholic areas such as France and Bavaria, most clock makers were Protestant; and the use of these instruments of time measurement and their diffusion to rural areas was far more advanced in Britain and Holland than in Catholic countries. Nothing testifies so much as time sensibility to the "urbanization" of rural society, with all that implies for diffusion of values and tastes.

This is not to say that Weber's "ideal type" of capitalist could be found only among Calvinists and their later sectarian avatars. People of all faiths and no faith can grow up to be rational, diligent, orderly, productive, clean, and humorless. Nor do they have to be businessmen. One can show and profit by these qualities in all walks of life. Weber's argument, as I see it, is that in sixteenth- to eighteenth-century northern Europe, religion encouraged the appearance in numbers of a personality type that had been exceptional and adventitious before and that this type created a new economy (a new mode of production) that we know as (industrial) capitalism.

History tells us that the most successful cures for poverty come from within. Foreign aid can help but, like windfall wealth, can also hurt. It can discourage effort and plant a crippling sense of incapacity. As the African saying has it, The hand that receives is always under the hand that gives. No, what counts is work, thrift, honesty, patience, tenacity. To people haunted by misery and hunger, that may add up to selfish indifference. But at bottom, no empowerment is so effective as self-empowerment.

Some of this may sound like a collection of clichés—the sort of lessons one used to learn at home and in school when parents and teachers thought they had a mission to rear and elevate their children. Today, we condescend to such verities, dismiss them as platitudes. But why should wisdom be obsolete? To be sure, we are living in a dessert age. We want things to be sweet; too many of us work to live and live to be happy. Nothing wrong with that; it just does not promote high productivity. You want high productivity? Then you should live to work and get happiness as a by-product.

Not easy. The people who live to work are a small and fortunate elite. But it is an elite open to newcomers, self-selected, the kind of people who accentuate the positive. In this world, the optimists have it, not because they are always right but because they are positive. Even when wrong, they are positive, and that is the way of achievement, correction, improvement, and success. Educated, eyes-open optimism pays; pessimism can only offer the empty consolation of being right.

2

Attitudes, Values, Beliefs, and the Microeconomics of Prosperity

MICHAEL E. PORTER

Attitudes, values, and beliefs that are sometimes collectively referred to as "culture" play an unquestioned role in human behavior and progress. This is evident to me from working in nations, states, regions, inner cities, and companies at widely varying stages of development. The question is not whether culture has a role but how to understand this role in the context of the broader determinants of prosperity. A large literature has explored the links between culture and human progress from various perspectives. In this chapter, I explore a subset of this broader territory—the role of what might be termed "economic culture" in economic progress. Economic culture is defined as the beliefs, attitudes, and values that bear on the economic activities of individuals, organizations, and other institutions.

Although the role of culture in economic progress is unquestioned, interpreting this role in the context of other influences and isolating the independent influence of culture is challenging. Treatments of the role of culture in economic prosperity tend to focus on generic cultural attributes that are deemed desirable, such as hard work, initiative, belief in the value of education, as well as factors drawn from macroeconomics, such as a propensity to save and invest. These are surely relevant to prosperity, but none of these generic attributes is unambiguously correlated with economic progress. Hard work is important, but just as important is what guides and directs the type of work done. Initiative is important, but not all initiative is productive. Education is crucial, but so is the type of education sought and what the education is used to accomplish. Saving is good, but only if the savings are deployed in productive ways.

Indeed, the same cultural attribute can have vastly different implications for economic progress in different societies, or even in the same society at different times. Frugality, for example, served Japan well until its recent prolonged recession; now it is an obstacle to recovery. The investigation of a wide range of successful nations, including the United States, Japan, Italy, Hong Kong, Singapore, Chile, and Costa Rica, reveals wide and subtle cultural differences associated with improving economic circumstances that further belie a simple connection between culture and prosperity.

In this chapter, I will explore the complex links between economic culture and economic progress. The focus here is on prosperity at the level of geographic units such as nations or states. Although I will often refer to nations, in many cases the relevant economic unit can be smaller. There are striking differences in economic prosperity among states and regions within virtually every nation, and some of the reasons may be related to attitudes, values, and beliefs. Many of the same influences can also be applied to thinking about the economic prosperity of groups that cut across geographic units such as, for example, ethnic Chinese.

I will begin by outlining some of the recent learning about the sources of economic prosperity in the modern global economy. I will then draw some tentative links between these sources and the types of beliefs, values, and attitudes that reinforce prosperity. Doing so confronts an important question: Why might unproductive cultures arise and persist? I examine this question in the context of prevailing economic thinking and circumstances over the last century. The chapter concludes with some reflections on the scope for cultural differences in the modern economy and on how the influence of culture may be shifting in light of the economic convergence triggered by the globalization of markets.

THE SOURCES OF PROSPERITY:
COMPARATIVE VERSUS COMPETITIVE ADVANTAGE

A nation's prosperity, or standard of living, is determined by the productivity with which it uses its human, capital, and natural resources. Productivity sets the level of sustainable wages and returns to capital, the principal determinants of national income per citizen. Productivity, then, is the basis of "competitiveness." It depends on the value of products and services produced by firms in a nation, deriving, for example, from quality and uniqueness, as well as on the efficiency with which they are produced. The central issue in economic development is how to create the conditions for rapid and sustained productivity growth.

In the modern global economy, productivity depends less on what industries a nation's firms compete in than on *how* they compete—that is to say, the nature of their operations and strategies. In today's global economy, firms in virtually any industry can become more productive through more sophisticated strategies and investments in modern technologies. Modern technologies offer major opportunities for upgrading in fields as disparate as agriculture, small package delivery, or semiconductor production. Similarly, there is scope for more advanced strategies in virtually any field, involving customer segmentation, differentiated products and services, and tailored value chains to deliver products to customers.

Hence, the concept of industrial targeting, in which government seeks to favor winning industries, is flawed. There is no good or bad industry in the new "productivity paradigm." Rather, the question is whether firms are able to employ the best methods, assemble the best skills, and utilize the best techniques to do whatever they do at an increasingly higher level of productivity. It does not matter if a country has an agricultural economy, a service economy, or a manufacturing economy. What does matter is a country's ability to organize itself effectively around the premise that productivity determines prosperity for the individuals of that country.

In the productivity paradigm, traditional distinctions between foreign and domestic firms also lose meaning. Prosperity in a nation is a reflection of what both domestic and foreign firms choose to do in that nation. Domestic firms that produce low-quality products using unsophisticated methods hold back national productivity, whereas foreign firms that bring in new technology and advanced methods will boost productivity and local wages. Traditional distinctions between local and traded industries, and the tendency to focus policy attention only on the traded industries, also become problematic. Local industries affect the cost of living for citizens and the cost of doing business for traded industries. Neglecting them, as in the case of Japan, creates serious disadvantages.

The productivity paradigm as the basis for prosperity represents a radical shift from previous conceptions of the sources of wealth. A hundred or even fifty years ago, prosperity in a nation was widely seen as resulting from the possession of natural resources such as land, minerals, or a pool of labor, giving the country a *comparative advantage* relative to other countries with less favorable endowments. In the modern global economy, however, firms can access resources from any location cheaply and efficiently, making resources themselves less valuable. The real value of resources is falling, evidenced by the steadily declining real prices of commodities over the past century. Similarly, cheap labor is ubiquitous, so that possessing a labor pool is not in and of itself a source of advantage. With rapidly declining transportation and communication costs, even favorable geographic location relative to markets or trade routes is less of a source of advantage today than it was in the past. A firm in Hong Kong or Chile, despite great distances from markets, can still be a major trading partner of the United States or Europe.

Comparative advantage has given way as the basis of wealth to *competitive* advantage residing in superior productivity in assembling resources to create valuable products and services. Countries that improve their standard of living are those in which firms are becoming more productive through the development of more sophisticated sources of competitive advantage based on knowledge, investment, insight, and innovation.

Ironically, in today's global economy it is the local things that are increasingly important and decisive in determining why a particular firm is more competitive and productive than one based elsewhere. This is because rapid flows of trade, capital, and information nullify the advantages that a firm gets from inputs sourced from elsewhere. If a firm in one country buys its machines from Germany, so can its competitor. If a firm sources capital from abroad, so can its competitor. If a firm buys raw materials from Australia, so can its competitor. All these approaches may be necessary, but they have essentially been neutralized as competitive advantages in today's global economy. The remaining sources of competitive advantage are increasingly local, including special supplier or customer relationships, unique insights about market needs gleaned from local customers or partners, special access to technology and knowledge from other local institutions, or production flexibility resulting from the use of a nearby supplier.

THE MICROECONOMIC
FOUNDATIONS OF PROSPERITY

Since many of the external sources of advantage for a nation's firms have been nullified by globalization, potential internal sources of advantage must be cultivated if a country wishes to upgrade its economy and create prosperity for its citizens. Attention is frequently focused on the importance of building a sound macroeconomic, political, and legal environment. However, macroeconomic conditions, while necessary, are not sufficient to ensure a prosperous economy. Indeed, there is less and less discretion about macroeconomic policies. Unless they are sound, the nation is punished by international capital markets.

Prosperity ultimately depends on improving the *microeconomic* foundations of competition. The microeconomic foundations of productivity rest on two interrelated areas: the sophistication of company operations and strategy and the quality of the microeconomic business environment. Unless companies operating in a nation become more productive, an economy cannot become more productive. Yet the sophistication with which companies compete is strongly influenced by the quality of the national business environment in which they operate. The business environment has much to do with the types of strategies that are feasible and the efficiency with which firms can operate. For example, operational efficiency is unattainable if regulatory red tape is onerous, logistics are unreliable, or firms cannot get timely supplies of components or high-quality service for their production machines.

Capturing the nature of the business environment at the microeconomic level is challenging, given the myriad of locational influences on productivity. In *The Competitive Advantage of Nations*,[1] I modeled the effect of location on competition via four interrelated influences: factor (input) conditions, the local context for strategy and rivalry, local demand conditions, and the strength of related and supporting industries. These form the microeconomic business environment in which a nation's firms compete and from which they draw their sources of competitive advantage. Economic development is the long-term process of building this array of interdependent microeconomic capabilities and incentives to support more advanced forms of competition.

Factor conditions refer to the nature and extent of the inputs that firms can draw upon to produce goods or services, including such things as labor, capital, roads, airports and other transportation and communication infrastructure, and natural resources. Factor inputs can be arrayed from basic (e.g., cheap labor, basic roads) to advanced (e.g., multi-modal systems of transportation, high-speed data communication infrastructure, specialized personnel with advanced degrees). The quantity of the inputs is not nearly as important as their quality and specialization. For example, if a country's infrastructure is tailored to the field in which that country competes, productivity will increase. Similarly, pools of untrained labor are not as valuable as a specially trained workforce with the skills to produce differentiated products and to operate production processes that are more advanced and productive. In general, successful economic development requires sustained improvements in the quality and specialization of a nation's inputs.

The quality of local demand is a second critical determinant of a country's microeconomic competitiveness. A demanding customer is a powerful tool for raising productivity. The pressures that the local customer places on a firm, on an industry, and on the nature of competition within local industries tend to raise productivity by enhancing the quality and value of the products, thereby improving the likelihood that those products will succeed in export markets. Demanding customers educate local firms about how to improve products and services and force them to upgrade these products and services in a way that will translate directly into higher value for customers and higher prices. On the other hand, if local demand is unsophisticated and a firm is simply imitating products developed elsewhere, productivity and international market prices will suffer.

The shoe industry in Italy is a good illustration of the importance of demanding clients. Italian women try on dozens of pairs of shoes before making a purchase. They carefully scrutinize the quality of leather and workmanship, the shape and size of the heel, the comfort, the fashion, and other qualities. Shoe manufacturers able to survive and prosper in such a local laboratory can feel confident that shoes that are successful in Italy are likely to be successful when exported globally.

The context for firm strategy and rivalry refers to the rules, incentives, and norms governing the type and intensity of local rivalry. Less-developed economies tend to have little local rivalry. Moving to an advanced economy requires that vigorous local rivalry develop and shift in character from minimizing costs and imitation to process efficiency and, ultimately, to innovation and differentiation. Healthy rivalry among local firms is fundamental to rapidly increasing productivity. If a firm cannot compete at home, it cannot compete abroad.[2] It will never be nimble and improve rapidly enough if it does not face intense local competition from locally based rivals. Anti-monopoly legislation and policies that support entrepreneurship and new business development are examples of tools that a nation can use to foster healthy local rivalry.

The final determinant of the strength of a country's microeconomic business environment is the extent and quality of local suppliers and related industries. Mid-level and advanced development depends on the formation of clusters. A cluster is a geographically concentrated network of industry competitors and their many related and supporting industries and institutions. Examples of strong clusters are Silicon Valley, Wall Street, and Hollywood. In fact, there are Hollywoods and Silicon Valleys all over the world, in virtually every advanced economy and in virtually every kind of industry. Clusters are an old phenomenon but one that appears to be increasingly important. The agglomeration of competitors, suppliers, and related businesses and institutions all in the same location occurs and persists because this form of organization is more productive than one that tries to assemble inputs and ideas from disparate locations in different parts of the world; also, it supports faster improvement and innovation.

Government's role in the productivity paradigm is different and more indirect than in other conceptions of competitiveness. Government responsibilities begin with creating a stable and predictable macroeconomic, political, and legal environment in which firms can make the long-term strategic choices required to boost productivity. Beyond this, government must ensure that high-quality factors (inputs) are available to firms (e.g., educated human resources, efficient physical infrastructure); establish overall rules and incentives governing competition that encourage productivity growth; facilitate and encourage cluster development; and develop and implement a positive, distinctive, and long-term economic upgrading program for the nation that mobilizes government, business, institutions, and citizens. Government and other institutions such as universities, standards agencies, and industry groups must work together to ensure that the business environment fosters rising productivity.

In the productivity paradigm, facilitating cluster development and upgrading is an increasingly important role for both government and the private sector. This approach contrasts sharply with the historical approach of industrial policy in which "desirable" industries or sectors were targeted for development by government. Industrial policy focused on domestic companies and was based on intervention by government in competition through protectionist policies, industry promotion, and subsidies. Decisions were highly centralized at the national level, reminiscent of central planning.

The cluster concept is very different. It rests on the notions that all clusters can contribute to a nation's prosperity, that both domestic and foreign companies enhance productivity, and that cross-industry linkages and complementarities are essential sources of competitive advantage that need to be encouraged. Although industrial targeting aims to distort competition in a nation's favor, cluster-based policies seek to enhance competition by fostering externalities and removing constraints to productivity and productivity growth. The cluster approach is also more decentralized, encouraging initiative at the state and local levels.

ECONOMIC POLICY AND THE
PROCESS OF DEVELOPMENT

Economic progress is a process of successive upgrading, in which the elements of a nation's business environment evolve to support increasingly sophisticated and productive ways of competing. The imperatives from a business environment perspective vary as a nation moves from low income to middle income to high income. In early-stage development, firms compete primarily on cheap labor and natural resources. The fundamental challenge is to escape from that situation. To move beyond poverty, a nation must upgrade its inputs, institutions, and skills to allow more sophisticated forms of competition, resulting in increased productivity. This requires such things as upgrading human capital, improving infrastructure, opening to trade and foreign investment, protecting intellectual property, raising regulatory standards to pressure improvements in product quality and environmental impact, and expanding regional integration.

To achieve the middle level of development, a country must focus increasingly on improving the quality of its human resources, enhancing the sophistication of home demand, developing its scientific base, ensuring local rivalry, and developing an advanced information and communications infrastructure. Government must work with the private sector, universities, and other institutions to build strong clusters. To reach the level of an advanced economy, the country must develop innovative capacity at the world technological frontier, on which firms can draw to create unique goods and services that can command high wages for citizens. This involves steps such as increasing investment in basic research, developing a growing pool of scientific and technical personnel, and expanding the availability of venture capital.

BUILDING PROSPERITY:
IMPLICATIONS FOR BELIEFS, ATTITUDES, AND BEHAVIOR

This discussion of the microeconomic foundations of competitiveness reveals some of the beliefs, attitudes, and values that support and promote prosperity. Prevailing beliefs about the basis for prosperity itself are among the most central. The attitudes of individuals and organizations and their economic behavior are strongly affected by what they perceive to be the way to win. Perhaps the most basic belief undergirding successful economic development is acceptance that prosperity depends on productivity, not on control of resources, scale, government favors, or military power, and that the productivity paradigm is good for society. Without such beliefs, rent seeking and monopoly seeking will be the dominant behavior, a pathology still afflicting many developing countries.

Another basic belief that supports prosperity is that the potential for wealth is limitless because it is based on ideas and insights, not fixed because of scarce resources. Wealth can be expanded for many by improving productivity. This belief supports productivity-enhancing steps in all parts of society that will expand the pie. In contrast, the view that wealth is fixed and not related to effort leads various groups to struggle over the distribution of the pie, a preoccupation that almost inevitably saps productivity. This zero-sum worldview is central to the theory of a universal peasant culture.[3]

The productivity paradigm gives rise to a whole series of supportive attitudes and values: Innovation is good, competition is good, accountability is good, high regulatory standards are good, investment in capabilities and technology is a necessity, employees are assets, membership in a cluster is a competitive advantage, collaboration with suppliers and customers is beneficial, connectivity and networks are essential, education and skills are essential to support more productive work, and wages should not rise unless productivity rises, among others. These can be contrasted with unproductive attitudes and values: Monopoly is good, power determines rewards, rigid hierarchy is needed to maintain control, and self-contained family relationships should determine partnership.

In any nation, there will be differences among groups and individuals in the beliefs and attitudes they hold. One can also view economic development as partly shaped by the tug-of-war between productivity-enhancing aspects of economic culture in a nation and productivity-eroding aspects of culture. Especially heavy weight is attached to the beliefs and attitudes of government leaders and the business elites. A strong government may impose a productive economic culture, at least for a time, but acceptance by business interests must develop or economic progress will be slow and reversible. Sustained development will require that productive beliefs, attitudes, and values spread to workers, institutions such as churches and universities, and ultimately to civil society. Otherwise, political support will be lacking for productivity-enhancing policies that challenge vested interests.

My work has revealed that one of the greatest challenges in enhancing national competitiveness in many respects is to modify economic culture. The policies and behaviors that support competitiveness are becoming better known—the problem is getting true acceptance of them. A big part of the task in economic development, then, is educational because many citizens and even their leaders lack a framework for understanding the modern economy, seeing their role in it, or perceiving their stake in the behavior of other groups in society. Lack of understanding often allows special interests to block changes that will widely benefit the nation's prosperity.

WHY DO NATIONS HAVE UNPRODUCTIVE CULTURES?

There is growing consensus about what determines prosperity and about the beliefs, attitudes, and values that foster economic progress. Why, then, do we have unproductive economic cultures? Why do these persist in certain societies? Do individuals and companies knowingly act in ways that are counter to their economic self-interest?

The answers to these questions are complex and present a fruitful area both for research and for practice. Clearly, individual and societal interests can diverge, and short-term horizons can lead to choices and behaviors that work against long-term interests. Let me suggest a number of broader answers, however. First, economic culture in a nation is strongly influenced by the prevailing ideas or paradigm about the economy. There have been numerous alternative theories of prosperity in this century, ranging from central planning to import substitution to factor accumulation. These ideas become deeply rooted in societies via the educational system, the influence of intellectuals and government leaders, and countless other means. At the same time, there is often ignorance about the international economy and its workings, even among political leaders. Ignorance creates a vacuum that allows these beliefs to persist.

What people believe about what it takes to be prosperous has much to do with how they behave. And beliefs become reflected in attitudes and values. Unproductive economic culture, then, often arises less from deeply embedded societal traits than ignorance or the misfortune of being guided by flawed theories. The acceptance of flawed theories is sometimes a matter of pure ideology, but sometimes it is a convenience related to desired modes of political control. Military regimes often like import substitution and self-sufficiency policies, for example, because they reinforce their power and control over citizens. Nations that are able to avoid flawed ideas, for whatever reason, have benefited in terms of economic prosperity.

Second, economic culture appears to be heavily derived from the past and present microeconomic context. True, individuals may act in ways that might hurt the collective interests of the society or national self-interest. But in my experience it is rare that individuals knowingly act in unproductive ways that are counter to their individual or company self-interest. The role of cultural attributes, then, is difficult to decouple from the influence of the overall business environment and a society's institutions. The way people behave in a society has much to do with the signals and the incentives that are created in the economic system in which they live.

For example, one often hears complaints about workers in developing countries as having a poor work ethic. But what if there is no reward for hard work? What if there is no advancement even if one works hard? A nation's work ethic cannot be understood independently of the overall system of incentives in the economy. Similarly, companies in developing countries often behave opportunistically and do not plan based on long time horizons. In fact, this short-term behavior often can be rational in an environment in which government policies are unstable and unpredictable. Rent seeking by companies, similarly, is usually associated with a political system that rewards it.

National characteristics ascribed to culture, then, often have economic roots. Good examples are Japan's lifetime employment system and its high savings rate. Lifetime employment was far from the norm in pre–World War II Japan and was originally instituted to control labor strife in the early post–World War II period. High savings is widely recognized as owing much to the memory of wartime deprivation and its aftermath, coupled with relatively early retirement, a poorly developed pension system, and exorbitant costs of home ownership requiring substantial capital accumulation.

Thus it is difficult to disentangle culturally derived behaviors from behaviors that have been enhanced or encouraged by the economic system. History, in this sense, places a strong imprint on economic culture, both from experiences during "good times" and those during "bad times." This dependence of culture on circumstance is supported by the success of people from poor countries who have moved to a different economic system. The case of some El Salvadorans in the United States who have achieved remarkable success is one of many examples.

Third, social policy choices can have a strong influence on economic culture because they influence the economic context. A good example is policies toward the social safety net. These directly affect attitudes toward work, personal savings behavior, and willingness to invest in self-education while they indirectly influence many other aspects of a nation's economic policies. Indeed, economic and social policies are inextricably intertwined.

Much economic culture, then, is learned directly or indirectly from the economy. Exceptions include those beliefs, attitudes, and values derived not from self-interest or economic interest at all but from purely social or moral choices. Societal attitudes toward older citizens, norms for personal interaction, and religious teachings are examples of social/moral attitudes and values that can shape economic culture independently. Such attitudes and values also have a large role in establishing a nation's social policy priorities. Even social and moral choices, however, can bear the imprint of past economic circumstances and learning. Religion and philosophy may well reinforce productive—or unproductive—economic culture.

These arguments, taken together, suggest great caution in dismissing the economic prospects of any society because of culture: "Country X is not successful because workers are lazy and companies are corrupt." What if the society learned different economic beliefs and instituted a different economic system? Similarly, it is dangerous today, in a global economy with access to advanced technology and knowledge, to rely solely on sweeping explanations for prosperity such as geography, climate, or religion.

All this suggests that economic culture is sticky and hard to change, but perhaps not as sticky as is sometimes supposed. Especially those beliefs, attitudes, and values that are unproductive can be changed if they are no longer reinforced by prevailing beliefs or by the contextual reality faced by citizens and companies. To be sure, there will be ignorance, suspicion, and inertia before giving up what has been learned. However, the experience of the recent decade suggests that nations can modify economic culture rapidly under the right circumstances.[4] There are reasons to suspect, which I will discuss, that the pace of potential change may be increasing.

GLOBAL CONVERGENCE AROUND
THE CULTURE OF PRODUCTIVITY

Historically, world political and economic circumstances offered scope for wide variations in economic culture. As noted, there have been widely differing economic models that have, in some cases, been pursued in nations for many decades. The persistence of these disparate models, with their resulting imprint on economic actors, reflected the then prevailing circumstances. The international economy was far less globalized over the past seventy to eighty years, so that national economies were less exposed to international competition. Protectionist policies in many countries created an even more self-contained world. Economies could continue unproductive policies and behaviors for decades, even if productivity was not improving. Military force and geopolitics distorted trade patterns, sending more false messages about economic prosperity. The protectionism of the developing world, in turn, taught poorer nations that they had to sell natural resources and cheap labor to Europe and the United States, stunting the upgrading of their economies. Global politics, shaped by the Cold War, further insulated nations from the need for economic change. Large amounts of foreign aid went into developing countries, propping up ineffective leaders and obscuring disastrous economic policies.

The persistence of unproductive economic cultures was reinforced by limits of knowledge and limits on the ability of poorer countries to improve. Citizens were often isolated and not exposed to alternate behaviors. The pace of technological change was slow enough that the costs of technological backwardness or late adoption were not as dramatic as they are today, which further perpetuated bad policies. There was relatively slow diffusion of economic and managerial knowledge and much less foreign investment. International dissemination of business knowledge was far more costly and less effective than today. Performance measurement and benchmarking across countries was rare. Old, flawed ideas about prosperity, economic policy, and management survived and in some cases were actively promoted. With many different economic models being implemented, cultural factors could play a large role in the approaches chosen and in the degree of a nation's success.

Today, however, we confront a radically different economic context. Complacency and tolerance for slow-paced development have given way to an overwhelming sense of urgency to meet the imperatives of the global economy. Theories of development at odds with the productivity paradigm have been discredited, unable to cope with open competition or to contend with the rapid pace of technological and managerial improvement. Differences of opinion about the bases of economic prosperity and the appropriate policy choices are narrowing. Knowledge about the elements of productive economic culture is being rapidly disseminated. Citizens are more exposed to successful behaviors elsewhere. There is, then, an increasing convergence of opinion around the globe about what it takes to be prosperous.

This growing convergence around the productivity paradigm is creating strong pressures on countries that fail to internalize it. Economic policies and behaviors are being increasingly measured and compared across countries. Financial markets penalize countries without sound policies; foreign investment dries up if nations do not provide a productive business environment; workers lose their jobs if they lack a good work ethic. Political leaders are increasingly accountable to wider economic forces, even if not to local citizens. The rapid advancement of technology is also raising the cost of being isolated from, or not embracing, international practices, thus amplifying these pressures.

The result is that many nations are striving, with differing degrees of success, to embrace the productivity culture. Take Central America. Centuries of nationalistic, inward-looking policies in most of the countries have given way to a process of opening and economic integration through coordinating transportation infrastructure, harmonizing customs practices, and many other steps. All the Central American countries are moving to embrace competition and productivity. The forces of globalization have led these small countries to put their nationalistic interests aside and to make large strides in changing long-standing practices.

At the same time that globalization provides a powerful discipline on unproductive behaviors; it is rewarding productive aspects of economic culture with unprecedented flows of capital, investment, technology, and economic opportunity. The same global economy is also enabling stunning rates of progress in those nations willing to embrace it. Knowledge and technology have become accessible and available as never before. Modern technology allows goods to be transported efficiently for long distances and commerce to be carried on efficiently in disparate climates. When caught in the comparative advantage mind-set, countries are limited by their endowment. In a world in which productivity, initiative, and learning are the determinants of prosperity, developing countries have unprecedented opportunities to enhance wealth.

Indeed, the forces in the new economy are so strong that it is no overstatement to suggest that economic culture is no longer a matter of choice. The question is, Will a country voluntarily embrace a productive economic culture by changing the old beliefs, attitudes, and values that are impeding prosperity, or will the change eventually be forced upon it? It has become a question of when and how fast a country's economic culture will change, rather than whether it will change. Although older citizens who grew up under past economic approaches often resist change, the generations of younger managers in their twenties and thirties have often been trained in the new economic culture, not infrequently at international business schools. Thus there are also forces for change from within the business elite in many developing countries.

In the modern economy, which exerts great pressure on societies to adopt beliefs, attitudes, and values consistent with the productivity paradigm, does culture today have the same influence in the economic sphere that it had under a different economic order? Historical accounts often include rich discussions of the impact of cultural attributes on societies and their development paths because historically these attributes were persistent and exerted considerable influence on the economic configuration of societies. Yet the convergence of economic ideas and the pressures of the global market have arguably reduced the scope for cultural variables to influence the economic paths societies choose.

What we are witnessing, in many ways, is the emergence of the core of an international economic culture that cuts across traditional cultural divides and will increasingly be shared. A set of beliefs, attitudes, and values that bear on the economy will be common, and the clearly unproductive aspects of culture will fall away under the pressure, and the opportunity, of the global economy. An important role for culture in economic prosperity will remain, but it may well be a more positive one. Those unique aspects of a society that give rise to unusual needs, skills, values, and modes of work will become the distinctive aspects of economic culture. These productive aspects of culture, such as Costa Rica's passion for ecology, America's convenience obsession, and Japan's passion for games and cartoons, will become critical sources of hard-to-imitate competitive advantage, resulting in new patterns of international specialization, as nations increasingly produce those goods and services in which their culture gives them a unique advantage.

Thus, although global convergence around the productivity paradigm is increasing, cultural differences will certainly remain. Globalization will not eradicate culture, as some have feared. However, instead of isolating some peoples in their economic disadvantage, these cultural differences can contribute the specialized advantages so important to improving the prosperity of nations in the global economy. In a global economy in which so many things can be easily sourced from anywhere, cultural differences that give rise to distinctive products and services should become more celebrated.

3

Notes on a New Sociology of Economic Development

JEFFREY SACHS

INTRODUCTION: THE GROWTH PUZZLE

The greatest puzzle in economic development is why sustained economic growth is so hard to achieve. Before 1820, there was essentially no such thing as sustained economic growth. Angus Maddison (1995) estimates that world growth of GDP per capita averaged around 0.04 percent per annum from 1500 to 1820. Whereas Western Europe and its colonies in North America and Oceania had pulled ahead of other regions by 1820, the gap between Western Europe and the world's poorest region (sub-Saharan Africa) was only three to one, according to Maddison's estimates.

All regions of the world experienced a rise in per capita income after 1820, with world growth rising to 1.21 percent per year between 1820 and 1992, but the growth has been very uneven. The two groups of nations already ahead in 1820, Western Europe and what Maddison terms the Western off-shoots (the United States, Canada, Australia, and New Zealand) pulled ahead still further, and today they constitute most of the developed world. Among the richest thirty countries in the world as of 1990, twenty-one were in Western Europe or were Western offshoots. Five were in Asia: Hong Kong, Japan, Korea, Singapore, and Taiwan. The other four countries include two small oil states (Kuwait and United Arab Emirates), Israel, and Chile. These thirty countries account for about 16 percent of the world's population. By the 1990s, the gap between the richest region (the Western offshoots) and the poorest (sub-Saharan Africa) rose to around twenty to one.

Three broad explanations may help to account for the growth puzzle.

- Geography: Certain parts of the world are geographically favored. Geographical advantages might include access to key natural resources, access to the coastline and sea—navigable rivers, proximity to other successful economies, advantageous conditions for agriculture, advantageous conditions for human health.

- Social Systems: Certain social systems have supported modern economic growth, whereas others have not. Precapitalist systems based on serfdom, slavery, inalienable landholdings, and so forth, tended to frustrate modern economic growth. In this century, socialism proved to be a disaster for economic well-being and growth wherever it was attempted. Similarly, colonial rule in the nineteenth and twentieth centuries was generally adverse to high rates of economic growth.

- Positive Feedback: Positive feedback processes amplified the advantages of early industrialization, thereby widening the gap between rich and poor. First, the early European industrializers exploited the laggard regions through military conquest and colonial rule. Many of the laggard societies collapsed when they were challenged militarily or economically by the richer nations. Second, the technological gap between the advanced and lagging countries has tended to widen rather than narrow over time. Technological innovation operates like a chain reaction in which current innovations provide the fuel for future breakthroughs.

Neoclassical economic theory does not answer the growth puzzle because it neglects the roles of geography, social institutions, and positive feedback mechanisms. Even the dynamics of innovation have been under-studied until recently. In neoclassical economics, development is really not much of a challenge. Market institutions are a given. Countries are assumed to save and accumulate capital, whereas technology and capital is assumed to flow readily across national borders. Since the marginal product of capital is higher in capital-scarce countries than in capital-rich countries, and since the technologically lagging countries can import the technologies of the richer countries, the poorer countries are expected to grow faster than the rich countries.

Neoclassical economics therefore has an ingrained optimism about the prospects for economic convergence—the tendency for the poor country to grow faster than the rich country and to narrow the gap in income levels. Of course, classical and neoclassical economists since Adam Smith have recognized that flawed economic institutions may hinder growth, but the optimism of neoclassical economics is sustained by the view that flawed economic institutions will be swept away by institutional competition or through public choice.

Neoclassical economics certainly helps explain various important episodes of rapid economic growth in the modern period. The rise of the East Asian economies in recent decades owes much to the rapid accumulation of capital and technology in a market-based, capital-scarce region. Similarly, the narrowing of the gap between northern Europe and southern Europe in the postwar period is clearly related to the convergence mechanisms stressed by neoclassical economics, again because the assumptions of the neoclassical framework have applied well in the Western European circumstances. The main problem is that these convergence mechanisms apply only in specific circumstances, not as general processes.

This chapter sketches a more extended sociological framework for understanding the uneven nature of world economic growth. I stress that an adequate theory must address physical geography and the evolution of social institutions, both through internal social change and through the interaction of societies across national borders.

THE ROLE OF GEOGRAPHY

If social scientists were to spend more time looking at maps, they would be reminded of the powerful geographical patterns in economic development. Two basic patterns stand out. First, the temperate regions of the world are vastly more developed than the tropics. (In the list of the thirty richest countries, only two, Hong Kong and Singapore—accounting for less than 1 percent of the combined population of the richest thirty countries—are in a tropical zone.) Second, geographically remote regions—either those far from the coasts and navigable rivers or mountainous states with high internal and international transport costs—are considerably less developed than societies on coastal plains or navigable rivers. Landlocked states in general face the worst problems. They are both distant from the coast and must cross at least one political border on the way to international trade. Although Europe boasts some rich landlocked economies (especially Austria, Luxembourg, and Switzerland), those countries have the advantage of being surrounded by rich coastal economies. In other regions of the world, landlocked countries are almost uniformly poor.

The reasons for the widespread impoverishment in the tropics are complex, but the phenomenon is general, occurring in all parts of the world. We don't really have a North-South division in the world; instead, we have a temperate-tropical division.

There are probably three major explanations for the persisting impoverishment of the tropics: agricultural factors, health factors, and factors relating to the mobilization of scientific resources. Tropical agriculture faces several problems that lead to reduced productivity of perennial crops in general and of staple food crops in particular: weak soils and high soil erosion and exhaustion under tropical rain forest conditions; difficulties of water control and risks of drought in the wet-dry tropics; very high incidence of agricultural and veterinary pests; high rate of food spoilage in storage; and reduced rates of net photosynthetic potential in regions with warm nighttime temperatures. The result seems to be an intrinsic limit on food productivity in large regions of the tropics. Exceptions include the alluvial and volcanic soil regions, such as the Nile Delta and Java, and intermontane valleys, where nighttime temperatures are lower. Highly populated tropical highland regions include Central America, the Andes, the Great Lakes and Rift Valley regions of East Africa, and the Himalayan foothills.

The burden of infectious disease is similarly higher in the tropics than in the temperate zones. Most infectious diseases in temperate zones are transmitted directly between humans (e.g., tuberculosis, influenza, pneumonia, sexually transmitted diseases). In the tropics, there are also major vector-borne diseases (malaria, yellow fever, schistosomiasis, trypanosomiasis, ochocerciasis, Chagas' disease, filariasis, among others), in which animals that flourish in the warm climate, such as flies, mosquitoes, and mollusks, play the critical role of intermediate hosts.

The combination of poor agricultural productivity and high incidence of infectious disease has had manifold adverse effects: a high proportion of the population in agriculture because of the absence of an agricultural surplus; low degree of urbanization; a high concentration in remote high-altitude regions (e.g., the Andean altiplano and the Great Lakes region of Africa) seeking to escape the problems of the hotter, tropical plains; lower life expectancy and a smaller accumulation of human capital.

A third disability may be associated with the tropics. Temperate regions have been more populated than tropical regions for at least 2,000 years. On very rough calculation, using the data in McEvedy and Jones (1978), the tropics have had about one-third of the world's population during the past two millennia. If productivity growth is related to the size of population and if productivity advances in one ecological zone do not easily cross into another zone, then the temperate zone might be advantaged by having a higher share of world population. Both of these assumptions seem realistic. Productivity growth is spurred by larger demand, and it is facilitated by a larger supply of potential innovators. Similarly, productivity advances in the temperate zone in areas such as agriculture, health, and construction are unlikely to be directly applicable to the very different ecological conditions of the tropics. Thus the higher rate of productivity advance in the temperate zone might not easily diffuse to the tropics.

From this perspective, commenting on Hong Kong and Singapore, two small economies in the geographical tropics (though only Singapore is in the ecological tropics), is worthwhile. These are, indeed, exceptions that help prove the rule. Both island city-states are concentrated in manufacturing and services. They don't have to grapple with low agricultural productivity or disease-carrying vectors.

Another major dimension of geography is the endowment of mineral resources, especially energy resources and precious minerals (e.g., gold, diamonds). In the nineteenth century, when transport costs were still very high in comparison to today, coal was a sine qua non of heavy industrialization. The Nordic countries, southern Europe, North Africa, and the Middle East were disadvantaged in heavy industry relative to the countries of the coal belt that stretches from Britain across the North Sea to Belgium, France, Germany, and Poland and into Russia. Of course, other regions could develop on the basis of agriculture and light industry, but they could not develop metallurgy, transport, and chemical industries. In the twentieth century, falling transport costs and the use of oil, gas, and hydroelectric power for the generation of energy have relaxed this constraint.

Geography is, no doubt, just one part of the puzzle. Several temperate-zone regions have not done well, as least not as well as Western Europe, East Asia (Japan, South Korea, Taiwan), and the Western offshoots. The lagging temperate-zone regions include North Africa and the Middle East, parts of the Southern Hemisphere (Argentina, Chile, Uruguay, and South Africa), and large parts of Central and Eastern Europe and the former Soviet Union that until recently were under communist rule. To understand these cases, we need to turn to social theory.

SOCIAL SYSTEMS AND ECONOMIC GROWTH

As an empirical matter, economic growth has been related to political, cultural, and economic factors and has been intimately connected with capitalist social institutions characterized by a state subject to the rule of law, a culture that supports a high degree of social mobility, and economic institutions that are market based and support an extensive and complex division of labor. Few societies have displayed this combination of political, cultural, and economic institutions. Moreover, history suggests that there is no strong tendency for societies to develop such institutions through internal evolution.

Indeed, so powerful are the barriers to evolutionary social change that fundamental institutional change typically results from external shocks rather than internal evolution. Most important in the past two hundred years have been the tumultuous interactions between economically advanced and economically lagging societies. These interactions cause profound social turmoil in the lagging societies that break the internal social equilibrium. The resulting turmoil may produce a reorientation of social institutions in a way that supports economic growth. Often, though, the result has been economic collapse and even the loss of sovereignty.

Max Weber's monumental sociology was the first to lay out an adequate description of the social institutions of modern capitalism. Weber drew "ideal type" distinctions between precapitalist and capitalist societies. In precapitalist societies, political authority is traditional and arbitrary, unbound by legal restraints. Social norms support hierarchical distinctions. Major markets do not exist, and the lesser markets that do are constrained by social or legal barriers. In capitalist societies, the state is bound by the rule of law. Social mobility is high. And economic exchange is heavily mediated through market institutions.

Weber's sociology was written at the start of the twentieth century. His field of inquiry was the emergence of capitalism in Western Europe and the reasons for its absence in other parts of the Old World. It is timely to update Weber's sociology at the beginning of the twenty-first century, asking a somewhat different question: Why did capitalism spread unevenly to other parts of the world?

Weber's comparative institutional analysis provides part of the framework for such an inquiry. Weber did not, however, deal adequately with three issues. First, he presented relatively static portraits of capitalist and non-capitalist societies, not the principles that govern their social evolution. Second, he did not deal adequately with intersocietal interactions, including institutional imitation or rejection, colonial rule, and military conflict. Third, he focused on precapitalist and capitalist societies. His sociological maps would have to be extended to at least three other broad types of social organization: colonial rule, socialist society, and collapsed societies. Let me offer a brief description of each.

In colonial societies, the essence of politics is exclusionary rule with the state apparatus controlled by the colonial power, the principal objective being maintenance of order. Traditional cultural institutions are systematically undermined in the interests of economic exploitation. Economic institutions are designed to ensure the terms of trade of the colonizer. Colonial rule was not a very good "school" for modern capitalism.

In socialist societies, politics is dominated by a repressive single-party organization. Traditional culture, especially religion, is suppressed, as are all private market activity and accumulation of private wealth. With the benefit of hindsight, we can now see clearly that socialism was economically destructive almost everywhere, with the possible exception of a few heavily subsidized remote areas within the Soviet empire.

There is another frequently occurring social condition, which we might call "social collapse," in which social institutions cease functioning and society is thrust into a Hobbesian war of all against all. Recreating any form of social order is typically very difficult after such an internal collapse. Since so much of the developing world has passed through such a state of social collapse, it is worth specifying its main features.

With respect to politics, state authority does not exist or is extremely limited, a condition often accompanied by violence. Cultural mechanisms of social trust break down, as do the market mechanisms of the economy. Black markets appear and monetary transactions may be replaced by barter.

One major goal of a revised sociology would be to explain the movements of society among these states (precapitalist, capitalist, colonial, socialist, and collapsed society). Why did some parts of the world make a relatively smooth transition to capitalism while others were colonized and still others collapsed? In which ways did the colonial experience prepare societies for capitalism, and in which ways did it frustrate the transition even beyond the colonial period itself? We are not yet in a position to answer these questions. The next section merely sketches some hypotheses.

PATTERNS IN THE DIFFUSION OF CAPITALISM

Marx and Engels were prescient in understanding the dynamism of the new capitalist system in Western Europe. They surmised, correctly, that capitalism would eventually spread to the entire world, based on the superiority of its economic productivity.

The bourgeoisie, by the rapid improvement of the instruments of production and the immensely expanded means of communication, draws all nations into civilization. The cheap prices of capitalism's commodities are the heavy artillery with which it batters down all walls and forces the "barbarians" to capitulate. It compels all nations, on pain of extinction, to adopt the bourgeois mode of production. It compels them to introduce "civilization" into their midst, that is, to become bourgeois themselves. It creates a world after its own image.

Yet the process was anything but rapid and smooth. We need a better sociological theory of institutional change if we are to understand this long, frequently bitter, and often violent process. Since we don't have a general theory of social evolution, or even a mapping of how capitalism did or did not diffuse from Western Europe to the rest of the world, I think it is most useful to offer some hypotheses, or at least informed speculation.

- Capitalist institutions are generally resisted by elites of non-capitalist societies because of the implications of capitalism for increased social, political, and economic competition. Thus, in virtually every type of society (precapitalist, socialist, colonial), elite actors try to frustrate or limit the institutionalization of the rule of law, the norms of social mobility, and the introduction of market institutions.
- Capitalist reforms are least likely to progress in highly stratified societies (e.g., Russia or the Ottoman Empire in the nineteenth century), since social elites are better positioned to resist change.
- Capitalist reforms tend to be resisted especially fiercely by political elites that have a weak claim on their own legitimacy. For example, the fact that nineteenth-century China was ruled by a foreign dynasty with dubious legitimacy (the Manchus) no doubt raised barriers to internal institutional change.
- Internal reforms in many regions were cut short by colonial rule. In general, colonial powers did not carry out market reforms in the colonized society, since this would have empowered local inhabitants and undermined foreign rule. Thus, the spread of capitalism was short-circuited by the European capitalist powers themselves, often for a century or more.
- Threatened societies often experienced internal collapse rather than reform, mainly because the outside threat leads to a financial crisis and hence a collapse of political power or because the outside threat delegitimized the internal rulers, or both.
- Internal collapse can be followed by a bewildering array of outcomes, including chronic chaos (à la Haiti). Social collapse is often the occasion of revolutionary change. In the wake of the financial and political collapse of the tsarist regime in 1917, Lenin was able to seize and consolidate power despite the absence of any broad-based political support. The Soviet system was then spread through military power into Eastern and Central Europe.
- The adoption of capitalist institutions is strongly favored by certain geographical conditions:

coastal states rather than hinterland states,
states proximate to other capitalist societies,
states on major international trade routes,
regions with fertile agriculture, which in turn supports a high level
of urbanization.
- Capitalist institutions are favored in societies linked to world markets through cultural connections (e.g., a dominant religion or a minority diaspora with links to other countries).

Modern capitalism began in the North Atlantic societies, especially England and Holland, after centuries of active trade and development in the Mediterranean. It was carried naturally to the lands of new settlement in North America and to Australia and New Zealand. These regions were distinguished by several factors, the most important of which were that they shared the same temperate zone ecological conditions as Britain and that native populations were sparse, even more so after decimation by European disease. Within Western Europe, capitalist institutions spread from west to east, carried by Napoleon's armies, by the Revolution of 1848, and by the example of British industrialization. By 1850, modern capitalism existed in Western Europe and the Western offshoots.

The remainder of the Americas deserves a special word. The Caribbean was settled as slave societies, mostly for sugar production. It remained colonized, with the important exceptions of Hispaniola (Haiti and the Dominican Republic) until the end of the nineteenth century (in the case of Cuba) or the middle of the twentieth century (in the Lesser Antilles and Jamaica). Most of the region was long characterized by white rule over an impoverished population of former slaves, and environmental degradation due to exhaustion of the tropical soils.

The Spanish colonies varied considerably. Argentina, Chile, and Uruguay, in the Southern Hemisphere temperate zone, are most similar to the lands of new settlement in North America and Oceania. Native populations were sparse. The climate was similar to that of Spain. Although these countries were politically unstable in the first decades of independence (from around 1820 to 1870), by 1870 they had become more or less capitalist societies with formal democratic structures, albeit with extremely unequal land distribution. In tropical Central America and the Andean countries, the situation was very different. Most of these societies had much larger indigenous Amerindian populations. Societies therefore developed with inequalities and social stratification between European-descended whites and native inhabitants plus imported slaves. These societies resisted capitalist institutions for much longer, due no doubt to their extreme inequalities.

The fiercest nineteenth-century battles over economic reform were fought in the Old World, in the great empires of China, Japan, Russia, and the Ottomans. Here the general principles observed earlier seem to be helpful. In three of the four cases (all but Japan), societies proved to be strongly resistant to capitalist reform, even when fundamentally threatened by Western European encroachments. Japan alone experienced a swift "capitalist revolution" after a coup in 1868. This transformation was favored by Japan's pre-existing commercial society; its cultural homogeneity; its coastal orientation, which allowed export-led growth; and even its coal deposits, which permitted early industrialization. In the other societies, a combination of political and cultural obstacles frustrated attempts at reform. Politics and culture worked in the same direction: Social elites resisted reforms that threatened their favored positions within long-standing social orders.

Almost all of the rest of the world—essentially the Old World tropics—fell under colonial rule. This was uniformly true in Africa after the spread of quinine opened the way for European settlement and conquest in malarial sub-Saharan Africa. North Africa, the Indian subcontinent, and Southeast Asia similarly fell under European rule. Japan colonized Korea and Taiwan, and Central Asia was absorbed within the Russian empire.

By 1900, there was a discernible if crude tally. Capitalism was prevalent in Western Europe, the Western offshoots, and, with some qualifications, the Southern Cone (Argentina, Chile, and Uruguay), and Japan. These countries accounted for approximately one-fifth of the world's population. The New World tropics (the Caribbean, Central America, and South America) were generally highly stratified, white-ruled societies in which much of the population lacked freedom, education, and social mobility. The Old World tropics and the Indian subcontinent were colonized by European powers. The three great empires—the Ottomans, tsarist Russia, and Ch'ing China—were all collapsing under the weight of European encroachments, declining legitimacy at home, and growing fiscal burdens from the external challenges.

Let me jump ahead sixty-five years—past the Bolshevik revolution, two world wars, and the Great Depression. Socialism had spread to much of the world. Decolonization was under way in Africa and was completed in the Indian subcontinent and much of Southeast Asia. I want to stress that little of the world, as late as 1965, was capitalist in orientation. Indeed, we could make the following rough tally:

- capitalist world: Western Europe, Western offshoots, Japan, Korea, Taiwan, Hong Kong, Singapore (21 percent of world population);

- socialist world: Soviet Union, Central and Eastern Europe, North Korea, China, Cuba (32 percent of world population);
- highly statist and in some cases one-party socialist rule: Argentina, Chile, Egypt, India, Indonesia, Iran, Mexico, Turkey (23 percent of world population);
- mixed capitalist/non-capitalist societies with extreme internal inequalities: tropical Americas, South Africa, Rhodesia (6 percent of world population);
- others: still colonized, traditional, and so on (18 percent of world population).

The general lesson, in summary, is that most of the world in modern history has been governed by non-capitalist institutions. The process of social reform was stymied in four ways: by the resistance of traditional Old World societies (mainly the major empires—the Ottomans, Russia, and China), by a period of colonial domination, by the adoption of socialism, and by social collapse. As late as 1965, only about one-fifth of the world could be counted as operating according to capitalist social institutions.

INCREASING RETURNS TO SCALE AS ANOTHER SOURCE OF WIDENING INEQUALITY

Another likely reason for the growing gap between rich and poor is that a major part of the economic development process—technological innovation—is characterized by increasing returns to scale. In theories of endogenous growth, new innovations are produced by the stock of existing technological "blueprints" in society. Ideas beget ideas. The dynamics of innovation may be characterized by increasing returns to scale, in which a kind of chain reaction takes place in response to an initial stock of ideas. Societies that have a critical mass of technological ideas may experience a takeoff into self-sustaining growth, whereas societies that fall short of that critical mass may experience continuing stagnation. The rich get richer because existing ideas are the source of new ideas.

There is surely some merit in this view. World science is even more unequally distributed than world income. The high-income regions (Western Europe, North America, Japan and the NICs, and Oceania) contain around 16 percent of world population and 58 percent of world GDP but account for around 87 percent of scientific publications and an astounding 99 percent of all European and U.S. patents.

SOME ECONOMETRIC EVIDENCE ON THE
SOURCES OF ECONOMIC DEVELOPMENT

There are sixty-one countries in the world with half or more of the population in temperate plus snow climatic zones. Of these, twenty-four countries were socialist during much of the post–World War II period. That leaves thirty-seven non-socialist temperate/snow zone countries. Of those, six are landlocked outside of Western Europe (Lesotho, Malawi, Nepal, Paraguay, Zambia, and Zimbabwe). Thus we have thirty-one temperate/snow zone economies that were neither landlocked nor socialist.

Of these thirty-one, all but seven are developed, if we use the threshold of $10,000 per capita in 1995 purchasing power parity (PPP) adjusted prices. The seven include four countries in North Africa and the Middle East (Lebanon, Morocco, Tunisia, and Turkey), and three Southern Hemisphere countries (Argentina, South Africa, and Uruguay). These seven countries are anomalous from a geographical viewpoint. Why have they not achieved economic development? Among culture, politics, economic institutions, which have been the major culprits?

The tantalizing possibility from a cultural point of view is that the lagging development of North Africa and the Middle East demonstrates a strong cultural component. Is there evidence here that, controlling for climate and geography, these Islamic countries face deeper internal obstacles to economic growth? Note that the cultural obstacles could be internal (e.g., opposition to market-based institutions emanating from within society) or they could be externally imposed (e.g., European discrimination against the region in trade policies). It is not possible at a macroeconomic level to disentangle such interpretations, assuming that either or both is actually correct.

The case for cultural factors in the other three countries is more dubious. Argentina and Uruguay are largely immigrant countries, sharing the cultural norms mainly of southern Europe. However, since these countries lag far behind southern Europe, we should suspect that geography and politics rather than culture per se is the predominant explanation of the lagging performance. Indeed, this is made more clear by the fact that Argentina was well above the income level of Italy as of 1929 ($4,367 compared with $3,026 in 1990 PPP adjusted dollars, according to the Maddison data). The shortfall in Argentina's performance occurred during the past half century and is clearly related to changes in domestic politics and economic strategy during and after the Perón regime. Uruguay's economic development followed closely upon that of its much larger neighbor. South Africa, finally, must be viewed mainly through the prism of colonial and racial policies rather than culture.

What about success stories among the tropical countries? Sadly, there are precious few. Only one tropical country (Singapore) plus one former colony now part of China (Hong Kong) rank among the top thirty countries. Suppose we focus our attention on the relative success stories: tropical countries that have a 1995 per capita income level at $6,000 or above. There are, in addition to Singapore and Hong Kong, eight such cases (out of a total of forty-six tropical countries), listed in order of income per capita: Malaysia, Mauritius, Gabon, Panama, Colombia, Costa Rica, Thailand, and Trinidad and Tobago. Two of these countries make the list mainly because of oil resources (Gabon and Trinidad and Tobago). Panama no doubt benefits mainly from its geographical distinctiveness rather than good government or cultural advantages. The more interesting anomalies therefore include Malaysia, Mauritius, Colombia, Costa Rica, and Thailand. Again, we should ask whether culture rather than politics has been decisive in the relatively strong performance of these countries.

Thailand and Malaysia have benefited strongly from export-led growth in the past thirty years, disproportionately concentrated among the overseas Chinese communities in those countries, and the links that the overseas Chinese communities have made with foreign investors from the United States, Japan, and Europe. More generally, the trade and financial linkages in Asia among the Chinese diaspora communities (especially Indonesia, Malaysia, Singapore, and Thailand) and Greater China (Hong Kong, Taiwan, and the Mainland) may well constitute a case in which cultural factors have contributed to successful development. (As always, there is an important ambiguity about the role that culture may play here. It may involve intrinsic factors within the belief systems of the community or it may rather provide a network of trusted economic connections). It is ironic, of course, that Weberian sociology pointed to China as a case of culturally arrested development set in contrast to growth under Protestant cultural norms. The evidence of the past half century, including China's own opening to market forces after 1978, strongly suggests that political factors and poor economic institutions, rather than culture per se, lie behind the many centuries of China's lagging economic development.

To summarize these points, the great divisions between rich and poor countries involve geography and politics (especially whether or not the country was socialist in the postwar era). If culture is in fact an important determinant of cross-country experience, it seems to play a subsidiary role to these broader geographical and political/economic dimensions. Nonetheless, there are indeed some hints of culturally mediated phenomena. Two are most apparent: the under-performance of Islamic societies in North Africa and the Middle East and the strong performance of tropical countries in East Asia that have an important overseas Chinese community. In each case, there is a deeper ambiguity of interpretation. Is the cultural signal related to beliefs within the community or rather to the international relations (and therefore trade prospects) of the countries in question?

Space limitations preclude a detailed treatment here of a regression analysis undertaken in 1999 to test these hypotheses. The conclusions: The basic variables are as expected—economic policy affects growth rates, temperate/snow zone economies grow faster than tropical countries, regions with falciparum malaria grow less rapidly than regions without the disease, and landlocked countries grow more slowly than countries with a coastline. The coefficients on Hindu and Muslim societies are small and statistically insignificant. There is, in short, no evidence that Hindu or Muslim populations achieved lower growth rates, controlling for economic policy variables or geography variables.

The same methodology can be used to show that former colonies do not demonstrate any sign of residual adverse effects of the colonial period in the sense that growth during 1965–1990 is not strongly affected by colonial status before 1965. Thus, although the colonial period was probably adverse for economic growth, there is no evidence of a longer-term adverse legacy. Clearly, though, more careful work should be carried out on that important question.

SUMMARY AND CONCLUSIONS

This chapter has discussed an approach to the sociology of economic development, including the possible role of cultural institutions in economic performance. It has argued that modern economic growth is intimately connected with capitalist institutions and favorable geography. There is only slight evidence that religious categories add explanatory power above those two broad classes of explanation of economic growth. There is some evidence that the Muslim countries of North Africa and the Middle East have under-performed over the long term relative to their favorable geography (temperate zone, specifically Mediterranean climate, and coastal orientation). However, there is no evidence that such under-performance has continued after 1965, and, at least in the past ten years, several Muslim countries have sharply outperformed the world average.

The cultural explanations of economic performance may be helpful in some circumstances, especially in accounting for resistance to capitalist reforms in the nineteenth century, but such explanations should also be tested against a framework that allows for other dimensions of society (geography, politics, economics) to play their role. Controlling for such variables sharply reduces the scope for an important independent role of culture. More broadly, there is considerable historical work remaining to develop a sound framework for measuring and studying the evolution of social institutions and the interactions of politics, culture, and economics in the course of social change. Equally important, we must better understand the role of cross-border factors in social evolution. The weight of international factors in social change has been extremely high for at least two centuries, and it is bound to increase in the future under the pressures of increasing globalization of society, politics, and economics.

REFERENCES

Kornai, Janos. 1992. *The Socialist System*. Princeton: Princeton University Press.

Landes, David. 1998. *The Wealth and Poverty of Nations*. New York: Norton.

Maddison, Angus. 1995. *Monitoring the World Economy, 1820–1992*. Paris: Organization for Economic Cooperation and Development.

McEvedy, Colin, and Richard Jones. 1978. *Atlas of World Population History*. New York: Penguin.

Weber, Max. 1979. *Economy and Society*. Berkeley: University of California Press.

Young, Crawford. 1995. *The African Colonial State in Comparative Perspective*. New Haven: Yale University Press.

4

A Cultural Typology of Economic Development

MARIANO GRONDONA

The process of economic development reaches a crisis when a nation passes from one stage to the next. It is at that moment when temptations arise. If the nation manages to resist these temptations, it will achieve development; otherwise, it will only enjoy a short period of enrichment.

When the cycle starting with labor and ending in reinvestment has yielded some fruit and people feel richer, they may be inclined to work less. On the other hand, consumption may rise at a pace that reduces the surplus, so that development turns into enrichment. Furthermore, even if the surplus is increased, a nation may decide not to return it to productive investment. It may instead spend it on those priorities to which nations have often surrendered, such as works that are monuments to leaders, wars of prestige, utopian plans of welfare, or outright corruption. Nations may also be tempted to preserve their stage of development through protectionist strategies or policies that discourage entrepreneurship and investment.

Every time a crucial temptation appears, a country may either overcome it or fall into it. Thus we may also define the process of economic development as an unending sequence of decisions favorable to investment, competition, and innovation that are made whenever the temptation to diverge arises.

A nation must transit the moments of temptation in ways favorable to economic development. It will do so if certain values prevail. Talcott Parsons writes that "value" may be considered an element within a conventional symbolic system that serves as a criterion for selecting among the alternatives available in a given situation.[1] Only those nations with a value system favorable to temptation-resisting decisions are capable of sustained, rapid development.

There are two categories of values: intrinsic and instrumental. Intrinsic values are those we uphold regardless of the benefits or costs. Patriotism, as a value, demands sacrifices and is sometimes "disadvantageous" as far as individual well-being is concerned. Nevertheless, hundreds of millions of people have died to defend their country throughout the course of history.

In contrast, a value is instrumental when we support it because it is directly beneficial to us. Let us assume that a country is dedicated to economic growth and to this end emphasizes work, productivity, and investment. If decisions favorable to development only answer to an instrumental value of an economic nature, such as increased wealth, the country's effort will decline as soon as the degree of wealth is attained.

Why should a nation go on acting as if it were poor once it is rich? The revolution of economic development occurs when people go on working, competing, investing, and innovating even when they no longer need to do so to be rich. This is only possible when the values pursued, which promote prosperity, do not vanish as prosperity arrives. Thus the values prevailing at the crucial moments of decisions leading to economic development must be intrinsic and not instrumental, since instrumental values are by definition temporary: Only intrinsic values are inexhaustible. No instrument survives its utility, but an intrinsic value always calls to us from an ever distant summit.

All economic values are instrumental. We want to have money as a means to some non-monetary end such as well-being, happiness, freedom, security, religion, or philanthropy. To make development unending, therefore, the accumulation process must not be suffocated by its own success. This means that the values driving constant investment cannot be of an economic nature; otherwise, they would vanish with economic success. When a nation is rich, something other than the pursuit of wealth must be present in its value system so that the wealth generated never suffices. This non-economic "something" may be salvation, survival, safety, excellence, prestige, or even empire: any value that will always be wanting.

However, the intrinsic values indispensable for sustained development, although non-economic, must not be anti-economic. They must be non-economic and pro-economic at the same time. Being non-economic, they will not be exhausted by economic success; being pro-economic, they will unceasingly push forward the process of accumulation.

The paradox of economic development is that economic values are not enough to ensure it. Economic development is too important to be entrusted solely to economic values. The values accepted or neglected by a nation fall within the cultural field. We may thus say that economic development is a cultural process.

Values fall within that province of culture we call "ethics." The behavior of someone who acts out of respect for an intrinsic value formerly accepted at will and later incorporated as an inner imperative is called "moral." A person is moral when answering to intrinsic values. If a country achieves economic development when responding to non-economic values that are nevertheless pro-economic, we can conclude that economic development is a moral phenomenon. Without the presence of values favorable to economic development, temptations will prevail. Temptations are the bearers of short-term expectations, but economic development is a long-term process. In the struggle between short and long term, the former will win unless a value intervenes in the decisionmaking process. This is the function of values: to serve as a bridge between short-term and long-term expectations, decisively reinforcing distant goals in their otherwise hopeless struggle against instant gratification.

In *Underdevelopment Is a State of Mind,*[2] Lawrence E. Harrison focuses on economic development from a cultural point of view. To illustrate his thesis, Harrison offers bilateral comparisons: Costa Rica and Nicaragua, the Dominican Republic and Haiti, Barbados and Haiti, Australia and Argentina, the United States and Latin America. The development gap between each pair is explained by cultural factors, whereas a chapter on Spain and Spanish America focuses on the cultural similarities and their consequences.

After reading Harrison's book, I felt inclined to venture beyond bilateral comparisons in order to produce a cultural typology in which two ideal types of value systems confront each other: one totally favoring economic development and the other totally resisting it. Under the theoretical umbrella of those two ideal types, Harrison's analysis would provide case studies.

Values can be grouped in a consistent pattern that we may call a "value system." Real value systems are mixed; pure value systems exist only in the mind, as ideal types. It is possible to construct two ideal value systems: one including only values that favor economic development and the other including only values that resist it. A nation is modern as far as it approaches the former system; it is deemed traditional as far as it approaches the latter. Neither of these value systems exists in reality, and no nation falls completely within either of those two value systems. However, some countries approach the extreme favorable to economic development, whereas others approach the opposite extreme.

Real value systems are moving as well as mixed. If they are moving toward the favorable value-system pole, they improve a nation's chances of developing. If they move in the opposite direction, they diminish a nation's chances of developing.

This typology embraces twenty factors that are viewed very differently in cultures that are favorable and those that are resistant to development. These differences are intimately linked to the economic performance of the contrasting cultures. In choosing a system of values closer to either the favorable or resistant ideal systems, people actually prefer the kind of economy that flows from those systems, and that is what they will have. This leads to a controversial conclusion: In the last analysis, development or underdevelopment are not imposed on a society from outside; rather, it is the society itself that has chosen development or underdevelopment.

TWENTY CONTRASTING CULTURAL FACTORS

Religion

Throughout history, religion has been the richest source of values. It was of course Max Weber who identified Protestantism, above all its Calvinist branch, as the root of capitalism. In other words, what initiated economic development was a religious revolution, one in which the treatment of life's winners (the rich) and losers (the poor) was centrally relevant. Weber labeled the religious (essentially Roman Catholic) current that showed a preference for the poor over the rich "publican," whereas he termed the current that preferred the rich and successful (essentially Protestant) "pharisaic."

Where a publican religion is dominant, economic development will be difficult because the poor will feel justified in their poverty, and the rich will be uncomfortable because they see themselves as sinners. By contrast, the rich in pharisaic religions celebrate their success as evidence of God's blessing, and the poor see their condition as God's condemnation. Both the rich and the poor have a strong incentive to improve their condition through accumulation and investment.

In the context of this typology, publican religions promote values that are resistant to economic development, whereas pharisaic religions promote values that are favorable.

Trust in the Individual

The principal engine of economic development is the work and creativity of individuals. What induces them to strive and invent is a climate of liberty that leaves them in control of their own destiny. If individuals feel that others are responsible for them, the effort of individuals will ebb. If others tell them what to think and believe, the consequence is either a loss of motivation and creativity or a choice between submission or rebellion. However, neither submission nor rebellion generates development. Submission leaves a society without innovators, and rebellion diverts energies away from constructive effort toward resistance, throwing up obstacles and destruction.

To trust the individual, to have faith in the individual, is one of the elements of a value system that favors development. In contrast, mistrust of the individual, reflected in oversight and control, is typical of societies that resist development. Implicit in the trusting society is the willingness to accept the risk that the individual will make choices contrary to the desires of government. If this risk is not accepted and the individual is subjected to a network of controls, the society loses the essential engine of economic development, namely, the aspiration of each of us to live and think as we wish, to be who we are, to transform ourselves into unique beings. Where there are no individuals, only "peoples" and "masses," development does not occur. What takes place instead is either obedience or uprising.

The Moral Imperative

There are three basic levels of morality. The highest is altruistic and self-denying—the morality of saints and martyrs. The lowest is criminal—disregard for the rights of others and the law. The intermediate morality is what Raymond Aron calls "a reasonable egoism"—the individual engages in neither saintly nor criminal behavior, reasonably seeking his or her own well-being within the limits of social responsibility and the law.

The highest morality is illustrated by Marx's slogan "from each according to his ability, to each according to his needs" and by the Roman Catholic Church's insistence on clerical chastity. Neither is consistent with human nature.

In development-favorable cultures, there is widespread compliance with laws and norms that are not totally exigent and are therefore realizable. Moral law and social reality virtually coincide. In development-resistant cultures, on the other hand, there are two worlds that are out of touch with each other. One is the exalted world of the highest standards and the other is the real world of furtive immorality and generalized hypocrisy. The law is a remote, utopian ideal that does little more than express what people might in theory prefer, whereas the real world, effectively out of touch with *all* law, operates under the law of the jungle, the law of the cleverest or the strongest, a world of foxes and lions disguised as lambs.

Two Concepts of Wealth

In societies resistant to development, wealth above all consists of *what exists*; in favorable societies, wealth above all consists of *what does not yet exist*. In the underdeveloped world, the principal wealth resides in land and what derives from it. In the developed world, the principal wealth resides in the promising processes of innovation.[3] In the resistant society, real value resides, for example, in today's computer, whereas the favorable society focuses on the generation of computers to come.

In the British colonies in North America, uninhabited lands were available to those who would work them. In the Spanish and Portuguese colonies to the south, all lands were claimed by the Crown. From the outset, wealth belonged to those who held power. Wealth thus did not derive from work but from the ability to earn and retain the favor of the king.

Two Views of Competition

The necessity of competing to achieve wealth and excellence characterizes the societies favorable to development, not only in the economy but elsewhere in the society. Competition is central to the success of the enterprise, the politician, the intellectual, the professional. In resistant societies, competition is condemned as a form of aggression. What is supposed to substitute for it is solidarity, loyalty, and cooperation. Competition among enterprises is replaced by corporativism. Politics revolve around the *caudillo*, and intellectual life has to adjust itself to the established dogma. Only in sports is competition accepted.

In resistant societies, negative views of competition reflect the legitimation of envy and utopian equality. Although such societies criticize competition and praise cooperation, the latter is often less common in them than in "competitive" societies. In fact, it can be argued that competition is a form of cooperation in which both competitors benefit from being forced to do their best, as in sports. Competition nurtures democracy, capitalism, and dissent.

Two Notions of Justice

In resistant societies, distributive justice is concerned with those who are alive now—an emphasis on the present that is also reflected in a propensity to consume rather than to save. The favorable society is likely to define distributive justice as that which also involves the interests of future generations. In such societies, the propensity to consume is often smaller and the propensity to save is often greater.

The Value of Work

Work is not highly valued in progress-resistant societies, reflecting a philosophical current that goes back to the Greeks. The entrepreneur is suspect but the manual laborer somewhat less so, since he must work to survive. At the top of the prestige ladder are the intellectual, the artist, the politician, the religious leader, the military leader. A similar prestige scale characterized Christendom until the Reformation. However, as Max Weber observed, the Reformation, and particularly the Calvinist interpretation of it, inverted the prestige scale, enshrining this work ethic. It is this same inverted value system that importantly explains the prosperity of Western Europe and North America—and East Asia—and the relative poverty of Latin America and other Third World areas.

The Role of Heresy

With his thesis of free interpretation of the Bible, Martin Luther was the religious pioneer of intellectual pluralism at a time when dogmatism dominated Christendom. The unpardonable crime at the time was not sin but heresy. Yet the questioning mind is the one that creates innovation, and innovation is the engine of economic development. Orthodox societies, including the former Soviet Union, suppress innovation. The collapse of the Soviet Union had more than a little to do with its insistence on Marxist-Leninist orthodoxy.

To Educate Is Not to Brainwash

We have seen that value systems favorable to development nurture the formation of individuals who are innovators, heretics. Education is the principal instrument of this nurturing. However, this must be a form of education that helps the individual discover his or her own truths, not one that dictates what the truth is. In value systems resistant to development, education is a process that transmits dogma, producing conformists and followers.

The Importance of Utility

The developed world eschews unverifiable theory and prefers to pursue that which is practically verifiable and useful. The intellectual traditions in Latin America focus more on grand cosmovisions, which put it at a developmental disadvantage. *Ariel*, the phenomenally popular book by the Uruguayan José Enrique Rodó that appeared in 1900, draws the distinction by using two characters from Shakespeare's *The Tempest*: the comely, spiritual Ariel, representing Latin America, and the ugly, calculating Caliban, representing the United States. However, it was the North Americans, not the Latin Americans, who opened the path to economic development. At the same time, we must note that utilitarianism suffers from a troubling lacuna, symbolized by the horrors of Nazi Germany and Soviet Russia.

The Lesser Virtues

Advanced societies esteem a series of lesser virtues that are virtually irrelevant in traditional cultures: a job well done, tidiness, courtesy, punctuality. These contribute to both efficiency and harmoniousness in human relations. They are unimportant in a resistant culture, partly because they impinge on the assertion of the individual's wishes and partly because they are overwhelmed by the great traditional virtues of love, justice, courage, and magnanimity. Nevertheless, the lesser virtues are characteristic of societies in which people are more respectful of the needs of others.

Time Focus

There are four categories of time: the past, the present, the immediate future, and a distant future that merges into the afterlife. The time focus of the advanced societies is the future that is within reach; it is the only time frame that can be controlled or planned for. The characteristic of traditional cultures is the exaltation of the past. To the extent that the traditional culture does focus on the future, it is on the distant, eschatological future.

Rationality

The modern world is characterized by its emphasis on rationality. The rational person derives satisfaction at the end of the day from achievement, and progress is the consequence of a vast sum of small achievements. The premodern culture, by contrast, emphasizes grandiose projects—pyramids, the Aswan Dam, revolutions. Progress-resistant countries are littered with unfinished monuments, roads, industries, and hotels. But it's not important. Tomorrow a new dream will arise.

Authority

In rational societies, power resides in the law. When the supremacy of the law has been established, the society functions according to the rationality attributed to the cosmos—natural law—by the philosophers of modernity (e.g., Locke, Hume, Kant). In resistant societies, the authority of the prince, the *caudillo*, or the state is similar to that of an irascible, unpredictable God. People are not expected to adapt themselves to the known, logical, and permanent dictates of the law; rather, they must attempt to divine the arbitrary will of those with power; thus the inherent instability of such societies.

Worldview

In a culture favorable to development, the world is seen as a setting for action. The world awaits the person who wants to do something to change it. In a culture resistant to development, the world is perceived as a vast entity in which irresistible forces manifest themselves. These forces bear various names: God, the devil, a powerful international conspiracy, capitalism, imperialism, Marxism, Zionism. The principal preoccupation of those in a resistant culture is to save themselves, often through utopian crusades. The individual in the resistant society thus tends to oscillate between fanaticism and cynicism.

Life View

In the progressive culture, life is something that I will make happen—I am the protagonist. In the resistant culture, life is something that happens to me—I must be resigned to it.

Salvation from or in the World

In the resistant conception, the goal is to save oneself *from* the world. According to traditional Catholicism, the world is "a vale of tears." To save oneself from it is to resist temptations in a quest for the other world, the world after death. But for the puritan Protestants, salvation in the other world depends on the success of the individual's efforts to transform *this* world. The symbol of the Catholic vision is the monk; that of the Protestant vision, the entrepreneur.

Two Utopias

Both progress-prone and progress-resistant cultures embrace a certain kind of utopianism. In the progressive culture, the world progresses slowly toward a distant utopia through the creativity and effort of individuals. In the resistant culture, the individual seeks an early utopia that is beyond reach. The consequence is again a kind of fanaticism—or cynicism. The latter utopianism is suggested by the visit of Pope John Paul II to India, where he insisted that all Indians have a right to a dignified life free of poverty and at the same time rejected birth control.

The Nature of Optimism

In the resistant culture, the optimist is the person who expects that luck, the gods, or the powerful will favor him or her. In the culture favorable to development, the optimist is the person who is resolved to do whatever is necessary to assure a satisfactory destiny, convinced that what he or she does will make the difference.

Two Visions of Democracy

The resistant culture is the heir of the tradition of absolutism, even when it takes the form of Rousseauistic popular democracy, which admits no legal limits or institutional controls. In this vision, the absolute power of the king accrues to the people. The liberal, constitutional democracy of John Locke, Baron de Montesquieu, James Madison, and the Argentine Juan Bautista Alberdi characterizes the vision of democracy in the progressive culture. Political power is dispersed among different sectors and the law is supreme.

CONCLUDING THOUGHTS

This list of twenty cultural factors, which contrasts a value system favorable to economic development and one that is resistant, is not definitive. It could be amplified by additional contrasts or it could be reduced, seeking only the most important differences. My criterion has been practicality, and these twenty factors are sufficient to obtain some idea of the contrasting visions from which the two value systems flow.

It is important to be mindful that neither the "favorable" nor the "resistant" exists in the real world. Rather, as Weber would say, they are *ideal types,* or *mental constructs,* that facilitate analysis because they offer two poles of reference that help us locate and evaluate a given society. The closer a society is to the favorable ideal, the more likely it is to achieve sustained economic development. Conversely, a society that is close to the resistant pole will be less likely to achieve sustained economic development.

An imaginary line runs between the resistant and favorable poles on which the real societies can be located. That location is not permanent, however, because no value system is static. There is continuous, albeit slow, movement on the line away from one pole and toward the other. Like two illuminated ports that call to the navigator from different directions, the ideal types permit a diagnosis of the course and speed of a given nation toward or away from economic development. Should it come close to the reefs of the resistant pole, it is time to consider what needs to be done to change the course and speed of the culture's value system to enhance the prospects of arriving at the opposite pole. Similarly, it should be possible to identify those values that, even if not wholly favorable to development, must be conserved because they preserve the identity of the society—so long as they do not block access to development.

Whether in the West or the East, development did not really exist before the seventeenth century. This was equally true for Europe and China, for pre-Columbian America and India. Productivity levels were low around the world because the societies were all agrarian. There were good years and bad years, mostly the result of climatic factors, above all rainfall, but there was no sustained economic development. The reason was cultural. Values that encouraged capital accumulation with a view to increased production and productivity did not exist. The value systems were anti-economic, emphasizing, for example, the salvation of the soul of the Egyptian pharaohs, art and philosophy in ancient Greece, the legal and military organization of the Roman Empire, mastery of traditional philosophy and literature in China, and the renunciation of the world and the quest for eternal salvation—often through war—of the Middle Ages in Europe.

It was the Protestant Reformation that first produced economic development in northern Europe and North America. Until the Reformation, the leaders of Europe were France, Spain (allied with Catholic Austria), the north of Italy (the cradle of the Renaissance), and the Vatican. The Protestant cultural revolution changed all that as heretofore second-rank nations—Holland, Switzerland, Great Britain, the Scandinavian countries, Prussia, and the former British colonies in North America—took over the reins of leadership. Economic development, in the form of the industrial revolution, brought wealth, prestige, and military power to the new leaders. Furthermore, the non-Protestant nations had to face the reality that their failure to pursue economic development would lead to their domination by the Protestant countries. They had to choose between Protestant hegemony and their traditional "resistant" values—their identity.

The responses varied across a spectrum from one non-Protestant country to another. At one extreme was Puerto Rico, which sold its Latin soul for the mess of pottage of economic development. At the other extreme is the Islamic fundamentalism of Iran, which ardently rejects Western-style development as a threat to an ancestral identity whose preservation is the chief goal of those in power.

Other nations pursued courses between these two extremes. Imperial China disdained the power of the West until it was subjugated by it. The Maoist communist revolution can be interpreted as China's first real accommodation to the West, albeit in the form of the Western heresy of Marxism. Deng took a further step in the direction of the West by opening the doors to capitalism, albeit within an authoritarian political system.

Following the visit of the U.S. naval squadron to Tokyo Bay in 1853, when it became apparent to the Japanese that they could not defend themselves against the West, Japan's new Meiji leadership staked out a different course: They would accept Western technology but not Western culture. Japan then built a formidable war machine that defeated China and Russia but was itself destroyed in World War II. That trauma was followed by an imposed democratization that has since taken root and a refocusing of Japanese priorities away from warfare toward industry and commerce—with astonishing results. A similar path has been followed by South Korea and Taiwan, both former Japanese colonies.

The Catholic countries of Europe have accepted the logic of economic development, particularly since World War II. As the rate of growth in the Protestant countries has declined, in part because of the waning of the earlier religious energy, France, Belgium, Italy, Ireland, and Spain have crossed the frontier that separates development from underdevelopment.

Is Catholic Latin America following the same path? In the 1980s—the "lost decade"—Latin America experienced an economic crisis precipitated by its resistant values. It remains to be seen whether Latin America will in fact achieve the lofty heights of economic development, democratization, and modernization.

5

Culture and the Behavior of Elites in Latin America

CARLOS ALBERTO MONTANER

Latin America has long suffered from manic-depressive cycles with respect to its political perceptions. There are times when, in a state of euphoria, the media announces that the continent has finally reached adulthood. We hear that Colombia is a new "Asian tiger," that Costa Rica is a surprising Silicon Valley in the heart of Latin America, or that Brazil is going to challenge the hemispheric hegemony of the United States. Then come the institutional catastrophes: coup attempts, hyperinflation, the failure of stabilization programs, and capital flight. We lapse into a state of gloomy depression, and foreign capital starts to flee. Depression then turns to despair, and we give up, concluding, "There's no way out!" Perhaps we should begin to talk about a cyclothymic culture.

As the twentieth century ends, we are in the depressive phase of the cycle. It is true that for the first time in history, all Latin American governments, with the exception of that in Cuba, have been elected freely. But there is a justified fear that our democracy is more fragile than we have appreciated. The same authoritarian Venezuelan lieutenant colonel, Hugo Chavez, who tried to take power by force in 1992, leaving four hundred dead in his wake, governs the country today with strong popular support. Ecuador, whose parliament had to get rid of a president, Abdala Bucaram, accused of "going mad," is now in the middle of an economic crisis that no one knows how to solve. The Brazilian currency lost half of its purchasing power in three weeks and, with this devaluation, the popularity of President Fernando Henrique Cardoso also plummeted. Mexico at times appears to be moving toward modern democracy, at times away from it. Colombia has been transformed into a series of urban islands precariously connected by airplanes. At least three armies impose their law: the central government army, the communist guerrilla army, and the paramilitary groups' army. At the same time but in varying degrees, these three armies are penetrated by a fourth power, the narcotraffickers, who buy consciences and weapons and control the actions of hundreds of hired killers. In Paraguay, the vice president, Luis María Argaña, an enemy of the president, Raúl Cubas, is murdered by his opponents; the president is then dismissed and escapes together with the putschist General Oviedo. But why belabor the point? We are simply in a depressive cycle.

THE ENDLESS DISCUSSION

The debate over the causes of Latin America's failures relative to the success of Canada and the United States has been a recurrent focus of Latin American intellectuals, and there are enough explanations to suit anyone. At the beginning of the nineteenth century, they put the blame on the Iberian inheritance with its intolerant Catholicism. Around the middle of that century, the shortcomings were attributed to the demographic weight of an apparently indolent native population opposed to progress. At the beginning of the twentieth century, and particularly with the Mexican Revolution in 1910, it was said that poverty and underdevelopment were caused by an unfair distribution of wealth, above all by the peasants' lack of access to land. Starting in the twenties and accelerating thereafter, "exploitative imperialism," mainly "Yankee imperialism," was blamed. During the thirties and forties, the view was espoused that Latin America's weakness was a consequence of the weakness of its governments, a condition that could only be corrected by turning them into "engines of the economy," converting public officials into businessmen.

All these diagnoses and proposals reached the crisis point in the eighties— "the lost decade"—when experience demonstrated that all of the arguments were false, although each may have contained a grain of truth. The rapid development of countries that were poorer than the Latin American average in the 1950s—South Korea, Singapore, Taiwan—proved that Latin America had fundamentally misunderstood the keys to prosperity. This inevitably led us back to the eternal question, Who is responsible?

One possible, although partial, answer is "the elites": the groups that lead and manage the principal sectors of a society; those who act in the name of certain values, attitudes, and ideologies which, in the Latin American case, do not favor collective progress. There is no single individual who is responsible; rather, a large number—a majority—of those who occupy leading positions in public and private organizations and institutions are the ones chiefly responsible for perpetuating poverty.

The idea that traditional cultural values and attitudes are a major obstacle to progress has gradually been gaining momentum. But how do these values and attitudes reflect themselves in the way people behave? In this chapter, I will suggest how they express themselves in the behavior of six elite groups: the politicians, the military, businessmen, clergy, intellectuals, and leftist groups. I want to stress at the outset that it is not fair to blame only the elites, who are, in large measure, a reflection of the broader society. If their behavior strayed radically from the norms of the broader society, they would be rejected. Moreover, within the elites, there are exceptions—people who are striving to change the traditional patterns of behavior that have brought us to where we are.

THE POLITICIANS

Let us begin with the politicians, since they are the most visible. Politicians are so discredited in Latin America today that to be elected, they have to demonstrate that they are not politicians at all but something quite different: military officers, beauty queens, technocrats—anything at all except politicians. Why is this so? Largely because public sector corruption with impunity is the norm throughout the region. It expresses itself in three forms:

- The classical form, in which government officials receive "commissions" and bribes for each project that is won or each regulation that is violated to benefit someone.
- The indirect form, in which the corruption benefits someone with whom you are allied, although you yourself may remain clean. Examples are Joaquín Balaguer in the Dominican Republic and José María Velasco Ibarra in Ecuador.
- The clientelism form—the most costly—in which public funds are used to buy large groups of voters.

It is as if politicians were not public servants elected to obey the laws but rather autocrats who measure their prestige by the laws they are able to violate. That is where the definition of true power resides in Latin America—in the ability to operate above the law.

The truth is that a large percentage of Latin Americans either nurture or tolerate relationships in which personal loyalty is rewarded and merit is substantially ignored. In Latin American culture loyalty rarely extends beyond the circle of friends and family. Thus the public sector is profoundly mistrusted and the notion of the common good is very weak. Consequently it is inevitable that the most successful politicians are those who pay off their allies and sympathizers.

To be sure, these noxious practices are not exclusive to Latin America. What is alarming, however, is the frequency and intensity with which they occur in the region and, above all, the people's indifference to these practices and the impunity with which wrongdoers engage in them. It is as if Latin Americans did not realize that they themselves are ultimately paying for the corruption and inefficiency that contribute so powerfully to the region's poverty.

THE MILITARY

The military is comparably culpable for Latin America's problems. In the advanced democracies, the role of the military is to protect the nation from foreign threats. In Latin America, the military has often assigned itself the task of saving the nation from the failures of the politicians, either imposing military visions of social justice by force or simply taking over the government and maintaining public order. In both cases, it has behaved like an occupying force in its own country.

It has been said that the behavior of the Latin American military reflects the influence of *la madre patria*, Spain. But the historical truth is that when the Latin American republics were established between 1810 and 1821, the putsches in Spain were exceptional and had little success. The time of the insurrections on the Iberian Peninsula coincided with similar phenomena in Latin America but did not precede them. Rather, the Latin American military *caudillos*, who provoked innumerable civil wars during the nineteenth century and prolonged dictatorships during the twentieth, seemed to be basically a Latin American historical phenomenon linked to an authoritarian mentality that had no respect for either the law or democratic values.

Although Latin America has known military dictatorships since the first days of independence early in the nineteenth century, in the thirties and forties the military, led by Getulio Vargas in Brazil and Juan Domingo Perón in Argentina, concluded that it was designated by Providence to undertake a new mission: to promote state-driven economic development, including the assignment of senior military officers as managers of state enterprises. The basic idea, which never really worked in practice, was that in nations with weak and chaotic institutions, as in Latin America, only the armed forces had the size, tradition, and discipline necessary to create large-scale modern industries capable of competing in the complex industrial world of the twentieth century.

This military involvement in state enterprises has cost Latin America dearly. Like politicians, military officers were corrupt. Their protected enterprises distorted the market, were often excessive in scale, and were vastly overstaffed. The result was inefficiency and obsolescence.

Although there have been a few civilian *caudillos*—for example, Hipólito Yrigoyen in Argentina and Arnulfo Árias in Panama—the *caudillo* tradition in Latin America has been dominated by the military. Rafael Leonidas Trujillo, Juan Perón, Anastasio Somoza, Alfredo Stroessner, Manuel Antonio Noriega, and Fidel Castro are good examples. The *caudillo* is more than a simple dictator who exercises power by force. He is a leader to whom many citizens, and practically the entire power structure, delegate full power of decision and control of the instruments of repression. The result is not only antithetical to democratic development but is also extremely costly in an economic sense and inevitably causes confusion of public and private property.

THE BUSINESSMEN

One of the greatest political ironies in Latin America is the frequent accusation that "savage capitalism" is to blame for the poverty of the 50 percent of all Latin Americans who are distressingly poor and survive in shacks with dirt floors and tin roofs. The real tragedy in Latin America is that capital is in limited supply, and a large part of what there is, is not in the hands of real entrepreneurs committed to risk and innovation but in those of cautious speculators who prefer to invest their money in real estate and expect that the vegetative growth of their nations will cause their properties to appreciate in value. These are not modern capitalists but rather landowners in the feudal tradition.

But even worse is the mercantilist businessman who seeks his fortune through political influence rather than market competition.[1] The mercantilist shares his profits with corrupt politicians in a vicious circle that produces both increasing profits and corruption. He often buys tariff protection, which results in higher prices and lower quality for the consumer. He may buy a monopoly position under the pretext of the national interest or economies of scale. Or he may also buy tax privileges, subsidies, preferential interest rates, loans that don't have to be repaid, and preferential rates for the purchase of foreign exchange.

These kinds of cozy relationships between mercantilist businessmen and corrupt politicians have been particularly shocking with respect to the sale of foreign currency at prime rates to import capital goods for local industries. In countries in which a dollar may have three different exchange rates, those with the appropriate relations can buy dollars at a prime rate, sell a portion of them secretly at a highly favorable rate, pay for the imported goods at yet another rate, and see their profits double as if by magic. And the richer they get, the more corrupt they become.

These harmful practices are not exclusive to Latin America, but the frequency and intensity with which this kind of corruption occurs in Latin America is very troubling, as is the indifference and impunity that accompanies it. The people don't seem to realize that the money acquired by mercantilist businessmen through the sale and purchase of influence comes either directly or indirectly from the pockets of taxpayers. Nor do they appreciate that this type of illicit activity increases the overall cost of transactions, substantially raising the cost of goods and services, further impoverishing the poor.

The fact is, with few exceptions, Latin America has never experienced the modern capitalism combined with political democracy that has produced the high levels of human well-being that are found in the prosperous nations of the West and increasingly in East Asia.

THE CLERGY

It is painful to have to include the clergy among the elites who are responsible for the misery of the masses. It is painful because those responsible are not all the clergy, only those who preach against market economics and justify anti-democratic actions. It is also painful because those clergy who behave this way do so out of altruism. But it is a quest for social justice that condemns the poor to permanent poverty—a true case of the road to hell being paved with good intentions.

In broad outline, since the second half of the nineteenth century the Catholic Church has lost most of its property, other than schools, hospitals, and a few mass media operations. Once the greatest landlord of the Western world, the Church long ago lost its major property role in the economic area. This does not mean that its influence has diminished, however, especially in moral terms. The Church can still legitimate or discredit given values and attitudes with profound impact on the prospects of the people.

But when the Latin American bishops' conference or the "theologians of liberation" or the Jesuits condemn "savage neoliberalism," they are propagating an absurdity.[2] "Neoliberalism" is nothing more than an array of adjustment measures designed to alleviate the economic crisis in the region: reductions in government spending, reductions in the public sector payroll, privatization of state enterprises, a balanced budget, and a careful control of monetary emission—pure common sense in the wake of an interventionist model that failed to produce widespread progress for the peoples of Latin America during more than half a century. These measures, so strongly criticized by the clergy, are no different from the ones the rich European countries demand of each other to qualify for the Euro. It is simply a matter of implementing a sensible economic policy.

The bishops, and particularly the liberation theology clergy, are even more destructive when they attack the profit motive, competition, and consumerism. They lament the poverty of the poor, but at the same time promote the idea that owning property is sinful, as is the conduct of people who succeed in the economy by dint of hard work, saving, and creativity. They preach attitudes that are contrary to the psychology of success.

For some liberation theology priests, poverty is inevitable, if for no other reason than the alleged imperialism of the rich countries, above all the United States. And the only way out of poverty is armed violence, which has been urged—and never publicly renounced—by liberation theology leader Gustavo Gutiérrez.[3]

THE INTELLECTUALS

There are few cultures in which intellectuals have as much visibility as in Latin America. This may come from the strong French influence on Latin American intellectuals; in France the same thing happens. Once a writer or an artist has achieved fame, he or she becomes an expert on all subjects, including war in the Balkans, the virtues of in vitro fertilization, and the disaster that is caused by privatizing state enterprises.

This characteristic of our culture would have no major significance, except for its destructive consequences. This "todology"—the faculty to talk about everything without modesty or knowledge—practiced by our intellectuals with great enthusiasm has a price: Everything they state and repeat turns into a key element in the creation of a Latin American cosmovision. This characteristic of our culture has serious consequences, since a significant number of Latin American intellectuals are anti-West, anti-Yankee, and anti-market. Moreover, no matter that their views are contrary to the experience of the twenty nations that are the most developed and prosperous on our planet, they nonetheless profoundly influence the Latin American cosmovision. The effect of their pronouncements is to weaken democracy and impede the development of a reasonable confidence in the future. If the intellectuals promote the vision of a frightening revolutionary dawn, we should not be surprised by the flight of capital nor the sense of impermanence that attaches to our political and economic systems.

Furthermore, what many intellectuals announce in newspapers, books and magazines, radio and television is repeated in the majority of Latin American universities. Most public Latin American universities and many private ones, with some exceptions, are archaic deposits of old Marxist ideas about economy and society. They continue to stress the danger of multinational investments, the damages caused by globalization, and the intrinsic wickedness of an economic model that leaves the allotment of resources to market forces. This message explains the close relationship between the lessons young scholars receive in the university and their link with subversive groups such as Sendero Luminoso in Peru, Tupamaros in Uruguay, Movimiento de Izquierda Revolucionaria in Venezuela, the M–19 in Colombia, or Sub-Comandante Marcos's picturesquely hooded Zapatistas in Mexico. The weapons these young men carried with them into the jungle, mountains, and city streets were loaded in the lecture rooms of the universities.

The Latin American university—with few and honorable exceptions—has failed as an independent creative center and has been a source of tireless repetition of worn-out and dusty ideas. But even more startling is the absence of a close relationship between what the students are taught and the real needs of society. It is as if the university were resentfully rebelling against a social model that it detests without any concern for the preparation of qualified professionals who could contribute to real progress. The failure of our universities is particularly appalling when we recognize that the majority of universities in Latin America are financed by the national budget—from the contribution of all taxpayers—in spite of the fact that 80 or 90 percent of the students belong to the middle and upper classes. This means that resources are transferred from those who have less to those who have more. This sacrifice then helps sustain absurd ideas that contribute to perpetuating the misery of the poorest.

THE LEFT

The final elite group consists of both labor unions that oppose market economics and private property and that peculiar Latin American category, the revolutionaries.

To be sure, there is a responsible labor movement dedicated to the legitimate interests and rights of workers. Sadly, this is often not the one that is dominant. The unions that burden Latin American societies are those that oppose privatization of state enterprises that have been losing money for decades while providing defective or nonexistent goods and services; the teacher unions that strike because they are opposed to their members taking standard competence tests; and the corrupt union aristocrats who loot retirement funds and health programs for their personal benefit.

Some unions fail to appreciate that the modern, competitive enterprise has to be flexible, capable of adapting to changing circumstances. When the unions make it difficult or costly to change staffing levels or when they establish rigid contracts, enterprises lose competitiveness and unemployment increases because businesses are reluctant to hire people under these conditions.

The revolutionaries are radicals who are convinced that they possess letters of marque that permit them to violate laws in the name of social justice. Some limit themselves to preaching revolution without taking any additional action to further the revolutionary cause. Others, for whom Che Guevara is often the patron saint, think that it is legitimate to engage in political violence without considering the consequences of their acts. For them, the state is illegitimate and must be attacked at all costs. Their vehicles are student strikes, street riots, sabotage, kidnapping, bombs, and guerrilla attacks.

What have the actions of this indomitable tribe of revolutionaries cost the Latin American nations? The amount is incalculable, but the revolutionary left has to be one of the principal causes of the region's underdevelopment, not just because of its destruction of existing wealth but because it has also interrupted that long and fragile cycle of savings, investment, profit, and reinvestment that produces the wealth of nations.

In conclusion, it is obvious that these elite groups do not exhaust the list of those who have kept Latin America in a state of poverty and injustice. But they figure very prominently. My hope is that by describing the behavioral expression of the traditional cultural values that have shaped them, by spotlighting that behavior, and by refuting their arguments, I may contribute to a process of change in Latin America in which these elites become forces *for* human progress, above all for those most in need: a Latin America where the dispossessed can reasonably hope for a life of freedom, dignity, justice, and prosperity.

6

Does Africa Need a Cultural Adjustment Program?

DANIEL ETOUNGA-MANGUELLE

The indicators of Africa's plight are staggering:

- Life expectancy is below sixty years in twenty-eight countries. Life expectancy is below fifty years in eighteen countries. Life expectancy in Sierra Leone is just thirty-seven years.
- About half of the more than 600 million people south of the Sahara live in poverty.
- Half or more of the adult populations of at least thirteen countries are illiterate.
- Half or more of women are illiterate in at least eighteen countries.
- Children under five die at rates in excess of 100 per 1,000 in at least twenty-eight countries. In Sierra Leone, the rate is 335 per 1,000.
- The population growth rate is 2.7 percent annually, almost four times the rate in the high-income countries.
- Among countries supplying such data to the World Bank (not all do), some of the most inequitable income distribution patterns are found in Africa. The most affluent 10 percent account for about 47 percent of income in Kenya, South Africa, and Zimbabwe, and about 43 percent in Guinea-Bissau, Senegal, and Sierra Leone.[1]

- And, obviously, democratic institutions are commonly weak or
  nonexistent throughout Africa.

Even in the face of all this human suffering, I cannot resist citing the story
of an African government minister carried away in his remarks: "When we
gained power, the country was at the edge of the abyss; since, we have taken
a great step forward!"

I cite this anecdote in part because we can no longer reasonably blame the
colonial powers for our condition. Several decades have passed during which
we have been in substantial control of our own destiny. Yet today Africa is
more dependent than ever on rich countries, more vulnerable than any other
continent to maneuvers aimed at giving with one hand and taking back with
the other. The World Bank, usually a great source of funds and advice, is itself short of ideas. Other than structural adjustment programs (whose efficiency has not yet been proven), there is silence.

The need to question our culture, the African culture, is evident. But what
characterizes the African culture? Is this culture compatible with the demands faced by individuals and nations at the beginning of the twenty-first
century? If not, what cultural reorientation is necessary so that in the concert
of nations we are no longer playing out of tune? *Does Africa need a cultural
adjustment program?*

WHAT WE ARE

It is never easy to speak of one's self, to reveal one's soul, especially when, as
is the case with the African soul, many different facets present themselves.
There are at least three dangers in this. The first is idealizing and embellish-
ing in order to appear to be more than we are. The second is to say nothing
that exposes the mysterious halo that people from all cultures wear. Finally,
who has the qualities and qualifications to speak in the name of us all? An
African proverb is correct in saying that he who looks from the bottom of a
well sees only a portion of the sky.

As legitimate as these concerns are, they should not prevent us from looking in the mirror. Do we dare to look ourselves in the face, even if it is difficult to recognize ourselves?

Fifty Africas, a Single Culture?

We long ago got into the habit of referring to Africa as a diverse entity,
and no one is surprised, in light of the balkanization of the continent, to
see works with titles like *Les 45 Afriques*[2] or *Les 50 Afriques*[3] because, as

J. Ki-Zerbo noted in the introduction to the latter, "Africa is palpable. It is also profitable."

The descriptions of African diversity are enough to make an Olympic skating champion dizzy. First, to better oppose them, we like to emphasize white Africa and black Africa: one north of the Sahara and the other south of it. But how do we then classify the Republic of South Africa and Zimbabwe, each with a powerful white minority? Behind the racial screen, one quickly discovers a far more important source of diversity—language. There is an Arabophone Africa, an Anglophone Africa, a Francophone Africa, a Lusophone Africa, a Hispanophone Africa, not to mention the scores of languages that have no relation to the languages of the European colonizers.

What can be said if we then dare to transcend frontiers resulting from colonial dismembering of real nationalities such as the Yorubas, Hausas, Peuls, Malinkes, to mention only a few, that straddle several states? To continue the census of African diversity based on the color of the epidermis or on language could lead to several thousand Africas! Next, we must confront the anthropologists. Are there as many cultures in Africa as there are tribes? Does their number coincide with the states as outlined by the colonial powers? Does generalizing about African culture as a whole make any sense at all?

I believe that it does. The diversity—the vast number of subcultures—is undeniable. But there is a foundation of shared values, attitudes, and institutions that binds together the nations south of the Sahara, and in many respects those to the north as well. The situation is analogous to that of Great Britain: Despite its Scottish, Welsh, and Northern Irish subcultures, no one would question the existence of a British culture.

The existence of this common base is so real that some anthropologists question whether imported religions—Christianity and Islam—have really affected African ancestral beliefs or given Africans different ways of understanding the contemporary societies in which they live. Modern political power has often assumed the characteristics of traditional religious ritual powers; divination and witchcraft have even made their way into courthouses. Everywhere on the continent, the bond between religion and society remains strong. As Felix Houphouët-Boigny, the late president of the Ivory Coast, told us (and he, as a Roman Catholic, knew what he was talking about): "From African archbishops to the most insignificant Catholic, from the great witch doctor to the most insignificant Moslem, from the pastor to the most insignificant Protestant, we have all had an animist past."[4]

African culture is not easily grasped. It refuses to be packaged and resists attempts at systemization. The following typology is not wholly satisfactory, but it gives some sense of what the African cultural reality is.

Hierarchical Distance

In the view of D. Bollinger and G. Hofstede, hierarchical distance—the degree of verticality—is generally substantial in tropical and Mediterranean climates, where the survival of the group and its growth depend less on human intervention than it does in cold and temperate countries.[5] In countries with substantial hierarchical distances, the society tends to be static and politically centralized. What little national wealth exists is concentrated in the hands of an elite. The generations pass without significant change in mind-set. It is the reverse in countries with short hierarchical distances. Technological changes happen because the group needs technical progress; the political system is decentralized and based on a representative system; the national wealth, which is substantial, is widely distributed; and children learn things that their parents never knew.

In the more horizontal cultures, subordinates believe that their superiors are people just like themselves, that all people have equal rights, and that law takes precedence over strength. This leads to the belief that the best way to change a social system is to redistribute power. In the more vertical societies, Africa among them, subordinates consider their superiors to be different—having a right to privilege. Since strength prevails over law, the best way to change a social system is to overthrow those who hold power.

To the extent that it covers many aspects of a society (e.g., political systems, religious practices, organization of enterprises), hierarchical distance would virtually suffice to explain underdevelopment. However, as Bollinger and Hofstede note, France, Italy (particularly in the south), and Japan are also countries of high hierarchical distance.

Control over Uncertainty

Some societies condition their members to accept uncertainty about the future, taking each day as it comes. There is little enthusiasm for work. The behavior and opinions of others are tolerated because deep down people feel relatively secure in the status quo.

In other societies, people are acculturated to conquer the future. This leads to anxiety, emotionalism, and aggressiveness, which produce institutions oriented toward change and the limitation of risks.

Africa, except for the southern tip of the continent, appears to belong entirely to the category of societies with weak controls over uncertainty. To create secure societies, three levers are available: technology, jurisprudence, and religion. We might say that African societies are societies of strong control over uncertainty; unfortunately, the control is exercised only through religion. In the final analysis, if Africans immerse themselves in the present and demonstrate a lack of concern for tomorrow, it is less because of the safety of community social structures that envelop them than because of their submission to a ubiquitous and implacable divine will.

The African, returning to the roots of religion, believes that only God can modify the logic of a world created for eternity. The world and our behavior are an immutable given, bequeathed in a mythical past to our founding ancestors, whose wisdom continues to illuminate our life principles. The African remains enslaved by his environment. Nature is his master and sets his destiny.

This postulate of a world governed by an immutable divine order in a universe without borders is accompanied by a peculiarly African perception of the notion of space and time.

The Tyranny of Time

The African sees space and time as a single entity. The Nigerians say, "A watch did not invent man." Africans have always had their own time, and they have often been criticized for it. As an example, Jean-Jacques Servan-Schreiber writes:

> Time in Africa has both a symbolic and cultural value that are very important in the manner in which it is lived and felt. This is frankly both a benefit and a handicap—a benefit to the extent that it is satisfying for individuals to live during a period at a rhythm that is their own and that they have no desire to give up. But it is also a handicap to the extent that they are in competition with countries that do not have the same work methods and for which competition at the level of productivity, for example, passes through a more rational use of time.[6]

Servan-Schreiber is right. In traditional African society, which exalts the glorious past of ancestors through tales and fables, nothing is done to prepare for the future. The African, anchored in his ancestral culture, is so convinced that the past can only repeat itself that he worries only superficially about the future. However, without a dynamic perception of the future, there is no planning, no foresight, no scenario building; in other words, no policy to affect the course of events. There can be no singing of tomorrows so long as our culture does not teach us to question the future, to repeat it mentally, and to bend it to our will. In modern society, everyone must prepare. Otherwise, as Servan-Schreiber reminds us, there will be no more seats on the train, no more money at the end of the month, nothing in the refrigerator for the dinner hour, and nothing in the granaries in between seasons.[7] All in all, daily life in Africa!

Indivisible Power and Authority

Over the course of several millennia, societies in the West evolved substantially outside of the influence of religion, leading to the separation of the things of this world from the spiritual world. This evolution also led to the advent of the power of the state, which was certainly still spiritual but detached from supernatural forces that no longer intervened in the governing of this world. In Africa, however, the force of religion continues to weigh both on individual and on collective destiny. It is common for African leaders to claim magical powers.

It is difficult to explain African passivity other than by the fear inspired by a God hidden in the folds of the clothes of every African chief. If a king or president escapes an attack (even a simulated one), the entire population will deduce that he has supernatural power and is therefore invincible. This propensity to equate all power with divine authority does not concern only the "fathers of the nation"; it affects every citizen—even the most ordinary— as soon as he is given any authority whatsoever. Take an African, give him a bit of power, and he will likely become bumptious, arrogant, intolerant, and jealous of his prerogatives. Constantly on his guard and an enemy of competence (not a criterion for electing gods), he is ruthless until an inopportune decree designates his successor. He ends his career entirely devoted to the cult of mediocrity. (It is a well-known fact in our republics that to end the career of a technocrat or a politician for good, you need only point out his excellence.)

The African will not accept changes in social standing: Dominant and dominated remain eternally in the places allocated them, which is why change in social classifications is often condemned. We complain about the difficulties in promoting the private sector in our states. These difficulties are rooted in the jealousy that dominates all interpersonal relations, which is less the desire to obtain what others possess than to prevent any change in social status.

In Africa, you must be born dominant; otherwise, you have no right to power except by coup d'état. The entire social body accepts, as a natural fact, the servitude imposed by the strong man of the moment. It has been argued that the underdeveloped are not the people, they are the leaders. This is both true and false. If African peoples were not underdeveloped (that is to say, passive, resigned, and cowardly), why would they accept underdeveloped leaders? We forget that every people deserves the leaders it gets.

The Community Dominates the Individual

If we had to cite a single characteristic of the African culture, the subordination of the individual by the community would surely be the reference point to remember. African thought rejects any view of the individual as an autonomous and responsible being. The African is vertically rooted in his family, in the vital ancestor, if not in God; horizontally, he is linked to his group, to society, to the cosmos. The fruit of a family-individual, society-individual dynamic, all linked to the universe, the African can only develop and bloom through social and family life.

How do we restore the degree of autonomy to the individual that is necessary for his affirmation as a political, economic, and social actor, while preserving this sociability that is the essence of the existence of the African? The suppression of the individual, the cardinal way of ensuring equality in traditional societies, is demonstrated in all areas—not only in economic matters, where the ultimate market price is a function of the presumed purchasing power of the buyer, but in cultural matters, where oral traditions have monopolized the transmission of culture. We might even wonder if it wasn't by design that Africans avoided the written word to assure the suppression of individualism. African thought avoids skepticism, another virus carried by the individual. Consequently, the established belief system remains absolute: As soon as ancestral beliefs are threatened, the only possible choice is between the established order and chaos.

The concept of individual responsibility does not exist in our hyper-centralized traditional structures. In Cameroon, the word "responsible" translates as "chief." Telling peasants that they are all responsible for a group initiative is to tell them therefore that they are all chiefs—which inevitably leads to endless interpersonal conflicts.

The death of the individual in our societies explains not only the culture of silence in which men like President Jerry Rawlings of Ghana rise up but also explains the contempt in which people hold all those that occupy an intermediate position in the hierarchy. Thus, in an African ministry, it is well understood that the only person who can solve any problem whatsoever, be it the most commonplace, is the minister himself. Supervisors, managers, and other officials are there only for show. Our ministers have no complaints. It is not good to delegate one's authority at the risk of encouraging the birth of a new political star who may eventually prove to be a competitor.

We must be realistic. Tribalism blooms in our countries because of both the negation of the individual and the precariousness of his situation in the absence of an operative set of individual rights and responsibilities. Should we then continue, while dancing and singing, to drift collectively toward hell

to safeguard a hypothetical social consensus? Or has the moment come to restore all rights to individuals?

Excessive Conviviality and Rejection of Open Conflict

The African works to live but does not live to work. He demonstrates a
propensity to feast that suggests that African societies are structured around
pleasure. Everything is a pretext for celebration: birth, baptism, marriage,
birthday, promotion, election, return from a short or a long trip, mourning,
opening or closure of Congress, traditional and religious feasts. Whether
one's salary is considerable or modest, whether one's granaries are empty or
full, the feast must be beautiful and must include the maximum possible
number of guests.

He who receives gives, but he who is received also gives in order to truly
participate in the joy or pain of his host. Sociability is the cardinal virtue of
all human beings; indeed, the African considers any person he meets a friend
until the contrary is demonstrated. Friendship comes before business; it is im-
polite, in a business discussion, to immediately go to the crux of the matter.
The African has an inexhaustible need for communication and prefers interpersonal warmth over content. This is the main reason for the inefficiency of
African bureaucracies. Each petitioner, instead of writing, seeks to meet in
person the official in charge of examining his file, thinking this eliminates all
the coldness of writing letters back and forth.

Differences that are the basis for social life elsewhere are not perceived or
are ignored to maintain ostensible social cohesion. It is the search for social
peace based on a shaky unanimity that pushes the African to avoid conflict—
although the continent is surely not free of it. In some African societies, the
avoidance of conflict means that justice cannot be rendered in the daytime.
In some Bamileke (West Cameroon) villages, the constituted bodies in charge
of security and justice are secret and meet at night. Members wear masks to
prevent being identified.

Conflict is inherent in human groups of whatever size, yet we try to sweep
it under the rug—and have been highly unsuccessful in doing so.

Inefficient Homo Economicus

In Africa, what classifies man is his intrinsic value and his birth. If the
African is not very thrifty, it is because his vision of the world attributes very
little importance—too little—to the financial and economic aspects of life.
Other than some social groups like the well-known Bamileke of Cameroon
or the Kamba of Kenya, the African is a bad *H. economicus*. For him, the

value of man is measured by the "is" and not by the "has." Furthermore, because of the nature of the rapport that the African maintains with time, saving for the future has a lower priority than immediate consumption. Lest there be any temptation to accumulate wealth, those who receive a regular salary have to finance the studies of brothers, cousins, nephews, and nieces, lodge newcomers, and finance the multitude of ceremonies that fill social life.

It should not come as a surprise that the urban elite embellish these spending traditions by behaving like nouveaux riches. They, of course, have access to large amounts of money, chiefly in government coffers, and to the relatives and friends who are the beneficiaries of our free-spending habits are added banks in Switzerland, Luxembourg, and the Bahamas. African governments are not, it is evident, any better at economic management than are African individuals, as our frequent economic crises confirm.

The High Costs of Irrationalism

A society in which magic and witchcraft flourish today is a sick society ruled by tension, fear, and moral disorder. Sorcery is a costly mechanism for managing conflict and preserving the status quo, which is, importantly, what African culture is about. Therefore, is not witchcraft a mirror reflecting the state of our societies? There is much to suggest this. Witchcraft is both an instrument of social coercion (it helps maintain and perhaps even increase the loyalty of individuals toward the clan) and a very convenient political instrument to eliminate any opposition that might appear. Witchcraft is for us a psychological refuge in which all our ignorance finds its answers and our wildest fantasies become realities.

Contrary to what some might believe, the Christian religion, far from putting an end to witchcraft in Africa, has legitimized it. The existence of Satan is recognized by the Bible and the White Fathers, thus confirming the existence of sorcerers and other evil persons.

Sects, usually based on the magical power of the leader or prophet, are proliferating in Africa. In Benin, a particularly religious land that is the cradle of Haitian and Brazilian voodoo, fifty-eight new sects were born between 1981 and 1986, bringing the total number of denominations in the country to ninety-two. In Kenya, there might be as many as 1,200 sects; in some rural districts, there are more churches than schools. Some prophets, their "temples" on the street, become affluent because of their ability to detect bad spirits. Others can protect against disease. Still others can help you protect your job and enhance your income.

An example I particularly like is that of Kombo, a transporter with a fleet of trucks serving the Ivory Coast and Burkina Faso. Kombo believes that to

European precautions—the regular maintenance of vehicles—it is necessary to add African precautions. What do these include? Well, his witch doctor gives him some porcupine-fish powder that he pours into his tires in order to prevent punctures. Why, you might ask? Because, when attacked, this thorny fish has the ability to inflate until it doubles in volume. The powder of this fish is therefore perfect for maintaining tire pressure.

Sorcery also extends to government. Witch doctors surround African presidents, and nothing that really matters in politics occurs without recourse to witchcraft. Occult counselors, responsible for assuring that authorities keep their power by detecting and neutralizing possible opponents, have power that the most influential Western advisers would envy. The witch doctors often amass fortunes, and they sometimes end up with official designations, enjoying the direct exercise of power.

Football, the opiate of Africans, competes with politics with respect to sorcery. The story made the rounds that the Elephants of Abidjan lost their match against Egypt for the African Cup because the captain of the team lost a magic charm on the field a little before halftime. The entire team searched for it in vain. Everyone believed that the Egyptians had found it and had made it disappear. Thanks to this deceit, they won the match, two goals to one.

The fact that Africa is not alone in celebrating irrationalism at the outset of the twenty-first century does not excuse our propensity to delegate to sorcerers and witch doctors the responsibility for solving our problems. Jean-François Revel has asked, "Might man be an intelligent being that intelligence does not guide?"[8] In my view, the African is the intelligent being that uses his intelligence least—so long as he is happy to live life as it comes. In an Africa that refuses to link knowledge and activity, our authentic cultural identity is operating when we say, as Revel notes, "Give us development in the form of subsidies, so as to spare us the effort of establishing an efficient relationship with reality."[9] That same culture lies behind our claim to the right to inefficiency in production, the right to corruption, and the right to disrespect basic human rights.

Cannibalistic and Totalitarian Societies

What Africans are doing to one another defies credulity. Genocide, bloody civil wars, and rampant violent crime suggest that African societies at all social levels are to some extent cannibalistic. Those who write laws and those who are responsible for enforcing them are those who trample on them. Thus, in almost all African countries, the day after gaining independence, investment codes designed to attract foreign investment were promulgated. Yet affluent Africans jostle each other at the counters of Swiss, French, Belgian, and English banks, giving the impression that they have no confidence in themselves, in their country, or in what they produce. They appear to destroy with their own hands what they have built.

The truth quickly becomes apparent. Seen from the inside, African societies are like a football team in which, as a result of personal rivalries and a lack of team spirit, one player will not pass the ball to another out of fear that the latter might score a goal. How can we hope for victory? In our republics, people outside of the ethnic "cement" (which is actually quite porous when one takes a closer look at it) have so little identification with one another that the mere existence of the state is a miracle—a miracle in part explained by the desire for personal gain. There is rarely any vision of a better future for all. At the same time, initiative and dynamism are condemned as signs of personal enrichment. The sorcerer wants equality in misery. There are numerous cases in which someone who has built a house has been told not to reside in it; others who have begun construction have been told to stop the work if they value their lives.

Was African totalitarianism born with independence? Of course not! It was already there, inscribed in the foundations of our tribal cultures. Authoritarianism permeates our families, our villages, our schools, our churches. It is for us a way of life.

Thus, faced with such a powerful, immovable culture, what can we do to change Africa's destiny? We are condemned either to change or to perish.

CULTURE AND CHANGE

Our first objective is to preserve African culture, one of the most—if not *the* most—humanistic cultures in existence. But it must be regenerated through a process initiated from the inside that would allow Africans to remain themselves while being of their time. We must keep these humanistic values—the solidarity beyond age classification and social status; social interaction; the love of neighbor, whatever the color of his skin; the defense of the environment, and so many others. We must, however, destroy all within us that is opposed to our mastery of our future, a future that must be prosperous and just, a future in which the people of Africa determine their own destiny through participation in the political process.

In doing so, we must be mindful that culture is the mother and that institutions are the children. More efficient and just African institutions depend on modifications to our culture.

The Four Revolutions We Must Lead

We need to undertake peaceful cultural revolutions in four sectors: education, politics, economics, and social life.

Education. The traditional education of the African child prepares boys and
girls for integration into their tribal community. To the child are transmitted
not only the habits customary for his or her age and sex, but all the values and
beliefs that are the cultural foundation of the group to which he or she belongs. In a system in which education is perceived above all as an instrument
of socialization, the traditional African child is educated by the entire community. The problem is that this system offers few incentives for children to improve themselves, to innovate, or to do better than their parents.

How then can we reform educational systems so strongly handicapped by
both a conservative culture and a lack of infrastructure and pedagogical fa-
cilities? (It is, for example, not unusual for there to be 125 students in a single classroom.) Very simply, by asserting the absolute preeminence of
education, by suppressing the construction of religious structures and other
palaces to the detriment of schools, and by modifying the content of the curricula, accenting not only science but especially the necessary changes of the
African society. This means critical thinking, affirmation of the need for sub-
regional and continental unity, rational development of manual as well as intellectual methods of work, and, in general, the qualities that engender
progress: imagination, dissent, creativity, professionalism and competence, a
sense of responsibility and duty, love for a job well done.

The African school should henceforth mold future businesspeople, and
therefore job creators, not just degree recipients who expect to be offered
sinecures. From the time the child is in elementary school, the young African
will have to be awakened to time management, not only in terms of production but especially in terms of maintenance of infrastructure and equipment.
The teaching of technological maintenance is surely more important than
courses on the role of the one-party system in national integration and on the
infallibility of the "Father of the Nation."

But change must not stop there. The role of the African woman—the
abused backbone of our societies—in society must also be transformed.
Women do not have access to bank accounts, credit, or property. They are
not allowed to speak. They produce much of our food, yet they have little access to agricultural training, credit, technical assistance, and so on.

In Africa as elsewhere, the emancipation of women is the best gauge of the
political and social progress of a society. Without an African woman who is
free and responsible, the African man will be unable to stand on his own.

Politics. Once education has been reformed, African political systems will change virtually by themselves. A new type of citizenship will emerge, one that gives more room to the individual, his worth as a social actor, his ability to adapt to his institutional environment, and the demands that progress puts on his community. African nations need to extend the pluralism that already exists in the diversity of their peoples to the political arena. They must cultivate tolerance and emphasize merit. Regional integration must replace nationalism.

Economics. To revolutionize our economic culture, we must understand that instead of depending on a world market that we are virtually excluded from, we must first establish integrated markets among ourselves. We must accept profit as the engine of development. We must recognize the indispensable role of individual initiative and the inalienable right of the individual to enjoy the fruits of his labor. We must understand that there can be no real or lasting economic growth without full employment. The entire African population must be put to work. It is impossible for anyone to be both unemployed and a good citizen, especially in countries with no social safety net.

Social Life. African civil society will not emerge without qualitative changes in behavior, first in the relationships among Africans and then with respect to behavior toward foreigners, to whom we generally feel inferior. We must have more self-confidence, more trust in one another, and a commitment to a progress that benefits all. We need more rigor and a systematic approach to the elaboration of strategies—and the implementation of decisions taken—whatever the costs.

CONCLUSION

We are now at a crossroads. The persistence and destructiveness of the economic and political crises that have stricken Africa make it necessary for us to act without delay. We must go to the heart of our morals and customs in order to eradicate the layer of mud that prevents our societies from moving into modernism. We must lead this revolution of minds—without which there can be no transfer of technology—on our own. We must place our bets on our intelligence because Africans, if they have capable leaders, are fully able to distance themselves from the jealousy, the blind submission to the irrational, the lethargy that have been their undoing. If Europe, that fragment of earth representing a tiny part of humanity, has been able to impose itself on the planet, dominating it and organizing it for its exclusive profit, it is only because it developed a conquering culture of rigor and work, removed from the influence of invisible forces. We must do the same.

part two

CULTURE AND
POLITICAL DEVELOPMENT

7

Culture and Democracy

RONALD INGLEHART

Building on the Weberian tradition, Francis Fukuyama (1995), Lawrence Harrison (1985, 1992, 1997), Samuel Huntington (1996), and Robert Putnam (1993) argue that cultural traditions are remarkably enduring and shape the political and economic behavior of their societies today. But modernization theorists from Karl Marx to Daniel Bell (1973, 1976) and the author of this chapter (1977, 1990, 1997) have argued that the rise of industrial society is linked with coherent cultural shifts away from traditional value systems. This article presents evidence that both claims are true:

- Development is linked with a syndrome of predictable changes away from absolute social norms, toward increasingly rational, tolerant, trusting, and postmodern values.
- But culture is path dependent. The fact that a society was historically Protestant or Orthodox or Islamic or Confucian gives rise to cultural zones with highly distinctive value systems that persist when we control for the effects of economic development.

Distinctive cultural zones exist and they have major social and political consequences, helping shape important phenomena from fertility rates to economic behavior and—as this chapter will demonstrate—democratic institutions. One major dimension of cross-cultural variation is especially important to democracy. As we will see, societies vary tremendously in the extent to which they emphasize "survival values" or "self-expression values." Societies that emphasize the latter are far likelier to be democracies than societies that emphasize survival values.

Economic development seems to bring a gradual shift from survival values to self-expression values, which helps explain why richer societies are more likely to be democracies. As we will see below, the correlation between survival/self-expression values and democracy is remarkably strong. Do they go together because self-expression values (which include interpersonal trust, tolerance, and participation in decisionmaking) are conducive to democracy? Or do democratic institutions cause these values to emerge? It is always difficult to determine causality, but the evidence suggests that it is more a matter of culture shaping democracy than the other way around.

MODERNIZATION AND CULTURAL ZONES

Huntington (1993, 1996) argues that the world is divided into eight or nine major civilizations based on enduring cultural differences that have persisted for centuries—and that the conflicts of the future will occur along the cultural fault lines separating these civilizations.

These civilizations were largely shaped by religious traditions that are still powerful today, despite the forces of modernization. Western Christianity, the Orthodox world, the Islamic world, and the Confucian, Japanese, Hindu, Buddhist, African, and Latin American regions constitute the major cultural zones. With the end of the Cold War, Huntington argues, political conflict will occur mainly along these cultural divisions, not along ideological or economic lines.

In a related argument, Putnam (1993) claims that the regions of Italy where democratic institutions function most successfully today are those in which civil society was relatively well developed centuries before. Harrison (1985, 1992, 1997) argues that development is strongly influenced by a society's basic cultural values. And Fukuyama (1995) argues that a society's ability to compete in global markets is conditioned by social trust: "low-trust" societies are at a disadvantage because they are less effective in developing large, complex social institutions. All of these analyses reflect the assumption that contemporary societies are characterized by distinctive cultural traits that have endured over long periods of time—and that these traits have an important impact on the political and economic performance of societies.

How accurate is this assumption?

Another major body of literature presents a seemingly incompatible view. Modernization theorists, including the author of this chapter, have argued that the world is changing in ways that erode traditional values. Economic development almost inevitably brings the decline of religion, parochialism, and cultural differences.

Using data from three waves of the World Values Survey (WVS), which now covers sixty-five societies containing 75 percent of the world's population, this article presents evidence that both claims are true. Economic development seems to be linked with a syndrome of predictable changes away from absolute social norms and toward increasingly rational, tolerant, trusting, and postmodern values. But culture is path dependent. The fact that a society was historically Protestant, Orthodox, Islamic, or Confucian gives rise to cultural zones with highly distinctive value systems that persist when we control for the effects of economic development.

These cultural differences are closely linked with a number of important social phenomena, of which we will focus on one: they are strongly linked with the extent to which a society has democratic institutions, as measured by scores on the Freedom House ratings of political rights and civil liberties from 1972 through 1997. Before I demonstrate this point, let us examine the evidence that enduring cross-cultural differences exist, even though economic development tends to bring systematic cultural changes.

TRADITIONAL/RATIONAL-LEGAL AND
SURVIVAL/SELF-EXPRESSION VALUES:
TWO KEY DIMENSIONS OF CROSS-CULTURAL VARIATION

To compare cultures in a parsimonious fashion requires a major data-reduction effort. Comparing each of the eight or nine civilizations on one variable after another, among the hundreds of values measured in the World Values Surveys (and the thousands that conceivably might be measured), would be an endless process. But any meaningful data-reduction process requires a relatively simple underlying structure of cross-cultural variation—which we cannot take for granted. Fortunately, such a structure does seem to exist.

In previous research (Inglehart 1997, chap. 3) the author of this chapter analyzed aggregated national-level data from the forty-three societies included in the 1990–1991 World Values Survey, finding large and coherent cross-cultural differences. The worldviews of the peoples of rich societies differ systematically from those of low-income societies, across a wide range of political, social, and religious norms and beliefs. Factor analysis revealed two main dimensions that tapped scores of variables and explained over half of the cross-cultural variation. These two dimensions reflect cross-national polarization between traditional versus secular-rational orientations toward authority and survival versus self-expression values. They make it possible to plot each society's location on a global cultural map.

This article builds on these findings by constructing comparable measures of cross-cultural variation that can be used with all three waves of the World Values Surveys, at both the individual level and the national level. This enables us to examine changes over time along these dimensions. The earlier analysis (Inglehart 1997) used factor scores based on twenty-two variables in the 1990–1991 surveys. We selected a subset of ten variables that not only had high loadings on these dimensions but had been utilized in the same format in all three waves of the World Values Surveys. This subset was used to minimize problems of missing data (when one variable is missing, an entire nation is lost from the analysis).

The factor scores generated by this reduced pool of items are highly correlated with the factor scores generated by the twenty-two items used earlier (Inglehart 1997, 334–335, 388). The traditional/secular-rational dimension used here is almost perfectly correlated with the factor scores from the comparable dimension based on eleven variables; the same is true of the survival/self-expression dimension. We are tapping a robust aspect of cross-cultural variation.

Each of these two dimensions taps a major axis of cross-cultural variation involving dozens of basic values and orientations. The traditional/secular-rational dimension reflects, first of all, the contrast between societies in which religion is very important and those in which it is not, but it also taps a rich variety of other concerns. Emphasis on the importance of family ties and deference to authority (including a relative acceptance of military rule) are major themes, together with avoidance of political conflict and an emphasis on consensus over confrontation. Societies at the traditional pole emphasize religion, absolute standards, and traditional family values; favor large families; reject divorce; and take a pro-life stance on abortion, euthanasia, and suicide. They emphasize social conformity rather than individualistic achievement, favor consensus rather than open political conflict, support deference to authority, and have high levels of national pride and a nationalistic outlook. Societies with secular-rational values have the opposite preferences on all these topics.

These orientations have a strong tendency to go together across the more than sixty societies examined here. This holds true despite the fact that we deliberately selected items covering a wide range of topics: we could have selected five items referring to religion and obtained an even more tightly correlated cluster, but our goal was to measure broad dimensions of cross-cultural variation.

Adherence to these values seems to have important consequences in the objective world. For example, societies that emphasize traditional values have much higher fertility rates than those that emphasize rational-legal values.

SURVIVAL/SELF-EXPRESSION VALUES

The survival/self-expression dimension involves the themes that characterize postindustrial society. One of its central components involves the polarization between materialist and postmaterialist values. Extensive evidence indicates that these values tap an intergenerational shift from emphasis on economic and physical security toward increasing emphasis on self-expression, subjective well-being, and quality of life (Inglehart 1977, 1990, 1997). This cultural shift is found throughout advanced industrial societies; it seems to emerge among birth cohorts that have grown up under conditions in which survival is taken for granted. These values are linked with the emergence of growing emphasis on environmental protection, the women's movement, and rising demands for participation in decisionmaking in economic and political life. During the past twenty-five years, these values have become increasingly widespread in almost all advanced industrial societies for which extensive time-series evidence is available. But this is only one component of a much broader dimension of cross-cultural variation.

Societies that emphasize survival values show relatively low levels of subjective well-being, report relatively poor health, are low on interpersonal trust, are relatively intolerant toward outgroups, are low on support for gender equality, emphasize materialist values, have relatively high levels of faith in science and technology, are relatively low on environmental activism, and are relatively favorable to authoritarian government. Societies that emphasize self-expression values tend to have the opposite preferences on all these topics. Whether a society emphasizes survival values or self-expression values has important objective consequences. As we will see, societies that emphasize self-expression values are much more likely to be stable democracies than those that emphasize survival values.

A GLOBAL CULTURAL MAP: 1995–1998

Let us now examine the location of each of our sixty-five societies on the two dimensions generated by the factor analysis we have just examined. The vertical axis on our global cultural map (see Fig. 7.1) corresponds to the polarization between traditional authority and secular-rational authority. The horizontal axis depicts the polarization between survival values and well-

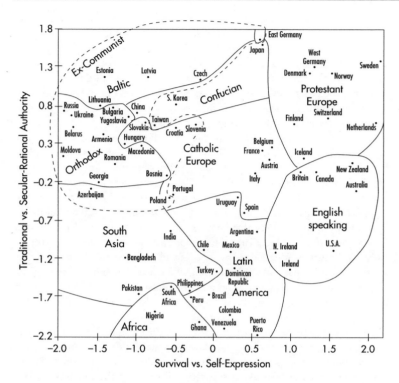

FIGURE 7.1   Locations of Sixty-Five Societies on Two Dimensions of
Cross-Cultural Variation

NOTE: The scales on each axis indicate the country's factor scores on the give
dimension.

SOURCE: The data for the following fifty societies are from the 1995–1998 World
Values Survey: U.S., Australia, New Zealand, China, Japan, Taiwan, South Korea,
Turkey, Bangladesh, India, Pakistan, the Philippines, Armenia, Azerbaijan, Georgia,
Great Britain, East Germany, West Germany, Switzerland, Norway, Sweden, Finland,
Spain, Russia, Ukraine, Belarus, Estonia, Latvia, Lithuania, Moldova, Poland,
Bulgaria, Bosnia, Slovenia, Croatia, Yugoslavia, Macedonia, Nigeria, South Africa,
Ghana, Argentina, Brazil, Chile, Colombia, Dominican Republic, Mexico, Peru,
Puerto Rico, Uruguay, Venezuela. Data for Canada, France, Italy, Portugal,
Netherlands, Belgium, Denmark, Iceland, Northern Ireland, Austria, Hungary, Czech
Republic, Slovakia, and Romania are from the 1990 World Values Survey. The
positions of Colombia and Pakistan are estimated from incomplete data.

being. The boundaries around groups of countries in Figure 7.1 are drawn using Huntington's (1993, 1996) cultural zones as a guide.

This map is remarkably similar to the one generated from the 1990–1991 surveys (Inglehart 1997, 93). We find distinct and coherent Protestant, Catholic, Latin American, Confucian, African, and Orthodox cultural zones, reflecting the fact that the societies within these clusters have relatively similar values. Although these surveys include only a few Islamic societies, they tend to fall into the southwest corner of the map.

Religious traditions seem to have had an enduring impact on the contemporary value systems of sixty-five societies, as Weber, Huntington, and others have argued. But religion is not the only factor shaping cultural zones. A society's culture reflects its entire historical heritage. One of the most important historical events of the twentieth century was the rise and fall of a communist empire that once ruled a third of the world's population. Communism has left a clear imprint on the value systems of those who lived under it. Despite four decades of communist rule, the former East Germany remains culturally close to what was West Germany, but its value system has been drawn toward the communist zone. And although China is a member of the Confucian zone, it too falls within a broad communist-influenced zone. Similarly Azerbaijan, though part of the Islamic cluster, also falls within the communist super-zone that dominated it for decades.

The influence of colonial ties is apparent in the existence of a Latin American cultural zone adjacent to Spain and Portugal. Former colonial ties also help account for the existence of an English-speaking zone containing Britain and the other English-speaking societies. All seven of the English-speaking societies included in this study show relatively similar cultural characteristics. Australia and New Zealand were not surveyed until 1995–1998, but they both fall into the English-speaking cultural zone that the author of this chapter found with the 1990–1991 data. Geographically, they are halfway around the world, but culturally Australia and New Zealand are neighbors of Great Britain and Canada.

The impact of colonization seems to be especially strong when reinforced by massive immigration from the colonial society. The fact that Spain, Italy, Uruguay, and Argentina are all relatively close to each other on the border between Catholic Europe and Latin America illustrates the point that though geographically remote from each other, the populations of Uruguay and Argentina are largely descended from immigrants from Spain and Italy. Similarly, Tom Rice and Jan Feldman (1997) find strong correlations between the civic values of various ethnic groups in the United States and the values prevailing in their countries of origin—even two or three generations after their families migrated.

HOW REAL ARE THE CULTURAL ZONES?

The placement of each society on Figure 7.1 is objective, determined by a factor analysis of survey data from each country. The boundaries drawn around these societies are subjective, guided by Huntington's division of the world into several cultural zones. How "real" are these zones? The boundaries could have been drawn in various ways because these societies have been influenced by a variety of factors. Thus, some of the boundaries overlap others—for example, the ex-communist zone overlaps the Protestant, Catholic, Confucian, Orthodox, and Islamic cultural zones. Similarly, Britain is located at the intersection of the English-speaking zone and Protestant Europe. Empirically, Britain is close to all five of the English-speaking societies, and we included it in that zone. But with only slight modification, we could have drawn the borders to put Britain in Protestant Europe, for it is also culturally close to those societies. Reality is complex. Britain is both Protestant and English speaking, and its empirical position reflects both aspects of reality.

Similarly, we have drawn a boundary around the Latin American societies that Huntington postulated were a distinct cultural zone: all ten of them do indeed show relatively similar values in global perspective. But with only minor changes, we could have drawn this border to define a Hispanic cultural zone including Spain and Portugal, which empirically are also relatively close to the Latin American societies. Or we could have drawn a boundary that included Latin America, Catholic Europe, and the Philippines and Ireland in a broad Roman Catholic cultural zone. All of these zones are both conceptually and empirically justifiable.

This two-dimensional map is based on similarity of basic values, but it also reflects the relative distances between these societies on many other dimensions, such as religion, colonial influences, the influence of communist rule, social structure, and economic level. The influence of many different historical factors can be summed up remarkably well by the two cultural dimensions on which this map is based. But because these various factors do not always coincide neatly, there are some obvious anomalies. For example, Japan and the former East Germany fall next to each other. This is appropriate in the sense that both societies are highly secular, are relatively wealthy, and have high proportions of industrial workers; but it is inappropriate in that Japan was shaped by a Confucian heritage, whereas East Germany was shaped by Protestantism. (To be sure, Harrison [1992] has argued that important parallels exist between Confucian and Protestant culture.)

Despite such apparent anomalies, societies with a common cultural heritage generally fall into common clusters. But their positions also reflect their level of economic development, their occupational structure, their religion, and other major historical influences. Their positions on this two-dimensional space reflect a multi-dimensional reality. The remarkable coherence between these various dimensions seems to reflect the fact that a society's culture has been shaped by its entire economic and historical heritage, which in turn shapes them.

Economic development seems to have a powerful impact on cultural values. The value systems of richer countries differ systematically from those of poorer countries. The overall structure of Figure 7.1 reflects the gradient from low-income countries (located near the lower left quadrant) to rich societies (located near the upper right).

Figure 7.2 demonstrates this point. A redrawn version of Figure 7.1, it shows the economic zones into which these sixty-five societies fall. All nineteen societies with annual per capita gross national products over $15,000 rank relatively high on both dimensions and fall into a zone at the upper right-hand corner. This economic zone cuts across the boundaries of the Protestant, ex-communist, Confucian, Catholic, and English-speaking cultural zones. Conversely, all of the societies with per capita GNPs below $2,000 fall into a cluster at the lower left of Figure 7.2, in an economic zone that cuts across the African, South Asian, ex-communist, and Orthodox cultural zones. The evidence suggests that economic development tends to move societies in a common direction, regardless of their cultural heritage. Nevertheless, distinctive cultural zones continue to persist two centuries after the industrial revolution was launched.

GNP/capita is only one indicator of a society's level of economic development. As Marx argued, the rise of the industrial working class was a key event in modern history. Furthermore, the changing nature of the labor force defines three distinct stages of economic development: agrarian society, industrial society, and postindustrial society (Bell 1973, 1976). Thus still another set of boundaries could be drawn around the societies in Figures 7.1 and 7.2. The societies with a high percentage of the labor force in agriculture are located near the bottom of the map, the societies with a high percentage of industrial workers near the top, and the societies with a high percentage in the service sector near the right-hand side of the map.

Modernization theory implies that as societies develop economically, their cultures will tend to shift in a predictable direction, and our data fit the implications of this prediction. Economic differences are linked with large and pervasive cultural differences. Nevertheless, we find clear evidence of the persistence of long-established cultural zones. Using the data from the latest available survey for each society, we created dummy variables to reflect whether a given society is predominantly English speaking or not, ex-communist or not, and so on, for each of the clusters outlined on Figure 7.1. Empirical

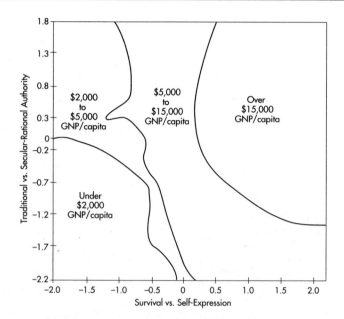

FIGURE 7.2   Economic Level of Sixty-Five Societies
Superimposed on Two Dimensions of Cross-Cultural Variation
NOTE: All but one of the sixty-five societies shown in Figure 7.1
fit into the economic zones indicated here: only the Dominican
Republic is mislocated.
SOURCE: Economic levels are based on the World Bank's
purchasing power parity estimates as of 1995; see *World
Development Report, 1997*, pp. 214–215.

analysis of these variables shows that the cultural locations of given societies
are far from random. Eight of the nine zones outlined on Figure 7.1 show statistically significant relationships with at least one of the two major dimensions
of cross-cultural variation (the sole exception is the Catholic Europe cluster; it
is fairly coherent but has a neutral position on both dimensions).

Do these cultural clusters simply reflect economic differences? For example, do the societies of Protestant Europe have similar values simply because
they are rich? The answer is no. The impact of a society's historical-cultural
heritage persists when one controls for GNP/capita and the structure of the
labor force in multiple regression analyses (Inglehart and Baker 2000).

To illustrate how coherent these clusters are, let us examine one of the key
variables in the literature on cross-cultural differences: interpersonal trust (a

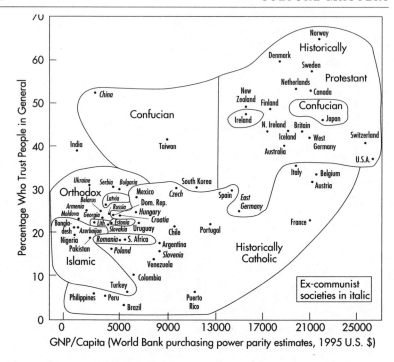

FIGURE 7.3   Interpersonal Trust by Cultural Tradition and Level of Economic
Development and Religious Tradition

Trust by GNP/capita: r = .60 p < .000

component of the survival/self-expression dimension). James Coleman
(1988, 1990), Gabriel Almond and Sidney Verba (1963), Putnam (1993),
and Fukuyama (1995) argue that interpersonal trust is essential for building
the social structures on which democracy depends and the complex social organizations on which large-scale economic enterprises are based. As Figure
7.3 demonstrates, virtually all historically Protestant societies rank higher on
interpersonal trust than virtually all historically Catholic societies. This holds
true even when we control for levels of economic development: interpersonal
trust is significantly correlated with the society's level of GNP/capita, but
even rich Catholic societies rank lower than equally prosperous historically
Protestant societies.

A heritage of communist rule also seems to have an impact on this variable, with virtually all ex-communist societies ranking relatively low. Accord-
ingly, historically Protestant societies that experienced communist rule, such
as East Germany and Latvia, show relatively low levels of interpersonal trust.

Of the nineteen societies in which more than 35 percent of the public believe that most people can be trusted, fourteen are historically Protestant, three are Confucian influenced, one is predominantly Hindu, and only one (Ireland) is historically Catholic. Of the ten lowest-ranking societies in Figure 7.3, eight are historically Catholic; none is historically Protestant.

In passing, we note the striking correlation of these data with the Transparency International Corruption Perceptions Index addressed in Chapter 9, by Seymour Martin Lipset and Gabriel Salman Lenz.

Within given societies, Catholics rank about as high on interpersonal trust as do Protestants. It is not a matter of individual personality, but the shared historical experience of given nations that is crucial. As Putnam (1993) has argued, horizontal, locally controlled organizations are conducive to interpersonal trust; rule by large, hierarchical, centralized bureaucracies seems to corrode interpersonal trust. Historically, the Roman Catholic Church was the prototype of a hierarchical, centrally controlled institution; Protestant churches were relatively decentralized and more open to local control.

The contrast between local control and domination by a remote hierarchy seems to have important long-term consequences for interpersonal trust. Clearly, these cross-cultural differences do not reflect the contemporary influence of the respective churches. The Catholic Church has changed a great deal in recent decades. Moreover, in many of these countries, especially the Protestant ones, church attendance has dwindled to the point where only a small minority of the population attend church regularly. The majority have little or no contact with the church today, but the impact of living in a society that was historically shaped by once-powerful Catholic or Protestant institutions persists, shaping everyone—Protestant, Catholic, or other—who is socialized into a given nation's culture.

Protestant and Catholic societies seem to display distinctive values today mainly because of the historical impact their respective churches had on the societies as a whole, rather than through the contemporary influence of the churches. This is why we classify Germany, Switzerland, and the Netherlands as historically Protestant societies (historically, Protestantism shaped them, even though today—as a result of immigration, relatively low Protestant birthrates, and higher Protestant rates of secularization—they may have more practicing Catholics than Protestants.

CULTURE AND DEMOCRACY

The idea that political culture is linked with democracy had great impact following the publication of *The Civic Culture* (Almond and Verba 1963) but went out of fashion during the 1970s for a variety of reasons. The political-culture approach raised an important empirical question: Did given societies have political cultures that were relatively conducive to democracy? Some critics alleged that this approach was "elitist" in finding that some cultures were more conducive to democracy than others. Any right-minded theory should hold that all societies are equally likely to be democratic. The problem is that tailoring a theory to fit a given ideology may produce a theory that does not fit reality, and consequently predictions will eventually go wrong; the theory will provide misleading guidance to those who are trying to cope with democratization in the real world.

By the 1990s, observers from Latin America to Eastern Europe to East Asia were concluding that cultural factors played an important role in the problems they were encountering with democratization. Simply adopting a democratic constitution was not enough.

Cultural factors have been omitted from most empirical analyses of democracy partly because, until now, we have not had reliable measures of them from more than a handful of countries. When cultural factors are taken into account, as in the work of the author of this chapter (Inglehart 1990, 1997) and Putnam (1993), they seem to play an important role.

Economic development leads to two types of changes that are conducive to democracy:

- It tends to transform a society's social structure, bringing urbanization, mass education, occupational specialization, growing organizational networks, greater income equality, and a variety of associated developments that mobilize mass participation in politics. Rising occupational specialization and rising education lead to a workforce that is independent minded and has specialized skills that enhance its bargaining power against elites.
- Economic development is also conducive to cultural changes that help stabilize democracy. It tends to develop interpersonal trust and tolerance, and it leads to the spread of post-materialist values that place high priority on self-expression and participation in decisionmaking. Insofar as it brings higher levels of well-being, it endows the regime with legitimacy, which can help sustain democratic institutions through difficult times. Legitimacy is an asset to any regime, but it is crucial to democracies. Repressive authoritarian regimes can hold on to power even when they lack mass support, but democracies must have mass support or they can be voted out of existence.

Positive outputs from a political system can generate mass support for political incumbents. In the short term, this support is calculated on the basis of "what have you done for me lately?" But if a regime's outputs are seen as

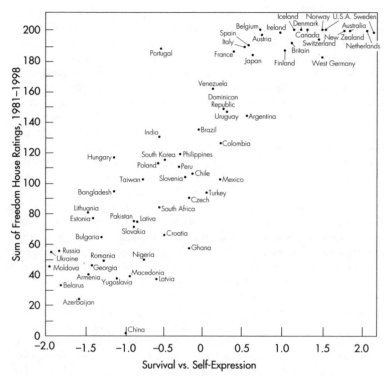

FIGURE 7.4   Self-Expression Values and Democratic Institutions

NOTE: Vertical axis is the sum of the Freedom House ratings for civil liberties and political rights from 1981 through 1998. Since these ratings give high scores for low levels of democracy, we reversed polarity by subtracting these sums from 236 (China, which had the maximum score of 235, has a score of 1 after this transformation). Horizontal axis reflects each country's mean factor score on the survival/self-expression dimension: It taps levels of postmaterialist values, trust, tolerance, political activism, and subjective well-being among each public. r=.88 N=63 p=.0000

SOURCE: Freedom House surveys reported in successive editions of *Freedom in the World*; survey data from the 1990 and 1995 World Values Surveys.

positive over a long time, the regime may develop "diffuse support" (Easton 1963)—the generalized perception that the political system is inherently good, quite apart from its current outputs. This type of support can endure even through difficult times.

The World Values Survey data make it possible to test this thesis on a worldwide scale. As Figure 7.4 demonstrates, a society's position on the survival/self-expression index is strongly correlated with its level of democracy, as indicated by its scores on the Freedom House ratings of political rights and civil liberties from 1972 through 1998. This relationship is powerful. It is clearly not a methodological artifact or merely a correlation because the two variables are measured at different levels and come from completely different sources. Virtually all of the societies that rank high on survival/self-expression values are stable democracies; virtually all the societies that rank low have authoritarian governments. We will not attempt to unravel the complex causal linkages in this chapter. For the moment, let us simply note that the powerful linkage shown in Figure 7.4 persists when we control for GNP/capita and spell out the main possible interpretations.

One interpretation would be that democratic institutions give rise to the self-expression values that are so closely linked with them. In other words, democracy makes people healthy, happy, tolerant, and trusting, and it instills post-materialist values (at least in the younger generation). This interpretation is extremely appealing. It provides a powerful argument for democracy and implies that we have a quick fix for most of the world's problems: Adopt democratic institutions and live happily ever after.

Unfortunately, the experience of the people of the former Soviet Union does not support this interpretation. Since their dramatic move toward democracy in 1991, they have not become healthier, happier, more trusting, more tolerant, or more post-materialist. For the most part, they have gone in exactly the opposite direction. Latin America's history of constitutional instability is another example.

An alternative interpretation is that economic development gradually leads to social and cultural changes that make democratic institutions increasingly likely to survive and flourish. This would help explain why mass democracy did not emerge until relatively recently in history and why, even now, it is most likely to be found in economically more developed countries—in particular, those that emphasize self-expression values rather than survival values.

The latter interpretation has both encouraging and discouraging implications. The bad news is that democracy is not something that can be easily attained by simply adopting the right laws. It is most likely to flourish in some social and cultural contexts than in others, and the current cultural conditions for democracy seem relatively unfavorable in Russia, Belarus, Ukraine, Armenia, and Moldova.

The good news is that the long-term trend of the past several centuries has been toward economic development, a process that has accelerated and spread around the world during the past few decades. Furthermore, economic development tends to give rise to social and cultural conditions under which democracy becomes increasingly likely to emerge and survive. If the outlook is discouraging concerning much of the former Soviet Union, the evidence in Figure 7.4 suggests that a number of societies may be closer to democracy than is generally suspected. Mexico, for example, seems ripe for the transition to democracy, since its position on the post-modern values axis is roughly comparable to that of Argentina, Spain, or Italy. A number of other societies are also in this transition zone, including Turkey, the Philippines, Slovenia, South Korea, Poland, Peru, South Africa, and Croatia.

Although China falls farther back on this dimension, it is experiencing rapid economic growth, which, as we have seen, seems to bring a shift toward self-expression values. The ruling Chinese communist elite are clearly committed to maintaining one-party rule, and as long as they retain control of the military they should be able to enforce their preferences. But the Chinese show a predisposition toward democracy that is inconsistent with China's very low ranking on the Freedom House ratings.

In the long run, modernization tends to help spread democratic institutions. Authoritarian rulers of some Asian societies have argued that the distinctive "Asian values" of these societies make them unsuitable for democracy (Lee 1994). The evidence from the World Values Surveys—not to mention the evolution of Japan, South Korea, and Taiwan to democracy—does not support this interpretation. It suggests that Confucian societies may be readier for democracy than is generally believed.

CONCLUSION

Economic development seems to bring gradual cultural changes that make mass publics increasingly likely to want democratic institutions and to be more supportive of them once they are in place. This transformation is not easy or automatic. Determined elites who control the army and police can resist pressures for democratization. But development tends to make mass publics more trusting and tolerant and leads them to place an increasingly high priority on autonomy and self-expression in all spheres of life, including politics, and it becomes difficult and costly to repress demands for political liberalization. With rising levels of economic development, cultural patterns emerge that are increasingly supportive of democracy, making mass publics more likely to want democracy and more skillful at getting it.

Although rich societies are much likelier to be democratic than poor ones, wealth alone does not automatically bring democracy. If that were true, Kuwait and Libya would be model democracies. But the process of modernization tends to bring cultural changes conducive to democracy. In the long run, the only way to avoid the growth of mass demands for democratization would be to reject industrialization. Few ruling elites are willing to do so. Those societies that do move onto the trajectory of industrial society are likely to face growing pressures for democratization.

The evidence suggests that culture plays a much more crucial role in democracy than the literature of the past two decades would indicate. The syndrome of trust, tolerance, well-being, and participatory values tapped by the survival/self-expression dimension seems particularly crucial. In the long run, democracy is not attained simply by making institutional changes or through elite-level maneuvering. Its survival also depends on the values and beliefs of ordinary citizens.

REFERENCES

Almond, Gabriel, and Sidney Verba. 1963. The *Civic Culture*. Princeton: Princeton University Press.

_____. 1990. *The Civic Culture Revisited*. Boston: Little, Brown.

Bell, Daniel. 1973. *The Coming of Post-Industrial Society*. New York: Basic.

_____. 1976. *The Cultural Contradictions of Capitalism*. New York: Basic.

Coleman, James S. 1988. "Social Capital in the Creation of Human Capital." *American Journal of Sociology* 94: 95–121.

_____. 1990. *Foundations of Social Theory*. Cambridge: Harvard University Press.

Diamond, Larry, ed. 1993. *Political Culture and Democracy in Developing Countries*. Boulder: Lynne Rienner.

Diamond, Larry, with Juan Linz and Seymour Martin Lipset. 1995. *Politics in Developing Countries*. Boulder: Lynne Rienner.

Easton, David. 1963. *The Political System*. New York: Wiley.

Fukuyama, Francis. 1995. *Trust: The Social Virtues and the Creation of Prosperity*. New York: Free Press.

Gibson, James L., and Raymond M. Duch. 1992. "The Origins of a Democratic Culture in the Soviet Union: The Acquisition of Democratic Values." Paper presented at the 1992 annual meeting of the Midwest Political Science Association, Chicago.

Gibson, James L., with Raymond M. Duch. 1994. "Postmaterialism and the Emerging Soviet Democracy." *Political Research Quarterly* 47, no. 1: 5–39.

Harrison, Lawrence E. 1985. *Underdevelopment Is a State of Mind—The Latin American Case*. Cambridge: Harvard Center for International Affairs; Lanham, Md.: Madison Books.

_____. 1992. *Who Prospers? How Cultural Values Shape Economic and Political Success*. New York: Basic.

_____. 1997. *The Pan-American Dream: Do Latin America's Cultural Values Discourage True Partnership?* New York: Basic.

Huntington, Samuel P. 1993. "The Clash of Civilizations?" *Foreign Affairs* 72, no. 3.

_____. 1996. *The Clash of Civilizations and the Remaking of World Order.* New York: Simon & Schuster.

Ingelhart, Ronald. 1977. *The Silent Revolution: Changing Values and Political Styles in Advanced Industrial Society.* Princeton: Princeton University Press.

_____. 1990. *Culture Shift in Advanced Industrial Society.* Princeton: Princeton University Press.

_____. 1997. *Modernization and Postmodernization: Cultural, Economic, and Political Change in Forty-Three Societies.* Princeton: Princeton University Press.

Inglehart, Ronald, and Wayne Baker. 2000. "Modernization, Cultural Change, and the Persistence of Traditional Values." *American Sociological Review*, February.

Lee Kuan Yew and Fareed Zakaria. 1994. "Culture Is Destiny: A Conversation with Lee Kuan Yew." *Foreign Affairs* 73, no. 2: 109–126.

Lipset, Seymour Martin. 1990. "American Exceptionalism Reaffirmed." *Tocqueville Review* 10.

_____. 1996. *American Exceptionalism.* New York: Norton.

Putnam, Robert. 1993. *Making Democracy Work: Civic Traditions in Modern Italy.* Princeton: Princeton University Press.

Rice, Tom W., and Jan L. Feldman. 1997. "Civic Culture and Democracy from Europe to America." *Journal of Politics* 59, no. 4: 1143–1172.

U.S. Bureau of the Census. *World Population Profile: 1996.* Washington, D.C.: Government Printing Office.

Weber, Max. 1958. *The Protestant Ethic and the Spirit of Capitalism.* New York: Scribner's.

Welzel, Christian, and Ronald Inglehart. Forthcoming. "Analyzing Democratic Change and Stability: A Human Development Theory of Democracy."

8

Social Capital

FRANCIS FUKUYAMA

Social capital can be defined simply as an instantiated set of informal values or norms shared among members of a group that permits them to cooperate with one another. If members of the group come to expect that others will behave reliably and honestly, then they will come to *trust* one another. Trust acts like a lubricant that makes any group or organization run more efficiently.

Sharing values and norms in itself does not produce social capital because the values may be the wrong ones. Southern Italy, for example, is a region of the world that is almost universally characterized as lacking in social capital and generalized trust, even though strong social norms exist. The sociologist Diego Gambetta tells the following story:

> A retired [Mafia] boss recounted that when he was a young boy, his Mafioso father made him climb a wall and then invited him to jump, promising to catch him. He at first refused, but his father insisted until finally he jumped—and promptly landed flat on his face. The wisdom his father sought to convey was summed up by these words: "You must learn to distrust even your parents."[1]

The Mafia is characterized by an extremely strong internal code of behavior, *omertà*, and individual Mafiosi are spoken of as "men of honor." Nonetheless, these norms do not apply outside a small circle of Mafiosi. For the rest of Sicilian society, the prevailing norms can be described more as "take advantage of people outside your immediate family at every occasion because otherwise they will take advantage of you first." And as the example cited by Gambetta suggests, even families may not be that reliable. Such norms obviously do not promote social cooperation, and the negative consequences for both good government and economic development have been documented extensively.[2] Southern Italy, one of the poorest parts of Western Europe, has traditionally been the source of the extensive corruption plaguing the country's political system.

The norms that produce social capital, by contrast, must substantively include virtues like truth telling, meeting obligations, and reciprocity. Not surprisingly, these norms overlap to a significant degree with those Puritan values that Max Weber found critical to the development of Western capitalism in his book *The Protestant Ethic and the Spirit of Capitalism.*

All societies have some stock of social capital; the real differences among them concern what might be called the "radius of trust." That is, cooperative norms like honesty and reciprocity can be shared among limited groups of people but not with others in the same society. Families are obviously important sources of social capital everywhere.

However, the strength of family bonds differs from society to society; it also varies relative to other types of social obligation. In some cases, there appears to be something of an inverse relationship between the bonds of trust and reciprocity inside and outside the family: when one is very strong, the other tends to be weak. In China and Latin America, families are strong and cohesive, but it is hard to trust strangers, and levels of honesty and cooperation in public life are much lower. A consequence is nepotism and pervasive public corruption. What made the Protestant Reformation important for Weber was not so much that it encouraged honesty, reciprocity, and thrift among individual entrepreneurs, but that these virtues were for the first time widely practiced outside the family.

It is perfectly possible to form successful groups in the absence of social capital, using a variety of formal coordination mechanisms like contracts, hierarchies, constitutions, legal systems, and the like. But informal norms greatly reduce what economists label "transaction costs"—the costs of monitoring, contracting, adjudicating, and enforcing formal agreements. Under certain circumstances, social capital may also facilitate a higher degree of innovation and group adaptation.

Social capital has benefits that go well beyond the economic sphere. It is critical for the creation of a healthy civil society—the groups and associations that fall between the family and the state. Civil society, which has been the focus of considerable interest in former communist countries since the fall of the Berlin Wall, is said to be critical to the success of democracy. Social capital allows the different groups within a complex society to band together to defend their interests, which might otherwise be disregarded by a powerful state.[3]

Although social capital and civil society have been widely praised as good things to have, it is important to note that they are not always beneficial. Coordination is necessary for all social activity, whether good or bad. The Mafia and the Ku Klux Klan are constituent parts of American civil society; both possess social capital, and both are detrimental to the health of the broader society. In economic life, group coordination is necessary for one form of production, but when technology or markets change, a different type of coordination with perhaps a different set of group members becomes necessary. The bonds of social reciprocity that facilitated production in an earlier time period become obstacles to production in a later time period, as is the case for many Japanese corporations in the 1990s. To continue the economic metaphor, social capital at that point can be said to be obsolete and needs to be depreciated in the society's capital accounts.

The fact that social capital can on occasion be used for destructive purposes or can become obsolete does not negate the widely shared presumption that it is generally a good thing for a society to have. Physical capital, after all, is not always a good thing, either. Not only can it become obsolete, but it can be used to produce assault rifles, thalidomide, tasteless entertainment, and a whole range of other social "bads." But societies have laws to forbid the production of the worst social bads, whether by physical or social capital, so we can presume that most of the uses to which social capital will be put will be no less good from a social standpoint than the products of physical capital.

And so it has been regarded by most people who have employed the concept. The first known use of the term "social capital" was by Lyda Judson Hanifan in 1916 to describe rural school community centers.[4] The term was also used in Jane Jacobs's classic work *The Death and Life of Great American Cities*, in which she explained that the dense social networks that existed in older, mixed-use urban neighborhoods constituted a form of social capital that encouraged public safety.[5] The economist Glenn Loury, as well as the sociologist Ivan Light, used the term "social capital" in the 1970s to analyze the problem of inner-city economic development: African Americans lacked the bonds of trust and social connectedness within their own communities that existed for Asian American and other ethnic groups, which went a long way toward explaining the relative lack of black small-business development.[6] In the 1980s, the term "social capital" was brought into wider use by the sociologist James Coleman[7] and the political scientist Robert Putnam. Putnam stimulated an intense debate over the role of social capital and civil society in Italy and the United States.

HOW DO WE MEASURE SOCIAL CAPITAL?

Neither sociologists nor economists have been happy with the spreading use of the term "social capital." Sociologists see it as part of the broader conquest of the social sciences by economics, and economists regard it as a nebulous concept that is difficult if not impossible to measure. And indeed, measurement of the total stock of cooperative social relationships based on norms of honesty and reciprocity is not a trivial task.

Robert Putnam has argued in *Making Democracy Work* that the quality of governance in the different regions of Italy is correlated with social capital, and that social capital has been in decline in the United States since the 1960s. His work illustrates some of the difficulties involved in the measurement of social capital, for which he uses two types of statistical measures. The first is information on groups and group memberships, from sports clubs and choral societies to interest groups and political parties, as well as indices of political participation such as voter turnout and newspaper readership. In addition, there are more detailed time-budget surveys and other indicators of how people actually spend their waking hours. The second type of data is survey research such as the General Social Survey (for the United States) or the World Values Survey (for over sixty countries around the world), which ask a series of questions concerning values and behavior.

The assertion that American social capital has been declining over the past two generations has been hotly contested. Numerous scholars have pointed to contradictory data showing that groups and group membership have actually been *increasing* over the past generation while others have argued that the available data simply do not capture the reality of group life in a society as complex as the United States.[8]

Aside from the question of whether it is possible to comprehensively count groups and group memberships, there are at least three further measurement problems with this approach. First, social capital has an important qualitative dimension. Although bowling leagues or garden clubs might be, as Tocqueville suggests, schools for cooperation and public spiritedness, they are obviously very different institutions from the U.S. Marine Corps or the Mormon Church in terms of the kinds of collective action they foster. A bowling league is not, to say the least, capable of storming a beach. An adequate measure of social capital needs to take account of the nature of the collective action of which a group is capable—its inherent difficulty, the value of the group's output, whether it can be undertaken under adverse circumstances, and so on.

The second problem has to do with what an economist would call the "positive externalities" of group membership, or what we might label the "positive radius of trust." Although all groups require social capital to operate, some build bonds of trust (and hence social capital) outside their own membership. As Weber indicated, Puritanism mandated honesty not simply toward other members of one's religious community but toward all human beings. On the other hand, norms of reciprocity can be shared among only a small subset of a group's members. In a so-called membership group like the American Association of Retired People (AARP), which has a membership of over 30 million, there is no reason to think that any two given members will trust each other or achieve coordinated action just because they have paid their yearly dues to the same organization.

The final problem concerns negative externalities. Some groups actively promote intolerance, hatred, and even violence toward non-members. Although the Ku Klux Klan, Nation of Islam, and Michigan Militia possess social capital, a society made up of such groups would not be particularly appealing and might even cease to be a democracy. Such groups have problems cooperating with each other, and the exclusive bonds of community uniting them are likely to make them less adaptive by sealing them off from influences in the surrounding environment.

It should be clear that coming up with a believable number expressing the stock of social capital for a large and complex society like the United States based on a census of groups is next to impossible. We have empirical data, of varying reliability, on only a certain subset of the groups that actually exist, and no consensus means of judging their qualitative differences.[9]

Alternatively, instead of measuring social capital as a positive value, it might be easier to measure the *absence* of social capital through traditional measures of social dysfunction, such as rates of crime, family breakdown, drug use, litigation, suicide, tax evasion, and the like. The presumption is that since social capital reflects the existence of cooperative norms, social deviance ipso facto reflects a lack of social capital. Indicators of social dysfunction, although hardly unproblematic, are far more abundant than data on group memberships and are available on a comparative basis. The National Commission on Civic Renewal has used this strategy to measure civic disengagement.

One very serious problem with using social dysfunction data as a negative measure of social capital is that they ignore distribution. Just as conventional capital is unevenly distributed within a society (i.e., as measured by wealth and income distribution studies), so social capital is also likely to be unevenly distributed—strata of highly socialized, self-organizing people may coexist with pockets of extreme atomization and social pathology.

THE GENEALOGY OF MORALS

Social capital is not, as sometimes portrayed, a rare cultural treasure passed down from one generation to the next, which, if lost, can never be regained.

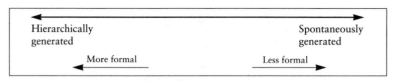

FIGURE 8.1   A Continuum of Norms

Rather, it is created spontaneously all the time by people going about their daily lives. It was created in traditional societies, and it is generated on a daily basis by individuals and firms in a modern capitalist society.

The systematic study of how order, and thus social capital, can emerge in a spontaneous and decentralized fashion is one of the most important intellectual developments of the late twentieth century. Leading the charge have been the economists—not a surprising development, given that the discipline of economics centers around markets, which are themselves prime examples of spontaneous order. It was Friedrich von Hayek who laid out the program of studying what he called "the extended order of human cooperation," that is, the sum total of all of the rules, norms, values, and shared behaviors that allow individuals to work together in a capitalist society.[10]

No one would deny that social order is often created hierarchically. But it is useful to see that order can emerge from a spectrum of sources that extends from hierarchical and centralized types of authority to the completely decentralized and spontaneous interactions of individuals. Figure 8.1 illustrates this continuum.

Hierarchy can take many forms, from the transcendental (e.g., Moses coming down from Mount Sinai with the Ten Commandments) to the mundane, as when a CEO announces a new "corporate ethos" that will govern customer relations. Spontaneous order has similarly diverse origins, ranging from the blind interaction of natural forces to highly structured negotiations among lawyers over underground water rights. By and large, the norms created spontaneously tend to be informal—that is, they are not written down and published—whereas norms and rules created by hierarchical sources of authority tend to take the form of written laws, constitutions, regulations, holy texts, or bureaucratic organization charts. In some cases, the boundary between spontaneous and hierarchical order is blurry; in English-speaking countries like Britain and the United States, for example, common law evolves spontaneously through the interaction of a myriad of judges and advocates, but it is also recognized as binding by the formal judicial system.

Besides arraying social norms along a continuum from hierarchically generated to spontaneously generated, we can overlay another continuum of norms that are the product of rational choice and norms that are socially in-

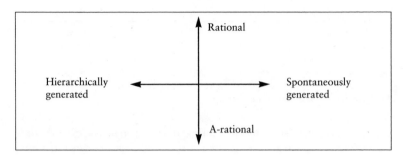

FIGURE 8.2   The Universe of Norms I

herited and a-rational in origin. Combining our two axes produces a four-quadrant matrix of possible types of norms, as illustrated in Figure 8.2. "Rational" as used here refers only to the fact that alternative norms are consciously debated and compared ahead of time. Clearly, rational discussion can lead to bad choices that do not serve the true interests of the people making them, whereas a-rational norms can be quite functional, as when religious belief supports social order or economic growth.

In many respects, this distinction between rational and a-rational corresponds to the disciplinary boundary between sociology and economics. Sociology is, in the end, a discipline devoted to the study of social norms. Sociologists assume that as human beings grow and mature, they are socialized into a whole series of roles and identities—Catholic, worker, deviant, mother, bureaucrat—defined by a series of complex norms and rules. These norms bind communities together and are tightly enforced by them, sharply limiting the kinds of choices people can make about their lives.

INSIGHTS OF THE ECONOMISTS

Over the past generation, economists have paid increasing attention to the importance of norms and rules in economic life. Ronald Heiner pointed out that as rational human beings we simply cannot make rational decisions at every point in day-to-day life. Were we to do so, our behavior would be both unpredictable and subject to paralysis as we perpetually calculated whether we should tip the waiter, stiff the cab driver of his fare, or put away a different amount of our paycheck every month in our retirement account.[11] In fact, it is rational for people to impose simplifying rules on their own behavior, even if these rules do not always yield correct decisions in every circumstance because decisionmaking is in itself costly and often requires information that is unavailable or faulty.

The entire sub-discipline within economics of the "new institutionalism" is built around the observation that rules and norms are critical to rational economic behavior. What the economic historian Douglass North labels an "institution" is a norm or rule, formal or informal, governing human social interaction.[12] He points out that norms are critical for reducing transaction costs; if we did not have norms, for example, requiring the respect of property rights, we would have to negotiate ownership rules on a case-by-case basis, a situation that would be conducive neither to market exchange, investment, nor economic growth.

Thus economists do not differ from sociologists in stressing the importance of norms. Where they do differ is in their self-perceived ability to give an account of the origins of norms and rules. Sociologists (as well as anthropologists) are, by and large, much better at describing social norms than explaining why they came to be that way. Many sociological descriptions paint a highly static picture of human society, observing, for example, that lower-class boys in Italian neighborhoods in New York are socialized by "peer group pressure" to join gangs.

But this kind of assertion simply begs the question of where those peer group norms came from in the first place. We can trace them back a generation or two into the historical past, but ultimately we face an absence of evidence for their more distant origins. There was for a time a school of "functionalist" sociology and anthropology that tried to find rational utilitarian reasons for the most bizarre social rules. The Hindu ban on eating cows was ascribed, for example, to the fact that cows were resources that had to be protected for other uses like plowing and dairy farming. What could not be explained is why the Muslims in India, who faced the same ecological and economic conditions, ate cows with gusto, or why the ban persists when a McDonald's in New Delhi can import all the beef it wants from Australia or Argentina.

Into the breech have stepped economists, who in recent years have not been shy about applying their methodology to ever wider aspects of social behavior. There is a large and well-developed branch of economics—game theory—that seeks to explain how social norms and rules come about. As noted above, economists do not deny that human action is bounded by all sorts of rules and norms: How human beings get to these norms, however, is for them a rational and therefore explicable process.

To oversimplify a bit, economic game theory starts from the premise that we are all born into the world as isolated individuals with bundles of selfish desires or preferences, not with lots of social ties and obligations to one another. In many cases, however, we can satisfy those preferences more effectively if we cooperate with other people and therefore end up negotiating cooperative norms to govern social interactions. People can act altruistically

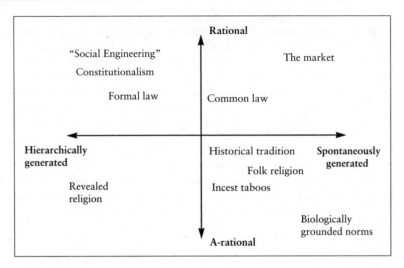

FIGURE 8.3   The Universe of Norms II

by this account, but only because they have calculated at some level that al-truism is of benefit to themselves (presumably because other people will then behave altruistically as well). The mathematics behind game theory simply seeks to understand in a formal way the strategies by which people can move from selfish interests to cooperative outcomes.

If we try to locate various types of norms within our previous four-quad-rant matrix, we come up with something like Figure 8.3.

The rules concerning car pools, for example, belong in the rational, spon-taneously generated quadrant. That is, the rules were evolved in a decentral-ized fashion, but presumably after some discussion and trial and error among the participants. Formal law, whether promulgated by dictatorships or democracies, belongs in the rational hierarchical quadrant, as does con-stitution writing, social engineering, and all other efforts to guide communi-ties from the top. Common law, on the other hand, is generated just like the car pool rules, spontaneously and rationally. Organized revealed religion usually comes from a hierarchical source—indeed, the ultimate hierarchical authority, God—and the rules it dictates are not adopted with rational de-bate. Some folk religions (e.g., Taoism and Shintoism in East Asia) and quasi-religious cultural practices may have evolved in a decentralized, a-ra-tional way. These forms of religious norms belong, therefore, in the lower left and lower right quadrants, respectively. Finally, certain norms are grounded in biology and belong firmly within the a-rational, spontaneously generated quadrant. The incest taboo is in this category. The most recent research indicates that human incest taboos, although conventional, draw upon natural aversions that human beings have to sexual relations between close relatives.

It is possible to hypothesize, as many have done, that as societies modernize, norms tend to be created less in the lower than in the upper quadrants, and particularly in the upper left one (i.e., by government authority). The terms that have classically been associated with modernization by theorists like Henry Maine, Max Weber, Émile Durkheim, and Ferdinand Tönnies—rationalization, bureaucratization, the shift from status to contract, and gemeinschaft to gesellschaft—all suggest that formal, rational legal authority, often vested in the state, becomes the chief source of order in modern societies. Yet as anyone who has tried to wade through the thicket of unwritten rules concerning gender relations in a modern American workplace or school knows, informal norms have not disappeared from modern life and are not likely to do so in the future.

Since people tend to be more aware of norms issuing from hierarchical authority than from Hayek's "extended order of human cooperation," it may be useful to look more closely at the two quadrants on the right side of Figure 8.2 to begin to understand the extent and limits of spontaneous order. "Self-organization" has become a buzzword not only among economists and biologists but also among information technology gurus, management consultants, and business school professors. Nevertheless, it can come into being only under certain distinct conditions, and it is not a universal formula for achieving coordination in human groups.

RULES FOR POOLS

Over the past generation, the greatest number of theoretical and empirical studies of spontaneous order have come out of economics and related fields like law and economics and public choice. Many early studies in this genre had to do with the origin of norms regarding property rights.[13] So-called common pool resources that are shared within communities—resources like meadows, fisheries, forests, underground water, and air—constitute especially difficult problems of cooperation because they are subject to what Garrett Hardin referred to as the "tragedy of the commons."[14] Hardin argued that the tragedy of the commons led to social disaster as seas were overfished and meadows overgrazed. According to him, the problem of sharing common resources could be solved only through hierarchical authority, presumably by a coercive state or even a supranational regulatory body.

In contrast to this hierarchical approach to norm generation, a number of economists have suggested more spontaneous approaches. The fountainhead of the entire law and economics field was Ronald Coase's frequently cited article, "The Problem of Social Cost," in which he argues that when transaction costs are zero, a change in the formal rules of liability will have no effect on the allocation of resources.[15] The problem of applying the Coase theorem to real-world situations is, of course, that transaction costs are almost never zero. It is usually costly for private individuals to work out fair agreements with one another, particularly when one is substantially richer or more powerful than the other.

On the other hand, transaction costs have been low enough in many cases that economists have been able to identify quite a number of intriguing cases of self-organization, whereby social norms have been created through a bottom-up process. Robert Sugden describes the rules for sharing driftwood on English beaches, where first come is first served, but only if a moderate amount is taken.[16] Robert Ellickson gives numerous examples of spontaneous economic rules. Nineteenth-century American whalers, for example, often faced potential conflicts when a whale harpooned by one ship would break free and be captured and sold by another ship that hadn't invested time and effort hunting it. Whalers developed an extensive set of informal rules to regulate such situations and divide the catch equitably.[17]

Much of the spontaneous-order literature tends to be anecdotal and does not give us a good sense of how often new norms are actually created in a decentralized manner. One exception is the work of Elinor Ostrom, who has collected well over 5,000 case studies of common pool resources, a sufficient number to allow her to begin making empirically grounded generalizations about the phenomenon.[18] Her broad conclusion is that human communities in a variety of times and places have found solutions to the tragedy of the commons much more often than is commonly predicted. Many of these solutions involve neither the privatization of common resources (the solution favored by many economists) nor regulation by the state (the solution often favored by non-economists). Rather, communities have been able to rationally devise informal and sometimes formal rules for sharing common resources in a way that is equitable and does not lead to their premature depletion or exhaustion. These solutions are facilitated by the same condition that makes a two-sided prisoner's dilemma soluble: iteration. That is, if people know that they have to continue to live with one another in bounded communities in which continued cooperation will be rewarded, they develop an interest in their own reputations, as well as in the monitoring and punishment of those who violate community rules.

It is clear from the work of Elinor Ostrom and others that spontaneous order occurs only under certain well-defined conditions and that in many situations it either fails to materialize or leads to situations that are not good from the standpoint of society as a whole. Ostrom notes that there are many instances of failed efforts to establish norms for the sharing of common pool resources. Her conditions for self-organization suggest several categories of reasons explaining why societies will not always be able to come up with spontaneous-order solutions.

Size. Mancur Olson pointed out that the free-rider problem becomes more severe as group size increases because it becomes increasingly difficult to monitor the behavior of any one individual. Members of a medical practice or partners in a law firm are likely to know if one of them is not pulling his or her weight; the same is not true in a factory employing 10,000 workers. Furthermore, when groups get larger than this, the system begins to break down. It becomes difficult to associate faces with reputations; monitoring and enforcement become increasingly costly and subject to economies of scale that dictate designating certain members of the group to specialize in these activities.

Boundaries. For spontaneous order to occur, it is important to put clear boundaries on group membership. If people can enter and exit the group at will or if it is not clear who is a member (and therefore who has a right to benefit from the common resources of the group), then individuals will have less incentive to worry about their reputation. This explains, among other things, why crime rates tend to be higher and levels of social capital tend to be lower in neighborhoods with a great deal of transience, such as those undergoing rapid economic change or those around railroad or bus stations.

Repeated Interaction. Many of the communities studied by Elinor Ostrom that have successfully solved common pool resource problems are traditional ones with virtually no social mobility or contact with the outside world, such as mountain villagers, rice farmers, fishermen, and the like. People worry about their reputation only if they know they will have to continue to deal with one another for an extended period in the future.

Prior Norms Establishing a Common Culture. The establishment of cooperative norms often presupposes the existence of a set of prior norms held in common by the individuals making up the group. A culture provides a common vocabulary of not just words but also gestures, facial expressions, and personal habits that serve as signals of intent. Culture helps people distinguish cooperators from cheaters, as well as in transmitting behavioral rules that make action within a community more predictable. People are much more willing to demand the punishment of people who have broken the rules of their own culture than those of another. Conversely, new cooperative norms are much harder to generate across cultural boundaries.

Power and Justice. Informal social norms can frequently reflect the ability of one group to dominate another through its greater wealth, power, cultural capacity, intellectual ability, or through outright violence and coercion. Certain social norms may be seen as unjust, even though they are voluntarily accepted by the communities that practice them. The norms justifying slavery, or those subordinating women to men, are examples.

The Persistence of Bad Choices. Even if unjust, inefficient, or counterproductive norms came into being, one could argue that they would spontaneously disappear precisely because they did not serve the interests of the communities that practiced them. In the law and economics literature, there is often an explicit evolutionary assumption that whatever survives represents fitness in some sense and that there is therefore over time an "evolution toward efficiency." Evil, inefficient, or counterproductive norms can persist in a social system for generations, however, because of the influence of tradition, socialization, and ritual.

Social capital can be generated spontaneously in relatively small, stable groups, in which participants number in the hundreds or in some cases thousands. It can also emerge in larger populations in societies where government and the rule of law exist already, and indeed it is an important consequence of a rule of law. But when spontaneous groups get too large, various public goods problems (e.g., who will negotiate the rules, monitor free riders, enforce norms, and the like) become insuperable. Elinor Ostrom's catalog of rules regarding common pool resources constitute culture with a small *c*— small rules for small communities that we do not generally associate with large and important cultural systems. The spontaneous-order literature can give no account of norm formation that applies to the largest scale groups: nations, ethno-linguistic groups, or civilizations. Culture with a capital *C*— whether Islamic, Hindu, Confucian, or Christian—does not have spontaneous roots.

The four-quadrant matrix of Figure 8.2 is only a taxonomic framework for beginning to think about where social capital actually comes from in contemporary societies. People's views of where cooperative norms actually come from is highly colored by ideological preferences as to where they *ought* to come from: traditionalist conservatives think they ought to come from religion and other sources of a-rational hierarchy populating the lower left quadrant; liberals worried about the workings of "untrammeled markets" want them to come from the upper left (e.g., in the form of a state regulatory agency); and libertarians of the right and left hope they will arise from either of the spontaneous-order quadrants on the right side. It should be clear, however, that in contemporary societies each quadrant contains a non-trivial set of cases and that the four sources of social capital all interact with one another in complex ways.

Formal laws play an important role in shaping informal norms, as in the case of civil rights legislation in the United States, whereas informal norms make the creation of certain kinds of political institutions more or less likely. Religion remains an important source of cultural rules, even in apparently secular societies; at the same time, religious rules are subject to a spontaneous evolution as they interact with a society's given historical environment. Understanding these relationships, and providing an empirical map of the sources of actual cultural rules, is a project for the future.

9

Corruption, Culture, and Markets

SEYMOUR MARTIN LIPSET AND GABRIEL SALMAN LENZ

Widespread interest in the social requisites of democracy and economic development has stimulated a growing literature on the extent, sources, and consequences of corruption. This chapter seeks to integrate theoretical and empirical analyses of corruption. Following a cross-cultural and transhistorical discussion of corruption, it reports some empirical findings from the research literature. It then seeks to integrate these findings and some original research into two theoretical frameworks: the means-ends schema from Robert Merton's scholarship and particularistic assumptions derived from Edward Banfield.

What is corruption? Students of the subject provide different definitions. As Arnold Heidenheimer writes in *Political Corruption*, the word "corruption has a history of uniquely different meanings and connotations."[1] Political scientists and philosophers emphasize its presence in politics or the state: efforts to secure wealth or power through illegal means—private gain at public expense.

Corruption has been ubiquitous in complex societies from ancient Egypt, Israel, Rome, and Greece down to the present. Dictatorial and democratic polities; feudal, capitalist, and socialist economies; Christian, Muslim,

TABLE 9.1
Corruption Perceptions Index 1998

1. Denmark	23. Botswana	46. Brazil	69. Bolivia
2. Finland	24. Spain	47. Belarus	70. Ukraine
3. Sweden	25. Japan	48. Slovak Rep.	71. Latvia
4. New Zealand	26. Estonia	49. Jamaica	72. Pakistan
5. Iceland	27. Costa Rica	50. Morocco	73. Uganda
6. Canada	28. Belgium	51. El Salvador	74. Kenya
7. Singapore	29. Malaysia	52. China	75. Vietnam
8. Netherlands	30. Namibia	53. Zambia	76. Russia
9. Norway	31. Taiwan	54. Turkey	77. Ecuador
10. Switzerland	32. South Africa	55. Ghana	78. Venezuela
11. Australia	33. Hungary	56. Mexico	79. Colombia
12. Luxembourg	34. Mauritius	57. Philippines	80. Indonesia
13. United Kingdom	35. Tunisia	58. Senegal	81. Nigeria
14. Ireland	36. Greece	59. Ivory Coast	82. Tanzania
15. Germany	37. Czech Rep.	60. Guatemala	83. Honduras
16. Hong Kong	38. Jordan	61. Argentina	84. Paraguay
17. Austria	39. Italy	62. Nicaragua	85. Cameroon
18. United States	40. Poland	63. Romania	
19. Israel	41. Peru	64. Thailand	
20. Chile	42. Uruguay	65. Yugoslavia	
21. France	43. South Korea	66. Bulgaria	
22. Portugal	44. Zimbabwe	67. Egypt	
	45. Malawi	68. India	

Hindu, and Buddhist cultures and religious institutions have all experienced corruption but not, of course, in equal measure. The omnipresence, the persistence, and the recurrent character of corruption suggest that it cannot be treated as a dysfunction reducible by purposive human action. Research and study should try to explain why there is more corruption in one time, place, or culture than in others.

Until recently, empirical research in the field consisted primarily of case studies. In response to the growing needs of multinational companies, however, consulting firms have developed a number of corruption indices, transforming the study of corruption and allowing social scientists to test a number of hypotheses about both its causes and its consequences.

One of the commonly used indicators of political corruption is Transparency International's Corruption Perceptions Index (CPI). Table 9.1 is the 1998 listing of eighty-nine countries, ranked from the least to the most corrupt.

This index "is a 'poll of polls' drawing upon numerous distinct surveys of expert and general public views of the extent of corruption in many countries around the world."[2] The CPI subsumes credible indices of corruption for countries in which a minimum of three polls exist; in some cases the index averages as many as twelve. All sources use a similar definition of corruption involving the misuse of public power for private benefits. The CPI averages poll results that attempt to differentiate between political and administrative corruption and thus claims to represent the general perception of corruption. The CPI does not deal with the problems of commensurability—intersocietal and intracultural differences in corruption. Nor does it include measures of corruption in private organizations, such as insider trading.

CPI's methodology is subject to controversy, some authors assuming that it deals only with surveys of the attitudes of international executives toward corruption. In reality, however, it includes samples of the populations. The CPI only counts countries in its index for which at least one such population survey is available. In any case, the polls of executives and experts correlate very highly with the population surveys. The CPI is scaled from 0 (least corrupt) to 10 (most corrupt). Ronald Inglehart reports from the 1995 World Values Survey that the responses to a question inquiring about the extent of corruption in the respondents' countries correlate highly with CPI rankings.

The bulk of this chapter focuses on the relationship between values and corruption. The lack of cross-national quantitative data on values and attitudes has long hindered comparative study in the area. However, the World Values Surveys, conducted in 1981–1982, 1990–1993, and 1995–1996, provide social scientists with large samples of such information on a range of attitudes and values. The 1995–1996 survey sampled over sixty countries; the data set is unfortunately not yet available for analysis but soon will be. The analysis in this chapter uses the 1990–1993 survey, which was carried out in forty-three countries containing 70 percent of the world's population. They include nations with per capita incomes as low as U.S.$399 per year to those as high as $30,000 per year. The quality of the samples varies greatly. The surveys carried out in some less developed and former Soviet countries are drawn disproportionately from the urban, literate populations, which tend to have orientations relatively similar to those found in industrial societies.[3] The findings thus probably underestimate the size of cross-national differences among First, Second, and Third World nations.

ECONOMICS AND CORRUPTION

Hard evidence has documented corruption's detrimental effect on many aspects of economic development. Research indicates that higher levels of corruption significantly reduce GNP growth rates. Paolo Mauro's regression analysis found that a 2.4 decline in the corruption index (scaled from 1 to 10) is associated with a four percentage point increase in the per capita growth rate.[4] The effect of corruption on growth seems to result in part from reduced levels of investment. The negative impact on investment may derive from the added risk that corruption brings to investors' calculations. Corruption may also reduce economic growth by reducing public spending on education. A 2.38 drop (one standard deviation) in the corruption index is associated with an increase in government spending on education by around half a percent of GDP.[5]

Why does corruption influence education? Research suggests that governments plagued by corruption spend relatively more money on items that facilitate the exaction of graft.[6] Corrupt public bureaucrats may shift government expenditures to those areas in which they can collect bribes more efficiently. Larger, hard-to-manage projects, such as airports or highways, facilitate fraud. However, in areas such as education, expenditures and their products are more visible and should presumably be less open to corruption.

Other research ties corruption to income inequality. Cross-national studies have found a strong relationship among corruption, income inequality, and poverty. The lower a country's score on the corruption index, the more likely it is to have a high Gini coefficient, meaning greater income inequality. A 0.78 increase in the growth rate of corruption is linked to a drastic decline in the rate of income growth among the poor—7.8 percentage points per year.[7]

The variable most robustly associated with corruption in international comparisons is per capita income.[8] The wealthy and most economically developed countries are the least politically corrupt. The top twenty, as measured by the Transparency International 1998 Corruption Perceptions Index, have a per capita income in purchasing power of U.S.$17,000 or more (see Table 9.1 for the corruption scores), whereas the twenty most corrupt have a per capita income of $4,000 or less. The latter draw largely from the ranks of the less developed and formerly communist countries. Only six Western European states fall outside the upper twenty.

A number of assumptions may explain the corruption-income relationship. Greater income may reduce corruption by changing the incentive structures of public officials: Increased wealth would seem to reduce the marginal value of expected monetary gains from corruption. At the same time, the cost of penalties—imprisonment, criminal record, embarrassment, loss of future job prospects—probably rises with income.

Economic development may also reduce corruption through its important and positive impact on democracy, which, evidence suggests, reduces corruption.[9] Additionally, development increases levels of education, which may improve the odds of catching abuse.[10] The degree to which a country is integrated into the world economy, as measured by international trade, should also be negatively associated with corruption. Incorporation into the global community exposes nations and citizens to the norms of more economically developed societies regarding personal and market behavior, and groups like the EU and NAFTA condition membership on the adoption of these norms.

CULTURE AND INSTITUTIONS

Systematic cross-national research into the ways that cultural and political variables affect the potentialities for corruption is largely a recent phenomenon. Quantitative evidence points to a link between corruption and social diversity, ethno-linguistic fractionalization, and the proportions of a country's population adhering to different religious traditions. In a sophisticated comparative study, Daniel Treisman found strong evidence that a number of cultural and institutional factors has reduced levels of corruption. In harmony with studies of factors related to democratization, his analysis suggests that a greater percentage of Protestants and a British colonial history are two of the most important factors associated with low levels of national corruption—second only to GNP.

Possible mechanisms by which Protestantism affects such behavior will be discussed below. With respect to British colonial origin, Treisman argues that it infused a lasting emphasis on procedure rather than authority. To quote Harry Eckstein, "Procedures, to them [the British], are not merely procedures, but sacred rituals."[11] The willingness by judges and public officials to follow the rules, even when doing so threatens authority, would seem to increase the chances of exposing corruption. British heritage may also reduce corruption through its positive relationship to democracy.

Two sociological approaches help illuminate the relationships between culture and corruption. The first stems from the work of sociology's founding figure, Émile Durkheim, as extensively reformulated by Robert K. Merton. In his *Social Theory and Social Structure*, Merton presents a means-ends schema that can account for variations in norm violations.[12] A second relates to the family. Political scientist Edward Banfield developed an intriguing analysis of the ways in which a strong familial orientation, as in southern Italy and Sicily, helps explain high levels of corruption.[13] The underlying theory stems from Plato, who pointed out that the inherent relations among family members, especially parents and children, press them to give particularistic preferences (nepotism). Banfield noted that corruption is linked to the strength of family values involving intense feelings of obligation.

THE MEANS-ENDS SCHEMA

Merton's theory implies that corruption is motivated behavior stemming from social pressures that result in norm violations. He emphasizes that all social systems set cultural goals—objectives—that human actors seek to achieve, as well as approved means to gain them (i.e., institutionalized norms). Those seeking to secure the goals by socially approved means are conformists, to use Merton's formulation. However, social systems also press many who have little access to the opportunity structure—whether because of their race, ethnicity, or from a lack of skills, capital, material, and other human resources—to seek the dominant goals from high income to social recognition. Many achievement markets are inherently organized so as to create a large gap between demand (goals and values) and supply (means). Consequently, many, who recognize early on that they have little access to opportunity, will reject the rules of the game and try to succeed by unconventional (innovative or criminal) means. Merton notes the ways this analytic framework helps explain variations in deviant behavior between higher and lower classes and among different ethnic groups in America, generalizations documented by Daniel Bell.[14]

Merton's theory implies that cultures that stress economic success as an important goal but nevertheless strongly restrict access to opportunities will have higher levels of corruption. This hypothesis finds support in data from the cross-national 1990–1993 World Values Survey, which yield evidence for the hypotheses derived from Merton on the relationship between achievement motivation, as measured by a scale of World Values Survey items, and corruption. The extreme cases conform to the analytic framework. The less affluent countries with high achievement motivation are the most corrupt. For instance, Russia, South Korea, and Turkey have the highest levels of achievement orientation according to the scale. These countries are also among the more corrupt.

Conversely, as anticipated by Merton's framework, countries that are relatively low on achievement motivation and high on access to appropriate means should have relatively low levels of corruption. Denmark, Sweden, and Norway fit the bill best. Surprisingly, they are the least achievement oriented according to our scale and are also the least corrupt. Presumably, the means-ends strain is weak among them.

The Scandinavian pattern is produced by the relationship between achievement motivation and structurally differentiated access to opportunity. Surprisingly, the achievement scale is strongly—but negatively—correlated with per capita income. This suggests a conundrum: The richer a country, the lower the level of achievement motivation. These results may appear to counter Weber's cultural theory. However, in dealing with the impact of religious values on economic development, Weber anticipated that the positive relationship with Protestantism would decline once high productivity had been institutionalized. It may be suggested that although today's wealthy nations were once among the most achievement motivated (i.e., before development), their citizens, now affluent, are led, as John Adams anticipated, to pursue non-work-related goals—music, art, literature—to become post-materialists, to use Ronald Inglehart's terminology.[15] The elites and middle classes of some less developed nations, on the other hand, reacting to an awareness of their inferior economic status, may be incited toward higher levels of achievement motivation.

A multiple regression analysis relating the 1990 World Values data to the Corruption Perceptions Index as the dependent variable was undertaken to test the hypothesis. As noted, Merton's theoretical analysis implies that serious corruption will plague countries with high levels of achievement orientation and low access to means. The actual relationship is reasonably strong and statistically significant at conventional levels. A 1.1 change in a country's achievement index score (one standard deviation, scaled from 1 to 5) is associated with almost a half-point change in a country's corruption score. The model's goodness-of-fit is high, explaining a good deal of the variation in corruption. The linkage between these two variables remains strong when controlling for other key factors.

Many indices of the availability of economic resources and of economic freedom have been developed. We primarily use the 1997 Index of Economic Freedom (IEF) published by the *Wall Street Journal* and the Heritage Foundation. Scaled from 1 (no freedom) to 5 (totally free), the index purports to measure the degree to which a government supports the free market. It includes several factors: freedom to hold property, freedom to earn a living, freedom to operate a business, freedom to invest one's earnings, freedom to trade internationally, and freedom to participate in a market economy. In a regression analysis, a 0.75 change (one standard deviation) in the Index of Economic Freedom is associated with almost a one and a half point change in a country's corruption score.

Like the IEF, per capita income may be an indicator of the availability of economic resources and even of the extent to which the bulk of the population is economically satisfied. Thus the fact that per capita income relates so powerfully to corruption further supports the idea that the availability of institutionalized means to achieve desired ends lowers levels of corruption, reinforcing the validity of Merton's assumptions. This model, combining the 1997 Index of Economic Freedom and per capita income, explains a good deal of the variance in corruption. Achievement's relationship to corruption remains robust when controlling for variables that relate to corruption—like per capita income and the percentage Protestant and of British national origin—suggesting that this scale captures an important factor.

AMORAL FAMILISM

The second major cultural framework, one derived from Plato via Banfield, assumes that corruption is in large part an expression of particularism—the felt obligation to help, to give resources to persons to whom one has a personal obligation, to the family above all but also to friends and membership groups. Nepotism is its most visible expression. Loyalty is a particularistic obligation that was very strong in precapitalist, feudal societies. As Weber implied, loyalty and the market are antithetical. The opposite of particularism is universalism, the commitment to treat others according to a similar standard. Market norms express universalism; hence, pure capitalism exhibits and is sustained by such values.

Plato contended two and a half millennia ago that family ties, especially those between parents and children, are the chief forces underlying institutionalized social classes and ascription.[16] He argued that to create an egalitarian society, a communist one, such ties—the family itself—would have to be eliminated. Children would have to be reared from birth in public institutions, not knowing their parents. Plato, of course, could not have believed that a society without parental ties was viable, but his discussion points up the social power he attached to the family.

In trying to understand capitalism's initial rise in Protestant cultures, Weber noted that the pre-industrial norms in Catholic societies were communitarian, requiring above all that the society, the family, and the dominant strata help the less fortunate. He believed that these values worked against the emergence of a rationally driven market economy. Conversely, a stress on individualism, concern for self, is more conducive to capital accumulation. Calvinism and Protestant sectarianism fostered such behavior. Sectarians believe that God helps those who help themselves. Weber pointed out that "the great achievement of . . . the ethical and ascetic sects of Protestantism was to shatter the fetters of the sib [the extended family]."[17] As Lawrence Harrison notes, "There is evidence that the extended family is an effective institution for survival but an obstacle to development."[18] Solidarity with the extended family and hostility to the outsider who is not a member of family, the village, or perhaps the tribe can produce a self-interested culture.

Edward Banfield, studying southern Italy, carried the analysis further with the concept of "amoral familism": a culture that is deficient in communitarian values but fosters familial ties. He writes: "In a society of amoral familists, no one will further the interest of the group or community except as it is to his private advantage to do so."[19] There is little loyalty to the larger community or acceptance of behavioral norms that require support of others. Hence, familism is amoral, gives rise to corruption, and fosters deviance from norms of universalism and merit. Anything goes that advances the interests of one's self and family. The Mafia is an extreme example of amoral familism. Banfield, in effect, argues that corruption in southern Italy and comparable traditional societies is an expression of forces similar to those that sustain the Mafia.

The World Values Survey 1990, together with aggregate statistics from the World Bank, provide data that we employ to create a scale of familism. The first item in the scale deals with unqualified respect for parents, measured by the percentage of people who agreed that regardless of the qualities and faults of one's parents, a person must always love and respect them. The second item is the percentage of people who think that divorce is unjustifiable. The third, from the World Bank, is the mean number of children per woman.

Those nations that score high on this scale tend to be among the more corrupt. Known for their strong familial ties, most Asian nations rank among the more corrupt. On the other hand, Scandinavians are by far the lowest on the familism scale—as noted, these countries are considered the least corrupt. Regression analysis affirms the association. The familism scale and CPI relate strongly. The relationship remains significant when controlling for per capita income. A model that includes the familism scale, the achievement scale, and purchasing power parity explains a great deal of the variation in the CPI.

In short, this analysis affirms the amoral familism thesis. In another model, we added a variable for the percentage of Protestants. Treisman has shown that this measure is powerfully linked to perceptions of corruption. This result suggests that familism is an intervening variable between religion and corruption. In other words, Protestantism reduces corruption, in part because of its association with individualistic, non-familistic relations.

RELIGION, CULTURE, AND CORRUPTION

In the preceding discussion we showed that cultural variables help explain and predict levels of corruption. But what explains culture? Dealing with this complex question is far beyond the limits of this chapter. However, the social science consensus that religion is an important determinant of variations in larger secular cultures offers some helpful suggestions. Countries dominated by Protestants are less corrupt than others. The Protestant religious ethos is more conducive to norm-adhering behavior. Protestants, particularly sectarians, believe that individuals are personally responsible for avoiding sin, whereas other Christian denominations, particularly the Catholic Church, place more emphasis on the inherent weakness of human beings, their inability to escape sin and error, and the need for the church to be forgiving and protecting. The Catholic, Anglican, and Orthodox

Churches tend to be more accepting of human weakness because the clergy have the authority to relieve the individual of some sense of responsibility. Given a more tolerant attitude toward the possibility of "sinning," acceptance of human frailty and of the assumption that no one can be a saint are natural consequences.

The sectarian ethos and the evangelical ethos, on the other hand, are more likely to foster adherence to absolute values, especially with respect to morals. They encourage adherents to press hard to attain and institutionalize virtue and to reduce, if not destroy, the influence of evil people and wicked institutions and practices. Politically, they tend to view social and political dramas as morality plays—battles between God and the devil—with compromise virtually unthinkable.

Protestants have retained important elements of their evangelical origins. Most denominations expect adherence from children of practitioners as a result of a conscious voluntary decision on reaching adulthood. Some require a conversion experience (rebirth) as a sign of sincere faith. Good standing in these groups has been contingent on righteous living in accordance with precepts that are sometimes very concrete. In a number of countries, the more ascetic branches of Protestantism have supported measures to inhibit or limit alcoholic beverages and outlaw gambling.

Protestantism is strongly linked to perceptions of corruption. The relationship remains significant when controlling for per capita income but becomes somewhat less so. This suggests that up to a quarter of the relationship between Protestantism and the CPI is linked to higher incomes or more advanced levels of economic development of Protestants. On the other hand, this finding also implies that as much as 75 percent of Protestantism's relationship to corruption may result from cultural factors.

An analysis of the relationship between our achievement scale and the percentage of Protestants in a country is congruent with the assumption that Protestants have become less achievement oriented. Although Weber stressed that Protestants tend to be more achievement oriented than Catholics or other traditionalists, this may no longer be the case. Now that most Protestant nations are wealthy, the evidence suggests that they have changed their value foci. The achievement scale correlates negatively with the percentage Protestant in a given country, meaning that the more Protestants, the lower the level of achievement motivation. This provides us with another reason to expect lower corruption levels among Protestant nations as compared to Catholic ones.

According to Merton's logic, the availability of institutionalized means in wealthier societies (in this case the accessibility of economic resources) also implies lower corruption scores in Protestant countries, which on average are more affluent. Catholic governments also tend to be more interventionist, limiting economic freedom, whereas Protestant countries are more market oriented, with some partial exceptions (e.g., Scandinavia). As expected, the Index of Economic Freedom correlates positively with Protestantism, meaning that the higher the percentage of Protestants, the greater the freedom.

Finally, Banfield's amoral familism thesis provides an even more basic explanation for why Catholic countries may be more corrupt than Protestant ones. According to conventional wisdom, Catholic countries are more communitarian and familistic, whereas Protestants emphasize individualism and self-reliance. The World Values Survey data support these ideas. The familism scale correlates with Protestantism in the expected direction. As discussed above, the analysis suggests that familism, or the lack thereof, is a major intervening variable between Protestantism and corruption.

DEMOCRACY AND CORRUPTION

What can be done to reduce corruption, other than increasing productivity and becoming more "modern"? For answers, we may look to Weber's discussion of the effects of a politically open society on limiting state power—more democracy, individual freedom, and the rule of law. Democracy—which entails political opposition, freedom of the press, and an independent judiciary—fosters potentially powerful corruption-reducing mechanisms. Opposition parties have an interest in exposing corruption in government in order to win elections. In a democracy, a ruling party or government that fails to reform may lose elections. One-party states, on the other hand, lack such incentives. Mikhail Gorbachev, while still a reformist communist, publicly voiced on at least two occasions his misgivings about the potential for abuse inherent in a one-party system. As a communist, of course, he did not advocate a multiparty system. Rather, he urged the Soviet press and the intellectuals to fulfill the role of the opposition in exposing norm violations.

The 1999 resignation of European Union commissioners over charges of fraud, cronyism, and mismanagement highlights some of the potential cleansing effects of democracy. The democratically chosen European Parliament—a volatile mixture of political parties, national, regional, and sectoral interests—launched an onslaught against the unelected commission's "Mediterranean [corrupt] practices, stemming from southern, more Catholic Europe."[20] The victory of this representative institution "mark[ed] a radical shift in power from the non-elected bureaucracy—the Commission—to the elected European Parliament."[21]

An analysis of the relationship between corruption and democracy broadly confirms these hypotheses. The data on democracy come from Freedom

House's Annual Survey of Political Rights and Civil Liberties.[22] Scaled from 1 (most free) to 7 (least free), the index consists of two parts. The first, political rights, includes responses to the following questions: Are the head(s) of state and legislative representatives elected through free and fair elections? Do citizens have the right to form competitive political parties or other organizations? Is there a significant opposition vote or a realistic opportunity for the opposition to increase its support? The second index, civil liberties, includes a measure of freedom and independence in the media, freedom of speech, assembly, equality under the law, access to an independent, non-discriminatory judiciary, and protection from political terror, unjustified imprisonment, and so on.

The combined Freedom House index of democracy (averaging both indices), taken over the lifetime of the index, 1972–1998, correlates highly and inversely with CPI 1998. In a regression analysis, this combined index of democracy remains significant when controlling for purchasing power parity in per capita terms. However, the unstandardized coefficient loses about half of its value, and when other key factors are entered into the equation, it becomes insignificant. This suggests that about half of the negative correlation between democracy and corruption results from the fact that democracies tend to be wealthier (i.e., provide more access to opportunity).

Although the average Freedom House score may not relate robustly to corruption, Treisman found that the number of consecutive years a country had been a democracy remained related to perceptions of corruption, even when controlling for key factors. Thus, democracy is an important factor in predicting national corruption levels. There is some indication that the civil liberties indicator, particularly the rule of law enforced by an independent judiciary, is more important than political rights.

CONCLUSION

The emergence of developed economies was facilitated by emphases on rationality, small family size, achievement, social mobility, and universalism—elements that characterize modernity as distinct from traditionalism. Ideally, they were marked by the decline of familism, of values that sustain particularistic mutual-help systems, which run counter to those functional for a market economy. Values that sustain and express the logic of the market followed on the breakdown of feudal-type stratification systems that stressed obligation and loyalty.

The strong emphasis of Asian countries on group obligation, especially to the family, which is much more powerful in the most recently feudal country, Japan, than in America or Europe, implies a high level of corruption. The

Transparency estimates indicate that most large East Asian countries do score high on corruption, well above the median. Japan, of course, seemingly is a major exception. It has an extremely low crime rate. Interpretations of Japan suggest that rules and the law are less often violated there because doing so disgraces one's family or other in-groups and shames the malefactor. However, reports of high-level business and political corruption keep surfacing. In Transparency's 1998 Corruption Perceptions Index, Japan ranks twenty-fifth, lower than Chile, Portugal, Botswana, and Spain, and only slightly above Costa Rica, Belgium, Malaysia, Namibia, Taiwan, and Tunisia.

The former communist countries, except for Hungary and the Czech Republic, all rank below the median. They share, to various degrees, an amalgam of familism, statist communitarianism, hierarchical religious cultures (Catholicism and Orthodoxy), and party particularism, which produced a high level of corruption under communism. They are also, for the most part, poor.

We have focused on two explanations of corruption, the Mertonian means-ends schema and the Banfield emphasis on familism. The issues that Merton and Banfield identified—inadequate means to attain prescribed goals and particularistic norms inherent in the family—will continue to affect the behavior of nations. If rationally oriented economic values and the rule of law become dominant in less developed and former communist countries, and if they foster development, levels of corruption should fall, as they have in the three now well-to-do and highly market oriented and relatively law abiding Chinese societies: Hong Kong, Taiwan, and Singapore.

part three

THE ANTHROPOLOGICAL DEBATE

10

Traditional Beliefs and Practices—Are Some Better than Others?

ROBERT B. EDGERTON

For those of us who are besieged daily by headlines and television reports concerning gang violence, the endangered environment, homelessness, child abuse, the threat of drugs, AIDS, and divisive political partisanship, the idea that some things people do may be harmful to themselves and others is unlikely to seem controversial. More and more surveys rate various cities in the United States in terms of their relative quality of life, and the same thing is being done of foreign countries.

Political systems are evaluated as well. Many people would surely be troubled by any relativistic insistence that the political systems of Iraq, Hitler's Germany, or the Khmer Rouge in Cambodia were, or are, as good for the people who live in them or near them as those in Norway, Canada, or Switzerland, for instance. Most people would probably also react with disbelief to the anthropological assertion that there is no scientific basis for the evaluation of another society's practice of (for instance) human sacrifice, genocide, or judicial torture, except as the people in that particular society themselves evaluate these practices. Nevertheless, that is exactly what many proponents of cultural relativism and adaptivism have asserted—and these principles continue to be strongly held, especially in anthropology.

These ideas are rooted in the belief that "primitive" societies were far more harmonious than "modern" ones. Misery, fear, loneliness, pain, sickness, and premature death are commonplace in America's urban ghettos and among its homeless people, just as they are in South Africa's black townships, the starving villages of the Sudan, the slums of Brazil, and the "ethnically cleansed" regions of the Balkans. People in such places are seen to be the hapless victims of various kinds of social, cultural, and environmental pressures, including governmental neglect, racism, corruption, ethnic, religious, and political strife, as well as economic exploitation.

However, many prominent scholars in anthropology and other disciplines believe that this sort of misery is not natural to the human condition. They believe that people in smaller, more homogeneous "folk" societies have historically lived in far greater harmony and happiness, and that people in many small societies continue to do so today. The belief that primitive societies are more harmonious than modern ones, that "savages" were "noble," that life in the past was more idyllic than life today, and that human beings once had a sense of community that has been lost is not only reflected in the motion pictures and novels of our popular culture but is deeply engrained in scholarly discourse as well.

THE HAPPY SAVAGE

In this view, human misery is the result of divisive social disorganization, ethnic or religious diversity, class conflict, or competing interests that plague large societies, particularly nation-states. Smaller and simpler societies, on the other hand, have developed their cultures in response to the demands of stable environments; therefore, their way of life must have produced far greater harmony and happiness for their populations. Anthropologist Robin Fox, for example, vividly described the upper Paleolithic environment of big-game hunters as one in which "there was a harmony of our evolved attributes as a species, including our intelligence, our imagination, our violence and, our reason and our passions—a harmony that has been lost" (1990, 3). When a small society that lacks this kind of harmony is found, social scientists often conclude that this condition must be the result of the disorganizing effects of culture contact, particularly economic change and urbanization. Like cultural relativism, this idea has been entrenched in Western thought for centuries (Nisbet 1973; Shaw 1985).

When Robert Redfield published his now well-known folk-urban typology in 1947, he lent the authority of anthropology to this ancient distinction

(Redfield 1947). The idea that cities were beset by crime, disorder, and human suffering of all sorts while folk societies were harmonious communities goes back to Aristophanes, Tacitus, and the Old Testament. It received renewed support in nineteenth-century thought from such influential figures as Ferdinand Tönnies, Henry Maine, Fustel de Coulanges, Émile Durkheim, and Max Weber. Others joined them in creating a consensus that the moral and emotional commitment, personal intimacy, social cohesion, and continuity over time that characterized folk societies did not survive the transition to urban life, in which social disorganization and personal pathology prevailed.

During the twentieth century, the contrast between folk "community" and urban "society" became one of the most fundamental ideas in Western thought, taking hold among social philosophers, political scientists, sociologists, psychiatrists, theologians, novelists, poets, and the educated public in general. As a case in point, Kirkpatrick Sale answered criticisms of his recent book *The Conquest of Paradise* (which examines the European conquest of the native peoples of America) by insisting that unlike the cultures of Europe, the "primal communities" of preconquest America were markedly more "harmonious, peaceful, benign and content" (Sale 1991).

Some folk societies were harmonious, but others were not. There is a pervasive assumption among anthropologists that a population's traditional beliefs and practices—their culture and their social institutions—must play a positive role in their lives or these beliefs and practices simply would not have persisted. Thus it has often been written that cannibalism, torture, infanticide, feuding, witchcraft, female genital mutilation, ceremonial rape, headhunting, and other practices that may be abhorrent to outsiders must serve some useful function in the societies in which they are traditional practices. Impressed by the wisdom of biological evolution in creating such adaptive miracles as protective coloration or feathers for flight, most scholars have assumed that cultural evolution too has been guided by a process of natural selection that has retained traditional beliefs and practices that meet people's needs. Therefore, when a society was encountered that appeared to lack a beneficial system of beliefs or institutions, it was usually assumed that the cause must lie in the baneful influence of other peoples—colonial officials, soldiers, missionaries, or traders—who had almost always been on the scene before anthropologists arrived.

The frequency with which traits that may have been maladaptive occurred in small-scale societies is simply not known because ethnographic accounts so seldom address the possibility that some of the beliefs or practices of the people being described might be anything other than adaptive. If one were to select a substantial number of ethnographic monographs more or less at random, one would probably find, as I did, that no more than a handful would contain an analysis of the maladaptive consequences of any particular belief or practice. Instead, if seemingly bizarre, irrational, inefficient, or dangerous beliefs or practices are described at all, they are usually presumed to be adaptive and are treated as if they must serve some useful purpose. For example, even the most extreme forms of penile mutilation— slashing open the urethra, scourging it with abrasive stalks of grass or other plants, mutilating the glans or infibulating it—have typically been analyzed in the ethnographic literature (if not the psychiatric) not as irrational, nonadaptive or maladaptive practices, but in terms of their positive social, cultural, or psychological consequences (Cawte, Djagamara, and Barrett 1966; Favazza 1987).

RATIONALIZING ADAPTIVENESS

The cumulative impact of relativistic and adaptivist assumptions has led generations of ethnographers to believe that there simply must be a good social or cultural reason why a long-established belief or practice exists. If it has endured for any length of time, it must be adaptive—or so it has been either implicitly or explicitly assumed by most of the people who have written what we know about the lives of people in small traditional societies.

Not everyone has made this assumption, however. Some ecologically oriented ethnographers, for example, have provided descriptions that carefully assess how adaptive a particular population's beliefs or institutions may be. Walter Goldschmidt's ethnography of the Sebei of Uganda is a good example. After analyzing the relatively positive social and cultural adaptations that the Sebei made during their recent history, he described what he referred to as "disequilibria and maladaptation," especially "the failure of the Sebei to establish a social order capable of maintaining their boundaries, and the failure to develop a commitment to a relevant set of moral principles" (1976, 353). His analysis went on to specify the changing socioeconomic circumstances that led to these "failures."

Similarly, Klaus-Friedrich Koch, writing about the then unacculturated Jalé, who in the mid-1960s lived in the remote eastern Snow Mountains of Irian Jaya before foreign influence changed their lives, concluded that the disputes and killing that were so common and so divisive among them resulted because Jalé methods of conflict management were "very few and very inefficient" (Koch 1974, 159). Others, most notably C. R. Hallpike, have pointed to similarly maladaptive practices in other societies (1972, 1986). However, even ecologically oriented ethnographers have typically paid scant attention to maladaptation. Instead, the emphasis has been placed on showing the adaptive fit between various economic activities and the environment.

For the most part, when the costs and benefits of a particular belief or institutionalized practice are discussed in ethnographic writing, the result is vintage Dr. Pangloss. For example, if it is acknowledged that a certain belief system, such as witchcraft, may have costs for a population, it is quickly asserted that it also has benefits that far outweigh them. When Clyde Kluckhohn and Dorothea Leighton wrote their classic ethnography, *The Navaho*, they concluded that the traditional Navaho belief in the existence of witches among them engendered fear, led to violence, and sometimes caused innocent people to suffer "tragically." Even so, they argued that witchcraft beliefs "keep the core of the society solid" by allowing the Navaho to redirect all the hostility they felt toward friends and relatives onto witches. What is more, these beliefs prevented the rich and ceremonially powerful from attaining too much power and, in general, served to prevent socially disruptive actions (Kluckhohn and Leighton 1962, 240). Kluckhohn and Leighton did not consider why the Navaho required witchcraft beliefs to achieve these ends with the fear, violence, and tragic suffering that resulted for many people, when less conflicted solutions for the same problems had been found by other societies.

They were not alone in this. Most ethnographers appear to agree with psychologist Donald T. Campbell, who wrote in favor of an assumption of adaptiveness because no matter how "bizarre" a traditional belief or practice might seem, once it is understood it will make "adaptive sense" (Campbell 1975, 1104). Others have agreed with Marvin Harris's declaration that there is no need to *assume* that beliefs or practices are adaptive because it has already been demonstrated that sociocultural systems are "largely if not exclusively" composed of adaptive traits (1960, 601). Both the assumption that culture must always be adaptive and the assertion that it has already been shown that cultures consist largely or exclusively of adaptive traits fly in the face of considerable evidence to the contrary. With the partial exception of economic practices, there has been no demonstration of such widespread adaptiveness (Edgerton 1992).

This issue is not of interest only to anthropologists—a tempest confined to an exotic, "primitive" teacup. The ethnographic record is important for anyone who has an interest in understanding why human societies, including our own, sometimes do not function as well as they might. It is undeniable that some folk societies have been relatively harmonious and that some still are, but life in smaller and simpler societies has hardly been free of human discontent and suffering. Although there is not enough space here to document my assertion, some small populations have been unable to cope with the demands of their environments, and some have lived in apathy, conflict, fear, hunger, and despair. Others have embraced practices like feuding that led to their destruction. Nevertheless, the belief persists that small-scale societies are better adapted to their ecological circumstances than we are. Some may be, but others decidedly are not.

Humans in various societies, whether urban or folk, are capable of empathy, kindness, even love, and they can sometimes achieve astounding mastery of the challenges posed by their environments. But they are also capable of maintaining beliefs, values, and social institutions that result in senseless cruelty, needless suffering, and monumental folly in their relations among themselves as well as with other societies and the physical environment in which they live. People are not always wise, and the societies and cultures they create are not ideal adaptive mechanisms, perfectly designed to provide for human needs. It is mistaken to maintain, as many scholars do, that if a population has held to a traditional belief or practice for many years, then it must play a useful role in their lives. Traditional beliefs and practices may be useful, may even serve as important adaptive mechanisms, but they may also be inefficient, harmful, and even deadly.

THE VALUES AND DISVALUES OF CULTURAL RELATIVISM

The principle of cultural relativism is not without historical value. It has helped to counter ethnocentrism and even racism. It has also provided an important corrective to ideas of unilinear evolution, which presumed that all societies passed through the same stages of "progress" until they eventually reached the near perfection of one or another version of Western European "civilization." Moreover, the relativists' insistence on respect for the values of other people may have done more good for human dignity and human rights than it has done harm to science. Even the overheated assertions of the so-called epistemological relativists have been useful, by reminding anyone audacious enough to compare the adequacy of cultures that any sociocultural system is a complex network of meanings that must be understood in context and, as much as possible, as its members understand it (Spiro 1990). They may even be right in arguing that some understandings and emotions are unique to a particular culture, and that the meanings and functions of some practices may remain permanently beyond the comprehension of outside observers of the foreign culture.

However, epistemological relativists not only claim that each of these worlds is wholly unique—incommensurable and largely incomprehensible—they assert that the people who inhabit them are said to have different cognitive abilities. In what Dan Sperber has referred to as "cognitive apartheid" and Ernest Gellner has called "cognitive anarchy," various postmodern relativists and interpretivists postulate fundamental differences from one culture to the next in cognitive processes involving logic, causal inference, and information processing (Gellner 1982; Sperber 1982). The existence of such basic cognitive differences has yet to be demonstrated, and if the history of research into human cognition and intersubjectivity is any guide, it will not be.

The history of cultural relativism or adaptivism is the more remarkable because some of the world's most respected anthropologists, all of whom had earlier endorsed the principle of cultural relativism, eventually published anti-relativistic evaluations of folk societies. For example, in 1948 Alfred Kroeber, then the doyen of American anthropology, not only rejected relativism but declared that as societies "progressed" from simple to more complex, they became more "humane," and he asserted—in language calculated to make present-day anthropologists' hair stand on end—that "the mentally unwell in modern advanced cultures tend to correspond to the well and influential in ancient and retarded cultures" (1948, 300). Furthermore, Kroeber continued, "progress," as he referred to cultural evolution, not only involved advances in technology and science but the abandonment of practices such as ritual prostitution, segregating women at parturition or menstruation, torture, sacrifice, and belief in magic or superstition. Two years later, Ralph Linton, another leading anthropologist, who possessed perhaps the most encyclopedic understanding of world ethnography of anyone then alive, wrote that there could be universal ethical standards, a position that Clyde Kluckhohn, by then no longer a committed relativist, endorsed three years later (Kluckhohn 1955; Linton 1952).

Robert Redfield, famous for his folk-urban comparison, agreed with Kroeber by declaring in 1953 that primitive societies were less "decent" and "humane" than more "advanced civilizations": "On the whole the human race has come to develop a more decent and humane measure of goodness—there has been a transformation of ethical judgment which makes us look at noncivilized people, not as equals, but as people on a different level of human experience" (1953, 163).

In 1965, George Peter Murdock, then the world's leading figure in comparative cultural studies, wrote that Benedict's relativistic idea that a cultural belief has no meaning except in its context was "nonsense" and that Melville Herskovits's assertion that all cultures must be accorded equal dignity and respect was "not only nonsense but sentimental nonsense" (1965, 146). He added that it was an "absurdity" to assert that cannibalism, slavery, magical therapy, and killing the aged should be accorded the same "dignity" or "validity" as old-age security, scientific medicine, and metal artifacts. All people, Murdock insisted, prefer Western technology and would rather be able to feed their children and elderly than kill them (1965, 149). With a very few exceptions, anthropologists not only did not embrace these anti-relativistic views, they held even more strongly to the belief that culture is and must be adaptive.

MALADAPTIVENESS

There are many reasons why some traditional beliefs and practices may become maladaptive. Environmental change is one. Others are more complex, having to do with various aspects of human problem solving. There is ample evidence, for example, that in many societies people can provide no rational reason for clinging to certain beliefs or practices, and that some of their most important decisions—where to hunt, when to raid an enemy, when to fish, what to plant—are based on prophecies, dreams, divination, and other supernatural phenomena. One southern African kingdom was utterly destroyed when its cherished prophets urged that all its cattle be killed and no crops be planted. The result was predicted to be a millennium; instead, it was starvation, as a more rational belief system would have predicted (Peires 1989).

Even when people attempt to make rational decisions, they often fail. For one thing, no population, especially no folk population, can ever possess all the relevant knowledge it needs to make fully informed decisions about its environment, its neighbors, or even its own social institutions. What is more, there is a large body of research involving human decisionmaking, both under experimental conditions and in naturally occurring situations, showing that individuals frequently make quite poor decisions, especially when it comes to solving novel problems or ones requiring the calculation of the probability of outcomes. These are precisely the kinds of problems that pose the greatest challenges for human adaptation.

Most humans are not greatly skilled in assessing risk, especially when the threat is a novel one, and they tend to underestimate the future effects of warfare and technological or economic change. Even when disasters such as droughts, floods, windstorms, or volcanic eruptions recur periodically, people consistently misjudge the consequences (Douglas and Wildavsky 1982; Lumsden and Wilson 1981). Nor do they readily develop new technology, even when environmental stress makes technological change imperative (Cowgill 1975). Western economists employ the concept of "bounded rationality" to refer to people's limited ability to receive, store, retrieve, and process information, and economic decision theory takes these limitations into account. Because of their cognitive limitations, along with imperfect knowledge of their environment, people inevitably make some imperfect decisions (Kuran 1988).

Humans are often non-rational, a point vividly made by Dan Sperber, who wrote that "apparently cultural beliefs are quite remarkable: they do not appear irrational by slightly departing from common sense, or timidly going beyond what the evidence allows. They appear, rather, like down-right provocations against common sense rationality" (1985, 85). As Sperber and others have pointed out, people in many folk societies are convinced that humans or animals can be in two places at the same time, can transform themselves into other kinds of creatures or become invisible, and can alter the physical world in various ways through their own beliefs. They also think magically at least some of the time; indeed, it is very likely that the principles of sympathetic magic are universally present because the human mind evolved to think in these ways (Rozin and Nemeroff 1990).

Moreover, all available evidence indicates that humans, especially those who live in folk societies, make their decisions using heuristics that encourage them to develop fixed opinions, even though these opinions are based on inadequate or false information. These same heuristics also encourage people to cling to their opinions, even when considerable evidence to the contrary becomes available. As R. A. Shweder has concluded, human thought is "limited to its scientific procedures, unsophisticated in abstract reasoning, and somewhat impervious to the evidence of experience" (1980, 76).

RATIONALITY AND IRRATIONALITY

None of this should be surprising, really, for no less rational a thinker than Aristotle was convinced that male babies were conceived at times when a strong north wind blew, and despite many generations of secular education, contemporary Americans continue to be less than fully rational. Various surveys have reported that 80 percent of contemporary Americans still believe that God works miracles, 50 percent believe in angels, and more than a third believe in a personal devil (Gallup and Castelli 1989; Greeley 1989; Wills 1990). Furthermore, as I mentioned earlier, our ability to identify the risks in our environment is limited. As Mary Douglas and Aaron Wildavsky noted, all populations concentrate on only a few of the dangers that confront them and ignore the remainder, including some that are manifestly dangerous. The Lele of Zaire, for example, faced many serious dangers, including a large array of potentially life-threatening diseases. Still, they concentrated on only three: bronchitis, which is less serious than the pneumonia from which they also suffer; infertility; and being struck by lightning, a hazard that is a good deal less common than the tuberculosis from which they frequently suffer yet largely ignore (Douglas and Wildavsky 1982). According to the Science Advisory Board of the Environmental Protection Agency, Americans do the same, worrying most about relatively unimportant environmental threats while largely ignoring potentially much more dangerous risks.

Thomas Gilovich has described the cognitive processes that allow even highly educated Americans to hold fervently to demonstrably false beliefs. Noting surveys of American college students that indicate that as many as 58 percent believe that astrological predictions are valid while 50 percent think that the Egyptian pyramids were built with extraterrestrial assistance, Gilovich describes the many ways in which contemporary Americans distort reality by their tendency to impute meaning and order to random phenomena, remembering only those instances that confirm their established beliefs while forgetting those that are at variance with them (Gilovich 1991).

If modern Americans are less than rational calculators—and these examples hardly exhaust the catalog of folly contributed to by those among us who are thought to be most rational, such as our engineers, physicians, scientists, and educators—then it is unreasonable to expect people whose cultures are even less secular than ours to be more efficient problem solvers than we are. I am not arguing that people in folk societies make less than rational decisions or hold maladaptive beliefs because they are cognitively less competent than people in literate, industrialized societies.

C. R. Hallpike, among others, has concluded that the thought processes of people in small-scale societies are incapable of comprehending causality, time, realism, space, introspection, and abstraction as utilized in Western science (Hallpike 1972). Whether so-called primitive thought is less abstract, more magical, or less able to assess marginal probabilities is an issue that continues to be debated, but its resolution is largely irrelevant to the point I am attempting to make. I am asserting that most people in *all* societies, including those most familiar with Western science, sometimes make potentially harmful mistakes and tend to maintain them. It is possible that people in small-scale societies make more mistakes of this kind, but maladaptive decisions are made in all societies.

IDENTIFYING PROBLEMS

For people to optimize the adaptiveness of their beliefs and practices, they must not only think rationally but must be able to identify the problems that need to be solved. This is often difficult. Some problems, like changes in climate or soil erosion, develop so gradually that by the time they can be identified, no human response is effective. Others, like the encroachment of diseases or the hazards of dietary change, may not be perceived as problems at all. Humans lived with the deadly hazard of malaria for millennia before it was finally understood very late in the nineteenth century that it was trans-

mitted by mosquitoes. Many populations still do not understand the causes
of the deadly diseases that plague them. And still other phenomena may be
perceived as problems but prove to be insoluble because the society is torn by
conflicting values or interest groups. How much energy are people willing to
expend to increase their food supply? Will people give up a tasty but un-
healthy diet for one that is more nutritious but less flavorful? Will leaders
willingly give up some of their privileges to benefit the society as a whole?
Will men do so to benefit women? Will elders yield some of their authority
and rights to younger men? Will men yield rights to women?

This is not to say that people in various societies do not worry about what
they perceive to be problems; societies with recognized leaders, councils, or
bureaucracies often do make decisions that are intended to be solutions.
Members of the Hawaiian priesthood and aristocracy abolished their system
of food taboos in an effort to resolve what they perceived as a problem, and
a Pawnee chief tried to abolish human sacrifice. Among the Sebei of Uganda,
a prophet named Matui instituted a new ritual, translated as "passing the
law," in which all men of a parish gathered together and swore not to commit a number of acts (Goldschmidt 1976, 204). Matui's innovation was
probably adaptive for the Sebei because it reduced interclan violence, but
such farsighted leadership must have been uncommon in human history. The
wisdom of various leaders' decisions over the entire course of human evolution is unknown, but if the written record of history is any guide, few of
them led to optimally beneficial outcomes. On the contrary, as Barbara Tuchman pointed out in *The March of Folly*, a great many were horrifically counterproductive (Tuchman 1984). Marvin Harris, long a leading proponent of
the view that virtually all traditional beliefs and practices are adaptive, recently reached the surprising conclusion that "all major steps in cultural evolution took place in the absence of anyone's conscious understanding of what
was happening." And, he adds, "the twentieth century seems a veritable cor-
nucopia of unintended, undesirable, and unanticipated changes" (Harris
1989, 495).

Rational, calculated decisions intended to resolve a people's problems seldom occur in small societies. Most of the time, how people hunt, fish, farm,
conduct rituals, control their children, and enjoy their leisure are not matters
for discussion at all or at least not discussion about how to make these activities more efficient or pleasurable. People complain incessantly about various
things in their lives. They may sometimes try something new, but only rarely
do they attempt any fundamental change in their traditional beliefs or practices. Large changes, if they occur at all, are typically imposed by some external event or circumstances—invasion, epidemic, drought. In the absence of
such events, people tend to muddle through by relying on traditional solu-

tions that arose in response to previous circumstances. Most populations manage to survive without being rational calculators in search of optimal solutions. It appears, for example, that folk populations typically adopt strategies that assure a life-sustaining but less than maximal yield of food, and they resist changes that entail what they perceive to be risks, even though these new food-providing practices would produce more food.

The reluctance of people to change has led some anthropologists to refer to their economic strategies in terms of "minimal risk" and "least effort." Beliefs and practices tend to persist not because they are optimally beneficial but because they generally work just well enough that changes in them are not self-evidently needed. Given all that we know about the sometimes astoundingly bad judgment of "rational" planners in modern nations, it seems unlikely that people in smaller and simpler societies who lack our scientific and technological sophistication would always make optimally adaptive decisions, even should they try to do so. Furthermore, even if a population somehow managed to devise a nearly perfect adaptation to its environment, it is unlikely that it could maintain it for any length of time.

My assertion is not that traditional beliefs and practices are never adaptive and that they never contribute to a population's well-being, and I am not claiming that people never think rationally enough to make effective decisions about meeting the challenges posed by their environments. Nor am I arguing that human behavior is driven solely by the socially disruptive aspects of biological predispositions such as paranoid ideation and selfishness. Humans are often driven by greed, lust, envy, and other attributes that challenge the common good. But people are also predisposed to cooperate, to be kind to one another, and sometimes even to sacrifice their interests for the well-being of others (Edgerton 1978, 1985).

However, if maladaptive beliefs and practices are as common as they appear to be, their existence poses a challenge to the prevailing adaptivist paradigm. Subsistence activities must be reasonably efficient for a population to survive, but they need not be optimal (in the sense of providing the best possible nutrition for the least expenditure of time and energy). It is highly unlikely that any population has achieved an optimal economic adaptation; indeed, it is not at all clear that any population has even attempted to do so. Social organization and culture will be affected by the technology available to a population and by its economic activities, but neither social institutions nor cultural belief systems have commonly led to anything that could be considered maximally adaptive utilization of the environment. Nor have they unfailingly enhanced the well-being of all members of that population.

Just as no population has yet devised an optimal means for exploiting its environment, so it is most unlikely that all members of a population have agreed about what an optimal environmental exploitation should be. More-over, no population yet reported has met the needs of all its members to their own satisfaction. All, including those whose members are healthiest, happi-est, and longest-lived, could do better; all could improve health and safety; all could further enhance life satisfaction. There has been no perfect society and no ideal adaptation—only degrees of imperfection. Sometimes know-ingly and sometimes not, populations adjust their ways of living in efforts to better their lives, but none has yet created the optimal society. Not only are humans capable of errors and of misjudging the ecological circumstances that they must learn to cope with, but they are given to pursuing their own interests at the expense of others and to preferring the retention of old cus-toms to the development of new ones. Culture may tend to be adaptive, but it is never perfectly so.

It should thus not be assumed, as it so commonly is, that any persistent, traditional belief or practice in a surviving society must be adaptive. Instead, it should be assumed that any belief or practice could fall anywhere along a continuum of adaptive value. It may simply be neutral or tolerable, or it may benefit some members of a society while harming others. Sometimes it may be harmful to all.

In closing, I quote British anthropologist Roy Ellen: "Cultural adaptations are seldom the best of all possible solutions and never entirely rational" (1982, 251).

REFERENCES

Campbell, D. T. 1975. "On the Conflicts Between Biological and Social Evolution and Between Psychology and Moral Tradition." *American Psychologist* 30: 1103–1126.

Cawte, J., N. Djagamara, and M. G. Barrett. 1966. "The Meaning of Subincision of the Urethra to Aboriginal Australians." *British Journal of Medical Psychology* 39: 245–253.

Cowgill, G. L. 1975. "On Causes and Consequences of Ancient and Modern Popula-tion Changes." *American Anthropologist* 77: 505–525.

Douglas, M., and A. Wildavsky. 1982. *Risk and Culture: An Essay on the Selection of Technological and Environmental Dangers.* Berkeley: University of California Press.

Edgerton, R. B. 1978. "The Study of Deviance—Marginal Man or Everyman?" In *The Making of Psychological Anthropology,* edited by G. D. Spindler, pp. 444–476. Berkeley: University of California Press.

_____. 1985. *Rules, Exceptions, and Social Order.* Berkeley: University of California Press.

_____. 1992. *Sick Societies: Challenging the Myth of Primitive Harmony.* New York: Free Press.

Ellen, R. 1982. *Environment, Subsistence, and System: The Ecology of Small-Scale Social Formations.* New York: Cambridge University Press.

Favazza, A. R., with B. Favazza. 1987. *Bodies Under Siege: Self-Mutilation in Culture and Psychiatry.* Baltimore: Johns Hopkins University Press.

Fox, R. 1990. *The Violent Imagination.* New Brunswick, N.J.: Rutgers University Press.

Gallup, G., Jr., and J. Castelli. 1989. *The People's Religion: American Faith in the Nineties.* New York: Macmillan.

Gellner, E. 1982. "Relativism and Universals." In *Rationality and Relativism,* edited by M. Hollis and S. Lukes, pp. 181–256. Oxford: Basil Blackwell.

Gilovich, T. 1991. *How We Know What Isn't So: The Fallibility of Human Reason in Everyday Life.* New York: Free Press.

Goldschmidt, W. R. 1976. *The Culture and Behavior of the Sebei.* Berkeley: University of California Press.

Greeley, A. 1989. *Religious Change in America.* Cambridge: Harvard University Press.

_____. 1990. *The Human Career.* Cambridge: Blackwell.

Hallpike, C. R. 1972. *The Konso of Ethiopia: A Study of the Values of a Cushitic Society.* Oxford: Clarendon.

_____. 1986. *The Principles of Social Evolution.* Oxford: Clarendon.

Harris, M. 1960. "Adaptation in Biological and Cultural Science." *Transactions of the New York Academy of Science* 23: 59–65.

_____. 1989. *Our Kind: Who We Are, Where We Came From, and Where We Are Going.* New York: Harper & Row.

Kluckhohn, C. 1955. "Ethical Relativity: *Sic et Non.*" *Journal of Philosophy* 52: 663–677.

Kluckhohn, C., and D. Leighton. 1962. *The Navaho.* Rev. ed. Garden City, N.Y.: Doubleday. Published in cooperation with the American Museum of Natural History.

Koch, K. F. 1974. *War and Peace in Jalémo: The Management of Conflict in Highland New Guinea.* Cambridge: Harvard University Press.

Kroeber, A. L. 1948. *Anthropology.* New York: Harcourt, Brace.

Kuran, T. 1988. "The Tenacious Past: Theories of Personal and Collective Conservation." *Journal of Economic Behavior and Organization* 10: 143–171.

Linton, R. 1952. "Universal Ethical Principles: An Anthropological View." In *Moral Principles of Action: Man's Ethical Imperative,* edited by R. N. Anshen. New York: Harper.

Lumsden, C. J., and E. O. Wilson. 1981. *Genes, Mind, and Culture.* Cambridge: Harvard University Press.

Murdock, G. P. 1965. *Culture and Society.* Pittsburgh: University of Pittsburgh Press.

Nisbet, R. 1973. *The Social Philosophers: Community and Conflict in Western Thought.* New York: Crowell.

Peires, J. B. 1989. *The Dead Will Arise: Nongqawuse and the Great Xhosa Cattle-Killing Movement of 1856–6.* London: Curry.

Redfield, R. 1947. "The Folk Society." *American Journal of Sociology* 52: 293–308.

_____. 1953. *The Primitive World and Its Transformations.* Ithaca: Cornell University Press.

Rosaldo, R., R. A. Calvert, and G. L. Seligmann. 1982. *Chicano: The Evolution of a People.* Malabar, Fla.: Krieger.

Rozin, P., and C. Nemeroff. 1990. "The Laws of Sympathetic Magic: A Psychological Analysis of Similarity and Contagion." In *Cultural Psychology: Essays on Comparative Human Development,* edited by J. W. Stigler, R. A. Shweder, and G. Herdt, pp. 205–232. New York: Cambridge University Press.

Sale, Kirkpatrick. 1991. Letter to the editor. *New York Times,* 25 July.

Shaw, P. 1985. "Civilization and Its Malcontents: Responses to *Typee.*" *New Criterion,* January, pp. 23–33.

Shweder, R. A. 1980. "Rethinking Culture and Personality Theory, Part 3, From Genesis and Typology to Hermeneutics and Dynamics." *Ethos* 8: 60–94.

Sperber, D. 1982. "Apparently Irrational Beliefs." In *Rationality and Relativism,* edited by M. Hollis and S. Lukes, pp. 149–180. Oxford: Basil Blackwell.

_____. 1985. "Anthropology and Psychology: Towards an Epidemiology of Representations." *Man* 20: 73–89.

Spiro, M. E. 1990. "On the Strange and Familiar in Recent Anthropological Thought." In *Cultural Psychology: Essays on Comparative Human Development,* edited by J. W. Stigler, R. A. Shweder, and G. Herdt, pp. 47–61. New York: Cambridge University Press.

Tuchman, B. 1984. *The March of Folly.* New York: Knopf.

Wills, G. 1990. *Under God: Religion and American Politics.* New York: Simon & Schuster.

11

Culture, Childhood, and Progress in Sub-Saharan Africa

THOMAS S. WEISNER

Every economic system consists of a world of social beings living out cultural careers, who bring their goals, motives, capacities, and cultural models of the world to economic life. Cultures around the world imagine and try to guide children into wonderful and varied cultural careers in hopes of producing the kinds of social beings they value. Cultural careers start before we are born and are foreshadowed in childhood pathways. Are the cultural careers of children in the less developed world significantly hindering economic market activity or new forms of civil society, and if so, should parenting and child life become a focus for change efforts intended to encourage economic progress?

My comments focus on sub-Saharan Africa—the "except-for" continent (Roe 1999)—that part of the world seemingly least economically favored and farthest from the ideal of a pluralist polity. In my view, there is nothing fundamental in the parenting and child care practices in Africa today that would prevent economic development under some version of a market model or a local version of a more pluralist society. Many values and practices in African family life and child care are at least compatible with economic de-

velopment and political pluralism. These include the shared, socially distributed caretaking of children; the high value placed on combining schooling
and shared family work for children; the evidence that parents want their
children to show a *mix* of individual cleverness and compliance to elders;
and the advantages of social networks that can mediate between rural and
urban settings.

Furthermore, parents actively debate how to raise children and try out new
practices and family arrangements. Hence, there are children and families
potentially ready for a variety of economic and political activities. The task is
to put such activities and institutions in place rather than fundamentally
change the values and practices of African parents and families. There will be
children and young adults there to engage in those activities once they are in
place.

Finally, the conception of culture and values as rather inflexible traits that
are inculcated early and become part of a national cultural "character" is
mostly wrong. Cultural beliefs and practices are tools for adaptation, not
simply fixed patterns that determine institutions. Culture is a mix of shared
values and beliefs, activities organized in daily routines of life, and interactional experiences that have emotional meaning. Cultures often raise children
in ways that cause them problems when they become adults that then have to
be solved anew. Western children are taught to be all they can be and to expect reasons for everything. They are offered choices and are expected to negotiate rules. As adults, they may struggle to compromise and work well in
social groups at work, and to realize that no one can perfectly realize every
childhood dream.

African children learn to be interdependent, to share resources, and to live
within family and community authority systems with at best covert questioning of them. As adults, they may struggle to break away from those very beliefs to be autonomous, curious, searching for new alliances. Beliefs, values,
activities, and experience are never perfectly integrated during childhood and
across developmental stages.

Children acquire cultural knowledge through mostly nonverbal channels
of participation and modeling—verbal tuition and language are important
but are not the dominant mode by any means. These channels for acquiring
culture do not necessarily give consistent information, and in times of
change, these levels of cultural experience and modes of acquisition can be
quite inconsistent. What all children learn about their culture and what
parents try to inculcate is always experienced ambivalently, is filled with
mixed messages, and is often resisted. Cultures may have a clear central
tendency and normative pattern, but they are hardly monolithic and uniform.

PARENTS, CHILDREN,
AND CHANGE IN EAST AFRICA

There certainly are conditions in the political economy of nation-states and the international economy that inhibit economic growth in Africa. Africa is the place where all the plagues of the economically poor nations are exponentially compounded (Landes 1998, 499; UNICEF 1992; Weisner 1994). Development and change are presumably occurring in much of the world, "except-Africa" (Roe 1999). Fertility rates have declined and development proceeds at least somewhat in most places, presumably except for Africa (although the fertility transition is actually under way in many places [Bradley 1997; Robinson 1992]). Economic growth exemplars can be found in most every continent, except for Africa (but some exist). Roe characterizes the "except-Africa" trope as part of a "narrative" that itself leads to negativity about development. He suggests a variety of positive "counternarratives" of development that focus on variety, surprise, unpredictability, and the complexity of circumstances on the ground.

But concerns over "narrativity" hardly capture the deeply felt and serious economic and social problems Africans face. Daniel Etounga-Manguelle outlines the problems facing African communities in this volume, and I share many of his concerns. He personally experiences the conditions that inhibit the desires for change and progress for millions in Africa. Etounga-Manguelle sees cultural features as the cause of these negative African institutions: "Culture is the mother and . . . institutions are the children. More efficient and just African institutions depend on modifications to our culture."

In Africa, as anywhere, culture can be oppressive and destructive. Although I agree that many experience the cultural patterns Etounga-Manguelle describes as harmful, and tens of millions of Africans hope they will change, I think that he is wrong to argue that culture *precedes* resource-based, institutional, and politico-economic factors. Rather, these factors are loosely coupled within a complex.

Africa is *not* the except-for case as far as parenting and child development beliefs and practices are concerned, and child care practices can hardly be blamed as among the *primary* conditions blocking economic and social progress. We should begin instead with the region's ecological constraints, and with the regional, national, and international institutions restricting and channeling the potential capacities of African children and youth, instead of proposing to change ways children are being raised and the values and goals parents have for their children.

My argument is not blindly optimistic in the face of the obvious poverty and problems plaguing so much of sub-Saharan Africa, nor does it absolve culture from a role in understanding the past and shaping the future progress of African communities. The absence of conditions in which families and communities can organize a sustainable daily life for themselves is the single most important factor inhibiting children and families from raising their economic level and is a fundamental concern of anthropological studies (Weisner 1997a). Tens of millions of children and parents in Africa and elsewhere around the world do not have the most basic conditions of health, security, and stability; nor do they have opportunities for acquiring literacy and other skills that would put them in a *position* to engage in a wider civic polity or make much economic progress. With Etounga-Manguelle, I deeply believe that African children deserve these basic material and social goods and the opportunity to find activities and institutions in their societies they can engage in to promote those goals.

Those who argue that African cultural values and practices are the reasons why these basic material and social goods are not available propose changing African cultural values. But the evidence from studies of families and children suggest that such change has been under way for at least two generations and that there is ample variety and heterogeneity within African communities to provide individuals who are ready for change. Provide *basic* support for children and then let them and their parents adapt to change, including turning to new child rearing values and practices.

Some would argue, however, that the evident variations in values and practices within cultures, although interesting, are irrelevant to the larger argument about relationships between culture and economic progress because so many sub-Saharan African states show slow or declining economic development and slow or no evidence of the emergence of democratic society. Ecological, cultural, and historical circumstances certainly play some role in these comparative differences, but the connections are at best only loosely coupled. Understanding local cultural change and variability is essential for understanding what is really going on among families and children within African societies. How else can we know what to do—how and whether and at what level and in which community to intervene? Only studies of real contemporary cultural circumstances can address that issue. This is a research program that, it seems to me, should be given the highest priority.

CHILD REARING, PARENTAL GOALS, AND ECONOMIC PROGRESS IN THE DEVELOPED WORLD

There is an association between certain core parental beliefs and child care practices, and economic progress in the developed world. Those beliefs and practices have not necessarily caused economic progress but are often associated with them in the West. A "pedagogical" developmental model (LeVine et al. 1994) emphasizes stimulation and responsiveness in the service of boldness, exploration, verbal skills, and literacy. It is characterized by a concern with individual child stimulation and active engagement of the child with others, exploratory behavior, active recognition of cognitive and verbal signs of intelligence, verbal communication, and question-response exchanges.

Individualism, autonomy, self-reliance, and self-expression are also encouraged in children. Parents look for signs of precocity in children and openly boast or glow in the admiration of others who remark on such precocity. There might be a steady drumbeat of praise and encouragement: "Good job!" "Way to go!" "Nice try!" "Be all you can be!" "You're so smart/athletic/beautiful." Parents interpret typical developmental milestones as signs of intelligence or unusual abilities. For instance, babies everywhere in the world begin to display a social smile at around three months of age. Many African parents interpret it as a sign of physical health. Western parents interpret this as an early sign of intellectual understanding and intelligence.

Along with these parental goals of energetic precocity, however, Western parents may worry over whether the child has sufficient and secure basic trust within a stable social network, attachment security, and enough "self-esteem." There is variation across North America and Europe in such beliefs, and commitment to this ideal-typical set of practices is not uniform (Harkness and Super 1996). However, this model is recognized as among the acceptable, desirable ways to raise children and is not questioned or challenged. There is quite high consensus about its desirability and normality.

African parents of course have equivalent hopes and goals for achievement and success for their children. But rather than individual verbal praise, parents are more likely to emphasize integration into a wider family group and show acceptance through providing opportunities for such integration, through giving food and other material possessions, and through physical affection and contact with their younger children. Parents encourage children to learn through observation and cooperation with others instead of providing active, adult-child verbal stimulation, and they encourage interdependence skills rather than individualistic autonomy. Robert Serpell (1993) has called this a socially distributed model for socialization of children.

Many African parents and children today actually have a much more mixed model of parenting, incorporating pedagogical, autonomy-centered, and sociocentric developmental goals. In addition, individual variation in children (in temperament and other constitutional capacities) and in families inevitably leads to heterogeneity in these patterns, ensuring that there are children growing up all the time who are in concord as well as in conflict with traits similar to those of the pedagogical/autonomy models.

I do not mean to gloss the obviously wide diversity of cultures and families across the African continent, but these are useful summary patterns for illustrative purposes. These patterns certainly fit, at least in part, child life in many regions of Africa as a central tendency with substantial variations and local differences around those tendencies. I share Etounga-Manguelle's view that there is of course very significant diversity across Africa, but also "a foundation of shared values, attitudes, and institutions that bind the nations south of the Sahara together, and in many respects those to the north as well."[1] Diversity across Africa around this central cultural pattern strengthens my argument that there are children and families throughout Africa ready to engage in new forms of market activity and civic life.

THERE IS SOME CONTINUITY IN ECONOMIC PROBLEMS

Africa in the nineteenth and early twentieth centuries consisted of dynamic and expansionist political economies. Eastern African cultures steadily expanded into new territories, had active trading networks into Arabia and the Middle East (as well as regionally within Africa), and intermarried with neighboring groups. It took savvy and ambition to be socially and economically successful under the very difficult circumstances of that era, just as it still does in the contemporary era.

The economic problems that faced parents and children in African communities then are still present now. Allen Johnson and Timothy Earle summarize these as the four universal politico-economic problems of production risks, warfare and raiding (security), inefficient resource use, and resource deficiencies (1987). Such problems remain omnipresent. Communities face the task of finding other solutions in a world of global markets, regionalization, dramatically increased access to information, and increasing inequality. The task is how to find a better fit between solutions useful in the past that still characterize parenting and child care and new solutions requiring new child care practices and parental goals, rather than the de novo creation of awareness of such problems. This search for new solutions seems to be happening in parenting and family life today.

Furthermore, communities need a variety of talents in children, not just narrow economic skills as contemporary Western market economies may define them. When we think about the fit between the need for economic progress, parental goals for children, and child socialization, it is not only entrepreneurial talent, competence in literacy and numeracy, or basic health that matter. Dealing with security, risk, and inefficiency problems requires individuals with varying talents and socialization experiences in a community, not only those with a single-minded preparation for economic innovation or wide social networks with an exclusively cosmopolitan outlook.

MARKET PRICING IS A UNIVERSAL PRINCIPLE OF SOCIAL RELATIONS AND MENTAL LIFE

A market economic calculus may well be among a small number of universal principles available in all societies and learned and used by all children to some degree (Fiske 1991, 1992). Alan Fiske sets out four such universal principles of social relations: communal sharing (solidarity, unity in a group), authority ranking (status, inequality, hierarchy in social relations), equality matching (egalitarian, peer relations among separate coequals), and market pricing (exchange relationships determined by pricing or utility). These elementary relational structures are likely universal properties of the mind as well as of social organization.

If the four forms are universal properties of both mind and society, all humans from childhood are prepared to appraise and relate to others using one or combinations of these four. Market calculus may not be as salient in mind and society as those interested in economic progress might want, but it seems that social beings everywhere learn how to balance among these four kinds of social relationships. Here again, the problem for those interested in economic development is not to create a sense of market thinking and social relations de novo in children and their parents but rather to develop and extend what is already available.

CULTURAL VALUES DO NOT DEFINE CULTURES OR THE POTENTIALS FOR CHANGE

Cultural values do not define or constitute a culture, although they are often thought to be the key cultural barrier to economic progress. Clyde Kluckhohn, a founder of the anthropological study of values, described values in abstract terms as "conceptions of the desirable"—shared ideas about what is good (D'Andrade 1995, 3). Kluckhohn actually opposed culture to "life" and to adaptation, and he did not consider values systems as determinative (Edmonson 1973; see also Kluckhohn and Strodtbeck 1961, 21).

Life [Kluckhohn] regarded as essentially disorderly and chaotic. Culture involved order imposed on life, and for the human species, was necessary for life to continue. . . . It was clear enough to him that not all individuals are made healthy and happy by their cultures, that in the long run not all societies are insured growth or survival by their cultures, and that successful societies do not indefinitely preserve their cultures intact but must change them. (Fischer and Vogt 1973, 8)

Barth (1993) argues that we should not reify values by concentrating on their institutional expression but should focus on their uses in socialization. However, values *do* affect behavior when they inhere in institutions; cultural values are therefore powerful and should be taken seriously at institutional and social action levels. But they are adaptive tools, subject to negotiation and change; they do not determine or constitute culture.

Values matter in how they guide social action. They do so by accounting for the world as it is constructed—making *sense* of it and why we should even act in it at all in a meaningful way; by providing a guide to *attentional* appraisal processes (e.g., what should we be attending to?); by providing socially sanctioned rationales for actions that are *justified* to oneself and others by invoking shared values; and by providing a form of *social identification* and labeling—the belief that I am a person with spiritual values, for instance, as compared to others who do not share those values (D'Andrade 1991).

Values serve different functions for different people. Respect for authority and one's elders might help children know who to attend to but would not help explain the nature of the contemporary changing world or serve as a primary social identification. Women may use values concerning respect for authority to know what they have to attend to, but they may not share with male authority the justifications and social identifications that such values imply.

A UNIVERSAL STANDARD FOR ASSESSING CULTURES WITH REGARD TO CHILDHOOD: WELL-BEING AND BASIC SUPPORT LEAD TO THE POTENTIAL FOR SUSTAINABLE CULTURAL LIFE

Cultures should be judged on their ability to provide well-being, basic support, and sustainable daily lives for children and families. I do not have a relativist stance with regard to these features of child life. We can certainly give our advice and ally ourselves with those in a society who share our visions of meaningful goals and cultural practices. But we should leave it to the internal mechanisms of change and debate within communities as to how, with what specific content, and toward what cultural goals these three conditions should be achieved.

Well-being for children is the ability to engage in the activities deemed desirable by their community, and the positive psychological experiences produced thereby. Resilience and the potential for change depend on such engagement by children and their families. Market economic activity or participation in shared civil society depends on such cultural well-being more than on the provision of particular values or beliefs (Weisner 1997b), although the content of beliefs of course matters as well.

Children and parents also require *basic support*. Support systems for children have certain features recognizable around the world. These include affection, physical comfort, shared solving of problems, provision of food and other resources, protection against harm and violence, and a coherent moral and cultural understanding of who can and should provide support, and the appropriate ways to do so (Weisner 1994).

Cultures provide basic support in different ways and mean different things by it. What is important to assess across cultures is whether children have culturally coherent, reasonably predictable support. Tens of millions of children and parents in Africa and elsewhere do not have this basic level of support.

Well-being and basic support combine to provide a sustainable daily routine of life for children. Sustainable routines of family life have some stability and predictability, have meaning and value with respect to parents' and children's goals, can minimize or balance inevitable conflicts and disagreements within a family and community, and have an adequate fit to the available resources of the family. If parents and children can create sustainable routines, the cultural basis for change, new competencies, and innovation is present. Without this, no intervention is likely to succeed (Weisner 1997a).

CHANGING PARENTING AND
CHILDHOOD SOCIALIZATION IN EAST AFRICA

African family and child care practices differ in emphasis from Western, middle-class parental goals and child care, yet they are not incompatible with versions of market economic activity and change in political life. More importantly, they can promote well-being and sustainable family life through socially distributed parenting and child care, flexible and changing moral debates about family resources and authority, an emphasis on childhood traits combining independence with respect, and expanding family social networks associated with increased modernity and less stress.

Socially Distributed Parenting and Care of Children

Socially distributed support in shared management family systems can be found in many places around the world (Weisner 1997a). Some of the characteristics of this culture complex include the following:

- Child caretaking often occurs as a part of indirect chains of support in which one child assists another, who assists a third. Support is often indirect and delayed, not necessarily organized around exclusive relationships between child and parent.
- Children look to other children for assistance and support as much or more than to adults.
- Girls are much more likely to do caretaking and domestic tasks than boys. Boys clearly provide support, caretaking, and nurturance to other children as well, although more infrequently as they reach late middle childhood.
- Mothers provide support and nurturance for children as much by ensuring that *others* will consistently participate in doing so as by doing so directly themselves; fostering and other forms of sharing children are common.
- Care often occurs in the context of other domestic work done by children.
- Aggression, teasing, and dominance accompany nurturance and support and come from the same people; dominance of these kinds increases with age.
- Food and material goods are a powerful cultural concern and are used to threaten, control, soothe, and nurture.
- Verbal exchange and elaborated question-framed discourse rarely accompany support and nurturance for children; verbal negotiations regarding rights and privileges between children and dominant caretakers are infrequent.
- Social and intellectual competence in children is judged in part by a child's competence in managing domestic tasks, demonstrating appropriate social behavior, doing child care, and nurturing and supporting others—as well as through signs of school achievement.
- Children are socialized within this system through apprenticeship learning of their family roles and responsibilities.

This pattern of African life promotes deference to older siblings and adults, training in sociability and nurturance toward others, jealousy and anger toward these same community members, competitive striving, and some distrust of those outside of one's home community.

Socially distributed support is part of a culture complex—a set of loosely coupled ecological circumstances, beliefs, and practices that interrelate and contribute to each other. It is almost always the case that persistent, stubborn, and hard-to-change features of a culture are that way in part because they are embedded in a culture complex that is an emotionally learned, high-consensus, tacit, cultural model of the world. The shared support culture is loosely coupled with features like high fertility; concerns over child health and mortality; expanded, extended, or joint household family patterns; a high maternal workload; and multiple affect and attachment patterns of diffused emotional and social behavior. Analyzing the entire, contextualized culture complex is essential. Change is unlikely to occur by simply pointing to one or another part of a culture complex and expecting it to take place in that particular feature.

Socially distributed caretaking certainly might inhibit individualism and autonomy in children, through diffusing affective ties and contributing to a more "sociocentric" sense of personhood and self that might limit autonomy. Early child labor contributions to the family estate can conflict with schooling, time for play, and social development. Control of children's work effort might conflict with their autonomy and explorations of new kinds of work and learning.

Although these characteristics are related, the connections are loose and situational, and they vary across families and individual children. For example, children participating in shared caretaking do a bit better in school. Competence in school abilities does not decline due to either boys' or girls' participation in socially distributed caretaking. Child fostering is another practice in which effects are positive or mixed. Fostering reinforces the female social hierarchy as children move from lower- to higher-status households. Effects on the child depend in part on whether the foster mother requested the child (such children seem to do well) or whether a child was forced by circumstances into a move (Castle 1995).

There Is a Varied and Complex Moral Discourse About Parenting and Children

Cultural change is far more difficult when cultural values and practices are so deeply held and tacitly accepted that minds and discourses are closed. But African debate seems quite open. Carolyn Edwards has presented an interesting version of open debate over the value of shared support in her story of "Daniel and the School Fees" (Edwards 1997, 50–51). Her informants mix notions of basic "reasonableness" and flexibility in family decisions with values of "respect."

In this moral dilemma, Daniel completes his secondary school education because his brother helps pay his school fees. Daniel then gets a wage job in Nairobi while his wife and children live in the rural community. Eight years later, Daniel's son is ready to start school and needs fees. Daniel's parents come to him and say that the brother who paid for Daniel's school has had an accident and the brother's child (who is the same age as Daniel's child) now needs school fees, and Daniel should pay them. But Daniel has only enough money to pay for one child. His wife says that he should pay for their own son first. What do you think Daniel and others should do? Why?

Edwards presented this dilemma to "moral leaders" in two Kenya rural communities—individuals recognized as responsible, honest, and available for wise advice. About half were non-schooled and half had some secondary school. She also interviewed secondary school students. Her sample comes from two communities in Kenya: Abaluyia and Kipsigis. She found that

> all the men—young and old, married and unmarried—shared a common vocabulary for talking about the underlying issues and moral conflicts raised by the dilemmas. The core values of respect, harmony, interdependence, and unity were not only alive and well, they were stressed over and over as the central virtues of family living. . . . The ideal of seeking "reasonableness" in one's thinking and behavior seemed more prominent among the [Abaluyia] men, whereas maintaining "respectful" relations . . . seemed to preoccupy the Kipsigis elders and students. (Edwards 1997, 82)

There were clear differences in moral reasoning due to generation, cultural community, and religious and cultural background. For example, the better-educated secondary school students were less likely to use authority criteria in evaluating the moral stories. Those from the Abaluyia, a community that had more education and was influenced by Quaker/Protestant missions, more often mentioned reasonableness.

Although arguments regarding what to do about the school fees differed, there was a shared basic moral and values vocabulary sufficient to have a meaningful debate. This common framework meant that arguments pro and con were grasped by everyone. There was flexibility in debates, multiple available scripts for understanding, and an openness to change in people's use of values justifications to account for different decisions by Daniel or others. Similar kinds of debates occur about economic strategies or the distribution of family resources to children (Super and Harkness 1997).

Such moral debates regarding child rearing are going on in Kenyan communities every day. The ambiguities and ambivalence in choosing the "best" strategies about what is "right" can be heard in the moral debates about such matters. Cultural beliefs and moral ideals regarding how to organize family life and child rearing are not based on rigid values.

Parental Goals for Children's Behavior

Traits parents desire for their children are also changing. Beatrice Whiting identified eight character traits that mothers prefer their children to have based on community interviews with Kikuyu mothers in Central Kenya. Four—confidence, inquisitiveness, cleverness, and bravery—were selected as character traits that were considered good for success in school by Kikuyu mothers and by students (and perhaps in market economic life and political participation as well). Four others—good-heartedness, respectfulness, obedience, and generosity—were chosen as examples of characteristics that stressed harmonious interaction in a hierarchical, patrilineal, mixed rural and peri-urban community.

Both clusters of traits are considered at least somewhat desirable. The dimension contrasts the relative advantages for schooling only, not their overall cultural desirability. Furthermore, these traits are desired for both boys and girls. These parents try to train children for a mix of traits. Since there is already expectable temperamental and other variation within sibling groups, and since there is variation in modernity across households, there are many children relatively more likely to display one or the other cluster of attributes, as well as many who are quite balanced in both.

Parents were asked which of these traits they could actually train in their children and which were more likely to be innate and inborn. Parents understood that both nature and nurture matter in development, as do parents around the world. Generally, children's traits that are visible in everyday cultural practices—those that are learned through "guided participation" or various forms of apprenticeship and informal learning—are more likely to be thought amenable to direct parental influence.

Most parents thought that curiosity, good work habits, industriousness, obedience, and respect for adults could all be trained. The reason? Children could learn these traits by being put to work in the household or sent to others for work. Kikuyu parents said that they definitely could allow children to ask questions and learn the answers through tuition at home or in schools. They could encourage curiosity through practices they could establish in their own daily routines. But being clever or brave, generous or good-hearted—these traits are inborn, a part of core personality (Whiting 1996, 22–25).

Whiting also developed a composite index of modernity, which included parents' education, mother's knowledge of Kiswahili and/or English, radio ownership, Christian church membership, and other items. Parents with these characteristics were more likely to value traits in their children such as confidence, inquisitiveness, cleverness, and bravery; they were relatively less likely to value being generous, obedient, and respectful. But again, most parents want both clusters of traits in their children.

Modernity Is Associated with Increased Social Connectedness and Affiliation with New Groups

Finally, more modern attitudes are found among families with ties to both rural and urban communities, rather than to only one or the other. Since 1970, I have followed families from western Kenya who tried to colonize both the cities and other rural areas to achieve economic and social gain (Weisner 1997a). Compared to families living mostly in Nairobi, families that had relatives in multiple locations and moved back and forth between those settings along with their children had lower levels of reported psycho-physiological stress and similar levels of overall modernity in their attitudes. The children in cities had higher levels of child-child and parent-child conflict and aggression, and lower levels of sociability and nurturance compared to rural-resident children or rural-urban commuting children. Parental strategies for deploying their children and other kin for survival and security varied. Families and children with socially distributed networks across generations and places were doing as well or better than their counterparts trying to make it in only one location.

CONCLUSION

Let parents and children around the world decide how to innovate and experiment with their cultural practices. If those with the means to do so can provide activities and new institutional contexts encouraging market accumulation or pluralism in political life, the evidence suggests that we will find many families and children there to engage in those activities. If such new institutions and community activities are planned and prepared with local cultural understanding in mind (Klitgaard 1994), they can and will find their place. If market economic activities and new and more positive forms of civic political life become available, there will be children and parents in contemporary African communities sufficiently well fitted to engage in those new activities.

Of course, like all cultural ways of life, socially distributed socialization has costs as well as benefits for individuals and for economic development. This is the case, for example, for the continuing gender segregation that restricts the cultural careers of boys and girls and the institutionalized jealousy and fears of neighbors and other cultural groups outside one's own. Although parents often say that boys and girls are equally likely to have this mix of traits (and greater formal education and economic success increases the likelihood that parents say this), the cultural careers of boys and girls keeps gender segregation highly salient, although increasingly fragmented and changing in the direction of increased equality. Local beliefs certainly can make equitable distribution of wealth and interventions on behalf of children and families difficult and complex (Howard and Millard 1997).

Millions of African parents and children are prepared for change, are increasingly cosmopolitan or at least aware of alternatives, and creatively do change their family life and child care practices. Yet many resist change at the same time. Parents and communities are, of course, ambivalent. They have "the impulse to defend the predictability of life . . . a fundamental and universal principle of human psychology" (Marris 1975, 3). Parenting and child care are changing and adapting, but there clearly are powerful, emotionally felt cultural models that make such change both possible yet difficult.

Given the cultural importance, personal intimacy, and ambivalence that attach to parenting and child rearing, why focus on changing the values and practices of children's cultural careers that families both defend and are struggling to change? Indeed, I have to wonder why those interested in achieving economic development and new forms of civic life displace our attention by focusing on the details of how parents should raise their children.

Families could be helped so much more easily through the provision of the means to establish basic and universally desired social supports and thereby the wherewithal to achieve meaningful daily routines of family life. There is little basis for prescribing interventions and new-values orientations that require specific changes in parental goals or child care practices within the family system, given the evidence that change is already widely occurring and that there is inherent individual variability built in to the child development process. But there certainly is reason to provide a foundation that establishes *any* culture's ability to provide well-being for children: the basic social supports of security, stability, health, and resources that permit families to achieve for their children a sustainable daily routine in their community that meets their goals. That is progress.

REFERENCES

Barth, F. 1993. "Are Values Real? The Enigma of Naturalism in the Anthropological Imputation of Values." In *The Origin of Values,* edited by Michael Hechter, Lynn Nadel, and Richard E. Michod, pp. 31–46. New York: Aldine de Gruyter

Bradley, C., and T. S. Weisner. 1997. "Introduction: Crisis in the African Family." In *African Families and the Crisis of Social Change,* edited by T. S. Weisner, C.

Bradley, and P. Kilbride, pp. xix-xxxii. Westport, Conn.: Greenwood Press/Bergin & Garvey.

Bradley, C. 1997. "Why Fertility Is Going Down in Maragoli." In *African Families and the Crisis of Social Change,* edited by T. S. Weisner, C. Bradley, and P. Kilbride, pp. 227–252. Westport, Conn.: Greenwood Press/Bergin & Garvey.

Castle, S. E. 1995. "Child Fostering and Children's Nutritional Outcomes in Rural Mali: The Role of Female Status in Directing Child Transfers." *Social Science and Medicine* 40, no. 5: 679–693.

D'Andrade, R. 1991. Afterword to *Human Motives and Cultural Models,* edited by R. D'Andrade and C. Strauss, pp. 225–232. Cambridge: Cambridge University Press.

_____. 1995. *The Development of Cognitive Anthropology.* New York: Cambridge University Press.

Edmonson, M. S. 1973. "The Anthropology of Values." In *Culture and Life: Essays in Memory of Clyde Kluckhohn,* edited by W. Taylor, J. L. Fischer, and E. Z. Vogt eds., pp. 157–197. Carbondale: Southern Illinois University Press.

Edwards, C. C. 1997. "Morality and Change: Family Unity and Paternal Authority Among Kipsigis and Abaluyia Elders and Students." In *African Families and the Crisis of Social Change,* edited by T. S. Weisner, C. Bradley, and P. Kilbride, pp. 45–85. Westport, Conn.: Greenwood Press/Bergin & Garvey.

Fischer, J. L., and E. Z. Vogt. 1973. Introduction to *Culture and Life: Essays in Memory of Clyde Kluckhohn,* edited by W. Taylor, J. L. Fischer, and E. Z. Vogt, pp. 1–13. Carbondale: Southern Illinois University Press

Fiske, A. P. 1991. *Structures of Social Life: The Four Elementary Forms of Human Relations.* New York: Free Press.

_____. 1992. "The Four Elementary Forms of Sociality: Framework for a Unified Theory of Social Relations." *Psychological Review* 99: 689–723.

Goldschmidt, W. 1990. *The Human Career.* London: Routledge & Kegan Paul.

Harkness, S., C. M. Super, and R. New, eds. 1996. *Parents' Cultural Belief Systems.* New York: Guilford.

Howard, M., and A. V. Millard. 1997. *Hunger and Shame: Poverty and Child Malnutrition on Mount Kilimanjaro.* New York: Routledge.

Johnson, A. W., and T. Earle. 1987. *The Evolution of Human Societies: From Foraging Group to Agrarian State.* Stanford: Stanford University Press.

Klitgaard, R. 1994. "Taking Culture into Account: From 'Let's' to 'How.'" In *Culture and Development in Africa,* edited by I. Serageldin and J. Taboroff, pp. 75–120. Washington, D.C.: World Bank. Proceedings of an international conference held at the World Bank, Washington, D.C.

Kluckhohn, F. R., and F. L. Strodtbeck. 1961. *Variations in Value Orientations.* Evanston, Ill.: Row, Peterson.

Lancy, D. 1996. *Playing on the Mother-Ground: Cultural Routines for Children's Development.* New York: Guilford.

Landes, D. 1998. *The Wealth and Poverty of Nations: Why Some Are So Rich and Some So Poor.* New York: Norton.

LeVine, R. 1973. "Patterns of Personality in Africa." *Ethos* 1, no. 2: 123–152.

LeVine, R., S. Dixon, S. LeVine, A. Richman, P. H. Leiderman, C. H. Keefer, and T. B. Brazelton. 1994. *Child Care and Culture: Lessons from Africa.* Cambridge: Cambridge University Press.

Marris, P. 1975. *Loss and Change.* New York: Doubleday Anchor.

Robinson, W. C. 1992. "Kenya Enters the Fertility Transition." *Population Studies* 46: 445–457.

Roe, E. 1999. *Except-Africa: Remaking Development, Rethinking Power.* New Brunswick, N.J.: Transaction.

Serpell, R. 1993. *The Significance of Schooling: Life-Journeys in an African Society.* New York: Cambridge University Press.

Super, C. M., and S. Harkness. 1997. "Modernization, Family Life, and Child Development in Kokwet." In *African Families and the Crisis of Social Change*, edited by T. S. Weisner, C. Bradley, and P. Kilbride, pp. 341–353. Westport, Conn.: Greenwood Press/Bergin & Garvey.

UNICEF. *The State of the World's Children, 1992.* New York: UNICEF.

Weisner, T. S. 1984. "A Cross-Cultural Perspective: Ecocultural Niches of Middle Childhood." In *The Elementary School Years: Understanding Development During Middle Childhood*, edited by Andrew Collins, pp. 335–369. Washington, D.C.: National Academy Press.

_____. 1994. "The Crisis for Families and Children in Africa: Change and Shared Social Support for Children." *Health Matrix: Journal of Law-Medicine* 4, no. 1: 1–29.

_____. 1997a. "Support for Children and the African Family Crisis." In *African Families and the Crisis of Social Change,* edited by T. S. Weisner, C. Bradley, and P. Kilbride, pp. 20–44. Westport, Conn.: Greenwood Press/Bergin & Garvey.

_____. 1997b. "The Ecocultural Project of Human Development: Why Ethnography and Its Findings Matter." *Ethos* 25, no. 2: 177–190.

Weiser, T. S., with C. Bradley and P. Kilbride, eds. 1997. *African Families and the Crisis of Social Change.* Westport, Conn.: Greenwood Press/Bergin & Garvey.

Whiting, B. B. 1996. "The Effect of Social Change on Concepts of the Good Child and Good Mothering: A Study of Families in Kenya." *Ethos* 24, no. 1: 3–35.

Wildavsky, A. 1994. "How Cultural Theory Can Contribute to Understanding and Promoting Democracy, Science, and Development." In *Culture and Development in Africa*, edited by I. Serageldin and J. Taboroff, pp. 137–164. Washington, D.C.: World Bank. Proceedings of an international conference held at the World Bank, Washington, D.C., 1994.

12

Moral Maps, "First World" Conceits, and the New Evangelists

RICHARD A. SHWEDER

ECONOMISTS' BRAINS: $2.39 A POUND!

Does cannibalism have nutritional value or is it just a form of high cuisine? Although this question is a topic of solemn debate in anthropology, at grand ceremonial occasions anthropologists are known to have a sense of humor. Being an anthropologist, I thought I would begin this chapter with an admittedly baroque variation on an old joke about the market for brains in Papua New Guinea.

This guy from the "First World" walks into a gourmet food store in Papua New Guinea. He goes to the meat section, where he sees a bill of fare designated "assorted westerners." It contains two general offerings: evangelical missionaries (religious and secular), who think it is their mission in life to make our world a better place by their moral lights, and romantic relativists, who think whatever is, is, is okay and actually seem to like it here. He notices many delicacies, all neatly arranged in bins.

The first bin has a sign that says "Economists' Brains from the World Bank: $2.39 a Pound!" The label on the bin reads, "These people want to loan us lots of money at very favorable rates (which of course we are never going to pay back), if only we will do things more like the way they do things in the West. They want us to formalize contracts, create an independent judiciary, and prohibit the preferential hiring of members of one's own ethnic group. And that's just for starters."

The sign on the second bin says "Protestant Ethicists' Brains: $2.42 a Pound." The label reads, "These people want us to change our work habits and our ideas about the good life. They want us to stop wasting our time on elaborate rituals for dead ancestors. They want to loan us lots of money at very favorable rates (which of course we are never going to pay back), if only we will start thinking about things the way they think about things in the West (or at least in the very northern sections of the West). Northern Western folk are convinced that everything is nefarious except the impersonal pursuit of work and that only the rich will be saved. They tell us that 'sustainable growth' is the contemporary code word for the adoption of Protestant values. They believe that God blesses men in the sign of their material prosperity, especially their purposefully amassed wealth. They want us to be saved. They want to save us."

The sign on the third bin says "Monocultural Feminists' Brains: $2.49 a Pound." The label reads, "These people want us to change our family life, gender relations, and reproductive practices. They want us to devalue the womb, which is associated in their minds with 'bad' things such as big families, domesticity, and a sexual division of labor. They want us to revalue the clitoris (which is associated in their minds with 'good' things such as independence, equality, and hedonic self-stimulation) as the biological essence of female identity, and as the symbol and means of female emancipation from men. And they want NATO to send in a 'humanitarian' invasion force unless we promise to join the National Organization of Women and the League of Women Voters."

The sign on the final bin says "Anthropologists' Brains: $15.00 a Pound." The label reads, "These people think we should just take the money and run!"

Dismayed, our visitor walks over to the guy behind the counter and he says, "What's this! Haven't you heard about the moral superiority of the West (or at least of the northernmost sections of the West)? Don't you know that the reason we [in the 'First World'] are better than you [in the 'Third World'] is that we are humanists who endorse the United Nations Declaration of the Rights of Man? Don't you know that when it comes to brains there is basic oneness to humankind? Don't you know that the major reason for differences in the world [variations in 'human capital'] is that people in the southern sections of the globe grow up in impoverished cultures ['cultures of poverty']? That is why they are badly equipped for life on the information highway and in the global fast lane. That is why they are untrustworthy, corrupt, undisciplined, unskilled, and poor. Okay, I can understand a slight difference in price for economists' brains, Protestant ethicists' brains, and monocultural feminists' brains ($2.39 a pound/$2.42 a pound/$2.49 a pound), but $15.00 a pound for anthropologist's brains? That's ridiculous! It's illogical! It's unfair! It defies 'transparency'!"

The guy behind the counter replies: "Do you know how many anthropologists we had to kill before we could find a pound of brains?"

So I admit to feeling a bit brainless writing for a volume whose contributors include so many distinguished scholars and evangelists from disciplines other than my own. Lawrence Harrison recruited me to this effort by stating, with characteristic candor, that he wanted me to write as a skeptic and critic because he thought I believed in "culture" but not in "progress." He said that he was planning to invite other types of skeptics and critics as well, such as those who believe in "progress" but not in "culture."

I do believe in progress, at least in a limited sense (more on that below). And I suspect that the precise sense in which I believe in culture (more on that too) may not seem very helpful (or even sensible) to those who have argued here that "culture matters."[1]

What does it mean to say that "culture matters?" It depends on who is speaking. The theme of this volume is expressive of an intellectual stance known as "cultural developmentalism." For a cultural developmentalist, the assertion that "culture matters" is a way of saying that some cultures are impoverished or backward, whereas others are enriched or advanced. It means there are good things in life (e.g., health, domestic tranquillity, justice, material prosperity, hedonic self-stimulation, and small families) that all human beings ought to want and have but that their culture keeps them from wanting and/or having.

Here is how you can tell if you are a cultural developmentalist. Do you like to inspect the globe with an ethical microscope and draw "moral maps" of the world? Or, doing what amounts to pretty much the same thing, do you like to construct "quality of life" indicators that can be used to rank cultures, civilizations, and religions from better to worse? If you are a cultural developmentalist, you probably feel deeply disturbed by the staying power and popularity of various ("archaic") ways of life and ("superstitious") systems of belief because you think they are relatively devoid of truth, goodness, beauty, or practical efficiency. You probably want to "enlighten" the residents of the "dark continents" of the world. You probably want to lift them up from error, ignorance, bad habits, immorality, and squalor, and refashion them to be more progressive, more democratic, more scientific, more civic-minded, more industrious, more entrepreneurial, more reliable, more rational, and more like (the ideal) us.

Culture matters for me too but in a rather different sort of way: If I were ever to refer to a "culture of poverty," I would probably reserve the expression for ascetic communities in which the renunciation of wealth and the repudiation of worldly goods had been positively valued as an objective good. Furthermore, given my conception of precisely how culture counts, I might even try to find some merit in that conception of the good.

Although the idea of an "impoverished culture" is not exactly an oxymoron, it has played almost no part in my own field research. To make matters worse, my commitment to the very idea of "culture" has its source in an interest in other cultures as sources of illumination (Shweder 1991, 1993, 1996a, 1996b, 1997; Shweder et al. 1998). I have never put much stock in the view that holds that a good reason for becoming interested in other cultures is that they are impediments to the realization of some imagined universal aspiration of all people to be more like northern Europeans. And while I certainly believe in the importance and moral decency of our way of life, I do not believe in our moral superiority over all the rest.[2]

Thus I do not think that northern Europeans have a corner on the market for human progress. I do not believe that cognitive, spiritual, ethical, social, political, and material progress go hand in hand. Societies in command of great wealth and power can be spiritually, ethically, socially, and politically flawed. Many vital, intellectually sophisticated, and admirable cultures, places where philosophers live in mud huts, have evolved in environments with rudimentary technology and relatively little material wealth. Hence, I do not believe that either "we" or "they" have implemented the only credible manifestation of the good life.

Obviously, I am one of the heretics at this revival meeting and it is not the greatest of feelings. So let me continue my presentation with a couple of confessions, which will perhaps reduce some of my anxiety over being drafted as a designated skeptic.

CONFESSION 1: I AM AN ANTHROPOLOGIST

My first confession, of course, is that I am an anthropologist. Unfortunately, given all the turmoil in the profession of anthropology these days, this confession is not very informative. It carries no implications (as it would have fifty years ago or even twenty years ago) for how I might feel about the concept of culture, whether I am for it or against it or whether it makes me laugh or cry.[3]

For the sake of accuracy in describing the current scene in anthropology, let me note that there was a time in anthropology when such words as "primitive," "barbarian," "savage," or even "underdeveloped" were put in quotation marks, if they were used at all. There was a time when the idea that there is only one way to lead a morally decent and rational life, and it's our way, would have been seen, quite frankly, as obscene.

But things have changed. Monocultural feminism has put an end to any facile relativism in anthropology and has given a new meaning to the idea of "political correctness." So, along with the international human rights movement and various agencies promoting Western-style globalization (UNICEF, WHO, perhaps even NATO), there are plenty of anthropologists these days who take an interest in other cultures mainly as objects of scorn. The slogan "It is not cultural, it's [fill in the blank: criminal, immoral, corrupt, ineffi-cient, barbaric]" (or alternatively, "It is cultural and it's [fill in the blank: criminal, immoral, corrupt, inefficient, barbaric]") has become the rallying cry for cultural developmentalists, Western interventionists of all kinds, and some schools of cultural anthropology as well.

I regret this ironic turn of events. Cultural anthropology was once a disci-pline that was proud of its opposition to ethnocentric misunderstanding and moral arrogance as well as its anti-colonial defense of other ways of life. That was yesteryear.

These days there are plenty of anthropologists (the post-culturalists) who want to disown the concept of culture. They think the word "culture" gets used in bad faith to defend authoritarian social arrangements and to allow despots to literally get away with murder. Indeed, as the world of theory in cultural anthropology turns, it seems to be "déjà vu all over again." Despite a century of objections by anthropological pluralists, relativists, and contex-tualists such as Franz Boas, Ruth Benedict, Melville Herskovits, Robert LeVine, Clifford Geertz, and others, an intellectual stance reminiscent of late nineteenth-century "white man's burden," cultural developmentalism is back. The self-congratulatory, up-from-barbarism theme of (certain versions of) Western liberalism (including the sensational accusation that African mothers are bad mothers, human rights violators, and mutilators of their daughters) has once again become fashionable on the anthropological scene, at least among those anthropologists who are the most politically correct.[4]

The current scene within anthropology is sufficiently complex (and per-verse) that there are even anthropologists who think they own the concept of "culture" but do not want anyone, including themselves, to do anything with it. I am not one of them. Regardless of whether the idea of culture makes me laugh or cry, I like it a lot. I can't get rid of it. I find we can't live by ecu-menism alone. Membership in some particular tradition of meanings is an essential condition for personal identity and individual happiness. In my view, "thick ethnicity" and cultural diversity both have their place and are part of the natural and moral order of things. I do not think Mother Nature wants everyone to be alike.

What do I mean by "culture"? I mean community-specific ideas about what is true, good, beautiful, and efficient. To be "cultural," those ideas about truth, goodness, beauty, and efficiency must be socially inherited and customary; and they must actually be constitutive of different ways of life.

Alternatively stated, culture refers to what Isaiah Berlin called "goals, values and pictures of the world" that are made manifest in the speech, laws, and routine practices of some self-monitoring group.

There is a lot more packed into that definition than I can unpack in a single chapter. There is the notion that actions speak louder than words and that "practices" are a central unit for cultural analysis. That is one reason I don't much like value questionnaires and find it hard to feel enthusiastic about research based on the analysis of official creeds or on endorsement patterns for abstract stand-alone propositions.[5]

Furthermore, one of the things "culture" is certainly not about is "national character." I am not going to have much to say about "national character" studies here, but they went out of fashion about forty years ago, and for good reason. They went out of fashion because it is far better to think about human behavior and motivation the way rational choice theorists or sensible economists do, rather than the way personality theorists do. Rational choice theorists think about action as something emanating from "agency." That is to say, action is analyzed as the joint product of "preferences" (including goals, values, and "ends" of various sorts) and "constraints" (including "means" of various sorts, such as causal beliefs, information, skills, and material and non-material resources), all mediated by the will of rational beings. This stands in contrast to the way in which personality theorists think about behavior. Personality theorists think about action as "forced." They try to explain action as the joint product of two types of vectors, one pushing from "inside," called "person" (described in terms of generalized motives and "sticky" global traits), and the other pushing from "outside," called "situation."

Looking for types of persons as a way of explaining cultural practices has not proved very useful. If one tries to characterize individuals in terms of personality traits or generalized motives, one usually discovers that "individuals within cultures vary much more among themselves than they do from individuals in other cultures" (Kaplan 1954). One also discovers that if there is any modal type at all (e.g., an "authoritarian personality type" or a personality type with a "need for achievement"), it is typically characteristic of no more than about one-third of the population. It has long been recognized among psychological anthropologists and cultural psychologists that (quoting Melford Spiro 1961) "it is possible for different modal personality systems to be associated with similar social systems, and for similar modal personality systems to be associated with different social systems." Looking for types of personalities to explain differences in cultural practices is a dead end (see Shweder 1991).

CONFESSION 2: I AM A PLURALIST

My second confession is that I am a cultural pluralist. My version of cultural pluralism begins with a universal truth, which I refer to as the principle of "confusionism." A "confusionist" believes that the knowable world is incomplete if seen from any one point of view, incoherent if seen from all points of view at once, and empty if seen from "nowhere in particular." Given the choice between incompleteness, incoherence, and emptiness, I opt for incompleteness while staying on the move between different ways of seeing and valuing the world.

This version of cultural pluralism is not opposed to universalism. Culture theorists do not divide into only two types, those who believe that anything goes (the "radical relativists") and those who believe that only one thing goes (the "uniformitarian universalists"). I strongly believe in "universalism," but the type of universalism I believe in is "universalism without the uniformity," which is what makes me a pluralist. In other words, I believe there are universally binding values but that there are just too many of them (e.g., justice, beneficence, autonomy, sacrifice, liberty, loyalty, sanctity, duty). I believe that those objectively valuable ends of life are diverse, heterogeneous, irreducible to some common denominator such as "utility" or "pleasure," and that they are inherently in conflict with each other. I believe that all the good things in life can't be simultaneously maximized. I believe that when it comes to implementing true values there are always trade-offs, which is why there are different traditions of values (i.e., cultures) and why no one cultural tradition has ever been able to honor everything that is good.[6]

Cultural pluralism has other implications, some of which are highly provocative. For example, there is the claim that the members of the executive board of the American Anthropological Association did the right and courageous thing in 1947 when they decided not to endorse the U.N. Declaration of the Rights of Man on the grounds that it was an ethnocentric document. In 1947, anthropologists were still proud of their anti-colonial defense of alternative ways of life (see Shweder 1996b).

PROGRESS AND PLURALISM: CAN THEY COEXIST?

Pluralism does not imply the rejection of the ideas of progress and decline. Progress means having more and more of something that is "desirable" (i.e., something that should be desired because it is "good"). Decline means having less and less of it. Name a specific "good" (e.g., taking care of parents in old age, eliminating contagious disease), and we can make objective judgments about progress with respect to that "good." If maximizing the likelihood of child survival during the first nine months after birth is the measure of success, then the United States is objectively more advanced than Africa and India. If maximizing the likelihood of child survival during the first nine months after conception (in the womb) is the measure of success, then Africa and India (where abortion rates are relatively low) are objectively more advanced the United States (where abortion rates are relatively high).

Of course there is much that is discretionary (i.e., not dictated by either logic or evidence) in any decision about how to name and identify specific "goods" and thus morally map the world. For example, the sheer quantity of life, or "reproductive fitness," is the measure used by evolutionary biologists for estimating the success of a population. By that measure of success—the genetic reproduction of one's tribe or ancestral line—how are we to evaluate the birth control pill, the legalization of abortion, and the reduction of family size in the high-tech societies of the First World? Do we narrate a story of decline?

Or, to select a second example, what type of story should we tell about "quality of life" measures such as life expectancy at birth? The longer lived a population, the greater the frequency of chronic illness, the greater the likelihood of functional impairment, and hence the higher the aggregate amount of pain (a true qualitative measure) experienced by that population. Good things (e.g., more years of life, no physical pain) do not always correlate. A longer life is not unambiguously a better life, or is it? Or, if longevity is a measure of success, then why not also numerousness or sheer population size, with China and India at the top of the list?

And why life expectancy at birth? What principle of logic or canon of inductive science dictates that standard for drawing moral maps and for assessing cultural progress? Why not life expectancy at age forty or, for that matter, at conception? Why not take the more comprehensive life-course perspective of the fetus and not just its later viewpoint as a newly born infant? As noted, if one considers the hazards of the womb the First World and former Second World look worse off than many societies in Africa and Asia. Consider how different our life expectancy tables would be if we factored in the 20 to 25 percent abortion rates in the United States and Canada or the 50-plus percent abortion rates in Russia, as compared to rates as low as 2 to 10 percent in India, Tunisia, and some other parts of the "underdeveloped" world.

The pro-life/pro-choice debate (I am pro-choice) is not the issue here. The issue is the discretionary aspect of moral mapping and the degrees of freedom one has in deciding whose ideals are going to be selected as the gold standard of the good life. As societies become technologically sophisticated, rates of abortion often rise, thereby lowering the life expectancy rate of the population (assuming that life expectancy is calculated from the point of conception rather than at birth). In some parts of the world, often in those parts of the world where reproductive success and large families are valued, early childhood is a relatively dangerous time of life. In other places, often in high-tech places where small families are valued and the womb is no longer thought of as a sanctified ground, the real dangers come earlier in life, and if you are an unwanted child, the womb can be hazardous to your health.

Once a particular "good" is selected and named, objective assessments of advance and decline can be made. That type of value-specific assessment is quite different, however, from any form of triumphal progressivism, which tries to pick out some one cultural tradition as superior to all the rest. Things can be made to seem either better or worse, depending on the criteria of value that you choose to select. When it comes to reviewing all the many potentially good things in life, cultural pluralists believe that there are pluses and minuses to most long-standing cultural traditions (see Shweder et al. 1997). And when it comes to constructing narratives about progress, they believe that there is lots of room for discretion (and ideology) in how one tells the story of who is better and who is worse.

It is also possible to make such value-specific judgments about progress without believing in the overall superiority of the present over the past, or that most changes are for the good. It is even possible to make criterion-specific judgments of progress and decline while being a "neo-antiquarian," that is, someone who rejects the idea that the world woke up, emerged from darkness, and became good for the first time yesterday or three hundred years ago in northern Europe. A "neo-antiquarian" does not think that newness is a measure of progress and is quite prepared, in the name of progress, to revalue things from distant places and from out of the distant past.

Pluralists do make critical judgments. Indeed, the "stance of justification" is so central to my style of cultural analysis that I would define a "genuine" culture, a culture deserving of appreciation, as a way of life that is defensible in the face of criticism from abroad. Pluralism is the attempt to provide that defense of "others," and not only as a corrective to the partiality and exaggerations of various modern forms of ethnocentrism and chauvinism (including the claim that the West is better than all the rest), although that is reason enough. Right now, with the fall of communism and the rise of global capitalism, including the expansion of our Internet, we (in the West) feel full of ourselves. It is at times such as these that we might do well to remember that Max Weber, the author of *The Protestant Ethic and the Spirit of Capitalism*, did not voice a preference for Protestantism over Catholicism or for the North over the South. He was a critical pluralist who put out warnings about the "iron cage" of modernity, about the impersonal rules of the bureaucratic state that redefine one's moral obligations to kith and kin as a form of "corruption," and about the hazards of an unbridled economic rationality.

Throughout history, whoever is wealthiest and the most technologically advanced thinks that their way of life is the best, the most natural, the God-given, the surest means to salvation, or at least the fast lane to well-being in this world. In the sixteenth century, Portuguese missionaries to China believed that their invention of clocks, of which they were very proud, was knock-down proof of the superiority of Catholicism over other world religions (Landes 1998, 336–337). For all I know, their mechanical timepiece may have been counted as an argument in favor of absolute monarchy. Dazzled by our contemporary inventions and toys (e.g., CNN, IBM, Big Mac, blue jeans, the birth control pill, the credit card) and at home in our own way of life, we are prone to similar illusions and the same type of conceits.

MILLENNIAL PROPHECIES:
THREE IMAGES OF THE "NEW WORLD ORDER"

These are confusing times, especially when one tries to imagine the broad outlines of the "new world order" that is likely to replace the old capitalist/communist/underdeveloped "three worlds" scheme.

One reason for the confusion is that the self-congratulatory, "enlightenment" origin story about the ascent of secularism, individualism, and science has taken its lumps in the 1990s and may not be all that useful for predicting the direction of change in the early twenty-first century. Thirty years ago, many social scientists predicted that, in the modern world, religion would go away and be replaced by science. They predicted that tribes would go away and be replaced by individuals. They were wrong. That has not and will not happen, either globally or locally. Multiculturalism is a fact of life. The former Second World, once an empire, is now many little worlds. The development of a global world system and the emergence of local ethnic or cultural revival movements seem to go hand in hand. At the limit, political succession may even have its rewards for cultural minority groups. The potential rewards include direct receipt of financial aid and military protection from various power centers, and perhaps even a voice at the United Nations.

Moreover, many of us now live in nation-states composed, as Joseph Raz has put it, "of groups and communities with diverse practices and beliefs, including groups whose beliefs are inconsistent with each other." We will continue to do so, if for no other reason than the reality of global migration and the fact that community and divinity are essential goods and must be acknowledged for the sake of individual identity and human progress. Of course, life in such a world can be hazardous, especially for members of immigrant or minority groups living in multicultural states or for members of different civilizations or cultures who are in geopolitical conflict. In such a world, one hopes that it is not just culture that matters but also a particular pluralistic conception of culture because the right conception of culture can be useful in minimizing some of the risks associated with "difference" and with multicultural life.

There is a second reason these are confusing times. It would be nice to have in hand a valid general causal explanation for the wealth and poverty of peoples, cultures, or nations, but we don't. If by "causation" we mean what J. S. Mill meant by it—all the necessary conditions that are jointly sufficient to produce an effect—I think we must admit that we do not really know what causes economic growth. Sicily in the fifteenth century, Holland in the sixteenth century, Japan today; social scientists can pick a people, culture, or nation and tell a plausible story about some of the reasons for economic failure or success, in that case. But that is a far cry from a general causal theory. Try listing all the potential causal conditions for wealth production mentioned by David Landes (1998) in his monumental economic history of the world. Then ask yourself this question: Are any of those conditions sufficient to produce economic growth? The answer is no. Are any of those conditions even necessary?

Having guns did it here. Having Jews did it there. In this case it was immigration policy; in that case it was having access to quinine. In this case it was freeing the serfs; in that case it was the availability of fossil fuel. In this case it was the weather; in that case it was willingness to trade with outsiders. In this case it was having good colonial masters; in that case it was high consumer demand. In this case and that case it was luck. Singapore is not a liberal democracy, but it is rich. India is the world's most populous democracy, but it is poor. Sweden in the eighteenth century was a sparsely populated democracy, and it was poor too. People who are religiously orthodox and don't believe in "gender equality" (e.g., Hasidic Jews) can be rich. Fully secularized egalitarian societies (e.g., former communist countries in Eastern Europe) may fail to thrive from an economic point of view. In 1950, Japan had "Confucian values" (which at the time didn't look very "Western") and was poorer than Brazil. In 1990 Japan had the same "Confucian values," which all of a sudden seemed very "Protestant-like," as Japan outstripped Brazil. If I were a cynic, I would say that our most able economic historians are really good at identifying some of the unnecessary conditions that might have been jointly sufficient to produce wealth in any particular special case. Less cynically, I think it is fair to say that despite many impressive post hoc historical accounts of the case-specific conditions that have promoted growth, one is entitled to feel confused about the general causes of economic success, if by "causation" we mean what J. S. Mill meant when he defined the term.

How then are we to grasp the big changes that are taking place in the "world order"? What is the relationship between "globalization" (the linking of the world's economies), "westernization" (the adoption of Western ideas, ideals, norms, institutions, and products), and economic growth? If you keep your ear to the ground these days, you can hear many prophecies or speculations about the shape of the "new world order." I will conclude by mentioning three.

Prophecy 1: The West Is Best and Will Become Global (or at Least It Should Try to Take Over the World)

The prediction here is that Western-like aspirations will be fired up or freed up by globalization and will be the cause and the concomitant of economic growth. Western-like aspirations include a desire for liberal democracy, the decentralization of power, free enterprise, private property, individual rights, gender equality, and so on, and perhaps even a taste for Western products. With regard to "globalization," "westernization," and "economic growth," this prediction imagines causal effects in all directions. Basically, this is the Western "enlightenment" origin story universalized and projected into the future.

Prophecy 2: Others Will Have a "Piece of the Rock" and Hold On to Their Distinctive Culture Too

In the early 1970s, I had a Sudanese student who did his Ph.D. on attitudes toward modernization among African students, using a beliefs and values questionnaire. He discovered that the "materialism" factor in his questionnaire was orthogonal to the "individualism" factor; one could value material wealth without giving up the collectivist values of the tribe. The Saudi Arabians liked that message so much they hired him to teach in their universities. Perhaps that is why Samuel Huntington's thesis (1996) that the West is unique but not universal and that other civilizations do not need to become like us to benefit from the technologies of the modern world is so popular in the non-Western world. This prediction imagines globalization and economic growth without deep cultural penetration from the West. Cultures and civilizations are encouraged to remain diverse while everyone gets a piece of the pie.[7]

Prophecy 3: A Liberal Ottoman-Style Empire with Two "Castes" (Cosmopolitan Liberals and Local Non-Liberals)

I associate the first prophecy with Francis Fukuyama (1992) and the second with Samuel Huntington (1996). Let me conclude with my own augury. Imagine a world order that is liberal in the classical sense. Its leaders assume a "stance of neutrality" with regard to substantive cultural issues. They don't condition aid and protection on changes in local gender ideals, forms of authority, kinship structures, or coming of age ceremonies. They don't try to tell the members of different cultural groups that they have to live together or love each other or share the same emotional reactions, aesthetic ideals, and religious beliefs. They don't try to tell them how to run their private lives or that they must have private lives. Imagine that in this world order various sanctioning mechanisms make it possible to enforce minimal rules of civility: exit visas are always available, and no aggression is permitted across territorial boundaries. Imagine that such a world system is set up to support decentralized control over cultural issues and hence to promote local cultural efflorescence. Such an emergent "new world order" might look like a postmodern Ottoman "millet system" on a global scale.

I imagine this system would be two tiered and operating at two levels, global and local. I imagine its personnel will belong to two "castes." There will be the cosmopolitan liberals, who are trained to appreciate value neutrality and cultural diversity and who run the global institutions of the world system. And there will be the local non-liberals, who are dedicated to one form or another of thick ethnicity and are inclined to separate themselves from "others," thereby guaranteeing that there is enough diversity remaining in the world for the cosmopolitan liberals to appreciate. The global elite (those who are cosmopolitan and liberal) will, of course, come from all nationalities. In the new universal cosmopolitan culture of the global tier of the world system, your ancestry and skin color will be far less important than your education, your values, and your travel plans. It is already the case in the postmodern cosmopolitan world that you don't have to grow up in the West to be Western any more than you have to grow up in the southern world to adopt an indigenous Third World point of view. Finally, I imagine that it would be possible in this "new world order" for individuals to switch tiers and castes in both directions, moving from global liberalism to local non-liberalism and back, within the course of a single life.

With regard to globalization, westernization, and economic growth, I would hazard this guess. If it should turn out as an empirical generalization that economic growth can be pulled off relying only on the shallow or thin aspects of Western society (e.g., weapons, information technology, Visa cards), then cultures won't converge, even as they get rich. If economic growth is contingent on accepting the deep or thick aspects of Western culture (e.g., individualism, ideals of femininity, egalitarianism, the Bill of Rights), then cultures will not converge and will not develop economically because their sense of identity will supersede their desire for material wealth.

REFERENCES

Fukuyama, Francis. 1992. *The End of History and the Last Man.* New York: Free Press.

Harrison, Lawrence E. 1992. *Who Prospers? How Cultural Values Shape Economic and Political Success.* New York: Basic.

Huntington, Samuel P. 1996. "The West Unique, Not Universal." *Foreign Affairs* 75: 28–45.

Kaplan, B. 1954. *A Study of Rorschach Responses in Four Cultures.* Papers of the Peabody Museum of Archaeology and Ethnology, 42:2. Cambridge: Harvard University Press.

Landes, David S. 1998. *The Wealth and Poverty of Nations: Why Some Are So Rich and Some Are So Poor.* New York: Norton.

Obermeyer, C. M. 1999. "Female Genital Surgeries: The Known, the Unknown, and the Unknowable." *Medical Anthropology Quarterly* 13: 79–106.

Obiora, L. A. 1997. "Rethinking Polemics and Intransigence in the Campaign Against Female Circumcision." *Case Western Reserve Law Review* 47: 275.

Shweder, Richard A. 1991. *Thinking Through Cultures: Expeditions in Cultural Psychology.* Cambridge: Harvard University Press.

_____. 1993. "Cultural Psychology: Who Needs It?" *Annual Review of Psychology* 44: 497–523.

_____. 1996a. "True Ethnography: The Lore, the Law and the Lure." In *Ethnography and Human Development: Context and Meaning in Social Inquiry* edited by R. Jessor, A. Colby, and R. A. Shweder. Chicago: University of Chicago Press.

_____. 1996b. "The View from Manywheres." *Anthropology Newsletter* 37, no. 9: 1.

Shweder, Richard A., ed. 1998. *Welcome to Middle Age! (and Other Cultural Fictions).* Chicago: University of Chicago Press.

Shweder, Richard A., with M. Mahapatra and J. G. Miller. 1990. "Culture and Moral Development." In *Cultural Psychology: Essays on Comparative Human Development*, edited by J. S. Stigler, R. A. Shweder, and G. Herdt. New York: Cambridge University Press.

Shweder, Richard A., with N. C. Much, M. Mahapatra, and L. Park. 1997. "The 'Big Three' of Morality (Autonomy, Community, Divinity) and the 'Big Three' Explanations of Suffering." In *Morality and Health*, edited by P. Rozin and A. Brandt. New York: Routledge.

Spiro, M. 1961. "Social Systems, Personality, and Functional Analysis." In *Studying Personality Cross-Culturally*, edited by B. Kaplan. New York: Harper & Row.

Stolzenberg, N. M. 1997. "A Tale of Two Villages (or, Legal Realism Comes to Town)." In *Ethnicity and Group Rights—Nomos XXXIX*, edited by I. Shapiro and W. Kymlicka. New York: New York University Press.

Richard Shweder's note 1 (see below) evoked reactions by Daniel Etounga-Manguelle, Carlos Alberto Montaner, and Mariano Grondona. Their comments appear after the footnote, along with a further comment by Richard Shweder.

Among the many fascinating remarks heard at the conference were several "indigenous" testimonials from cosmopolitan intellectuals out of Africa and Latin America. These representatives from the "Third World" played the part of disgruntled "insiders," bearing witness to the impoverishment of their own native cultures, telling us how bad things can be in the home country. That role has become increasingly complex, even dubious, in our postmodern world, where the outside is in and the inside is all over the place (think of CNN, VISA, and the Big Mac). For most globe-hopping managers of the world system, including cosmopolitan intellectuals from out of the "Third World," travel plans now matter more than ancestry. Consequently, one feels inclined to raise doubts about any claims to authority based on an equation of citizenship (or national origin) with "indigenous" voice. After all, whose voice is more "indigenous"? The voice of a "Western-educated" M.B.A. or Ph.D. from Dakar or Delhi, who looks down on his or her own cultural traditions and looks up to the United States for intellectual and moral guidance and material aid? Or the voice of a "Western" scholar who does years of fieldwork in rural villages in Africa or Asia and understands and sees value in the traditions of "others"?

COMMENTS OF MONTANER, ETOUNGA-MANGUELLE, AND GRONDONA, WITH FURTHER COMMENTS BY SHWEDER

Carlos Alberto Montaner

Richard Shweder's comment is typical of those who expect Third World reactions from Latin Americans. He simply doesn't understand that Latin America is an extension of the West. I don't understand why Shweder thinks that we ought to resign ourselves to authoritarian governments and economic models that condemn half of our people to misery when the entire world—beginning with the Japanese—believes that it was admirable when Japan copied the production techniques and social organization of the West. Perhaps the Brazilian *favelas,* with their infinite, barbaric misery, seem picturesque to him. I cannot accept those subhuman conditions. I believe that they must be eradicated and that the people living in them must have a chance for a better, more human life.

How do I know what Latin Americans want? It's very simple: by following migration trends. Surveys demonstrate that half or more of the populations of Mexico, Colombia, and Guatemala, among others, would abandon their countries for the United States. Why? Because the United States offers them what they don't find in their own countries.

What Shweder says of "these representatives from the 'Third World' play[ing] the part of disgruntled 'insiders'" could also be applied to the Americans who are concerned about improving subhuman conditions in the black and Puerto Rican ghettos. If he is to be consistently uncritical of the values and attitudes of a culture, then he should have no problem with the Sicilian *omertà*.

Daniel Etounga-Manguelle

As a "disgruntled insider" and "cosmopolitan intellectual" from Africa, I appreciate the opportunity to comment on Richard Shweder's note. I do so with some diffidence. After all, I am responding to a Western scholar who identifies himself as more "indigenous" than I am because he "has done years of fieldwork in rural villages in . . . Asia and understands and sees value in the traditions of 'others.'"

I have to confess that I failed to receive the "intellectual and moral guidance and material aid" I expected at the Harvard symposium, so I am going to tell the truth: We Africans really enjoy living in shantytowns where there isn't enough food, health care, or education for our children. Furthermore, our corrupt chieftaincy political systems are really marvelous and have permitted countries like Mobutu's Zaire to earn us international prestige and respect.

Moreover, surely it would be terribly boring if free, democratic elections were organized all over Africa. Were that to happen, we would no longer be real Africans, and by losing our identity—and our authoritarianism, our bloody civil wars, our illiteracy, our forty-five-year life expectancy—we would be letting down not only ourselves but also those Western anthropologists who study us so sympathetically and understand that we can't be expected to behave like human beings who seek dignity on the eve of the third millennium. We are Africans, and our identity matters!

So let us fight for it with the full support of those Western scholars who have the wisdom and courage to acknowledge that Africans belong to a different world.

Mariano Grondona

There is a methodological difference between Richard Shweder and Latin Americans like Carlos Alberto Montaner and myself. Shweder's goal, were he focused on Latin America, would be to understand it. We want to change it. Anthropologists need the societies they study to remain relatively static and predictable, like an entomologist studying bees or ants. Montaner and I, on the other hand, have an existential approach to our region: It is "our" world—where we come from—which we love. Because of our commitment to it, we want it to advance to new levels of human fulfillment, closer to those in the developed world.

One must ask who represents Latin America better, Shweder and other foreign social scientists or Montaner and myself? We belong to our region. We feel it. The fact that millions of Latin Americans are "voting with their feet" as they migrate to the developed countries and that the overwhelming electoral majorities are supporting progressive governments throughout our region eloquently testifies that our views and concerns are widely shared.

To be sure, we travel back and forth between Latin America and the developed countries. But these experiences do not alienate us from Latin America. Rather, they both increase our concern about conditions, particularly for poor people, in Latin America and focus us on what needs to be done to change those conditions. Like the vast majority of our countrymen, we want our nations to have the democratic stability, justice, opportunity for advancement, and prosperity that we find in the advanced countries.

Richard A. Shweder's Reply to Montaner, Etounga-Manguelle, and Grondona

As far as I can tell nothing in note 1 (or in my chapter) recommends authoritarian rule, a life of squalor, or death at an early age. In authoritarian power orders, those in power act in such a way that only their own interests are served, and no one can stop them from doing so. I think the world would be a far better place if there were no such orders of power. And nothing suggests that we must be uncritical or accepting of the received ideas, attitudes, and practices of any cultural tradition, including our own. As I state in my chapter, "Pluralists do make critical judgments. Indeed, the 'stance of justification' is so central to my style of cultural analysis that I would define a 'genuine' culture, a culture deserving of appreciation, as a way of life that is defensible in the face of criticism from abroad."

If one truly cares to achieve some appreciation of a cultural tradition, one must usually engage in some participant observation and in a process of sympathetic understanding. One initially tries to bracket all ethnocentric reactions and discover what is good, true, beautiful, or efficient in the ideas, attitudes, and practices of "others." There is no guarantee that appreciation will be achieved. There is no guarantee that everything that is, is okay or "genuine." Ideas, attitudes, and practices that are demonstrably bad, false, ugly, or inefficient should be criticized and perhaps even changed. So much for red herrings and the bogeyman of radical relativism. My essay is in fact a critique of both radical relativism ("whatever is, is okay") and ethnocentric monism ("there is only one way to lead a morally decent, rational and fulfilling life, and it's our way"), although by my lights I did not see many radical relativists at the conference.

In a moment I will respond to one or two other points raised by Carlos Alberto Montaner, Daniel Etounga-Manguelle, and Mariano Grondona. First, however, I want to focus on what was actually said in note 1, namely, that in the postmodern world, one should be skeptical of all claims to authority based on the equation of citizenship (or national origin) with "indigenous" voice. And I want to tell you a story, which illustrates that point.

Rabindranath Tagore is modern India's most acclaimed poet. He was a recipient of the Nobel Prize for Literature in 1913, a spokesman for the India nationalist movement, and an admirer, interpreter, and literary beneficiary of the classical Sanskrit literatures of India. In 1877, Tagore visited England for the first time. He was sixteen years old. He went there to study law. In his book *India and Europe: An Essay in Understanding*, Wilhelm Halbfass quotes Tagore's impressions:

> I had thought that the island of England was so small and the inhabitants so dedicated to learning that, before I arrived there, I expected the country from one end to the other would echo and re-echo with the lyrical essays of Tennyson; and I also thought that wherever I might be in this narrow island, I would hear constantly Gladstone's oratory, the explanation of the Vedas by Max Mueller, the scientific truth of Tindall, the profound thoughts of Carlyle and the philosophy of Bain. I was under the impression that wherever I would go I would find the old and the young drunk with the pleasure of "intellectual" enjoyment. But I have been very disappointed in this.

Apparently, the young Tagore, a political and civic "outsider" to the British Isles, was culturally more English and spoke the English language far better than most Englishmen. His reference to Max Mueller is highly pertinent to note 1 because it was Max Mueller, a German philologist and "orientalist" who taught at Oxford, to whom Hindu Brahmans turned to learn about Sanskrit and their own classical literary traditions.

This situation of "outsiders" and "insiders" trading places and keeping each other's valuable cultural heritages in play is not unusual, especially in the contemporary world. We live in a world where Afro-Caribbean scholars translate ancient Greek texts, where scholars from Africa, Asia, and Europe write perceptive books about the United States, and where the Max Mueller effect is alive and well. For example, Gusii intellectuals from Kenya, some of whom are quite expert in Western philosophy and science, read Robert LeVine's work (conducted from the 1950s through 1990s) to learn about the meaning, value, and history of Gusii norms and folkways. The main point of this observation is a simple one: Statements about the pros and cons of a cultural tradition do not gain authority and should not be granted authority on the basis of claims to ancestry, membership, or national origin.

Note 1 was an aside, a parenthetical remark about my fascination with one aspect of the structural organization of the conference. The conference was choreographed in such a way that there was one session in which all the speakers from the "Third World" participated, and they spoke pretty much with one voice, supporting the idea that "Western civilization" is superior to all the rest. Now, of course, this idea is not unpopular in many capitals of Asia, Africa, and Latin America. It is especially popular among those Western, westernized, or westernizing elites who tend to view the received beliefs, attitudes, and everyday practices of non-Western peoples, even their own countrymen, as unenlightened, superstitious, magical, authoritarian, corrupt, or otherwise unworthy or embarrassing. But that type of wholesale acceptance of "Western modernity" over non-Western "traditionalisms" of various kinds has never been the only voice in town in either the "West" or the "East," the "North" or the "South," the "developed" or the "underdeveloped" world. Had there been other types of voices in the session, the voice of "Third World" intellectuals who might speak with pride and admiration about "indigenous" ideas, attitudes, and practices, the session would perhaps have been less fascinating. Perhaps I would not have been led to wonder about the use of "insider" testimonials from the "Third World" to lend authority to the idea that the Protestant "First World" really got it right.

Carlos Alberto Montaner and Mariano Grondona are impressed by migration patterns, by the fact that "millions of Latin Americans are 'voting with their feet'" in favor of the "developed" world. The first time I ever heard the "voting with your feet" argument was in the 1960s, when a famous conservative made the argument that black migration patterns into South Africa far exceeded black migration patterns out of South Africa. He interpreted this as evidence that black Africans were voting with their feet in favor of the apartheid government of South Africa over other African states! I suspect they were not voting or expressing their moral and cultural preferences at all—just going where there were higher-paying jobs.

Daniel Etounga-Manguelle seems to imply that one cannot live a dignified life and a life that is distinctively African at the same time. As I stated in my essay, I am not a fan of broad categories such as "Latin American" or "African" as ways of identifying cultural communities—Bahia is not San Paolo, the Yoruba are not the Masai. Nevertheless, I do believe, as did Edward Sapir, that "the societies in which different societies live are distinct worlds, not merely the same world with different labels attached." For a pluralist, "distinctness" or "difference" is not a term of disparagement. With complete respect for all three of my critics, whose sincerity I never doubted, whose company and conversation I much enjoyed, and whose testimonials and arguments I found fascinating, I fully confess to rejecting the idea that the only or very best way to be dignified, decent, rational, and fully human is to live the life of a North American or a northern European.

part four

CULTURE AND GENDER

13

Culture, Gender, and Human Rights

BARBARA CROSSETTE

Over the last decade, no other nations have been drawn into such comprehensive and profoundly important debates about cultural identity and human rights as the United States and Canada. In the press, in academia, in ethnic communities, and among major religious organizations, there is a palpable sense of shift in North American civilization. It is sometimes welcomed and often feared.

That there are apprehensions should not be surprising. No country in history has voluntarily changed its ethnic profile in such a short time as the United States has. We need only look at early Hollywood films and the television programs of the 1950s to see the mental image that used to be conjured up by the word "American." Across most of the United States there were largely two kinds of faces, European and African, and in those heads and hearts people shared, for better or worse, a similar mainstream culture that was more American and less like that of any of their ancestors. At the beginning of the twenty-first century, however, American faces reflect virtually all the world's ethnic communities and many minds and hearts are determined not to lose—or if necessary to reinvent—ancestral cultures. Does that fragment us or does it make us the first truly planetary nation?

Whatever it does, our changing mix draws us with greater frequency into debates about broader definitions of human rights and their relationship to cultural bottom lines. The new environment should also lead us into more informed, clear-sighted, and judicious considerations of human rights problems abroad. But just as the linguistic diversity of our ancestors has not made us a multilingual nation, a variety of cultural backgrounds has yet to make us—the media included—better judges of distant practices, traditions, or causes, which also appear on our shores in the luggage of immigrants. Two imperatives collide: to salvage a core American culture while making way for different modes of life, without always having the necessary information to comprehend them. Reactions to cultural practices may thus be contradictory in different contexts and places—in Africa and Afghanistan, for example, which are approached with inconsistent attitudes.

An era of reexamination in the United States coincides with a new age of cultural awareness abroad, at worst spawning the destructive ethnicity (further fueled by economic troubles and political uncertainty) seen in Africa, the Balkans, and Indonesia. At the same time, countries in every region are also feeling the effects of significant social change. The burgeoning assertion of women's rights will have long-run effects on traditional social practices. The intense pressure of overpopulation in the world's poorest nations puts the essentials of life—food, water, and air—under greater strain every year.

The world is belatedly discovering that women and natural resources are not unrelated. In countries like Bangladesh and Indonesia, more authority in female hands has shown that lower birthrates follow, along with rising demands for education, better farming techniques, and more investment in the land and villages. In Africa, UNICEF (the United Nations Children's Fund) found in its *State of the World's Children 1999* report that mothers are beginning to band together to demand schools, seeing them as the key to a better life for their children and often for themselves. In Burkina Faso, where only 9 percent of women over the age of fifteen can read, women have formed twenty-three Pupils' Mothers Associations to monitor the enrollment and attendance of girls in school. In Pakistan and Egypt, among other places, local communities have found ways to train teachers for village schools.

The results are quick to discern: "A 10 percentage-point increase in girls' primary enrollment can be expected to decrease infant mortality by 4.1 deaths per 1,000, and a similar rise in girls' secondary enrollment by another 5.6 deaths per 1,000. This would mean concretely in Pakistan, for example, that an extra year of schooling for 1,000 girls would ultimately prevent roughly 60 infant deaths." But in no small number of traditional societies, listening to women would still be taking a momentous cultural step.

With the world in social ferment, intellectual disputes over culture and human rights have become more frequent in recent years, particularly when issues take on international dimensions. Major international human rights groups, once considered fringe activist organizations by many governments, have built solid reputations for their legal and investigative work. They have pushed long-dormant international covenants to the center of public debate, lobbied successfully for permanent institutions (e.g., an international criminal court), and generally moved into the foreign policy establishment. They are now consulted by State Department officials, invited to set up university centers, and listened to by the Council on Foreign Relations. But these human rights experts, largely well-trained lawyers, are almost by nature purists and universalists who are loath to bend principles to fit cultural wrinkles. Moreover, their frequent insistence on the preeminence of civil and political rights defined in concrete ways has brought them into conflict with those who believe that economic and social rights come first or, more broadly, that cultures outside the Western mainstream see politics and civil society differently and must hew to their own values when setting priorities and codifying principles.

To add to the mushrooming controversies over rights and cultures worldwide, those who argue for cultural exceptions to international human rights models are themselves coming under attack from dissenters within their own societies. In Southeast Asia, for example, some well-known promoters of "Asian values" are on the streets battling the forces of *reformasi*—a situation that not many would have predicted a few years ago. Dissidents, energized as well as outraged by hard economic times, say that they have had enough of the kind of Asian values that brought corruption and cronyism and stifled political growth. In the Muslim world, where militancy once seemed inexorable, a question being heard more often from North Africa through the Middle East and South Asia to the Pacific is, Who speaks for Islam? Pluralism is in the air, and the voices of dissent are both female and male.

THE KEY ROLE OF WOMEN

Some of the most intense efforts to rethink and realign the mix of religion, rights, and culture are indeed being made today by Muslim women, but they are not alone. In the months leading up to the 1995 U.N. Fourth World Conference on Women, local and regional meetings in Africa, Asia, Europe, and the Americas were organized to write agendas for Beijing, where both the formal conference and a parallel unofficial gathering of nongovernmental organizations were held. The impassioned speeches and papers presented by regional assemblies from widely different cultural and geographic settings included some astonishingly similar goals. Building on the 1994 Conference on Population and Development in Cairo, women were clarifying and defining a genre of rights universal to them.

Their demands cut across old sectors, rendering irrelevant some timeworn disputes about civil or economic rights. Women spoke pragmatically of the right to own and inherit property or to start a business, and the need to establish and protect these activities by law—an economic demand coupled with a political call for more women in legislatures. Women also sought changes in family laws to give them rights equal to those of spouses or parents. They demanded the right to say no to unwanted children or unwanted sex, putting control over their own bodies and reproductive lives in the category of fundamental freedoms. "Women's rights are human rights" became a familiar slogan. In Beijing, a Nepali housewife who raided her small savings account to travel to China could meet farmers from Tanzania, writers from Teheran, and inner-city Americans in a variety of occupations. Most of these women from diverse backgrounds found that they had more in common than they had expected. Back home, buoyed by their newfound networks, many of these women took a new look at the cultural assumptions surrounding them.

For women, the interplay between a prevailing culture or ethos and their daily lives is not a hypothetical topic. Despite great political and economic gains in many places, women around the world still have good reason to be sensitive to how cultures affect them. Indeed, for large numbers of women, cultural sensitivity is not an intellectual exercise or a social attitude taught in seminars by consultants. Cultural shifts and the political use of traditional practices can create intolerable, if not life-threatening, situations for women. Over the last two decades, middle-class women in Iran, Afghanistan, and Algeria have discovered how quickly life can turn upside down and how powerless they can suddenly become in the face of tumultuous change.

THE DOMINANCE OF MEN

In many societies, the cultural rules are unambiguously made by men who frequently choose, deliberately or otherwise, to use women as the symbols of their beliefs or policies. When leaders or policies change, so can cultures. Women are told what to wear, where to go or not go, how to live. Although the collarless shirt (with a necktie ban) became the male uniform of Islamic piety among Iranians and the Taliban of Afghanistan enforce a regulation length for men's beards, in both countries—one Shiite, one Sunni—it is the life of women that is most constrained by dress codes and restrictions on work and play. Saudi Arabia falls into the same category of nations, in which the holiness of men is measured by the degree to which various parts of women are made invisible and their smallest hopes—to drive a car, for example—are denied.

The phenomenon is not confined to conservative Islamic cultures. Mennonite and Amish girls in Pennsylvania are still told of Biblical strictures against wearing trousers, though few of them may be listening to the warnings and their chances of being physically abused for defiance are very slight. In Laos, for many years wearing a sarong to work in government offices was mandatory for women, whereas men dressed pretty much as they liked, apparently without fear of diluting the national character. When the rebel soldiers who overthrew Mobutu Sese Seko entered Kinshasa, the Zairian capital, in 1997, they ordered women in jeans off the streets and brandished their bayonets, at least for a few heady days. Guerrilla armies, various breeds of ideologues, perhaps even fashion designers get into the business of making social or political statements by dressing the female body in one way or another.

Women, who are rarely in a position to make the religious or social rules, tend to be swept up into a culture in the broadest sense, which takes in religion, the economy, the arts, the law, and entertainment, as well as the often subtly defined rules of social behavior involving public life, family relationships, and the place of children. A male-dominant culture is, in short, the atmosphere in which most women live all the time, with fewer lines of definition between work and home, career and family, than many men in most countries enjoy.

Furthermore, any cultural milieu may generate unpredictable, even paradoxical results for women. A free society in political terms does not necessarily mean a better life, as more than 100 million poor, illiterate, and often victimized women in India who are unable to escape the cultural apartheid of caste could demonstrate. Living in a notably tolerant, even egalitarian, culture does not necessarily liberate women either. In countries like Thailand, where women have made considerable gains in the economy and society, and Cambodia, a freewheeling atmosphere can actually make the sexual enslavement of women and girls easier because prostitution on a grand scale, catering to every need and fetish, is not very shocking.

The complexity of women's lives within the context of their varying cultures is only beginning to be understood, as development experts focus more on the centrality of people, not projects, in both the poorer countries of the global South and in pockets of underdevelopment in the richer industrial nations of the North. What is certain now is that countries ignore the lives of women at their economic and social peril.

India, a nation aspiring to rank among the world's leaders, is in trouble on this point, according to its own development experts. Its population is nearing the 1 billion mark, and it is likely to overtake China as the world's most populous nation in the first half of the twenty-first century. But the numbers of the disadvantaged are huge. Barely half of India's population is literate, a necessary step by most measures toward a fully productive society; little more than a third of its women can read and write. Up to a half of births are not registered, putting millions of children in an official limbo where they may be denied basic services because officially they do not exist. Moreover, development studies report that the broader social indicators in India are pulling the South Asian region down to or below the level of sub-Saharan Africa.

The problems are most acute in northern India. In its *State of the World's Children 1999*, UNICEF reports that no women are literate in many villages in the poor state of Bihar. Nationwide, again led by the northern tier of states, half of India's children are malnourished, with nearly one in five affected to the point of stunting. Twenty percent of children under five years of age are severely underweight; less than 30 percent of the population has access to sanitation—any kind of toilet, including a rudimentary latrine—and 20 percent of the population lacks clean water. According to UNICEF, the World Bank, and other organizations, unless women are involved in development at the local level, the country's much publicized middle class will be perched on top of a larger and larger number of disadvantaged people, who already number in the hundreds of millions. As gaps in the living standard grow and resources shrink, social unrest may become inevitable.

FEMALE CIRCUMCISION/MUTILATION

Precisely how new theories of development that place women at the center translate into pivotal roles for women in defining the dominant culture, whatever it may be, is harder to decide. Nowadays, when neither feminism nor human rights constitutes a monolithic concept with all-purpose formulas applicable worldwide, looking at cultural practices of any kind demands a certain relativism. Furthermore, as women and men do not inevitably see their culture through the same eyes, adding women to the mix only makes the picture more complicated. Men may also control culture by controlling power, from the village police on up to the national government, and they tend to dismiss the complaints of women in the name of tradition. In many places, women make progress only when a prominent man—the village elder, a supreme court judge, a president—has a change of heart.

These complexities are reflected in the intellectual battle over what is termed either female circumcision or female genital mutilation—the choice of language reveals the position one takes. To follow the logic of Aziza Hussein, an Egyptian family planning expert and a founder of the Egyptian Society for the Prevention of Practices Harmful to Women and Children, the evolution of genital cutting is more or less as follows.

The first premise is that the practice has long served men by rendering the women they marry uninterested in sex or unappealing and inaccessible to any other man—a safe, albeit damaged, piece of property. Next comes the rationalization/belief that no girl or woman will be marriageable unless she has submitted to this process. Peer group pressure begins to kick in. By this time, women, not men, may be the enforcers of the practice, enshrining it and validating it within a certain culture. But, says Hussein, that does not erase the basic truth, which is that this is a procedure invented on behalf of men that most women would rather not experience. A doctor in a Cairo children's hospital told me that it was "pointless, not to mention cruel and dangerous, to mutilate a woman in the name of destroying desire." Moreover, she added, "All impulses, including sexual impulses, start in the brain."

When, from a distance, the argument is made that the genital cutting of females (which often involves the mutilation of the entire genital area, leading to lifelong and life-threatening infections and incontinence) must be a tradition of worth because people support it, whose voices are we hearing? What people? Hussein argues that, at some point, the cultural argument is no longer valid and societies have to make their decisions based on science and medicine—and perhaps a contemporary understanding of human sexual behavior, since depriving a woman of the possibility of sexual arousal and orgasm is taking away part of her life.

In December 1997, Egypt's highest court agreed. Upholding a ban on the practice in government hospitals imposed in 1996—admittedly only a start in ending the procedure legally—the court dismissed the arguments of some Islamic scholars that there were religious grounds for the tradition. "Circumcision of girls is not an individual right under *Sharia*," the court said. "There is nothing in the Koran that authorizes it."

One of the inconsistencies found in Western responses to the human rights of women in the Islamic world is that some influential scholarly and cultural experts who are willing to find validity in genital cutting rites in Africa are absolutely unwilling to give an inch of ground to the Taliban in Afghanistan when these Muslim zealots bar women from schools and jobs. It is not going too far to say that U.S. Afghan policy rests almost entirely at this point on the issue of how women are treated. Again the question is, Whose voices are we hearing? In this case, the answer is the articulate, middle-class women of Kabul and a few other urban centers. Not men this time, but not village women either.

Where is our cultural sensitivity here? Incremental improvements in the lives of Afghan women have been ruled out by feminist absolutism, boldly enunciated by Hillary Rodham Clinton and Secretary of State Madeleine Albright: Either the Taliban give in on women's rights or there will be no diplomatic recognition or aid. The Taliban, who have heard the West's message face-to-face from a number of international officials (including Emma Bonino, speaking for the European Union, and Carol Bellamy, the executive director of UNICEF), have tried to make the case for assistance in rebuilding Afghanistan's education system to conform with Islamic principles and their conservative vision of Muslim culture. They want new teacher-training institutes and duplicate schools for boys and girls. In some areas of the country, the Taliban have allowed home schools for girls to operate with minimal or no interference behind the scenes. In some villages, girls have more of a chance of getting a rudimentary education now than they did when a quarrelsome coalition of holy warriors ruled the country and kept it in a state of civil war for nearly a decade. These holy warriors, the mujahedeen who brought down the Soviet army, had American and European support.

THE CASE OF BHUTAN

Considering the case of Bhutan reduces the debate over culture and human rights to one of its most esoteric yet instructional cases. This small Buddhist kingdom in the Himalayas, wedged between China and India, is the last of its cultural breed—a Tibetan, Tantric monarchy that once counted Ladakh, Sikkim, and, above all, Tibet, among its ranks. From the mid-1970s, when Prime Minister Indira Gandhi and her intelligence networks undermined Sikkim's Buddhist monarchy and engineered the country's collapse and absorption into India, until the late 1980s, when an ethnic Nepali, largely Hindu, fifth column similar to the movement that had delivered up the Sikkimese seemed poised to do to the same for Bhutan, the Buddhist Bhutanese elite began to panic. They were incapable of policing a long land border with India, over which ethnic Nepali migrants were entering as illegal immigrants to swell the ranks of the local minority population.

Instead, the Bhutanese tried a policy of cultural enforcement. To be Bhutanese meant wearing a prescribed national costume, building homes in a certain style, and accepting the leadership of the Buddhist monarchy. Bhutanese Nepalis were justifiably distressed, but before they could make their peace with Bhutan's king, Jigme Singye Wangchuck, not an intolerant man, they were drawn into a larger pro-democracy movement flourishing in Nepal. Bolstered by flying squads of radical students from across Asia, many Bhutanese Nepalis were persuaded to join a revolt against the monarchy. Later, fleeing Bhutan to refugee camps in Nepal by way of India, which initially did nothing to stop the campaign, the Bhutanese Nepalis created a public relations nightmare for Bhutan that continues to this day. Using questionable data from essentially Nepali sources, organizations like Freedom House consistently rank Bhutan very low in civil and human rights, although in terms of human development, as measured by U.N. agencies, the country is outpacing most of its neighbors.

Western human rights organizations were at first convinced that a Himalayan ethnic cleansing was in train. Western nations, unrepresented in the isolated Buddhist kingdom because India insisted on controlling its foreign policy, fell back on diplomats in Katmandu, Nepal's capital, who were in turn under the influence of Nepali human rights groups or of foreign organizations with branches in Nepal. These organizations, often barred from Bhutan by a short-sighted government, portrayed the situation as a struggle of democratic forces against an absolute tyranny.

On their side, the Bhutanese saw it as a last-ditch struggle to preserve an endangered culture. Years passed before major international rights organizations recognized the king of Bhutan's story as being closer to the truth than the lurid tales told by his enemies who, incidentally, see in Bhutan a large under-populated stretch of fertile Himalayan land into which the excess population of Nepal might conveniently spill. Inexplicably, the army of westerners willing to demonstrate on behalf of the Dalai Lama's claim to Tibet have been all but silent in the face of the cultural annihilation of Bhutan. The issue remains unresolved, and many Bhutanese are perplexed and angry. "What exactly do you want from us?" an enraged Bhutanese official once shouted at me as I asked about reports of violence against Nepalis in his district. Good question.

THE TAMIL, EAST TIMOR, AND
KASHMIR QUESTIONS

The terrain on which cultural values and human rights interact often conceals land mines. Special interest groups whose principal goals are not necessarily the improvement of human rights have learned to manipulate the media and legislatures by championing causes in one-dimensional terms. In an age of information overload, a heart-rending story may not always be checked too carefully.

For years, the Sinhalese-led, Buddhist-dominated government of Sri Lanka was on the defensive because of persuasive ethnic Tamil propaganda abroad that a kind of genocide was being carried out against their community. Tamils, both Hindus and Christians, were winning asylum abroad only to use it, the Sri Lankan government said, to raise money and arms for a particularly brutal organization known as the Liberation Tigers of Tamil Eelam—Tamil Eelam being the name of an area they intended to carve out of northeastern Sri Lanka for a homeland. Other Tamils, separated by history and caste, who dominate the island's tea plantations in the central hills, did not support them. Eventually, the world caught up with the atrocities of the Tamil Tigers, now listed as a terrorist organization in the United States. But for years, sheer ignorance of events in Sri Lanka, despite extensive news coverage, allowed westerners to make cultural assumptions about the country that were often wide of the mark or told only part of the story.

The misperception was encouraged by India, which for years helped to arm and train the Tamil guerrillas against the Sri Lankan government—at least until the Tamils turned their guns on Indian peacekeeping troops, who tried to reverse New Delhi's course and eventually assassinated (or so those in New Delhi believe) Rajiv Gandhi, the former prime minister, who had sent Indian forces numbering up to 50,000 to the beleaguered island. Prominent Sri Lankans, among them Neelan Tiruchelvam, the leading Tamil moderate and internationally recognized constitutionalist, who was working on an autonomy plan for the Tamil areas that the Tigers deemed not radical enough, were also ruthlessly murdered.

Much of Sri Lanka's conflict was and is political, economic, or even ideological, not strictly ethnic and not religious. However, culture does play a significant role in both East Timor and Kashmir. In East Timor, a combination of Portuguese-inspired Catholicism and indigenous religious and ethnic differences with Muslim Java, Indonesia's Javanese-dominated military, and settlers from other ethnic communities, particularly the Bugis of South Sulawesi, pose fundamental problems, even without politically inspired violence.

In Kashmir, which has been fought over by Pakistan and India since 1947, the people are also ethnically and linguistically separate, and they are not at home in either country. Kashmiris are Muslims, but they have little in common with the Muslims of India or large parts of Pakistan, and their problems in the Kashmir valley, the setting of a decade-long war with Hindu India, are not primarily religious, but rather cultural and political.

Both East Timor and Kashmir are considered disputed territories by the United Nations. But the Timorese, with strong support from Catholics and the European-based organizations that supported revolutionary groups in other Portuguese colonies (Mozambique and Angola in particular), have enjoyed a high profile. Indonesia, on the other hand, has been made a pariah in a way that India was not when it marched into Portuguese Goa and annexed it without a hint of democratic ritual.

CONCLUSION

More recently, the sometimes problematic role of cultural touchstones has been revealed in the controversy over the life of the Guatemalan Nobel laureate Rigoberta Menchu. Scholars and investigative journalists now say that her childhood and youth, although certainly harsh, were not as full of deprivation and tragedy as first portrayed. It also seems that cultural stereotypes played a large part in creating an irresistible account of a poor Guatemalan Indian girl at the mercy of a heartless "European" military dictatorship. This image made her—and used her as—a cultural icon representing indigenous people across the region. Even now, there are those who argue that this overarching cultural symbolism is more important than mere facts.

Scholarship, journalism, the human rights establishment—and history—demand a higher standard. The way Americans deal with complex ethnic conflicts abroad (or political conflicts in ethnic trappings) often seems to indicate that our cultural sensitivity stops at the water's edge. Ironically, campaigns waged with the best intentions are often shallow or poorly informed, and they are as much politically motivated by their leaders in this country as by their counterparts in distant societies.

In the end, there must be a meaningful link between our value system—including the importance we attach to honesty and a truth not colored by ideology—and our foreign policy. After all, central elements of that value system, rooted in both Western and Eastern cultures, have acquired a universality through the U.N. Declaration of Human Rights.

14

Culture, Institutions, and Gender Inequality in Latin America

MALA HTUN

Gender discrimination has been a remarkably consistent feature of most cultures. Women everywhere have been accorded inferior economic, social, and legal status. The universality of sex-based inequality and the diversity of national cultures make any simple connection between sex discrimination and cultural attitudes dubious. The important question is whether and what cultural attributes contribute to and sustain progressive changes in gender relations.

This chapter analyzes the role played by culture in contemporary changes in the position of women in Latin America. Though traditional models of cultural influences on economic development and democracy are convincing in many ways, they cannot explain the impetus for change in gender relations across countries and cultures. Anglo-Protestant culture, held by some scholars to be particularly conducive to capitalist development and liberal democracy, has historically been compatible with systematic gender discrimination. Major progress in gender relations in the United States since the 1960s is less attributable to culture than to economic transformations, women's movements, and changing Supreme Court jurisprudence. In Latin America, by contrast, the cultural heritage has been deemed hostile to private capital accumulation and liberal democracy. Yet this heritage has not prevented Latin America from making great strides in gender equality over the past twenty years.

The second part of the chapter explores two ways in which cultural attributes contribute to and sustain changes in gender relations. First, underlying cultural values account for the diverse ways in which different societies conceive of achieving gender equality. Second, cultural attributes related to the performance and efficiency of state institutions affect the sustainability of changes in gender relations. If there is a significant gap between policy and enforcement, a widespread feature of Latin America, advances in women's rights in politics and the law may prove ephemeral.

CULTURE AND GENDER IN NORTH AND
SOUTH AMERICA COMPARED

Prominent social and political theorists from Tocqueville and Weber to many of the distinguished contributors to this volume have postulated that culture exerts a decisive influence on a people's economic and political development. Scholars such as Howard Wiarda and Lawrence Harrison argue that Latin America's cultural particularities account for the distinctive historical trajectory of the region, characterized by cycles of authoritarian rule and pronounced social inequality. Anglo-Protestant values, by contrast, are deemed responsible for the capacity of Anglo-American societies to generate wealth and support stable democratic institutions. As Harrison argues, "I believe that there is no other satisfactory way to explain the sharply contrasting evolution of the North and the South in the [Western] Hemisphere than culture—the strikingly different values, attitudes, and institutions—that have flowed from the Anglo-Protestant and Ibero-Catholic traditions."[1]

My intention is not to evaluate the claim that culture accounts for national variation in economic development and democracy, but merely to urge caution in using cultural arguments to explain differences in gender relations between the United States and Latin America. Anglo-Protestant culture's vigorous work ethic, propensity to save, and valorization of individual rights may have contributed to the good things of capitalism and democracy, but they were historically compatible with laws and policies that severely discriminated against women. Major changes in women's status are relatively recent. Consider the institution of coverture. Long after the founding of the republic, U.S. laws continued to uphold coverture rules that granted a husband legal representation of and exclusive control over the body and the property of his wife. Beginning with Married Women's Property Acts in the mid- to late-nineteenth century, some elements of coverture were eradicated, but male prerogatives in marriage and the family remained firmly entrenched well into the twentieth century. The last remnants of coverture were only abolished by the U.S. Supreme Court's 1992 decision in *Planned Parenthood v. Casey*, which held that "women do not lose their constitutionally protected liberty when they marry."[2]

For centuries, Anglo-Protestant culture in the United States condoned, and the judiciary tolerated, differential and discriminatory treatment of women in the workplace and the exclusion of women from certain professions. Prior to the Equal Pay Act of 1963 and the enactment of Title VII of the Civil Rights Act of 1964, statutes, rules, and regulations that discriminated by gender were widespread in many states and federal agencies. Enforcement of these laws has been instrumental in expanding women's employment opportunities, although many de facto discriminatory practices have been upheld by courts employing loose standards of scrutiny.

Bureaucratic invasion of personal and marital privacy on issues like sexuality and reproduction also seems to violate liberal values. Still, only in 1965 did the U.S. Supreme Court rule that a constitutional right to marital privacy prevented states from outlawing the use of contraceptives by married couples.

Violence against women is another area in which state action has been relatively recent. The Violence Against Women Act (VAWA), which creates federal penalties for crimes of violence against women and provides funds to states for prevention and treatment programs, was only enacted in 1994. Economic equality, recognition of women's rights to exercise control over fertility, and official condemnation of violence against women are not part of the Anglo-Protestant cultural heritage but are relatively recent events provoked by social changes and feminist movements.

Adherents of the culture and development school believe that Latin America's Ibero-Catholic culture is less conducive to capitalism and democracy than the Anglo-Protestant culture of the United States. As Wiarda puts it,

> [Latin America's] economy was and remains mercantilist and state-directed rather than capitalist and individually directed; its social structure was two class rather than multi-class and pluralist; its political institutions were hierarchical and authoritarian rather than democratic; its culture and religion were orthodox, absolutist, and infused with Catholic-Thomist precepts as contrasted with the religious nonconformity and pluralist precepts of the North American colonies.[3]

When seen in light of the traditional sexism of Roman Catholic ethics and secular ideologies like *machismo* and *marianismo,* the authoritarian and hierarchical features of Ibero-Catholic culture appear to be particularly hostile to women's advancement. As one scholar has remarked, Latin America's gender relations are "harsh patriarchal systems whose endurance is rivaled only in the Arab world."[4] Though some data show that Latin American cultural values have remained coherent and stable over time,[5] recent changes in gender relations and women's status have been remarkable. Shifts in society, law, and policy are no less revolutionary than what has happened in the United States since the 1960s. There are signs of a convergence in women's position among countries with different cultural heritages, as well as persisting variation among countries within the same cultural zone.

In politics, economics, education, and the law, changes in gender relations in Latin America are impressive. In the region today, women represent an average of 15.4 percent of the members of Congress, the second highest regional average in the world and ahead of the 13 percent in the United States (the world average is also 13 percent). In some countries, women's presence is very high, such as Argentina and Cuba (28 percent); Costa Rica (19 percent); Ecuador, El Salvador, and Mexico (17 percent); and the Dominican Republic (16 percent). Women's participation in the economy has skyrocketed. Region-wide, women made up 20 percent of the labor force in 1970. By 1995, this had grown to around 35 percent (U.S. women make up 45 percent of the labor force).

The wage gap between women and men continues to be significant but is not much different from the wage gap registered in industrialized countries. In the early 1990s, women's wages were between 20 and 40 percent lower than men's. However, the wage gap is much smaller for younger women. According to one study, women workers between twenty-five and thirty-four years of age earned 80 to 90 percent of men's salary. Women have made impressive gains in literacy and in education. Illiteracy among women has dropped substantially, and women make up about half of students in primary, secondary, and post-secondary education. In several countries, women represent more than half of university students. In the United States, women constitute 50 percent of secondary students and 55 percent of post-secondary students.[6]

Latin Americans have made notable progress in implementing legal reforms to grant women formal equality. The constitutions of several Latin American countries recognize the equal rights of women and men: constitutions in Brazil, Cuba, Ecuador, Guatemala, Mexico, and Paraguay include gender equality as a basic principle. Civil codes have been reformed to eliminate the institution of marital power *(potestad marital)* and to grant women equality in the management of common property, household decisionmaking, and authority over minor children.

At least twelve Latin American countries have adopted new laws stipulating penalties for domestic violence and expanding the authority of law enforcement to protect victims. Hundreds of police stations staffed by female law-enforcement officers specially trained in domestic violence and sex crimes have been established throughout the region. Nineteen Latin American countries have ratified the U.N. Convention on the Elimination of Discrimination Against Women (CEDAW), and Argentina has incorporated CEDAW into its national constitution. In the same year that the U.S. Congress enacted the Violence Against Women Act, members of the Organization of American States adopted the Inter-American Convention on Violence Against Women, subsequently ratified by at least twenty-six OAS member states.[7]

However, Latin American countries continue to exhibit significant variation regarding women in terms of political representation, economic opportunities, education, and legal position. Although women occupy 28 percent of the seats in Argentina's Congress, they make up merely 3 percent of Paraguay's Congress and 6 percent of Brazil's. Women account for 41 percent of the labor force in Uruguay, but merely 26 percent in Ecuador. In countries like Bolivia, Guatemala, and Peru, in which a substantial portion of the population is indigenous, rural women's illiteracy is much higher than men's. In Peru, for example, 46 percent of rural women are illiterate, compared to 10 percent of rural men. The situation of women's health exhibits tremendous variation across countries. In Costa Rica, the maternal mortality rate is 60 per 100,000 live births; in Bolivia, the rate is 650 per 100,000 live births. Whereas in Uruguay a 1946 civil code reform granted married women full legal agency and equality in marriage, in Chile the old institution of marital power continued to structure the default regime of property relations between husband and wife in 1999. Costa Rica and Venezuela legalized divorce in 1886 and 1904, respectively, but pro-divorce reformists only achieved their goals in Brazil in 1977 and in Argentina in 1987. There is also substantial variation in the status of women across social class and color within each country.

These examples point to two conclusions. First, in terms of aggregate participation in the economy, education, and politics, the status of women in Latin America and the United States is converging. In spite of cultural differences between the two regions, there are growing structural similarities in the position of women. Second, there is persistent and marked variation in women's position among Latin American countries with a similar cultural heritage. There is no simple relationship between culture and gender, for cultural attributes appear to have little explanatory power for shifts in gender relations. The cultural valorization of gender equality seems to be the product, rather than the cause, of changes in the structure of gender relations. When gender relations change, culture moves in response.

CULTURAL FRAMES AND THE
SUSTAINABILITY OF WOMEN'S ADVANCEMENT

Although culture cannot be posited as a cause of major change in gender relations, cultural factors nonetheless profoundly affect the character and the durability of advances in women's position. Cultural norms and values provide frames within which changes in gender relations are interpreted and determine how different societies conceive of achieving gender equality. In the United States, progressive changes in women's rights are strongly marked by our values. Laws on the family, divorce, and abortion, for example, reflect an individualist ethos to a much greater extent than laws on the European Continent and in Latin America. Whereas U.S. courts have decided that individual liberty and self-determination are the supreme values to be protected, judges and legislators in continental Europe "are more deeply engaged in an ongoing moral conversation about abortion, divorce, and dependency" and more likely to moderate individual rights with "attention to social context and individual responsibility."[8] The United States has gone further than any other Western country in making marriage freely terminable at the will of either party, in casting the issue of abortion as a matter of individual privacy and self-determination until fetal viability, and in articulating a constitutional right to marital privacy.

Latin America's different cultural heritage has meant that changes in women's rights are less marked by liberal individualism and the principle of non-state intervention than in the United States. On the one hand, this creates hurdles for feminists and liberals aiming to relax existing prohibitions on abortion. Abortion is considered a crime in every Latin American country except Cuba, although the majority of countries permit abortions to be performed to avert a threat to the mother's life or when the pregnancy results from rape. Clandestine abortion is widespread in the region, but campaigns to legalize abortion have not received widespread public support. Clearly, moral and political pressure from the Roman Catholic bishops is a major factor impeding the liberalization of abortion laws. Yet the absence of a cultural and juridical tradition defending the right to privacy and self-determination also makes it difficult to advance the claim that women's interest in controlling their reproductive lives trumps the state's interest in protecting the fetus.

On the other hand, affirmative action to secure women's presence in public decisionmaking is widespread in Latin America, a policy measure that would be virtually unthinkable in the United States. In the 1990s, nine Latin American countries—Argentina, Bolivia, Brazil, Costa Rica, the Dominican Republic, Ecuador, Panama, Peru, and Venezuela—passed national laws establishing quotas for women's participation as candidates in general elections. Quota laws require that 20 to 40 percent of the candidates fielded by political parties be women. After quota laws were enacted, women's presence in Congress increased from 5 to 28 percent in Argentina, from 7 to 12 percent in Bolivia, from 16 to 19 percent in Costa Rica, and from 10 to 16 percent in the Dominican Republic. Latin America's corporatist tradition, inherited from Thomist thought and the social teachings of the papal encyclicals, provides a favorable cultural environment for advancing claims about women's right to representation as a group. Cultural attributes modulate the movement toward gender equality in different societies, prioritizing some issues over others and casting a distinct tone to national debates on women's rights.

THE GAP BETWEEN LAW AND BEHAVIOR

Although changes in aggregate statistics and national law and policy are crucial components of the movement toward gender equality, they do not tell the whole story. The sanctioning of laws by democratically elected representatives attests on one level to a cultural endorsement of gender equality. Rhetorical and symbolic changes in law and policy communicate messages about equality throughout society at large. Still, the contradiction between well-intentioned bureaucratic policy and uneven bureaucratic application and enforcement is a widespread feature of Latin American societies. The problem is not gender specific, since tendencies toward corruption, human rights abuses, tax evasion, and arbitrary law enforcement reduce the efficacy of state institutions in many areas.

The gap between law and behavior is at least as severe when it comes to gender-related laws, and it thwarts the sustainability of recent advances in women's rights. On the one hand, laws long abolished continue to influence behavior, such as the "legitimate defense of honor" used to acquit men who murder their adulterous wives in Brazil. On the other hand, newly adopted laws, such as recent reforms on sexual and domestic violence in most countries of the Latin American region, are not implemented. Narrowing the gap between law and practice requires cultural adjustments as well as deeper changes within legal institutions.

THE "LEGITIMATE DEFENSE OF HONOR" IN BRAZIL

The legitimate defense of honor thesis in Brazil became famous in the late 1980s, when a jury in the southern state of Paraná voted to acquit a man of murder on the grounds that he had acted legitimately to defend his honor when he killed his estranged wife and her lover. The state court of appeals upheld the decision, but the Supremo Tribunal da Justiça, Brazil's highest court for civil and criminal matters, annulled the jury's decision in 1991 and ordered a new trial. When the case was retried in Paraná later that year, another jury acquitted the defendant on the grounds of a legitimate defense of honor. The jury's decision prompted domestic and international outrage, and a special mission of Human Rights Watch was sent to Brazil to investigate the problem of violence against women.

The legitimate defense of honor thesis has no explicit basis in Brazilian law. In the colonial period, the Philippine Ordinances permitted men to kill wives discovered in adulterous acts, as well as their male companions. Later, the criminal code of the Brazilian Empire (adopted in 1830), the penal code of the First Republic (1890), and the current penal code (adopted in 1940) explicitly precluded homicide as a solution for the crime of adultery. Nonetheless, the 1940 code introduced the idea of legitimate defense against unjust aggression putting fundamental rights at risk, and some legal doctrines consider "honor" to be a fundamental good or right. The legal doctrine of legitimate defense and the existence of a tacit basis for the consideration of honor as a legal good gave way to a jurisprudential practice that permits men to murder their adulterous wives and be acquitted.

The law's valorization of honor stems from the importance of reputation in social relations. As a prominent interpretation of the penal code states:

> Good reputation is essential for men, constituting the indispensable base of their position and social effectiveness. Good men only surround themselves with men of good names. If anyone acquires a bad name, friends and acquaintances will desert him, and he will no longer be accepted in good social circles. He will be deprived of the confidence and prestige in which society holds gentlemen. Without a good reputation, moreover, it is impossible to attain or successfully exercise positions of merit, influence, or responsibility, because those with a bad name do not deserve confidence.[9]

A man with an adulterous wife, known in Brazilian slang as a *corno* (someone who wears the horns of a cuckold), stands to lose his good name, social position, and opportunities. The legitimate defense of honor is used by defense lawyers and is accepted by juries because resort to homicide in light of a threat to honor is seen as understandable. Jury behavior reveals that the honor and reputation of men and entire families depends on perceptions of women's morality and sexual behavior. Killing adulterous wives and their partners allows men to restore their honor in the face of society at large.

As early as 1955, higher courts in Brazil began to overturn lower court decisions acquitting murders on the grounds of a legitimate defense of honor. In Brazil's civil law system, however, higher court decisions do not establish a precedent that is formally binding on lower courts. Brazilian appellate courts therefore lack the institutional power to rectify the contradictory jurisprudence that has evolved over the honor defense. Furthermore, trial court judges have not always exercised their prerogative to instruct juries on what theories and defenses are permitted by the law. Instead, they have chosen to defer to the jury's sovereignty, even when the jury's reasoning has no basis in formal law. Use of the honor defense signals a persisting conflict within Brazilian culture over female sexuality and within Brazilian legal institutions over the status of honor and the scope of legitimate defense.

SEXUAL AND DOMESTIC VIOLENCE

In the 1990s, countries all over Latin America reformed their penal codes to reclassify the crime of rape and introduced new legislation aimed to punish and prevent domestic violence. Rape, historically considered a crime against custom, honesty, or decency, was recast as a crime against individual sexual freedom and dignity. Marital rape was penalized, and hundreds of women's police stations were created throughout the region to receive and investigate complaints of violence against women. As mentioned earlier, at least twelve countries adopted laws on domestic or intra-family violence that offer judges and law enforcement officials new competencies to resolve violent situations. These new laws and policies are the catalyst for a cultural shift. Violence against women and family members is increasingly seen as a violation of human rights and therefore as a policy problem, the family no longer being viewed as remaining outside the purview of state power and formal laws. However, the behavior of citizens and law enforcement officers has not kept up with the spirit of the new laws.

In the first place, incidents of sexual violence are severely underreported. Estimates from Mexico and Peru suggest that merely 10 to 20 percent of rape cases are reported to the police. Second, the rate of investigation, prosecution, and sentencing of violent aggressors is disturbingly low. Data from Brazil show that only one-third of violent incidents in the state of São Paulo were followed up with a police investigation, and few investigations actually led to prosecution or conviction. In Mexico, only 15 percent of offenders in one sample of rape cases studied were sentenced. Data from Ecuador show that just 1 percent of the total number of incidents of sexual violence reported to the authorities led to a conviction.[10] The reluctance to investigate and prosecute in cases of sexual violence contrasts sharply with the state's presumption of guilt and overzealous prosecution of suspects in other areas of criminal law.

Low prosecution and sentencing rates of violent aggressors stem from the insensitivity of law enforcement officers to victims of violence, reflecting the widely held sentiment that women victims must have deserved or consented to whatever happened to them. Analysis of court cases shows that judges are more favorable to virgins and frequently blame victims for provoking the rape. Many judges and prosecutors pressure women to reconcile with their partners instead of pressing charges. Rape victims have also complained that medical examiners question them extensively about their sexual history.[11]

On the other hand, victims themselves often fail to cooperate with the investigation or desist from prosecuting the perpetrators of violence. Some victims reconcile with their partners and therefore see no need to continue. Others fall subject to social pressure from friends and family members. In a 1997 case in Peru, a woman victim of a gang rape was pressured by family members into marrying one of her assailants to defend the family honor; charges against the rapist were dropped. (The penal code loophole that exempted rapists who married their victims was removed in April 1997, after domestic and international outcry.)

Although women's police stations were intended to mitigate some of the problems mentioned above, they suffer from a shortage of financial and material resources, lack a standard operating procedure for processing cases or dealing with victims, and are often inconveniently located. Working in women's police stations is also considered to be of low prestige within the police force as a whole. To sum up, the application and enforcement of existing laws represents the greatest challenge faced by women's rights advocates in Latin America.

CONCLUSION

Culture is an essential but insufficient concept for understanding the progress toward and prospects for gender equality in Latin America. Cultural values alone do not explain patterns of change and continuity on gender issues. In spite of long-standing cultural biases against women, women's capabilities and opportunities relative to men have substantially improved over the past few decades in Latin America. Although there is considerable variation among countries, the enactment of egalitarian laws and policies by democratic governments and legislatures reflects a growing cultural commitment to equal opportunity. However, the persistent gap between law and behavior attests to the resilience of discriminatory practices. Cultural changes did not provoke contemporary advances in women's status in Latin America, but cultural change is indispensable for guaranteeing the implementation and sustainability of these advances over the longer term.

What policy strategy points a way out of this dilemma? The exercise of presidential leadership has been an important engine of policy change. In fact, enthusiastic backing by the president and his party was the common denominator for some of the most sweeping changes in law and policy on gender in the 1990s. Presidential commitment also facilitated implementation. Without the executive decrees regulating implementation of Argentina's quota laws, for example, the quota would not have caused women's representation in Congress to rise from 5 to 28 percent. The institutional and normative powers in the hands of the president make the exercise of presidential authority effective for securing gender-related changes, even though the president's ideas about gender are not necessarily shared by everyone. However, by demonstrating a commitment not only to gender-equality rhetoric but also to practice, those at the pinnacle of political power may spearhead the broad transformations necessary to effect more fundamental progress in gender equality throughout Latin America in the twenty-first century.

part five

CULTURE AND
AMERICAN MINORITIES

15

Taking Culture Seriously: A Framework and an Afro-American Illustration

ORLANDO PATTERSON

THE CONTRADICTORY APPROACH TO CULTURE

There is something very odd about how the culture concept is used today. On the one hand, at no other time in the history of the concept has it been more popularly debated or more seriously considered. In academia the relatively new discipline of cultural studies flourishes. And in the American public arena, so-called culture wars have become what Hunter calls "a reality *sui generis* . . . the defining forces of public life."[1] And yet, at the same time, in academic and intellectual circles, including an influential group of professional anthropologists and nearly all sociologists, there is strong resistance to attempts to explain any aspect of human behavior in cultural terms.[2]

In the humanities and liberal circles generally, a rigid orthodoxy now prevails that can be summarized as follows: Culture is a symbolic system to be interpreted, understood, discussed, delineated, respected, and celebrated as the distinctive product of a particular group of people, of equal worth with all other such products. But it should never be used to explain anything about the people who produced it. In humanistic terms, culture is often likened to a text to be read and interpreted. Although explanations of the text are permitted, no claims of objectivity can be made for such explanations. The understanding of culture is wholly subjective and reflects as much about the interpreter as the interpreted.

In sociological circles, culture occupies what Mabel Berezin calls a "fissured terrain" in which there is "epistemological dissidence" between "scholars who privilege the possibility of explanation . . . and those who privilege exegesis or interpretation."[3] But even those who favor explanation tend to shun any causal role for culture. Typically, as in the so-called production-of-culture school, culture is the dependent variable, something to be described and, with all due caution, to be explained by organizational, economic, and other such "hard" independent variables. All attempts to reverse this explanatory equation and make culture or elements of culture the independent variable are inherently suspect. Oddly, this is the very opposite of what prevailed during the first half of this century, when the Parsonian theory of values as ends and normative regulators of action was predominant. However, as Ann Swidler has pointed out, because the general rejection of the Parsonian approach left sociologists "without an alternative formulation of culture's causal significance, scholars either avoid causal questions or admit the values paradigm through the back door."[4] Swidler proposed an approach to the problem that has won wide favor. Although it is a start in the right direction, her conception of culture as a "tool kit" from which people selectively draw their strategies of action as it suits their purposes is too open-ended and voluntaristic to offer real explanatory power. Cultural analysis is reduced to a mere supplement of rational choice theory.

The hostility to cultural explanations is especially marked in the study of Afro-Americans and the many problems that they face. There are good and bad reasons for this. Too many studies of Afro-American problems up to the late sixties—when the reaction set in—relied on a simplistic or untenable conception of culture that was used in a crudely deterministic way to explain Afro-American social problems. Afro-American culture was seen as an encrusted accretion of the Afro-American past that had become a fixed, explanatory black box invoked to explain anything and everything about the group. Outmoded nineteenth-century views of culture as some kind of "cake of custom" lingered in many writings. Hardly more palatable was the over-determining functionalism and values framework of the Parsonian school. Although the more sophisticated advocates of the culture of poverty school such as Oscar Lewis did not commit many of the errors that they are now routinely accused of, in the hands of non-specialists, cultural accounts of the group's problems were too often circular, reductionist, and static.

Unfortunately, it was and is still too often the case that cultural explanations are employed by reactionary analysts and public figures who attribute the social problems of the poor to their "values" and thereby wash their hands and the hands of government and the taxpayers of any responsibility for their alleviation. Indeed, perhaps the main reason why cultural explanations are shunned by anthropologists and sociologists—both very liberal disciplines—is the fact that they have been so avidly embraced by reactionaries or simple-minded public figures. Culture as explanation languishes in intellectual exile partly because of guilt by association.

This last is only the worst of some very bad reasons for the rejection of cultural explanations. Another of these is the liberal mantra, still frequently chanted, that cultural explanations amount to blaming the victim. This is sheer nonsense and a simple analogy reveals its silliness. Consider the all too common case of someone who has low self-esteem and behaves in extremely self-destructive ways as a direct result of having been sexually abused as a child. A sympathetic person might point to the person's psychological problems and urge him or her to seek therapy. It would be absurd to accuse that person of blaming the victim. Yet this is exactly what happens when a sympathetic analyst is condemned for even hinting that some Afro-American problems may be the tragic consequences of their cultural adaptation to an abusive past.

Another bad reason for the censorship of cultural explanations in the study of Afro-Americans is ethnic nationalism and so-called black pride. Ethnic pride, once a necessary corrective to centuries of ethnic dishonor and negative stereotyping, has now hardened into ethnic glorification and Afro-centrism, both given academic legitimacy by multicultural studies. Any scholar who invokes historico-cultural explanations for social problems is seen as an agent who comes to bury and not to praise, a threat to the feel-good insistence on a "usable past" and a proud, non-problematic culture that can hold its place and parade its laurels at the great American multi-cultural powwow.

Yet another reason for the suspicion of cultural explanations is the misunderstanding, especially on the part of policy specialists and others concerned with correcting social ills, that nothing can be done about culture. This misunderstanding springs from the view of culture as something immutable. Closely related to this reason for the rejection of cultural explanations is a conviction held by many that it is a racist view of a group. Behind this charge is a riot of intellectual ironies. The modern anthropological study of culture began as an explicitly anti-racist reaction against the racialism of social Darwinism, especially under the liberal influence of Franz Boas's cultural relativism. For the first half of this century, culture was precisely that which was not biological in human development. Cultural relativism, however, has a way of biting its own tail and descending into essentialism, as I pointed out in my critique of its use during the seventies by both ethnic revivalists in America and defenders of the apartheid regime of South Africa.[5] More recently, the same criticism has been made of the latest wave of ethnic celebration in America, Walter Benn Michaels stating flatly that the modern multi-cultural concept of culture and ethnic identity have simply become substitutes for racism.[6] Although critics of multi-culturalism such as Michaels condemn the multi-cultural use of culture as racist from a universalist standpoint, many multi-culturalists condemn cultural explanations in equally vehement terms as racist, as the long litany of attacks on Senator Daniel Patrick Moynihan and his report make clear. Thus in 1970 the liberal sociologist Robert Blauner labeled those of his colleagues who emphasized the lower class rather than ethnic distinctiveness of Afro-American life as "neo-racists."[7] Incredibly, then, the culture concept has become a term of abuse and has been condemned as racist by both universalists and relativistic multi-culturalists in their quarrels with each other.

A deeper irony in the attack on cultural explanations as racist is the fact that critics of the explanatory role of culture all make one quiet, backdoor exception to the causal use of the concept. The exception is its use in the intellectual war between environmentalists and genetic determinists. In the so-called Bell Curve Wars a few years ago, when the IQ controversy went through its latest cycle in America, Richard Herrnstein and Charles Murray, although losing the war, grievously injured one of the mainstays of the liberal defense of the environmental position, namely, that the persistent single standard deviation difference in IQ scores between Afro-Americans and Euro-Americans is to be explained *primarily* in socioeconomic terms. Herrnstein and Murray drew on the vast body of accumulated evidence to show that this position is no longer tenable. Structural explanations of IQ differences were often vitiated by what Arthur Jensen has called "the sociological fallacy," namely, the fact that the presumably independent structural variables explaining away the IQ effects were themselves partly the effects of subjects' IQs.

I do not intend to rehash the IQ controversy here except to note that when the dust had settled one major point emerged with crystal clarity, and it has both a negative and a positive aspect. The negative aspect is that although genetic factors can explain only a small part of the differences in social and economic outcomes that exist between Afro-Americans and Euro-Americans, neither can standard socioeconomic variables such as family income. This important point, which nearly got lost in the heat of the debate, has been reinforced by more recent findings, especially those reported in a work that is of far greater scientific integrity than *The Bell Curve*, namely, *The Black-White Test Score Gap*, edited by Christopher Jencks and Meredith Phillips. The general conclusion of this group of scholars is that, first, the test-score gap between Afro-Americans and Euro-Americans is indeed important in explaining later occupational status and income, although what it is measuring is not so much innate intelligence as learnable cognitive and educational skills. Second, this test-score gap is only partly explained by the class or social background of students. The still substantial income difference between Afro-Americans and Euro-Americans explains, at best, about one point of the large ethnic gap in students' test scores. And when all socioeconomic background factors are considered, such as wealth and occupation, no more than a third of the ethnic gap is explained, which is about the same as Herrnstein and Murray estimated.[8]

If the answer to the skill gap is to be found neither in the g-loading on IQ scores nor in the socioeconomic differences between the two groups, where is it to be found? Here we come to the positive side of what emerged from the Bell Curve controversy. The answer, in a nutshell, is culture. "Cultural beliefs and practices," writes psychologist Howard Gardner in his critique of the Bell Curve, "affect the child at least from the moment of birth and perhaps sooner. Even the parents' expectations of the unborn child and their reactions to the discovery of the child's sex have an impact. The family, teachers, and other sources of influence in the culture signal what is important to the growing child, and these messages have both short- and long-term impact."[9]

Significantly, Meredith Phillips and her collaborators found large effects on children's test scores resulting from parenting practices, accounting for over 3.5 points of the test gap between Afro-Americans and Euro-Americans. What's more, their controls strongly indicated that these practices were wholly environmental.

Psychological studies bear out these findings. It is remarkable that, barely five years before *The Bell Curve* was published, Arthur Jensen, unquestionably the most sophisticated defender of the genetic view of ethnic differences, had very nearly thrown in the towel with his concession that "the genetic hypothesis will remain untested in any acceptably rigorous manner for some indeterminate length of time, most likely beyond the life span of any present-day scientists."[10] Psychologist Nathan Brody, in an exhaustive review of the state of knowledge on the subject, concluded that the "reasons for the differences are probably to be found in the distinctive cultural experiences encountered by black individuals in the United States."[11] Responding to Herrnstein and Murray, another distinguished psychologist, Richard Nisbett, arrived at much the same conclusion. Arguing that there "are systematic differences in the socialization of black and white children that begin in the cradle," he reviewed several studies, one of which concerned children of mixed marriages:

> Under the assumption that mothers are more important than fathers to the intellectual socialization of their children and that socialization practices of whites favor the adoption of skills that result in high scores on IQ tests, one would expect that the children of unions where the mother is white and the father is black would have higher IQs than the children of unions where the mother is black and the father is white. And in fact, this is the case. Children of black-white unions have IQs nine points higher if it is the mother who is white.[12]

Although selection factors could not be discounted, they seemed to work in both directions and cancel themselves out. Nisbett quite reasonably concluded that "the higher IQs of the children born to white mothers would have to be attributed largely to socialization."[13]

There is a profound irony in the uses and responses to the kind of findings just cited. When used in the IQ debate to defend the liberal, environmental position they are acceptable, even eagerly embraced. But in any other context the use of these same findings would be viewed with outrage. Why? Because findings like these are anathema to notions of ethnic pride, identity politics, and the prevailing relativism of liberal academic circles. In any other context statements by Phillips and her collaborators that for "parents who want their children to do well on tests (which means almost all parents), middle-class parenting practices seem to work" or that "racial differences in parenting practices also appear to be important," as well as Nisbett's argument that the cultural practices of Euro-American mothers are more effective than those of Afro-American mothers, would condemn them as certifiable racists and unregenerate cultural chauvinists on any campus in America.

This is a ridiculous state of affairs. Afro-Americans and their academic supporters simply cannot have it both ways. If cultural factors are to be given prime explanatory status in the IQ wars, they cannot be reduced by multicultural and liberal sociological critics to what Margaret Archer has called "a position of supine dependence."[14] This selective censorship of the causal use of the culture concept has distorted the study of Afro-American social history and contemporary issues.

The plain truth, of course, is that there is no necessary conflict between the causal use of culture and its treatment in purely descriptive or dependent terms. Usually the conflicts can be resolved once it is understood that different conceptions of culture are being used and that causal studies often proceed at quite different levels of analysis from those that approach it in symbolist or descriptive terms. Furthermore, a cultural explanation does not preclude social causes. Often what's most interesting and useful in any analysis is to identify and disentangle the complex explanatory interplay between cultural and non-cultural factors, an interplay in which both sets of factors can be both independent and dependent in one's causal model. Above all, it should be understood that to explain is not to be deterministic. As Goodenough wisely points out, "Biology helps explain human behavior but does not determine it. Similarly, culture helps explain behavior but does not determine it, either."[15]

THE CULTURE CONCEPT

By culture I mean a repertoire of socially transmitted and intra-generationally generated ideas about how to live and make judgments, both in general terms and in regard to specific domains of life. It is an information system with varying levels of specificity: on one level it is as broad as a set of ideas about styles of public self-presentation; on another level, it is the micro-information system prescribing the best way to make bagels, curried chickpeas, or Jamaican jerk pork. This information system is more than "what people must learn in order to be able to function acceptably as members of a social group in the activities in which members of the group engage with one another,"[16] as Goodenough originally phrased it in a seminal statement. For one thing, as Eugene Hunn has pointed out, the "culture concept must address not only what is formally appropriate, but also what is ecologically effective." Hence, "culture is what one must know to act effectively in one's environment."[17] For another, culture sometimes embraces transmitted antisocial behavior and not only what is acceptable to a group.[18] This point is of special importance to those who study the Afro-American experience, since often the cultural processes one wishes to understand are precisely those that are deviant and not acceptable to either the broader Euro-American society or to the Afro-American group. We cannot restrict the cultural exclusively to what is normative.

I take the very sensible advice of Roger Keesing that it is best "to narrow the concept of 'culture' so that it includes less and reveals more."[19] Thus Roy D'Andrade speaks of a "particulate theory of culture; that is, a theory about the 'pieces' of culture, their composition and relation to other things."[20]

Culture is acquired or learned by individuals; it is what they know. This, however, does not preclude a collective or shared dimension of culture. How can an individualist, internal view of culture be reconciled with any notion of culture as a shared group phenomenon? Through the notion of cultural models, which, as Keesing argues, "are at once cultural and public, as the historically cumulated knowledge of a people and the embodiments of a language, *and* cognitive, as paradigms for construing the world."[21]

These models, however, are not mere tool kits, as sociologist Ann Swidler argued in her frequently cited paper.[22] Although this view is valuable for sociologists in emphasizing the role of agency in cultural analysis, it nonetheless fails to capture two other critical aspects of culture. A tool kit is useless if there is nothing to make or do. Cultural elements are always, first, plans for living, blueprints for how to think, judge, and do things. A tool kit is also useless without the know-how or skill to use the tools. Cultural models are also rules for how to realize cultural plans.

There is some controversy about where these rules come from. It is likely that the same capacity for rule making that directs our acquisition of language also works with the acquisition of some cultural models, especially models of social behavior. Although some rules are inferred by one's innate rule-making capacity, others are taught, and some are derived from a combination of both methods.

Dorothy Holland and Naomi Quinn argue against any typology of cultural models into "models of" and "models for," as some have proposed, suggesting instead that

> underlying cultural models of the same order—and in some cases the same underlying model—are used to perform a variety of different cognitive tasks. Sometimes these cultural models serve to set goals for action, sometimes to plan the attainment of said goals, sometimes to direct the actualization of these goals, sometimes to make sense of the actions and fathom the goals of others, and sometimes to produce verbalizations that may play various parts in all these projects as well as in the subsequent interpretation of what has happened.[23]

In other words, cultural models are the sociological counterparts of biological stem cells.

How are these models acquired? In two ways. They are inherited from the preceding generation through socialization, and they are learned intra-generationally from peers and significant others through imitation and teaching, as well as indirectly from agents such as the media or popular figures. I agree with Robert Boyd and Peter Richerson that social learning is "the transmission of stable behavioral dispositions" and that stable means those "that are substantially divorced from environmental contingencies."[24] Although I will be drawing on the cultural theory of Boyd and Richerson in what follows, I differ from them by including within the cultural domain models of behavior that are learned through trial and error by individuals in their responses to interactions with others and other environmental or structural forces.

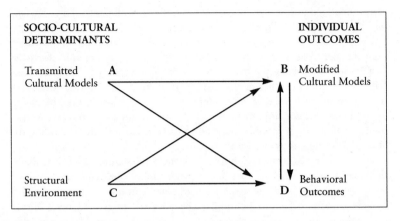

FIGURE 15.1   Interactions Among Cultural Models, the Structural Environment, and Behavioral Outcomes

Two further features of culture should be noted at this point. First, cultural models are not to be confused with behavior. Boyd and Richerson note that "two individuals with identical sets of culturally acquired dispositions may behave quite differently in different environments."[25] Second, culture changes and the forces that account for variations and instability are as important in any theory of culture as the forces leading to the transmission of stable models.

THE INTERACTIONAL APPROACH TO
CULTURE AND THE STRUCTURAL ENVIRONMENT:
AN AFRO-AMERICAN ILLUSTRATION

Let me illustrate the relationship between culture and social structure with an example from the Afro-American experience. Cultural models and structural or environmental factors have cultural and behavioral outcomes for individuals, yielding a causal matrix consisting of (A) cultural models inherited from the previous generation; (B) modified cultural models that are the outcome of changes in the inherited models due to transmission errors in teaching and imitation, as well as adjustments to new strategies of coping with the environment learned by trial and error; (C) the current set of environmental, especially structural, contingencies; and (D) the behavioral outcomes that we wish to explain. Figure 15.1 diagrams these causal interactions.

Let the problem to be explained (D) be the present high rate of paternal abandonment of children among Afro-Americans. This rate currently stands at 60 percent of all Afro-American children. It is the single greatest problem of the group, as well as the source of other major problems. What are the causal interactions accounting for this behavioral problem?

The present generation has inherited a cultural model (A) that originated in one earlier environment, slavery (c. 1640–1865), and was later adapted to, and transmitted through, a second environment, the sharecropping, or lien-crop, system (c. 1880–1940). The Africans imported as slaves would have brought with them well-defined models of kinship, gender roles, and notions of sexuality and paternity. Most of these models were devastated by the new order; in particular, the role of father and husband had no legitimacy or authority. Men had no custodial claims in their wives or children. However, the West African model of high fertility and the view that a man's masculinity and status were enhanced by the number of his children dovetailed with the demands of the slave system. A major preoccupation of the system was the need for a growing slave population, especially after the slave trade was abolished in 1807. Hence planters encouraged stable reproductive units. The result was a behavioral pattern in which two-thirds of all unions consisted of a man and a woman and their children and a third in which unattached women reared their children with the help of kinsmen.[26]

In *Rituals of Blood* I argued that to call the unions between slave men and women "marriages" and the households they fostered "stable nuclear families" is a sociological travesty. The revisionist scholarly focus on the structural form of slave unions has diverted attention from their functioning, from the nature of the relationships that constituted these unions and from the cultural models associated with them. Most men did not live regularly with their partners. Half of those in stable unions lived on other plantations and a third who had children had no such stable unions. Hence, even on the basis of the revisionist historians' own figures, at least two-thirds of adult men who had children did not live in the same residence and often did not even live on the same farm with their partners and progeny. In addition, there was on every estate a group of unattached men without children who constituted between 10 and 15 percent of all men and whose sexual needs had to be met somehow. Thus the great majority of men during slavery—at least three-quarters of them—lived most of their lives away from stable households with children, including a good number of those in so-called stable unions. Furthermore, whatever the nature of their unions, slaves rarely had time to interact with their children. The whole point of slavery was that slaves were worked like, well, slaves.

After two and a half centuries several cultural models emerged in response to this system. One was a model of compensatory sexuality. Denied any claims to status in the broader society or any legitimate claims to their partners or children, men reinforced the transmitted West African model of virility and high fertility as symbols of male pride and status. Closely related to this was the model of unsecured paternity. This was not African. Rather, it was a direct adaptation to the slave system. The master assumed the responsibility to provide for the slave's children and encouraged adults to have as many as possible. Some may even have engaged in deliberate breeding.[27] Because they wanted to own the product of their male slaves' sexuality, masters encouraged their male slaves to mate with slaves on their own plantations. Such unions also greatly reduced the cost of labor control, since slaves in such stable reproductive unions were less likely to run away. Even so, as noted earlier, only half of the regular unions of slaves were with partners on the same plantations.

Other models developed that complemented these two. One was the model of matrifocality, which highly valorized the mother–child relationship and exalted it over the father–child bond. Another was the model of female independence—a transmitted model that was reinforced and modified by the slave environment. Traditional West African societies were unusual for the level of economic participation and relative independence of women. This transmitted model was strongly reinforced by the economic gender neutrality of the slave system with regard to slaves. Women worked equally with men in the fields. The demand for more slaves highlighted their childbearing capacity. Although owners encouraged both sexes to reproduce, legal ownership of slave progeny was determined by the mother. Indeed, some owners strongly favored female familial ties, carefully preserving sororal, mother–daughter, and other matrifocal ties while ruthlessly selling off sons and brothers.[28]

Finally, there was the simple, brute fact that slave men lacked the one thing that all other men primarily relied on for their domination of women: control of property.

These women-related models greatly reinforced the two male models under study: compensatory sexuality and unsecured or resourceless paternity. Yet slaves also learned many other cultural models during slavery. American slaves were, of necessity, strongly influenced by the cultural models of their Euro-American owners. They adopted and modified their owners' language, religion, music (i.e., aspects of their music), and, naturally, their gender, marital, and familial models. Although some of these models, such as the stable patriarchal ideal of legitimate marriages and families in which the husband-father was the main provider, were beyond reach (and, as such, internalized mainly as ideals), others, such as the sexual double standard and predatory sexuality of many Euro-American Southern men would have been all too reinforcive of the emerging models of compensatory sexuality among the male slaves.

The sharecropping system that followed slavery included two features of special note. First, although the legal ownership of one person by another was abolished in 1865, the culture of slavery clearly was not. Indeed, if anything, it was powerfully reinforced after the end of reconstruction and maintained the public denial of Afro-American male honor and masculinity. The classic Southern method of achieving this was, of course, communal lynching which, as I have shown elsewhere, was a ritualized ceremony of human sacrifice culminating in the symbolic and literal castration of the Afro-American male.

The second important feature of the sharecropping system was the fact that although Afro-American men were denied most forms of meaningful employment as well as ownership of land, they nonetheless had access to whatever land they could farm as long as they agreed to the lien crop arrangement. This had several devastating consequences, which have been summarized by Tolnay:

> The personal "sacrifice" of delayed and slowed family formation often associated with establishment of households in agricultural economies was not only unnecessary for rural blacks but was also largely futile. Alternative economic opportunities were also restricted because of the relative unavailability of nonagricultural employment opportunities for blacks and the generally hostile racial atmosphere after the Civil War.[29]

These new features of the environment strongly encouraged a pattern of early marriage and high fertility. The only way a man could make his way was by applying as much labor as he could to the available land at his disposal, and the only way he could get this labor was from his wife and children. Thus slavery was followed by a behavioral tendency toward marriage and large families among the mass of poor Afro-Americans. Among the small middle class, as well as the not much larger urban working class, men and women were at last able to realize the dominant cultural ideal of marriage and respectable, patriarchal unions after slavery and did so, reinforced by their fundamentalist faith. But our concern here is with developments among the mass of rural sharecroppers.

What was going on among the mass of poor sharecroppers beneath their formal early marriages and large families? Tragically, this system reinforced the two male models that had evolved during slavery. First, it reinforced the model of unsecured paternity. Men did not have to take account of resources before having children. Land and other means of production were readily available. What they needed were hands—those of a good, strong woman and as many children as possible. Tragically, children ended up supporting their fathers rather than the other way around (households were best off during those periods when children were most exploited) and were frequently prevented from acquiring even a rudimentary education in order to serve this purpose.

Second, the nefarious targeting of Afro-American manhood by the dominant Euro-American community led to an even greater need for masculine compensation on the part of the mass of poor Afro-American males. Denied all opportunities to prove their worth in the broader society, confined to a semi-serf condition, mocked in blackface and the popular culture of minstrelsy in the northern half of the country, and brutalized into submission in public acts of humiliation and ritual castration in their own part of the country, poor Afro-American men could express their manhood in only one way: through their virility and control of their own women. The women they tried to control, however, were no pushovers. Two and a half centuries under the gender-neutral rack of slavery had seen to that. They deeply resented this compensatory behavior, especially when it took the form of marital infidelity. Unfortunately, most of them had little choice but to remain in their marriages on the tenant farm, since opportunities were as blocked for them as they were for the men. Instead they sought support and solace from their kinswomen. Within this context, according to Anita Washington, "the strong bonds that have been noted to exist between Black mothers and their children, the great value Black women have been noted to place on their roles as mothers, and the priority of this over their roles as wives and workers, are easily understood."[30]

Here, then, beneath the surface calm of two-parent units documented in the censuses, and the sole focus of revisionist historians, further incubated the tragic conflict between Afro-American men and women and the male cultural models engendered during slavery that were to be transmitted, via the great northern migration, to the present period of the central cities.

To this period we now turn.

Point C in the diagram indicates the largely structural explanation of behavior emphasized by social scientists. Unemployment, low income, and the neighborhood effects of segregated habitats, as well as ethnic and gender discrimination in employment, are the most obvious examples. Included also are government programs aimed at helping the poor: AFDC, earned income tax credit, and the like. Another important feature of this environment that is of special interest to Afro-Americans is the importance of the sports industry and the opportunities it offers to a few but enormously important athletic stars. These conditions, although important in any final explanation, can directly account for only a small part of D.

Many have argued that poor economic prospects for young, urban Afro-American men account for both their low marriage rate and the higher rate of out-of-wedlock births;[31] others have pointed to women's employment status in relation to that of their partners.[32] It may be true, as Katherine Newman recently observed, that men "who lack the wherewithal to be good fathers, often aren't."[33] But the fact remains that in nearly all other ethnic groups in America, including Mexican Americans with higher levels of poverty than Afro-Americans, and in nearly all other known human societies, including India with its vast hordes of people in grinding urban poverty and unemployment, poverty does not lead to the large-scale paternal abandonment of children. In fact, the best available data show little correlation between job availability and the marriage rate.[34] Economist George Akerlof recently argued that marriage explains men's labor force activity, along with a good many other social outcomes. Married men "have higher wages, are more likely to be in the labor force, less likely to be unemployed because they had quit their job, have lower unemployment rates, are more likely to be full-time, and are less likely to be part-year workers."[35] Akerlof thinks that changing social factors (by which he means mainly what we are calling cultural models) explain the sharp decline in the marriage rate over recent decades, a decline that in his estimation explains a good part of the increase in crime and other social problems. However, he makes no attempt to account for these cultural changes. His dismissal of economic variables may also be premature. An interactional model of the kind proposed here is better able to explain how cultural patterns interact with structural ones to produce undesirable outcomes.

The transmitted cultural model (AD) is one possible answer. It is certainly possible that a small minority of poor Afro-American men are simply actualizing the models of paternity they learned from the preceding generation. However, I consider such direct effects to be as secondary as direct structural ones. First, recall that models are not the same as behavior. Most Afro-American men exposed to these models have, in fact, adopted others and behave differently. I cannot too strongly overemphasize the following point: *The fact that 60 percent of Afro-American children are fatherless does not mean that anything near this percentage of Afro-American fathers have abandoned their children. Indeed, the great majority of Afro-American fathers behave responsibly toward their children and operate with mainstream models of paternity. Rather, a minority of usually poor men with limited education exhibit this behavior. But because of their higher rates of fertility, they end up creating a problem of fatherlessness for the majority of the younger genera-*

tion of the entire group. It is as great an error to underestimate the group-wide consequences of the reproductive behavior of this minority of men as it is to generalize about Afro-American fathers on the basis of the models and behavior of this minority.

Instead, the major explanations of the behavioral outcome D are the indirect paths CBD and ABD, as well as the more complex causal spirals such as CDBD.

Consider, first, the path CBD. Lee Rainwater gave us an early (and still the best) analysis of this path.[36] Lower-class culture, he argued, "represent[s] adaptations to [the] demands society makes for average functioning and the resources they are able to command in their own day-to-day lives."[37] While holding to mainstream norms, lower-class men and women develop "survival techniques for functioning in the world of the disinherited: Over time, these survival techniques take on the character of substitute games, with their own rules guiding behavior. But . . . these operating rules seldom sustain a lasting challenge to the validity of the larger society's norms governing interpersonal relations and the basic social statuses involved in marriage, parent-child relations, and the like."[38] Instead, "lower class sub-culture acquires limited *functional autonomy* from conventional culture just as the social life of the lower class has a kind of limited functional autonomy vis-a-vis the rest of society." Tragically, it is precisely the disjuncture between the persistent commitment to mainstream cultural models of paternal behavior, especially on the part of women, that leads to the behavioral outcome of marital dissolution and paternal abandonment. Men are only too happy to live with women who put up with their philandering. Afro-American lower-class women, to their great credit, refuse to do so, preferring single mothering than compromising their deeply held models of proper (essentially mainstream) marital and paternal behavior. An important dimension of CB is the fact that the modern urban environment, for the first time, offers relatively better economic opportunities for women as well as welfare support from the state. Unlike wives of the sharecropping era, then, they are not forced to put up with male cultural models and behaviors that offend their own cultural models and sense of independence. Hence CBD.

Note that this interpretation has the great merit of taking account of women's cultural models and socioeconomic condition, as well as men's models and behavior, instead of simplistically considering only male circumstances (CD) in accounting for D.

The path AB refers to the modification of the inherited models under the environmental pressure of C and in response to the adaptive strategies just discussed. We see now that both the models of unsecured paternity and compensatory sexuality are once again reinforced by the new set of structural contingencies. Both models are now fused into a new model, which sometimes has a misogynistic edge. Lower-class men, with their low educational attainment and unrealistically high reservation wages, are now irrelevant to the post-industrial society that has emerged. Worse, a new post-1965 influx of low-skilled immigrants have entered the system and in many of the large cities are favored by employers.[39] Black pride and aspirations have led to higher levels of alienation. The inherited model of compensatory sexuality acquires even greater urgency. The fact that women now have the means to resist, somewhat, simply heightens the satisfaction of sexual victory. Male pride is defined now more than ever in terms of the impregnation of women. The majority of Rainwater's respondents "indicated that boys either do not care and are indifferent to the fact that their girlfriends are pregnant, or with surprising frequency, they feel proud because making a girl pregnant shows that you are a man!"[40] A quarter of a century after this research was conducted in the mid-sixties, Elijah Anderson and others found identical cultural models, suggesting a system of cultural transmission.[41]

Another new feature of the environment, C, bears directly on the modification and intensification of these two inherited models. This is the elimination of the color bar in the sports industry, leading in turn to the rise of a significant number of young Afro-American super-star athletes, most coming from the ghettos. Although the actual numbers of these multi-millionaire stars are infinitesimally small in comparison with the mass of lower-class blacks, their influence is vast. As role models, however, they have reinforced both the cultural model of predatory sexuality and unsecured paternity. These developments are associated with another, largely cultural, phenomenon: the rise of hip-hop culture which, as with athletics, has seen the emergence of many super-stars from the ghettos. This culture has blatantly promoted the most oppositional models of urban lower-class life, celebrating in "gangsta-rap," as never before, predatory sexuality and irresponsible paternity. It is reasonable to conclude that among a large number of urban, Afro-American lower-class young men, these models are now fully normative and that men act in accordance with them whenever they can.

Thus we have A and C leading to intra-generational and inter-generational variants of B, both variants leading to a fused modified model of sexuality and paternity among young men, expressed in D, which, in turn, encourages attitudes toward mainstream society and work (DB) and a ghetto lifestyle that reinforces the modified models of compensatory-cum-predatory sexuality and unsecured paternity. In this context of opposition to mainstream norms, the likelihood of the modified sexual and paternal models being actualized in D is even greater.

CONCLUSION

My main objective in this chapter has been to bring the concept of culture as a causal factor back to the study of Afro-American problems without falling prey to the methodological, theoretical, and ideological problems of many previous works. I have argued that this task is now of paramount importance, since the best that sociology has to offer has taken us to the limits of purely structural explanations of these problems.

I briefly noted near the beginning that many sociologists are reluctant to take the causal role of culture seriously because of the persistence among them of the hoary old fallacy of cultural inertia. As I have emphasized in this chapter, however, although cultural continuities certainly exist, people are not slaves to them. They use them and they can change them if they really want to.

It is often the case that cultural models can be changed faster and more effectively than structural factors, and to point to their causal role is in no way to condemn oneself to the status quo. Indeed, the sociological critique becomes ironic when it is considered that the discipline's favorite explanation for most matters is class. But what could be more immutable than class?

Consider the fate of one important area of American culture and its class system over the second half of the twentieth century. During that time, the entire culture of Jim Crow—the system of legalized and culturally sanctioned overt social, economic, and political segregation and discrimination, built up during the previous three and a half centuries—was effectively abolished. During that period too there were fundamental changes in the cultural models of gender that had been built up over the previous millennia of human history.

But during that same period, American economic inequality—the class variable so beloved by sociologists as something always ripe for change—has grown greater than at any other time in the nation's history.

Has the time not come for us to start talking about the cake of class?

16

Disaggregating Culture

NATHAN GLAZER

The relationship between culture and the social and economic trajectories of the various minority, racial, and ethnic groups in the United States is embedded in a larger discussion of the role of culture in the fate of nations. The context has been set by such provocative theses on the causes of international conflict and the wealth of nations as those of Samuel Huntington, David Landes, Lawrence Harrison, and Francis Fukuyama, and by the extended debate on Asian values. In that larger discussion, we deal with categories rather grander than American ethnic groups, which for the most part begin their lives in America as fragments of much larger societies, nations, and civilizations and are soon enveloped through processes of acculturation and assimilation into the larger American society. In time, for most of these groups, the boundaries that once defined them fade through intermarriage, conversion, and changing identities. It becomes doubtful just what, if any, elements of cultural distinctiveness they retain, and they become part of a larger American society and civilization.

In the larger discussion that frames this chapter, we deal with world religions, world philosophies, world cultures, of continental scale, as well as with nations and societies. We consider the causes of international conflict, of national wealth and poverty. In the smaller discussion, we deal with less grand issues, such as the relative educational and economic success of various ethnic groups. In most cases, their histories cannot easily be followed beyond two or three generations in America.

What do the successes or failures of American ethnic and racial groups have to do with such large categories as world civilizations, world religions, and world cultures? What is the link between the large discussion and the small one? Whatever may explain the fate of nations and continents, can it help us understand the fate of American ethnic groups?

For example, what is the connection between a common fact that can be observed among American ethnic groups, such as their concentration in certain economic niches, and the larger civilizations from which they have come as immigrants? In New York City the newsstand business is the province of Asian Indians, and in California the doughnut shop has been colonized by Cambodians. Is there any connection between that Indian occupational concentration in New York and Hindu civilization? (We could also refer to other occupational concentrations of Indians, such as medicine and science, that might make the question less ridiculous.) Is there any connection between Khmer civilization and the Cambodian concentration in doughnut shops? Whatever we have in mind when we think of Khmer civilization—whether Angkor or the very different conditions of today—at initial glance it is clearly a far-fetched notion.

The shift in scale from Hindu civilization, with its three-thousand-year history, the billion people presently shaped in some respect by it, and its influence over great stretches of Asia, to the economic, social, and political characteristics of a million Indian immigrants in the United States, is mind-boggling. It leads us to realize that whatever we mean by culture or civilization in the large, we will have to have rather different things in mind when we consider its role in the fate of India and its role in the economic progress of American Asian Indians. My discussion in this chapter is shaped by the contrast between these two scales, and it tries to examine more closely what we might mean when we use the category "culture" as an explanation.

"CULTURE" IN THE TWENTIETH CENTURY

I begin with some preliminary remarks on the shifting status of culture as an explanation over the last century. We all realize that before we resort to culture today to explain the differences in economic progress or political attitudes among nations and ethnic groups, we prefer to find other explanations. Culture is one of the less-favored explanatory categories in current thinking. The least favored, of course, is race—genetic characteristics—which played such a large role over much of the first half of the century, with such evil consequences, and which still occasionally make an appearance. We prefer not to refer to or make use of it today, yet there does seem to be a link between race and culture, perhaps only accidental. The great races on the whole are marked by different cultures, and this connection between culture and race is one reason for our discomfort with cultural explanations.

There was a time when culture seemed a much more benign form of explanation of difference than race. Consider Ruth Benedict's *Patterns of Culture*, a highly respected work of the 1930s, read widely in American college classes in the 1950s and 1960s because it explained group difference in non-genetic, non-racial terms. Racial explanations have always been conservative or worse than conservative. They don't seem to allow for change. Progressive anthropologists resisted and attacked race as a category in social explanation. Cultural explanations, in contrast, seemed liberal, optimistic. One could not change one's race but one could change one's culture.

Culture as an explanatory variable is no longer considered so benign. First, as I pointed out, there is the inevitable link, not in logic but in fact, between race and culture. Second, it seems invidious to use culture to explain why a group or nation has not prospered. Since we all accept economic advancement as desirable, there must be something undesirable about a culture that hampers economic advance. It is true that some trends in contemporary thinking (e.g., those critical of the environmental consequences of economic development or of the cultural effects of globalization) may today look with favor on the cultures that hobble economic advance. For the most part, however, thinking runs the other way. Geographic interpretations are, I think, becoming more popular. Without having to resort to race or culture, they might, for example, explain the backwardness of Africa, where the few good natural harbors on its coastline limited trade and interchange, as compared to Greece or Europe.

On the political left, explanations based on differences in power and degree of exploitation are favored to explain differences among nations and continents, as well as differences among American ethnic and racial groups. Among radicals, and liberals too, cultural explanations are looked at suspiciously. They seem to "blame the victim."

Cultural explanations have thus lost the liberal and progressive aura they possessed in the days of Franz Boas, Ruth Benedict, and Margaret Mead. Then, race was unchangeable but culture was not. Today, we find culture almost as resistant to change as race. If we resort to world religions and civilizations whose origins we have to trace back two or three millennia to explain the nature of distinctive cultures, what hope do we have of really changing their basic characteristics? And on the smaller scale of American ethnic groups, if we resort to cultural explanations, what hope do we have for the progress of the backward groups?

Culture seems to us these days almost as resistant to change as race. The progressive anthropologists saw culture as changeable; today we are inhibited in thinking of culture this way. One reason is that we are chary of intervening in a culture to change its characteristics, assuming we knew how. At a time when we think of all cultures as worthy of equal respect, what justification would we have to intervene—whether that intervention is public or private—and change a cultural feature that we think limits economic development? What is our mandate for intervention? In addition, we are not very sure about how to intervene to change culture, or about what aspects of the culture of a group need changing. Culture is such a spongy concept covering so much—the original anthropological definition covered literally everything that distinguished a group, aside from its genetic inheritance—that we would be at a loss to know what in culture holds up economic progress. Is it family, religion, attitudes toward work, toward education? Furthermore, under each of these categories, we can find subcategories some think important to success.

This does not mean that social scientists should not use culture for understanding. But they should know they are engaged in a dangerous enterprise. To resort to culture as an explanatory variable raises political problems almost as serious as the resort to race. Before we get to these, however, we first have to consider the question of how we can use culture as an explanatory variable.

CULTURE AS AN ANALYTICAL TOOL

In shifting from the grand scale of continents, world religions, and nations to American ethnic groups, we need to make two major modulations. When we have gone through them, we may be left with very little to explain by way of culture, if we conceive it as culture in the large.

The First Modulation

Ethnic and racial groups in the United States are not randomly drawn from the large populations that bear or are characterized by a culture. The million Chinese in the United States do not represent a China a thousand times larger; and similarly with the million Asian Indians in the United States. This is the case with every ethnic or racial group in the United States, even if their descendants outnumber the inhabitants of the nation from which they came, as is true for the Irish and perhaps for some other groups as well. The visitor to Ireland who knows the Irish of Boston is immediately struck by some surprising differences. Is this owing to the regions or classes of Ireland from which American immigrants were drawn or to the effects of American civilization or culture affecting Irish immigrants and their descendants?

Immigrants come from distinctive areas, classes, subgroups in each society, often from areas and subgroups with a tradition of emigration. Emigration then sustains itself from these subareas socially and geographically through family connection and a chain of useful knowledge communicated from relatives and friends in the country of immigration to the potential emigrants. The immigrants who form an ethnic community in an immigrant nation sometimes come from surprisingly small areas of the country whose name identifies them. This seems to be true, for example, for the Bangladeshis in Britain. Immigrants may be drawn from segments of the elites of a society, as is the case with Asian Indian immigrants, or they may represent the enterprising and trading classes, as is the case with Lebanese and Syrians. They may on the contrary be drawn from humble and hardworking peasants, as is the case with the early Chinese, Japanese, and Sikh immigrants to this country. It is more likely that they represent the humble, even if the more enterprising humble, than the elites.

In what way then do they bear or represent their "cultures"? Of course they have cultures—everyone does. But if we are talking about culture in the large, what does Confucianism or Buddhism or Taoism tell us about Chinese emigrants, who come from the southern coastlands, were peasants, and did not speak Mandarin? What does Italy in the large tell us about the typical Italian immigrant, poor, from the south, uneducated? Are we to take him as an example of the culture and civilization of Catholic Europe, of the Mediterranean, of peasant life, all of which and more may be considered to mark him? From the point of view of explanation, all these categories are too large and diffuse. Catholic Europe has been contrasted with Protestant Europe by Max Weber and other analysts of the effort to explain economic development, but one wonders what connection there is between the Catholicism of Italy and the Catholicism of Ireland, the countries from which two of the largest immigrant Catholic groups in the United States come, and whether their common Catholicism will explain much about them.

My point about this first modulation is that culture in the large must be disaggregated to the very specific variants that characterize American immigrants, who came from distinct provinces, classes, and subgroups of the large culture. In the 1950s Robert Redfield and Milton Singer, anthropologists at the University of Chicago, developed the notion that in culture we deal with both a great tradition and the little traditions. The great tradition refers to the canonical texts, the ceremonies, the priesthood, and the great historical tradition, which may all mean very little to the people of the village, with their "little traditions," or to the burgeoning urban population. Parts of the great tradition do get transmitted, but in modified or distorted terms, mixing at the village level with autochthonous traditions that may have little to do with the great tradition and at the urban level with the universal culture of the mass media. When the people of the village or the people of the growing towns emigrate to the United States, we may indiscriminately label them representatives of the great tradition with little warrant. I think that if we went back to those studies and analyses, we would find much food for thought on the relationship between culture and the varying fates of immigrant groups in the United States. One thing that we would learn is that whatever the characteristics of the great tradition, it may have little bearing on the little traditions.

Another key point that would be brought home to us is that it was rare that the elite bearers of the great tradition were among the immigrants. The experience of Jewish immigrants is not untypical. In each wave of immigration, from the earliest Sephardic of the seventeenth century to the German of the nineteenth century to the East European of the late nineteenth century, there were few men of learning, few rabbis, few carriers of the great tradition that is the tradition we have in mind when we think of Jewish religion and culture, the tradition of classic texts and roles. I have therefore always felt it odd to find that the disproportionate Jewish achievement in higher education, which leads to the disproportionate role in science, scholarship, and the learned professions that has been so evident for the last half century, is attributed to the Jewish tradition of scholarship. That scholarship is a far cry from the contemporary learning and education in which Jews excel. Indeed, the Jewish "great traditions" looked on almost all contemporary learning with suspicion and distaste. Further, few practitioners of traditional Jewish learning came with the immigrants. In time, it is true, such adepts in the traditional high culture came, but I wonder what they, and their efforts to establish traditional rabbinic and talmudic learning in the United States, in which they succeeded, had to do with Jewish achievement in theoretical physics, law, medicine, and a host of other areas based on higher education.

I am perhaps particularly attuned to see the problems in this direct leap to Jewish tradition to explain Jewish achievement in science and scholarship because I am aware that persons of my generation who went on to substantial achievement came from families, as mine, in which parents had never attended a formal Western school and had little if any classic Jewish traditional education. Some of these parents were indeed illiterate, and many were not literate beyond the ability to read the prayer book. Some subtle moves are required to use their great tradition to explain the striking role of the children of East European immigrants in higher education in the early twentieth century.

There are thus many slips and gaps along the way in moving from a great tradition (which we can describe through its major canonic texts, its commentaries, its ceremonies, its history) to those who may practice various versions of it—little traditions, perhaps only distantly related. How much does the great tradition explain in the fate of those so distantly related to it?

I have been intrigued by a skeptical comment of the Singapore economist John Wong on the possible role of Confucianism in Asian and Singapore economic success. (There are not many such skeptical comments, which makes this one all the more interesting.) Wong writes that economists will not take the Confucian explanation seriously until

> it is expressed in a testable hypothesis. It is not enough to argue in general terms that the Confucian ethos is conducive to increased personal savings and hence higher capital formation. It must also be demonstrated forcefully and specifically whether such savings have been productively invested in business or industry or have been squandered in non-economic spending, such as the fulfillment of personal obligations, which is after all also a part of the Confucian value system. It must also be shown how Confucian values have actually resulted in effective manpower development in terms of promoting the upgrading of skills and not in encouraging merely intellectual self-cultivation or self-serving literary pursuits. A typical Confucian gentleman in the past would have shown open disdain for menial labor.[1]

What Wong is asking skeptically is whether we really can perform the exercise of moving from the great tradition of Confucianism to the success of those societies or, we may add, the success of ethnic groups that we can connect to it. I have asked the same question about the connection between the great tradition of Jewish learning and the disproportionate success of Jews in contemporary science, learning, and the high professions. It is too easy to leap from the great tradition to the current groups and individuals that can claim a historical connection. One may see among the current descendants of the great tradition little of its authentic reality.

And it is not only John Wong who is skeptical of the usefulness of the Confucian tradition or culture for economic development. Sun Yat-sen and other reformers and revolutionaries were not only skeptical about the value of Confucian traditions but decried them for playing a major role in keeping China backward and denounced Chinese traditional culture for holding back China's economic and political development. Were they wrong? Did Confucianism change, so that in one period it restrained China's modern development and in another facilitated it? Are we not engaged in an after-the-fact explanation, whether for the Chinese or the Jews? How much has Confucianism to do with the educational and economic success of Chinese people in America?

Of course, despite the attention given to the great traditions, the great religions, and the Protestant ethic and its equivalents around the world, we may be able to give a perfectly good explanation and defense of the role of culture in economic achievement of ethnic groups by resorting to the little traditions, the distinctive cultures of a trading and business community, for example, or of a hardworking and stable peasantry. Successful ethnic groups have come from both backgrounds, and others. But whatever the cultural background, a second modulation is necessary in connecting culture to economic success, and that is the circumstances immigrants found on their arrival, the state of the economy, the opportunities available, the character of the areas in which they settled, and the like.

Contemporary social scientists find the effect of a variable by holding all other things equal. Thus if we are trying to determine the role of prejudice or culture in explaining lower earnings among blacks, we will have to make such adjustments as comparing groups of the same age, the same education, and the same geographical area. Since wages differ by area, perhaps we will have to take into account differences in rural and urban residence, since wages are affected by that too, and the like. The result of such an exercise is generally to reduce, or "explain," a difference. A residual is produced, and it is there that we may find the effect of discrimination or the effect of culture. Sometimes indeed the entire difference can be explained away, and there is no residual. But whether there is or is not, how we factor in culture, as against discrimination, always remains a problem.

The Second Modulation

The problem occurs in setting up the explanatory model. How do we separate culture from non-cultural features that explain difference? Thus every element in the example given above of trying to explain black-white earnings differences mixes cultural with other elements. We want to explain differences in earnings, so we hold age constant. But is not the fact that one group is lower in age than another, or has more children, also a cultural feature? We want to hold geography constant—people will do better in cities than in the countryside, in the North and West than in the South. But aren't there cultural factors in migration and the selection of places to which to migrate? Our comparison will hold family structure constant, noting that the large proportion of female-headed families among blacks lowers average income. But is not family structure a cultural feature par excellence?

The point of such models used to analyze differences is to explain them, but they also have inevitable political consequences. A cultural explanation is generally rejected by the group in question, whether it is doing better or worse than some average. If it is doing better, it fears others will accuse it of pride and hubris. Paying attention to its presumably superior culture, it fears, will lead to envy, anger, and worse. If the group is doing worse, it fears the snobbish disapproval and disdain of the majority. It is of benefit, every group thinks, to be seen as victim, not as superior.

For example, a few decades ago it was already evident that Asian household incomes were as high as white, which would have seemed on the face of it to dispose of the discrimination issue. But then it was pointed out that if we put education in the model, Asian earnings are not as high as those of whites of the same educational level. There have been efforts to show that there is nothing special about high Jewish earnings. After all, Jews live in cities, where earnings are higher for all; their average age is higher and earnings rise with age; they go to better colleges and universities; they are more concentrated in the high-earning professions; they have smaller families, and so on. In the end, the Jewish earnings advantage may be erased by holding all these factors constant. But that does not dispose of the cultural explanation, which is inextricably mixed in with each feature we control to explain difference.

Jews have generally been concerned about the news of their earnings and income advantage getting out. The census does not ask for religion, and thus Jews do not appear in census statistics. The Jewish defense organizations generally oppose any question on religion in the census, for this and other reasons. Asians, all of whom are counted in the census as individual races, generally try to explain away the statistical evidences of their success for various reasons, among them the desire of some to hold on to victim status, which may give some benefits. (There are no benefits now to Asian identity for college admissions, but Asians are still considered an underprivileged minority for government contracts.) Others want to hold on to the possibility of a Rainbow Coalition of the colored peoples, and if Asians are better off than the average, their eligibility for this coalition falls into question.

We may observe some odd contortions in the effort to maintain the victim status of Asians—the claim that they are seriously and adversely affected by discrimination, despite their present income and occupational profile. For instance, consider a paper written by the Chinese American historian John Kuo Wei Chen.[2] He first tells us that he takes great pleasure every year in the announcement of the Westinghouse Science Talent Search winners because so many Asians are among them: "Yet as I have followed press coverage and public discussion of these students, I have become increasingly concerned about the dissonance between their actual high achievements and how those achievements have been construed, declaring Asians a 'model minority'—despite compelling evidence defying overgeneralization." He takes pride in their achievement but resists the idea they are a "model minority."

The nature of his concern over this reputation is not easy to divine. He writes that a follow-up article to the Westinghouse story in the *New York Times* dealt with Cardozo High School in Queens in New York City, which produced eleven semifinalists, all Asian. This article led to an op-ed piece by Stephen Graubard, editor of *Daedalus*. Kuo reports, disapprovingly, that Graubard makes stable, single-parent families "the primary cause of Asian student success. Then, in the spirit of social welfare planning, he speculated about what might be done for all those hundreds of thousands of children who did not live in such stable environs. . . . Graubard assumed that stable, single-family neighborhoods provided the prerequisites for success."

Why Kuo resists this seemingly unobjectionable and common interpretation is unclear. We get some hint when he quotes approvingly a letter to the *New York Times* from the Asian student winners at Cardozo in response to the Graubard article, which rejects any generalization to explain their success. The letter attacks Graubard's interpretations as "stereotyping . . . which in its most extreme form is the root of prejudice, a disease that can never be solved by science." The letter asserts that the parental role in the school careers of these students ranged from apathy to intense involvement, and the reasons for student participation and success in the Westinghouse contest were varied and individual. Kuo concludes: "This formulation of Asian student success turned a complex phenomenon into a simplistic and historical [perhaps he means unhistorical?] representation of the unchanging nature of Asian cultures." All this is prelude to the main body of his paper, a study of anti-Chinese prejudice in New York City in the nineteenth century. One is left to conclude there is some connection between the anti-Chinese prejudice of the nineteenth century and the myth of "model minority" success today.

THE KEY ROLE OF EDUCATION

I have suggested that it is not easy scientifically to locate the cultural factors in ethnic group success or failure and that it is not to anyone's advantage politically to insist on the role of cultural factors in ethnic group failure or success.

Despite the best methods and approaches of the contemporary social sciences, I believe that it is difficult to make a clear case that cultural factors distinctive to one ethnic group or another are responsible for economic success or failure. What we can do from the point of view of social science is to determine the factors that seem to be regularly connected with the economic fate of ethnic groups. The factor that emerges most sharply from research is education. This is also the favored measure for human capital. It correlates best with later success in the form of higher-prestige occupations and higher earnings.

The great differences among groups in educational and occupational achievement would seem to constitute a clear case for the significance of culture, since a taste for education would seem to be above all a cultural fact. But the matter is not so simple. The taste for education, and subsequent success, varies by class. Are we to encompass class in culture? We could, but then it is not ethnic culture that leads to the success—there is much in common in the working and middle classes of all groups. Further, as I have tried to suggest, when we try to trace back a taste for education to the high culture of a group (Jewish learning, for example), the connections raise some problems. Admittedly, an orientation to learning of some type may be transformed into an orientation to learning of a very different type, and this is what may have happened to Jews; to Brahmins, who may have given up Sanskrit for science; and to Chinese, who may have given up the Confucian classics for physics. All of these cases require closer examination than they have received.

The children of Japanese peasants and Vietnamese boat people have also done well in school. They are quite distant, one would think, from the great traditions of learning in their societies, and the reasons for their success would also bear examination.

One reason for examining the potential cultural factors in educational success, which has emerged as the key measurable factor for economic success, is the idea, as expressed in the op-ed article by Stephen Graubard referred to above, that we can learn from such cases. The learning is intended to guide interventions into the ways of life of the less successful groups. I believe in the possibility of such learning, but I wonder whether we want, for political reasons or even for scientific reasons, to label whatever we learn as part of the culture of some specific group. Thus many believe from research that reading to children will assist them in learning to read. That is a general factor not connected to any ethnic group. It would be best to advocate it and encourage it for itself, rather than because it contributes to the success of Chinese or Vietnamese children. (Indeed, useful as it may be, it could not have had much to do with the success of second-generation Jews, Chinese, or Japanese, most of whose parents could only have read to them in a non-English language and probably worked too much to read to them at all.)

Undoubtedly, strong support for education among parents is better for children than the reverse. (But recall the talent search–winning Chinese students' reference to the "apathy" of some of their parents.) Yet studies regularly show that African American parents strongly urge their children to take school seriously, urge on them the importance of school. All of these factors that may contribute to educational success can be called cultural, but we have to go into them very deeply before we find out why practices that seem similar or identical at first look seem to have such different effects in different groups.

I think culture does make a difference. But it is very hard to determine what in culture makes the difference, as these examples suggest. Whatever it is, I think it will be more subtle than the large characteristics of the great traditions of a culture, since too many different outcomes, at different times, seem compatible with each of the great traditions. They have all had their glories and their miseries, their massacres and their acts of charity, their scholars and their soldiers, their triumphs of intellectual achievement and their descents into silliness or worse. Rather, it makes more sense to think of them as storehouses from which practices suitable for and useful for all may emerge. In any case, they have gone through so much change that it is utopian to think that we can apply their lessons if we can agree on them, in the large. But the specific practices of ethnic and racial groups in the United States, empathetically explored, may well tell us something useful.

part six

THE ASIAN CRISIS

17

Law, Family Ties, and the East Asian Way of Business

DWIGHT H. PERKINS

During the Asian financial crisis that began in 1997 and then spread well beyond the boundaries of Asia, much was said about the close cooperation that existed between business and government in the region. The term most often heard was "cronyism," and the implication was that it was directly responsible for the crisis. If the economies of East and Southeast Asia had followed a different path, one based on the rule of law and an arms-length relationship between business and government, there never would have been a financial crisis; or so it was argued or implied.

By now there have been many studies of the origins and nature of the Asian financial crisis, and there is a consensus that the nature of government–business relations in the region did contribute to what happened.[1] A typical financial panic triggered by macroeconomic mismanagement in Thailand and later in South Korea started these economies on a downward spiral, but the depth of the decline had much to do with weaknesses in the systems of these two countries. The nature of government–business relations had even more to do with that sharp economic downturn suffered by Indonesia and Malaysia.

But was "cronyism" really the cause of the deep recessions in these four economies, or was it a symptom of something more fundamental? The main argument of this chapter is that close business–government relations were one manifestation of a broader phenomenon, the reliance on personal relationships to provide business transactions with the security that is an essential component of any successful commercial system.

Societies made up of self-contained villages or autonomous feudal estates do not have to worry much about the security of economic transactions. The village elders or the feudal lord can enforce whatever rules they choose. However, when trade takes place over long distances, local authority can no longer guarantee that a transaction will be carried out in accordance with a given set of rules. A trader can provide security for himself by shipping the goods in a boat that he controls and can insist on immediate payment in gold or silver. He can also hire a mercenary army to protect his goods along the way and to prevent the loss of his gold payments to bandits or rapacious local lords. Commerce handled in this way, however, has very high transaction costs and is justified only when the value of the goods per unit of weight is extraordinarily high. The first Portuguese, Dutch, and British trading ships that went to Asia for spices and silk, many of them not much different from pirates, fit this model.

For commerce in more ordinary goods of lesser value, there must be a way of bringing transaction costs down. A general authority must provide security along the road or river; each individual trader should not have to provide it on his own. Furthermore, a means of payment must be found that does not involve lugging large quantities of gold, silver, and copper back and forth. Specialists in trade, shipping, and finance are more efficient than generalists who handle all aspects of a transaction, but each must have some basis for depending on the good-faith actions of the others.

In Europe and North America, the required security was supplied by laws backed up by a judiciary that over time became increasingly independent of the other functions of government. This development of the rule of law backed up by an independent judiciary took place over centuries, and the process was well along by the eighteenth century. The main theme of this chapter is that there was no comparable development of this kind of legal system in East and Southeast Asia. There was, however, the development of long-distance commerce both within and between economies in Asia, and that commerce had to have something that substituted for the rule of law. That substitute drew on one of the strengths of East Asian culture: close personal relationships based on family ties, as well as ties that extended beyond the family.

THE HISTORICAL ORIGINS OF THE
EAST ASIAN WAY OF BUSINESS

The central role of the family in Chinese society dates back to at least Confucius and requires little elaboration here. The Confucian system establishes clear hierarchical relationships within the family and between the family and higher levels of the government, culminating in the emperor. This system is still a central component of Chinese, Korean, and Japanese culture. Because much of the business community of Southeast Asia is Chinese in origin, these same values play a central role in that region as well.

Early work on the relationship between Confucian family values and economic development argued that these values were a serious barrier to the growth of large, successful businesses.[2] The argument in essence was that close family ties led to nepotism, which was inconsistent with a modern corporate economy in which universalistic values replaced the particularistic values of family-based systems. This early literature, although widely debunked by subsequent China scholarship, could be seen as an early precursor of the modern arguments about the debilitating impact of cronyism.

China, of course, had laws throughout its history. Southeast Asia also had laws, most of which were provided by the colonial authorities. In the case of China, however, the laws were administered by the county magistrates, who were the lowest rung on the ladder of the central government system of administration and control. The magistrates thus possessed a wide range of powers, from taxation to the police to dispute resolution. Some magistrates saw protection of local merchants as one of their charges, but this was not the norm. Merchants seldom resorted to legal procedures to protect their contracts because the law was not designed to protect such contracts. Going to the judge was a formula for economic ruin in most cases.

Chinese merchants thus developed their own systems for sanctioning behavior that undermined the security of commerce. They formed guilds, and the guilds typically had a regional as well as an occupational foundation. Shanghai merchants from the city of Ningbo, for example, formed a guild, while bankers who originated from the province of Shanxi controlled China's banking system through the end of the nineteenth century. These associations were too large to be based on a single extended family, but they were based on ties that had many of the characteristics of Confucian relationships. It is easier to trust someone from your home province, since it is likely that you either know that person or know members of his family, as well as his reputation.

But it was not necessary to rely on reputation alone. Families in China were collectively responsible for the behavior of their members. In the case of the Shanxi bankers, family members were in effect held hostage to the behavior of an individual charged with the responsibility of handling other people's money. If that individual absconded with the money, he could not go back to his family. Although he could hide out in some distant city, without family ties, he was a nonentity in Chinese society. Shanxi bankers, as a result, were able to reliably transfer large sums of money from one part of China to another in relative safety.

Business relations within the overseas Chinese communities of Southeast Asia were similar to those in traditional China. Southeast Asia had fully developed legal systems administered by the British, Dutch, and French, but few overseas Chinese turned to these systems if they had any alternative. The systems were administered in a language that many of the overseas Chinese did not speak and by colonial judges whose culture and values the overseas Chinese did not understand. The overseas Chinese, for the most part, settled their differences within their own communities and regional associations. Generally, it was easier to resolve disputes within a regional association (e.g., Fujian, Guangdong, Hakka) than between associations. Business relationships, therefore, were heavily influenced by where one's family originated from in China.

This system evolved over time, and some overseas Chinese learned to work within the colonial legal systems. Much is made today of the role of the rule of law in Hong Kong. It reflects the fact that what was originally a British system run by and mainly for the colonial authorities gradually came to be a system run by and for the local population. In most of East and Southeast Asia, however, the colonial system came to an end long before local people came to value the colonial legal system as something of their own that served the interests of their own society.

CHANGES IN THE SYSTEM AFTER 1945

Whatever the strengths and weaknesses of the traditional Chinese and colonial systems of business relations and law, those systems were changed when the Communist Party came to power in China and colonial rule ended in Southeast Asia, Korea, and Taiwan.

The change was most radical in China, where the Communist Party–run government first imported the economic system of the Soviet Union, including many of its laws and regulations. During the Cultural Revolution, Mao Zedong led an effort that went to the extreme of abolishing most laws and all lawyers. There was little or no security for anyone, least of all for someone who was in business, even if the business was state owned. That radical experiment ended with Mao's death in 1976, but China had to begin building a new legal system essentially from scratch. It was a relatively straightforward matter to write large numbers of commercial laws and have them formally adopted. However, it was quite a different matter to create a legal system that was capable of administering the laws efficiently and fairly. Dispute settlement in China still depended mainly on the discretionary authority of ranking members of the Chinese Communist Party and the party-dominated government. Individuals interested in doing business in China had to take that reality into account.

In Southeast Asia and to some degree even in South Korea, the change in the system was not quite so radical as in China. For the most part, the colonial laws, particularly those that pertained to commerce, remained on the books. The responsibility for administering these laws, however, passed to the new independent governments. In some cases, such as Singapore and Malaysia, people having substantial experience with the colonial legal system ran the new governments, and—at least for a time—maintained the spirit as well as the letter of that system with respect to the commercial sphere.

In other cases, notably in Indonesia, the new government officials possessed little relevant experience with the old system, and the legal system deteriorated rapidly after independence. Decades of writing new laws and training lawyers left Indonesia at the end of the twentieth century with a legal system that was easily manipulated by money and political power. Elsewhere in the region, the tendency was for the legal system to come increasingly under the discretionary authority of the political leadership.

These changes in the way commercial law was administered in Southeast Asia, Korea, and Taiwan meant that members of the business community, particularly persons of Chinese origin, had to continue to rely on their own efforts to provide security for their transactions. Although they continued to rely on each other and their own associations, they increasingly began to build ties to their local governments—ties of a kind that were not really feasible in the colonial era, when the colonial authorities kept their distance from local businesses, particularly the businesses of the overseas Chinese.

The nature of these ties to government varied, depending in part on the degree to which the culture of the business community was compatible with the culture and interests of those who ran the government. In countries such as South Korea and Japan, members of the business community and government personnel came from the same ethnic group and even the same schools. In fact, it was not always easy to tell where the government left off and private business began. In Thailand, a political leadership that actively discriminated against the local Chinese community in the 1950s subsequently changed to an approach that fully integrated the local Chinese population into Thai society.

In Indonesia and Malaysia, in contrast, the gap between government and business was large and remained so throughout the latter half of the twentieth century. At the same time, however, both governments carried out an activist economic policy. Businesses, to prosper, had to build ties to the governments that controlled their access to licenses, capital, and much else. These ties, however, could not be built on Confucian-style family and regional loyalties, since such loyalties did not exist across the gulf that separated Malay and Chinese cultures. Trust was made even more difficult by a long history of communal violence.

The relationship between the local Chinese and the political authorities in countries like Indonesia and Malaysia, therefore, was based on marriages of financial convenience. Because the Chinese were often successful in business, the political leadership could turn to them for money, either to support their political party or for more personal uses. Several local Chinese in Indonesia, for example, got their start toward billionaire status by gaining access to licenses to log the tropical forests; they then built on those fortunes by establishing close business ties to various members of President Suharto's family. In the early years of the governing Alliance parties in Malaysia, much of the funding of political activity came from the Chinese business community. As the Malay, or Bumiputra, who dominated government gained confidence, however, they took steps to help develop Bumiputra-owned businesses that then became the main source of funding for the dominant party of the governing coalition, the United Malay National Organization, or UMNO.

A neoclassical economic purist might say that both Confucian extended family ties and the alliances formed between the overseas Chinese businesses and the local non-Chinese political leadership were based on expectations of an economic return from those relationships. But even if most motivation is reduced to a financial foundation, the ties that bound family members in a Confucian society were far stronger and were likely to last longer than the personal friendships formed across ethnic lines.

THE SYSTEM PRODUCED BY THESE VALUES

The business system produced by relying on family and other personal ties for security had many features in common throughout most of East and Southeast Asia. The businesses themselves were generally owned and controlled by single families. Even limited liability corporations that sold their shares on the local stock exchange were family controlled. Minority shareholders, and even a majority if they were non-family shareholders, had little say in the operation of the business, and there was little protection for minority shareholder rights.

Where possible, control was passed down from the founder to his sons or, in rarer cases, to a daughter or a son-in-law. Generational changes in Chinese-owned companies often threatened the health of those companies because the founder's descendants were frequently less competent or because the siblings did not get along with each other. Even by the end of the 1990s, very few private firms owned by local people in Korea, Taiwan, Hong Kong, and Malaysia had made the transition to a professional (as contrasted to a family-based) management and control system.

Throughout the East and Southeast Asian region there were many firms run by professional managers, but they were controlled by European, Japanese, and American investors, or they were state owned. Governments like those in Malaysia, Taiwan, and even Singapore relied on state ownership in part to ensure that the ethnic group controlling the government got its share of economic power. In Malaysia, it was the Bumiputra elite who benefited from state control and later privatization of certain heavy industries. In Taiwan, it was the mainland Chinese who had come to the island in 1949 who controlled the state-owned enterprises, whereas most of the private sector was in the hands of those born in Taiwan during the Japanese colonial period. In Singapore, it was the powerful civil service and political elite that ran the state enterprises, whereas much of the private sector was dominated by foreign direct investors.

Family and regional ties also heavily influenced relationships between businesses, as well as relationships within individual businesses. There is, however, little scholarly work on the networks of relationships that play such an important role in relations between overseas Chinese within and between countries in the region.[3] Because these relationships are informal and because they exist in an environment that is often perceived as hostile, it may never be possible to fully understand the nature and scope of these networks.

Where networks do not already exist, Chinese businesses spend time and resources trying to develop them, even across ethnic lines. A standard statement about business practices in China is that American and European businessmen show up with their lawyers and try to write and negotiate formal contracts that cover all contingencies. Chinese businessmen, in contrast, are prepared to spend years visiting, entertaining, and getting to know the foreigners before they are prepared to get down to carrying out actual transactions with or without formal contracts.

There is some variation across the region in business and government relations, some of which has been described above. Underlying many of the patterns, however, is the attempt to achieve security where the rule of law is absent and where governments are actively involved in trying to direct the economy. Over 80 percent of the early foreign direct investment in China, for example, came from Hong Kong investors or from other overseas Chinese businesses, and most of this investment went into Guangdong Province, where the families of most of these businessmen originated.

Even by 1997, when the legal system in China's coastal cities had begun to play an increasingly constructive role in business, total foreign direct investment from Europe and North America totaled only U.S.$8.4 billion. Foreign direct investment from Hong Kong alone, in contrast, was $21.55 billion. Taiwan's foreign direct investment was officially $3.3 billion but was actually much higher, while tiny Singapore's foreign direct investment was $2.61 billion.[4]

Chinese-owned businesses knew how to operate in a world in which legal contracts were often not enforced. They had established working relationships with local governments and could turn to them for help when needed. At a minimum, these close relationships with local governments could ensure that these governments would not interfere with business operations. The Americans and Europeans, on the other hand, who did not have these kinds of relationships, tried to turn to the underdeveloped legal system.

Where personal ties between government officials and businessmen were based on family and family-like relationships (e.g., school ties, origin in the same town or province), the line between the sphere of government and the sphere of business was often blurred. Graduates of the University of Tokyo took it for granted that they would staff the highest levels of the key economic ministries and would then retire at a relatively young age to lucrative positions in the companies that they had up to then regulated. Senior government officials in Korea moved easily to corporate think tanks or to head up business associations.

In Malaysia, the government had as one of its primary goals the creation of a Bumiputra billionaire elite, and government investments and licenses were directed to that purpose. As already noted, this elite was in turn expected to fund the politicians who led the government. Thai politicians, many of them former military officers, sat on the boards of many public and private enterprises. There was nothing secret or under the table about these relationships. Within the elite, at least, they were accepted as the normal way of doing business.

Where deep ethnic cleavages separated the ruling elite from business, government relations, as pointed out above, tended to be based more on the exchange of money in return for government support. These transactions were much more likely to be seen by both the general public and the participants themselves as illegal bribes.

THE IMPACT OF THESE RELATIONSHIPS ON ECONOMIC PERFORMANCE

This way of business served Asia well for more than three decades. East and Southeast Asia did not have to wait until they had a well-developed commercial law system before growth could accelerate. Investment climbed to a very high share of GDP in most of the countries of the region, and, with notable exceptions, that investment was used efficiently by international standards. High rates of investment would have been inconceivable if investors had feared they would lose their investments to rapacious governments and unscrupulous competitors. If security had been absent, these investors, like their counterparts in Latin America, would have sent much of their money to New York and Zurich, and growth would have been much slower. They could also have invested for short-term profits, but the long-term investments that are critical for sustained growth would have been ignored. Instead, they kept their money in the country and put it into factories and infrastructure.

It is also true, however, that this way of business did not always create institutions that stood up well to adversity, periods of which are an inevitable part of the growth process. Reliance on personal ties within a business or between private businesses was not the main problem. Individual companies might fail because the heir to the founder was incompetent or because long-standing personal ties led them to favor an inefficient supplier, but other companies would simply take their place. The economy-threatening problems occurred because of the nature of the relationship between business and powerful interventionist governments.

Because government and business ties were so close, businesses took it for granted that government would help out if they got into trouble. Given the pervasive nature of government's role in these countries' economies, there was little doubt in the minds of businessmen that government had the power to intervene in support of business in general and of individual businesses in particular. Governments would want to intervene because they would be helping out their friends and supporters. The businesses, therefore, felt confident that they could afford to take large risks in implementing their investment strategies. The positive side of this was that it contributed to the high rate of investment and many successful projects. The downside was that, in some circumstances, the risks taken would be excessive and could threaten the entire economy.

It is this downside, or "moral hazard," aspect of the government–business relationship that came to the fore in the financial crisis of 1997. The banks and non-bank financial institutions turned out to be particularly vulnerable. Many of the banks in Asia were owned outright by the state, and so they took for granted that the state would bail them out of a crisis. Many other private bank and non-bank financial institutions, like those in Thailand and Indonesia, were controlled by politically powerful figures, and so they to felt they could count on the government. And the governments in Thailand, Malaysia, and Indonesia did in fact try to help out.

The Thai decision to keep the exchange rate fixed until they nearly ran out of foreign exchange was driven in part by a desire to help the financial institutions that had borrowed so heavily abroad and would face a huge increase in debt denominated in baht if there were a large devaluation. In Indonesia, President Suharto's toying with a currency board was probably driven in part by a desire to help his friends escape the consequences of their speculation with foreign dollar- and yen-denominated debt. Malaysia's decision to end the convertibility of the Malaysian ringgit was also driven in part by a desire to keep the Bumiputra billionaires from going under because of their financial maneuvers.

These statements about the motivations behind these particular government interventions are controversial and cannot be proved. Many of the participants in these decisions would no doubt deny such intentions and would describe their motives in terms of general benefits to the society at large. Some outside analysts would simply see these rescue attempts as mistakes in judgment. No doubt, many other considerations played a role as well, but from what we know of the general motives of much of the political leadership of these three countries, the motives in the particular incidents described above are, at the very least, plausible.

Moral hazard clearly had a great deal to do with the risky investment behavior and the weakness of the financial institutions. That behavior in turn had much to do with the depth of the economic decline experienced during the Asian financial crisis. There is also little doubt that the moral hazard which was present resulted from the close ties between the government and business. But to describe this all as the result of "cronyism" is to imply that everyone would accept the interpretation that government corruption was responsible for what happened—that the Asian way of business was corrupt in some universal sense.

What I have tried to argue here is that the Asian way of business and business–government relations were, for a long time, a successful adaptation by business and government to a situation in which one of the prerequisites of growth, the rule of law, was missing. Although this system did create numerous opportunities for what almost anyone would describe as corruption, the system itself was not inherently corrupt, at least in terms of the values that prevailed in East and Southeast Asia in the last half of the twentieth century. The system also created moral hazard that led to some excessively risky and unwise investment behavior. Many kinds of insurance also create moral hazard situations, but we don't conclude that we should abolish them.

IMPLICATIONS FOR THE FUTURE

Personal relationships in business based on family and other ties served East and Southeast Asia well for over three decades but badly during the last three years of the twentieth century. It may take many more years before the financial systems created by this approach to development are made healthy, but recovery in these economies is likely to occur much sooner—indeed, it appears to be occurring in the summer of 1999. Does it follow then that the Asian approach to business and government–business relations simply hit a bump in the road and only needs to get back up on the bicycle and peddle on?

The main point of this chapter is not that personal ties based on family-type relationships are superior to alternative ways of providing security for economic transactions. For a time, these personal ties were an adequate substitute for the way in which most industrial and postindustrial societies achieve the same objective. There are at least two reasons, however, why achieving security through personal ties is not likely to serve East and Southeast Asia well in the future.

The first reason is that the Asian crisis revealed the full extent of the weakness of the financial systems that arose in this kind of environment. Among other problems, these financial systems, when opened up, were far too weak to withstand or moderate the kinds of capital movements that characterize the international economic system. They simply collapsed and took the economy with them.

There is now a wide-ranging effort and a growing literature on what the Asian nations need to do to repair their financial systems. Reliable accounting standards, strengthened prudential regulation, and competition from well-established international banks are among the many proposals. But the task is not simply a narrow technical one of rewriting the laws and training bankers. The Harvard Institute for International Development, among others, was involved in just such an effort in Indonesia over many years. The laws were rewritten, bankers were trained, private banks were authorized and proceeded to grow rapidly, and the commercial banks were given substantial autonomy from the central bank. And yet, as of 1999, all of Indonesia's banks were technically bankrupt.

Perhaps no banking system could have withstood an 80 percent devaluation of the nation's currency. Indonesia's banking problems, however, were also a result of a decade in which many of the banks had been the toys of the ruling elite and could not have withstood even a mild crisis without government support. The problem in 1998 was that the government was no longer in a position to provide that support. To prevent the recurrence of a similar crisis at some later date, the banks must stop being subject to the discretionary interventions of high officials in support of pet projects. As long as government is directly and heavily involved in promoting particular business projects, however, the banks will always be vulnerable, as even Japan in the

1990s has demonstrated. If government officials are to be restrained from these kinds of intervention, there must be some institution capable of enforcing that restraint. That institution, in most industrial and postindustrial societies, is the rule of law administered by an independent judiciary.

A second reason for believing that personal relations between government and business will not serve as well in the future is that the international economic system itself has changed. The rules of that system, as manifested in such institutions as the World Trade Organization, are geared to economic systems that are based on the rule of law. Perhaps the international economic system could have been designed differently, but it is not going to be fundamentally altered in order to accommodate developing countries. Small and poor developing economies can opt out of the system or can be treated as exceptions, but the nations of East and Southeast Asia are not small and they are no longer poor. Many of them are among the major trading nations of the world, and they want and need access to the markets of Europe and North America. Fairly or not, that access will require the nations of East and Southeast Asia to strengthen the degree to which their economic systems are governed by transparent laws instead of opaque discretionary actions by government officials.

Asian values served economic development well for nearly half a century. They are not likely to serve the region as well in the future. The challenge now is to complete the process of creating a strong modern economy built on a foundation of law.

18

"Asian Values": From Dynamos to Dominoes?

LUCIAN W. PYE

There is no example in history to match the dramatic reversals in fortune of the Asian economies during the second half of the twentieth century. Widely shared views about the fundamental cultural determinants of the Asian countries have been turned on their heads two times in four decades. First, the long-established assumption that Asian cultures lacked the capacity to generate economic growth was dramatically shattered in the 1970s and 1980s by the emergence of the "miracle" economies and especially the "four little tigers." As the region became the envy of the developing world, there was for a time much talk about an Asian model for economic development. But then, even more suddenly, in the late 1990s there came crises and collapses. First, Japan went into a severe recession, if not depression, that has lasted a full decade, and then the Southeast Asian and South Korean economies went from financial crises to more fundamental setbacks. A decade of hype about superior "Asian values" was tellingly deflated.[1]

After a decade of 10 percent annual growth rates, the Asian economies contracted 15 percent in 1998, their stock markets losing over half their value and their currencies 30 to 70 percent of their value. In 1996, some $96 billion in capital had flowed into the five countries of South Korea, Thailand, Malaysia, Indonesia, and Singapore, but in 1997 there was an outflow of over $150 billion. In one year, Indonesia's per capita GNP fell from $3,038 to about $600. The International Labor Organization estimated that some 10 million Asians lost their jobs.[2]

Thus, in a matter of a year, the future of Asian economies became uncertain, and the trumpets heralding the greatness of Asian practices were silenced. Yet the collapse of the "miracles" should not end the discussion about "Asian values" but should ignite a more sober and critical analysis of the importance of values in producing sustainable economic development. Instead of the somewhat obnoxious nationalistic chest beating that went with a great deal of the Singapore and Malaysia version of the "debate" over Asian values, what is now called for is an explanation of how the same set of cultural values could have produced both the dynamos and the dominoes. The fact that Asia could go from the extremes of stagnation to dynamic economic growth and then to collapse raises a serious challenge as to the validity of cultural factors for explaining national development. Clearly, the fundamental cultures did not change.

To examine this significant problem, we need first to expose some of the exaggerated rhetoric about the supposed superiority of Asian values and seek a more realistic understanding of the economic performance of the Asian countries. We also need to clarify some points in the theories about Asian cultures and economic development, including another look at what Max Weber had to say about Confucianism and the development of capitalism.

I will then propose two hypotheses that can help explain how the same cultural values can produce such dramatically different results. The first is that the same values, operating, however, in quite different circumstances, can and usually will produce different effects. That is, the values of the Asian cultures have remained the same but the contexts have changed, and hence what had been positive outcomes became negative ones.

The second hypothesis is that cultural values are always clusters of values that at different times can be combined in different ways and thus produce different effects. This is a tricky argument that must be made with care to avoid the danger of reinforcing the criticism that it is always possible to find some cultural considerations to "explain" whatever has happened. Valid explanations require appropriately solid cultural variables, as well as precise linking of cause and effect.

JUST THE FACTS, NOT THE HYPE
ABOUT "MIRACLE ECONOMIES"

It is easy to dismiss much of the rhetoric generated in the Asian values debate as just a manifestation of Asian triumphalism in the wake of success, which may have reflected a need to be heard over the din of the West's triumphalism about winning the Cold War. Yet the emergence of the "four little dragons" and the impending emergence of China as a potential new superpower, all in varying degrees emulating the Japanese model of state-guided capitalism, did provide the basis for claims of Asian distinctiveness. The combination of economic successes and authoritarian rule clearly suggested that the Asian countries had hit upon something deserving of attention. The concept of Asian values quickly became a shorthand explanation for economic achievements and a justification for authoritarian governmental practices.

The Asian values debate was further complicated by the fact that, in the 1970s, not just Asians but westerners got carried away with the vision of "miracle" economies in Asia and of a West in decline. There is thus a need to put into perspective some of the exaggerated claims about how exceptional the Asian achievements actually were.

First, there was a strange tendency in some quarters to think of Japan, the leader of the miracle economies, as a Third World country that almost overnight rose to become the second largest economy in the world. In fact, Japan began to industrialize with the Meiji Restoration in the last third of the nineteenth century. The United States started to industrialize at about the same time. Japan was a significant industrial power by the time of the First World War and was able to take advantage of disruptions in the European economies to capture markets for consumer goods and especially textiles, first in Asia and Africa and then in Europe and America.

By the 1920s, Japan had the world's third largest navy and a merchant marine of equal magnitude. By the late 1930s, its economy was the third or fourth largest in the world, depending on whether its investments in Korea, Taiwan, and Manchuria were included. Its prewar auto industry was the match of most in Europe, and of course it produced a very impressive military airplane, the Zero. Those who see the emergence of a powerful Japan only in the 1960s tend to forget the challenge Japan posed in the Pacific War.

The pre-miracle backwardness of other parts of Asia has also been overstated. It has been much too easy to treat Emperor Qianlong as a buffoon because of his arrogant letter to King George III, declaring that "we have never valued ingenious articles, nor do we have the slightest need of your country's manufactures." Yet at the time of his reign, the Chinese economy was in fact larger than Great Britain's. Indeed, before the industrial revolution transformed the world economy, and when agriculture was still king, the huge agricultural populations of Asia produced a disproportionate share of the world's economic output. At the end of the eighteenth century, Asia as a whole registered 37 percent of the world's economic output, and for all the hype about their miracle economies, by the mid-1990s Asia's share had dropped back to 31 percent. The outlook before the disasters struck was that Asia would not regain its earlier share until 2010.

What had impressed people in the last few decades was of course the growth rates of the Asian economies. With Asian economies boasting 10 percent rates and the West 3 percent or less, Asians were held in awe. But attention was all on the percentage figures and not on the net growth in absolute terms. For all the excitement about a "decade of 10 percent growth" in the Chinese economy, the fact remains that not during a single year of that decade did the growth produce an addition to the Chinese economy that matched the net growth of the U.S. economy for that year. Thus in every year in what was called its decade of growth, China was not catching up but was actually falling further behind. The inescapable fact of arithmetic is that 10 percent of a $600 billion economy is less than a third of 2.5 percent of a $7.5 trillion economy—$60 billion compared to $187.5 billion. The moral is that focusing on growth percentage figures without regard to the base numbers can produce seriously false impressions.

I make these points not to belittle the accomplishments of the Asians but rather to counter a tendency to think in magical terms about miracles. It is true that there has been a historic transformation in living conditions as Asian households benefited from the growth rates. For the Chinese, going from less than $100 per capita income in 1985 to $360 in 1998 has meant that now there is more than one color television set per household, whereas then fewer than one in five households owned one; whereas 7 percent had refrigerators then, 73 percent do now.[3] There have indeed been manifest improvements in living conditions, and the Chinese are justified in believing that their children's future will be brighter still.

WHAT MAX WEBER REALLY SAID

Having clarified the facts to some degree, I now turn to examine the theoretical considerations in the analysis of the relationship of Asian cultural values and economic development. As a preface, however, I will review what Max Weber had to say on that subject. Weber, of course, remains the unsurpassed master of the cultural origins of capitalism. As everyone knows, he found those origins in the Protestant ethic, which, on being popularized, has unfortunately come down to little more than a version of the Boy Scout oath, a banal listing of such virtues as hard work, dedication, honesty, thrift, trustworthiness, willingness to delay gratification, and respect for education. Weber, in fact, saw the cultural origins of capitalism in far more complex terms. In particular, he was intrigued with two paradoxes.

The first was the historical fact that monks, devoted solely to otherworldly considerations and living totally ascetic lives in their monasteries, created extraordinarily efficient organizations for making worldly profits. The second paradox was that the critical actors in creating capitalism were Calvinists who believed in predestination and not those Christians who believed that virtuous living and good deeds would be rewarded in the hereafter. Weber recognized that an account book approach to rewards and punishments got people off too easily, whereas with predestination there was a profound sense of psychic insecurity that would drive people to grasp for any possible sign that they might belong among the "elect." The key drive was psychic anxiety.

In his detailed analysis of Chinese culture and in his comparison of Confucianism with Puritanism, Weber emphasized the degree to which the ideal of the Confucian gentleman stressed "adjustment to the outside, to the conditions of the 'world.'"[4] Confucian culture idealized harmony without producing any intense inner tensions or psychic insecurities; none of the problems with "nerves," as Weber puts it, that Europeans have—a reference to the problems that Freud analyzed.

Weber goes into great detail describing Chinese character as being well adjusted, as having "unlimited patience" and "controlled politeness," of being "insensitive to monotony" and having "a capacity for uninterrupted hard work." But these, he insists, were not the qualities that could spontaneously produce capitalism. At the same time, Weber was remarkably prescient in recognizing that they were qualities that could make for great skill in emulating capitalistic practices. He wrote that "the Chinese in all probability would be quite capable, *probably more capable than the Japanese*, of assimilating capitalism which has technically and economically been fully developed in the modern culture area."[5]

Thus the criticism that the recent economic successes of the Confucian countries disprove Weber is an incorrect reading of his theories. Weber foresaw that China might indeed be able to emulate capitalistic practices in time. In fact in many ways Weber shared the Enlightenment's positive views about China. The historic fact remains, however, that the Asian successes came about through access to the world economic system and not as the result of internal, autonomous developments.

THE PARADOXICAL RELATIONSHIP BETWEEN CONFUCIAN VALUES AND ECONOMIC BEHAVIOR

Considering the assimilation of capitalism by Confucian cultures, we come upon some paradoxes that are the match of those in Max Weber's theories about the economic behavior of monks and Calvinists. For example, Confucianism formally placed the merchant near the bottom of the social scale, below even the peasant. However, as a consequence of having to live with this stigma, Chinese merchants had no choice but to excel at making money. True, they could educate their sons to pass the imperial examinations and become mandarin officials, but that would mean the successful business would last only one generation. Otherwise, they had no alternative but to specialize in a skill that the Confucian mandarin-scholars despised. As marginalized people in their own society, their situation was somewhat analogous to that of the Jews in feudal Europe.

A second paradox, and one that is troubling to Americans raised on Horatio Alger stories extolling hard work as the sure path from "rags to riches," is that Confucianism scorned hard work and all forms of physical exertion while idealizing leisure and effortlessness. The Confucian gentleman wore long fingernails to prove that he did not have to work with his hands. Taoism, of course, reinforced this view by elevating to the highest philosophical level the principle of *wu-wei*, or non-effort, of accomplishing things with the minimum expenditure of energy. In Chinese military thinking, the ideal was to win battles not by exerting prodigious effort but by compelling the opponent to exhaust himself. As far as I know, no other culture is the match of the Chinese in idealizing effortlessness and decrying the folly of hard physical work. For the Chinese, Sisyphus is not a tragedy but a hilarious joke. Certainly in Chinese culture, hard work is not a prime value in itself but only an imperative dictated by necessity.

Instead of idealizing hard work, Chinese emphasize the importance of "good luck," the likelihood of which can be increased by proper ritual acts. Again, it is Taoism with its concept of the Tao, the Way, or the forces of nature and history, that gives a philosophical foundation to the basic Chinese view that much of life is determined by forces external to the actors involved. Some people are more skilled than others in flowing with the current and thus being blessed with good luck. Others foolishly buck the tide and are born losers. This stress on good fortune does not, however, produce a fatalistic approach to life—there are always things that can be done to increase the chance of good luck, and if things turn out badly, it was only bad luck, which it is hoped will change in time.

This stress on the role of fortune makes for an outward-looking and highly reality-oriented approach to life, not an introspective one. People need to be ever alert to exploit opportunistically anything that might improve their chances for good fortune. This appreciation of the prime importance of external forces makes for extreme sensitivity to objective circumstances, to the lay of the land, and to the importance of timing in taking action. The focus of decisionmaking is on judging carefully the situation and exploiting any advantages.

Thus, what might seem at first an otherworldly emphasis on luck has the paradoxical effect of instilling a vivid appreciation of objective realities. This orientation has made the Chinese very appreciative of the character and structure of markets. Markets are not a theoretical abstraction for Chinese but are vivid and dynamic realities.

This readiness to think in terms of clearly conceptualized markets explains a critical difference between Chinese and Western capitalism. Western capitalism is technology driven—build a better mousetrap, and people will come to your doorstep. But the driving force in Chinese capitalism has always been to find out who needs what and to satisfy that market need. Western firms seek to improve their products, strengthen their organizational structures, and work hard to get name recognition. Chinese entrepreneurs try to diversify, avoid getting a reputation for producing just a prime product, and always be ready to change production in response to what the market wants. Americans know that they are being flooded by consumer goods from Taiwan and China, but they do not know the names of the companies producing those goods.

Although scorning physical exertion and hard work, Confucianism upheld the importance of self-improvement, and hence the culture respected achievement motivation. The concept of "need for achievement" as formulated by David McClelland describes an important Chinese cultural value. McClelland demonstrated that countries that have had success in development also rated high in "need for achievement," as measured in such ways as the motivations taught in children's books. Every attempt to measure need for achievement among Chinese people confirms what any general, impressionistic understanding of Chinese culture would suggest—that the Chinese rank high in such a drive. Chinese children are taught the importance of striving for success and the shame of not measuring up to parental expectations.

Yet, paradoxically, Chinese culture also stresses the rewards of dependency, a psychological orientation that goes against the grain of the Horatio Alger ideal of the self-reliant individual. The paradoxical combination of achievement and dependency was central to the traditional Chinese socialization practices, which sought to teach the child early that disciplined conformity to the wishes of others was the best way to security and that being "different" was dangerous. The result was a positive acceptance of dependency.

The combination of achievement and dependency dictated an implicit goal of the traditional Chinese socialization process, which was to strive to resolve achievement needs by diligently carrying out the assigned role within the family, and hence by being properly dependent. On this score, Chinese and Japanese family norms significantly differed. In China, achievement was rewarded within the family, and the Confucian duties of the sons to the father, and of the younger and older brothers to each other, were lifetime obligations. The tradition was thus inward looking, and there was a basic instinct to distrust people in the non-family world.[6] In Japan, however, the tests of achievement in both samurai and merchant families were in terms of competition against outside parties and forces. Moreover, a younger brother could strike out on his own; if successful, he become a *gosenzo*—the head of a new family line.[7]

The balancing of the need for achievement and the blessings of dependency is closely related to the operations of trust and the dynamics of personal relationships that provide the linkages that make possible social networks. In the case of Chinese culture, the bonds of family extend outward to the clan and then on to more general ties of *guanxi,* or personal connections based on shared identities. What is most significant about the Chinese practices of *guanxi* for economic development is that parties are expected to share mutual obligations even though they may not personally know each other well. It is enough that they were classmates or schoolmates, came from the same town or even province, belonged to the same military outfit, or otherwise had a common element in their backgrounds. The bases of *guanxi* ties are thus objective considerations that others can recognize as existing, not primarily the subjective sentiments of the parties involved.

The comparable Japanese ties of *kankei* are far more subjective and are based on deep feelings of indebtedness and obligation—the importance of *on* and *giri*. Outsiders can assume that two Chinese with a shared connection will have a *guanxi* relationship, whereas the Japanese ties depend more on personal experiences.

THE CULTURAL FACTOR IN ECONOMIC BEHAVIOR

As stated earlier, the central hypothesis of this chapter is that the same values will produce different consequences in different circumstances. The key values of reliance on social networks *(guanxi),* of taking the long-run view, of seeking market share rather than profits, of delaying gratification, and of aggressively saving for the future all have different consequences according to the state of the economy and its level of development.

The rules of family trust and of *guanxi* meant that in the earlier and more unstable political environment, Chinese enterprises were largely limited to family operations. Distrusting outsiders, family firms could not expand by having more branches than they had sons to manage them.[8] However, as the political environment in East and Southeast Asia became more stable, networking rapidly expanded along the lines of *guanxi* connections. Banking operations in the region in particular tended to be highly personalized and to follow the chain of personal connections. Unger makes the interesting argument that the overseas Chinese practices of networking gave them a form of "social capital" that was not the basis for democracy as Robert Putnam's social capital is, but rather a form of social capital that can provide the basis for economic development. Focusing on Thailand, Unger shows how the Chinese relied upon their connections to facilitate the flow of capital so as to make Thailand an economic "miracle."[9]

Guanxi is also fundamental in explaining the astonishingly rapid expansion of overseas Chinese investments in coastal China. With Deng Xiaoping's opening to the outside world, people from Hong Kong, Taiwan, and the Chinese communities in Southeast Asia went back to their ancestral hometowns and villages in China, and they were instantly accepted and encouraged to invest in the development of the local economies. Hong Kong people went into Guangdong, Taiwanese into Fujien, and others into Shanghai to set up joint ventures, usually with the local political leadership, for manufacturing export items. The result was the spectacular expansion of village and township enterprises. The deals were made on highly personalized bases, not legalistic ones. The overseas Chinese investors sought all manner of favored arrangements, from multiple years of tax exemptions to fixed low wages.

Thus for a time the tradition of informal networking worked wonders in moving capital rapidly into China for setting up new enterprises far faster than legalistic contractual negotiations could have. Even foreign bankers were caught up in the spirit of what they took to be Asian values and were prepared to make loans based on winks and nods from Chinese officials. Yet in time the lack of transparency or firm legal understandings led inevitably to crony capitalism and widespread corruption. The lack of legal foundations for business transactions, which may have facilitated deals when conditions were good, also meant that there were no clear procedures for handling bankruptcies if things went bad.

The tradition of networking in Japan set the stage for the pattern of close informal ties among businessmen, bureaucrats, and politicians that came to be called "Japan Inc." The patterns of mutual obligation and particularistic ties meant that huge amounts of credit could flow with minimum need for formal accounting or checks on the soundness of the projects. For a time, it was assumed that just as long as the state guidance "got the prices right," there was little need to worry about insider dealings and the possibilities for corruption. But then came the shocks: The Japanese elite were not as upright as they had been made out to be. The practice of close cooperation between government and business meant that when it came time for the state to engage in greater regulating of financial institutions, it seemed powerless in dealing with its former partners.

The practices of networking also encouraged the idea that making short-term checks on the profitability of enterprises was unnecessary. Rather, it was desirable to take a "long view" and seek to capture an ever larger share of the market. The supposed virtue of such long-term perspectives was reinforced by the cultural propensity to see great virtue in delayed gratification and the willingness to suffer in the short run in the expectation that in time there would be greater rewards for steadfastness. For a time, when all the economies were on the rise, there were benefits to be gained from this approach, and the successes of the Japanese made many Westerners believe that the Japanese had hit upon a superior strategy for producing wealth. Consequently, many elsewhere in Asia sought to emulate the Japanese drive to capture market share and to postpone worries about profitability.

In time, however, the approach proved disastrous because indebtedness piled up, and the compulsive drive to capture a greater share of the market produced gross excesses in capacity. The lack of transparency and legal norms in bank lending allowed for huge expansions in loans based on unrealistic expectations of what expanding production might bring. It turned out that the approach provided no effective checks on whether capital was being allocated rationally. In industry after industry, surplus capacity became the norm. It was strange that the world did not recognize that a crisis was in the making in 1995 when a leading Korean *chaebol* declared with exuberant hubris that it planned to invest $2.5 billion in a new steel complex, at a time when the world was already awash in more steel than it could use.

The Western accounting practice of quarterly profit-and-loss statements provides managers and investors with critical feedback as to whether capital is being efficiently allocated and thus provides a steering mechanism to guide the invisible hand of the market. The combination of a drive for greater market share above all else, a fixation on only the long run, and the notion that it is heroic to suffer the pains of delayed gratification—all essential Asian values—inspired economically useful behavior during the initial stages of economic development, but the combination led in time to serious problems of overcapacity and numerous bubble economies.

Indeed, nearly all the East Asian countries have had major real estate bubbles. In Japan it was said that real estate prices had reached such ridiculous heights that the Imperial Palace grounds in Tokyo were worth more than all the real estate in California. It was not just uninformed people who believed such talk; many supposedly serious Japanese bankers also believed it. In Shanghai, cranes were everywhere in the Putung district putting up skyscrapers—some Chinese liked to say that the crane had become the Chinese national bird. But the buildings finished in 1997 have only 15 percent occupancy, and those finished in 1998 have even fewer tenants. Buildings were still going up as investors felt that they must take the long view and bravely suffer the pains of delayed gratification.

Another dramatic example of how a cultural value can operate usefully under some conditions but then become a source of disaster is the East Asian propensity to save. The Chinese have one of the world's highest savings rates, some 30 percent in recent years, providing much of the capital for economic growth at the start of the reforms. The state banks welcomed the flow of savings that grew as prosperity spread, for they provided the funds necessary for bank lending to the state-owned enterprises (SOEs). But the SOEs have now become huge white elephants and the state banks have no hope of ever recovering their "loans." What keeps the system going is the citizens' propensity to save. The banks could no more honor the private accounts of the savers than the SOEs could honor their debts. However, as long as the people have nowhere else to put their money, the state banks will get it, and an otherwise failed system will manage to stay afloat.

The same propensity to save initially provided bountiful capital for the postwar Japanese economic recovery, but what was a virtue is now making it hard for Japan to get out of its prolonged recession. Japanese officials find it frustratingly difficult to generate a rise in demand that might pull the economy out of its stagnation because the Japanese people, with something of a peasant mentality, believe that if the times are bad, they should postpone consumption and increase savings. Even if fiscal and monetary policies are able to put more money into people's pockets, they refuse to spend more and may even try to save more in anticipation of further troubles ahead.

GETTING THE CONTEXT RIGHT IN
CULTURAL ANALYSIS

Although the story is too complex to tell in this chapter, it is clear that the ups and downs of the Asian economies have created serious problems for the advocates of Asian values. But these developments do not challenge a more sophisticated understanding of the relationship of culture to economic growth. Problems arise when an attempt is made to jump all the way from generalized cultural characterizations to economic outcomes without taking into account all the intervening variables and the situational contexts. It is thus unscientific to try to draw up a universal list of positive and negative cultural values for economic development. What may be positive in some circumstances can be quite counterproductive under other conditions.

Moreover, our current state of knowledge leaves us with many mysteries about the dynamics of economic development. Our theories do not provide us with sharp enough cause-and-effect relationships to make it possible to assign definite weights to specific cultural variables. Leaving aside all the general considerations such as geography, climate, resource endowment, capacity of the government, and the wisdom of its public policies, the general category of economic behavior is so broad as to make it impossible to be rigorous in evaluating the significance of any specific cultural value. Some behavior is tied to individual conduct, such as the initiative essential for entrepreneurship, while other behavior is more collective, defining the character and structure of the general society. We need to be somewhat humble in ascribing precise weights to cultural variables. We know that they are important, but exactly how important at any particular time is hard to judge. We are dealing with clouds, not clocks, with general approximations, not precise cause-and-effect relationships.[10]

Thus, as we pull these threads of analysis together, it is clear that the advocates of Asian values have grossly overstated the wonders of the Asian economies and the helplessness of the West. Nevertheless, it is true that Asia will continue to modernize and, in doing so, will produce forms and practices that are distinctive. This should not be surprising, for the West as the leader in modernization has not produced a homogeneous culture—there are dynamic differences among all the leading Western societies. Cultural differences will endure, and in most cases there is little point in trying to say which cultures are superior and which ones inferior. Their strengths and weaknesses will be in different areas and will involve different practices. Economic development is not a single event but an ongoing process of history, so there will be many ups and downs in all countries. Organizational forms that were effective in exploiting one state of technology can turn out to be liabilities with newer technologies.

This having been said, it is true that several of the East Asian economies have recovered more rapidly than many expected, and the recovery doubtlessly reflects in part the same cultural factors that contributed to the rapid growth of recent decades.

19

Multiple Modernities: A Preliminary Inquiry into the Implications of East Asian Modernity

Modernity is both a historical phenomenon and a conceptual framework. The idea of multiple modernities is predicated on three interrelated assumptions: the continuous presence of traditions as an active agent in defining the modernizing process, the relevance of non-Western civilizations for the self-understanding of the modern West, and the global significance of local knowledge.

In an exploration of economic culture and moral education in Japan and the four mini-dragons (Taiwan, South Korea, Hong Kong, and Singapore), the continuous relevance of the Confucian traditions in East Asian modernity is studied from cross-cultural and interdisciplinary perspectives. Each geographic area is greatly varied and each disciplinary approach (philosophical, religious, historical, sociological, political, or anthropological) is immensely complex, and the interaction among them layers the picture with ambiguities. A discussion of them together shows that an appreciation of the Confucian elite's articulation and the habits of the heart of the people informed by

Confucian values is crucial for an understanding of the political economy and the moral fabric of industrial East Asia.[1]

"MODERNIZATION"

Historically the term "modernization" was employed to replace "westernization" in recognition of the universal significance of the modernizing process. Although the modernizing process originated in Western Europe, it has so fundamentally transformed the rest of the world that it must be characterized by a concept much broader than geography. Including the temporal dimension in the conception reveals modernization as the unfolding of a global trend rather than a geographically specific dynamic of change.

The concept of modernization is relatively new in academic thinking. It was first formulated in North America in the 1950s by sociologists, notably Talcott Parsons, who believed that the forces unleashed in highly developed societies, such as industrialization and urbanization, would eventually engulf the whole world. Although these forces could be defined as "westernization" or "Americanization," in the spirit of ecumenicalism, the more appropriate and perhaps scientifically neutral term would be "modernization."

It is interesting to note that, probably under the influence of intellectual discussion in Japan, the Chinese term for "modernization," *xiandaihua,* was coined in the 1930s in a series of debates to address issues of development strategies, organized by the most influential newspaper in China, *Shenbao.* The three major debates, which centered on whether agriculture or industry, socialism or capitalism, or Chinese culture or Western learning should have priority in China's attempt to catch up with imperialist powers (including Japan), provide a richly textured discourse in modern Chinese intellectual history.[2] Furthermore, a focused investigation of the Chinese case will help determine the applicability of the concept of modernization to non-Western societies.

However, the claim that East Asian modernity is relevant to the modern West's self-understanding is built on the assumptive reason that if the modernizing process can assume cultural forms substantially different from those of Western Europe and North America, it clearly indicates that neither westernization nor Americanization is adequate in characterizing the phenomenon. Furthermore, East Asian forms of modernization may help scholars of modernization develop a more differentiated and subtle appreciation of the modern West as a complex mixture of great possibilities rather than a monolithic entity impregnated with a unilinear trajectory.

If we begin to perceive modernization from multiple civilizational perspectives, the assertion that what the modern West has experienced must be repeated by the rest of the world is no longer believable. Indeed, upon scrutiny, the modern West itself exhibits conflictual and contradictory orientations, a far cry from a coherent model of development. The difference between European and American approaches to modernization broadly defined gives ample evidence to the argument for diversity within the modern West. Actually, three exemplifications of Western modernity—Britain, France, and Germany—are so significantly different from one another in some of the salient features of the modernizing process that, in essence, none of the local knowledge is really generalizable. This by no means undermines the strong impression that virtually all forms of local knowledge that can be generalized, if not universalized, are Western in origin.

Nevertheless, we are at a critical juncture and must move beyond three prevalent but outmoded exclusive dichotomies: the traditional/modern, the West/the rest, and the local/global. Our effort to transcend these dichotomies has far-reaching implications for developing a sophisticated understanding of the dynamic interplay between globalization and localization. The case of East Asia is profoundly meaningful for this kind of inquiry. I will focus my attention on Confucian humanism as the basic value system underlying East Asian political economy. Let us begin with a historical observation.

Whether or not Hegel's philosophy of history signaled a critical turn that relegated Confucianism, together with other spiritual traditions in the non-Western world, to the dawn of the Spirit, the common practice in cultural China of defining the Confucian ethic as "feudal" is predicated on the strong thesis of historical inevitability implicit in the Hegelian vision. The irony is that the whole Enlightenment project as captured by the epoch-making Kantian question, "What is Enlightenment?" was actually an affirmation that cultural traditions outside the West, notably Confucian China, had already developed an ordered society even without the benefit of revelatory religion.

As understood by contemporary thinkers such as Jürgen Habermas, what happened in the nineteenth century when the dynamics of the modern West engulfed the world in a restless march toward material progress was definitely not the result of a straightforward working out of the Enlightenment. On the contrary, the perceived Enlightenment trajectory of rationality was thoroughly undermined by the unbound Prometheus, symbolizing an unmitigated quest for complete liberation from the past and thorough mastery of nature. The demand for liberation from all boundaries of authority and dogma may have been a defining characteristic of Enlightenment thinking; the aggressive attitude toward nature is also a constituent part of the Enlightenment mentality. To the rest of the world, the modern West, informed by the Enlightenment mentality, has been characterized by conquest, hegemony, and enslavement as well as by models of human flourishing.

Hegel, Marx, and Weber shared the ethos that despite all its shortcomings, the modern West was the only arena of progress from which the rest of the world could learn. The unfolding of the Spirit, the process of historical inevitability, or the "iron cage" of modernity, was essentially a European *Problematik*. Confucian East Asia, the Islamic Middle East, Hindu India, and Buddhist Southeast Asia were on the receiving end of this process. Eventually, modernization as homogenization would make cultural diversity inoperative, if not totally meaningless. It was inconceivable that Confucianism, or for that matter any other non-Western spiritual traditions, could exert a shaping influence on the modernizing process. The development from traditional to modern was irreversible and inevitable.

In the global context, what some of the most brilliant minds in the modern West assumed to be self-evidently true turned out to be parochial. In the rest of the world, and definitely in Western Europe and North America, the anticipated clear transition from tradition to modernity never occurred. As a norm, traditions continue to exert their presence as active agents in shaping distinctive forms of modernity, and, by implication, the modernizing process itself has continuously assumed a variety of cultural forms rooted in specific traditions. The recognition of the relevance of radical otherness to one's own self-understanding of the eighteenth century seems more applicable to the current situation in the global community than the inattention to any challenges to the modern Western mind-set of the nineteenth century and most of the twentieth century. In the twenty-first century, the openness of the eighteenth century as contrasted with the exclusivity of the nineteenth and twentieth centuries may provide a better guide for the dialogue of civilizations.

The current debate between the "end of history"[3] and the "clash of civilizations"[4] scratches only the surface of the *Problematik* I wish to explore. The euphoria produced by the triumph of capitalism and the expectation that the liberal democratic persuasion will be universally accepted is short-lived. The emergence of the "global village," at best an imagined community, symbolizes difference, differentiation, and outright discrimination. The hope that economic globalization engenders equality, either of consequence or opportunity, is simple-minded. The world has never been so divided in terms of wealth, power, and accessibility to information and knowledge. Social disintegration at all levels, from family to nation, is a serious concern throughout the world. Even if liberal democracy as an ideal is widely accepted as a universal aspiration by the rest of the world, the claim that it will automatically become the only dominant discourse in international politics is wishful thinking.

Although the "clash of civilizations" is based on the sound judgment that cultural pluralism is an enduring feature of the global scene, it is still rooted in the obsolete notion of pitting the West against the rest of the world. The credible proposition that only Western forms of local knowledge are generalizable, even universalizable notwithstanding, the thesis of Western exceptionalism is defensible. If the "clash of civilizations" is a strategy of enhancing the persuasive power of cherished Western values, its goal, in the last analysis, is comparable to the "end of history," except for the cautionary note that, as a process, the initial stage may be wearisome for the advocates of Western liberal democracy.

In a deeper sense, neither the end of history nor the clash of civilizations captures the profound concern of modern Western intellectuals. Despite all of the ambiguities of the Enlightenment project, its continuation is both necessary and desirable for human flourishing. The anticipated fruitful interchange between Habermas's communicative rationality and John Rawls's political liberalism is perhaps the most promising sign of this endeavor. The challenges to this mode of thinking indiscriminately labeled as postmodernism are formidable, but this is not the place to elaborate on them. Suffice it now to mention that ecological consciousness, feminist sensitivity, religious pluralism, and communitarian ethics all strongly suggest the centrality of nature and spirituality in human reflexivity. The inability of our contemporary Enlightenment thinkers to take seriously ultimate concerns and harmony with nature as constitutive parts of their philosophizing is the main reason for them to respond creatively to postmodern critique. Lurking behind the scene is the question of community. We urgently need a global perspective on the human condition that is predicated on our willingness to think in terms of the global community.

Among the Enlightenment values advocated by the French Revolution, fraternity—the functional equivalent of community—has received scant attention among modern political theorists. The preoccupation with establishing the relationship between the individual and the state since Locke's treatises on government is of course not the full picture of modern political thought, but it is undeniable that communities, notably the family, have been relegated to the background as insignificant in the mainstream of Western political discourse. Georg Hegel's fascination with the "civil society" beyond the family and below the state was mainly prompted by the dynamics of the bourgeoisie, a distinct urban phenomenon threatening to all traditional communities. It was a prophetic gaze into the future rather than a critical analysis of the value of community. The transition from gemeinschaft to gesellschaft was thought to have been such a rupture that Max Weber referred to "universal brotherhood" as an outmoded medieval myth unrealizable in the disenchanted modern secular world. In political and ethical terms, strenuous effort is required for the family of nations to rise above the rhetoric of self-interest to recapture the cosmopolitan spirit of interdependence.

The upsurge of interest in recent decades within North America regarding community may have been stimulated by a sense of crisis that social disintegration is a serious threat to the well-being of the republic, but the local conditions in the United States and Canada, precipitated by ethnic and linguistic conflicts, are visible throughout the highly industrialized, if not postmodern, First World. The conflict between globalizing trends, including trade, finance, information, migration, and disease, and localism, rooted in ethnicity, language, land, class, age, and faith, is not easily resolvable. We are compelled by brutal confrontations as well as encouraging reconciliation around the world to transcend the "either-or" epistemology and to perceive the imagined global community in a variety of colors and many shades of meaning. The case of East Asian modernity from a Confucian perspective helps us cultivate a new way of thinking.

CONFUCIAN HUMANISM

The revival of Confucian teaching as political ideology, intellectual discourse, merchant ethics, family values, or the spirit of protest in industrial East Asia since the 1960s and socialist East Asia more recently is the combination of many factors. Despite tension and conflict rooted in primordial ties (particularly ethnicity, language, cultural nationalism, and life orientation), the overall pattern in East Asia is integration based on values significantly different from the Enlightenment mentality of the modern West.

East Asian intellectuals have been devoted students of Western learning for more than a century. In the case of Japan the samurai-bureaucrats learned the superior knowledge of Western science, technology, manufacturing industries, and political institutions from the Dutch, British, French, Germans, and, in recent decades, Americans. In similar fashion, the Chinese scholar-officials, the Korean "forest intellectuals," and Vietnamese literati acquired knowledge from the West to build their modern societies. Their commitment to substantial, comprehensive, or even wholesale westernization enabled them to thoroughly transform their economy, polity, and society according to what they perceived, through firsthand experience, as the superior modus operandi of the modern way.

This positive identification with the West and active participation in a fundamental restructuring of one's own world according to the Western model is unprecedented in human history. However, East Asia's deliberate effort to relegate its own rich spiritual resources to the background for the sake of massive cultural absorption enhanced the need to appeal to the native pattern to reshape what they had learned from the West. This model of creative adaptation following the end of the Second World War helped them to strategically position themselves in forging a new synthesis.

The Confucian tradition, having been marginalized as a distant echo of the feudal past, is forever severed from its imperial institutional base, but it has kept its grounding in an agriculture-based economy, family-centered social structure, and paternalistic polity that are reconfigured in a new constellation. Confucian political ideology has been operative in the development states of Japan and the four mini-dragons. It is also evident in the political processes of the People's Republic of China, North Korea, and Vietnam. As the demarcation between capitalist and socialist East Asia begins to blur, the cultural form that cuts across the great divide becomes distinctively Confucian in character.

Economic culture, family values, and merchant ethics in East Asia and cultural China have also expressed themselves in Confucian terms. It is too facile to explain these phenomena as a postmodern justification. Even if we agree that the Confucian articulation is but an afterthought, the circulation of terms such as network capitalism, soft authoritarianism, group spirit, consensus formation, and human relatedness in characterizing salient features of the East Asian economy, polity, and society suggests, among other things, the transformative potential of Confucian traditions in East Asian modernity.

Specifically, East Asian modernity under the influence of Confucian traditions suggests a coherent vision for governance and leadership:

- Government leadership in a market economy is not only necessary but also desirable. The doctrine that government is a necessary evil and that the market in itself can provide an "invisible hand" for ordering society is antithetical to modern experience, West or East. A government that is responsive to public needs, responsible for the welfare of the people, and accountable to society at large is vitally important for the creation and maintenance of order.
- Although law is essential as the minimum requirement for social stability, "organic solidarity" can only result from the implementation of humane rites of interaction. The civilized mode of conduct can never be communicated through coercion. Exemplary teaching as a standard of inspiration invites voluntary participation. Law alone cannot generate a sense of shame to guide civilized behavior. It is the ritual act that encourages people to live up to their own aspirations.
- Family, as the basic unit of society, is the locus from which the core values are transmitted. The dyadic relationships within the family,

differentiated by age, gender, authority, status, and hierarchy, provide a richly textured natural environment for learning the proper way of being human. The principle of reciprocity as a two-way traffic of human interaction defines all forms of human relatedness in the family. Age and gender, potentially two of the most serious gaps in the primordial environment of the human habitat, are brought into a continuous flow of intimate sentiments of human care.

- Civil society does not flourish because it is an autonomous arena above the family and beyond the state. Its inner strength lies in its dynamic interplay between family and state. The image of the family as a microcosm of the state and the ideal of the state as an enlargement of the family indicate that family stability is vitally important for the body politic, and that a vitally important function of the state is to ensure organic solidarity of the family. Civil society provides a variety of mediating cultural institutions that allow a fruitful articulation between family and state. The dynamic interplay between the private and public enables the civil society to offer diverse and enriching resources for human flourishing.
- Education ought to be the civil religion of society. The primary purpose of education is character building. Intent on the cultivation of the full person, school should emphasize ethical as well as cognitive intelligence. Schools should teach the art of accumulating "social capital" through communication. In addition to the acquisition of knowledge and skills, schooling must be congenial to the development of cultural competence and the appreciation of spiritual values.
- Since self-cultivation is the root for the regulation of family, governance of state, and peace under heaven, the quality of life of a particular society depends on the level of self-cultivation of its members. A society that encourages self-cultivation as a necessary condition for human flourishing is a society that cherishes virtue-centered political leadership, mutual exhortation as a communal way of self-realization, the value of the family as the proper home for learning to be human, civility as the normal pattern of human interaction, and education as character building.

CONFUCIANISM AND MODERNIZATION

It is far-fetched to suggest that these societal ideals are fully realized in East Asia. Actually, East Asian societies often exhibit behaviors and attitudes just the opposite of the supposed salient features of Confucian modernity. Indeed, having been humiliated by imperialism and colonialism for decades, East Asia now, on the surface at least, blatantly displays some of the most negative aspects of Western modernism with a vengeance: exploitation, mercantilism, consumerism, materialism, greed, egoism, and brutal competitiveness. Nevertheless, as the first non-Western region to become modernized, the cultural implications of the rise of "Confucian" East Asia are far-reaching.

The modern West as informed by Enlightenment mentality provided the initial impetus for worldwide social transformation. The historical reasons that prompted the modernizing process in Western Europe and North America are not necessarily structural components of modernity. Surely, Enlightenment values such as instrumental rationality, liberty, rights consciousness, due process of law, privacy, and individualism are all universalizable modern values, but as the Confucian example suggests, "Asian values" such as sympathy, distributive justice, duty consciousness, ritual, public-spiritedness, and group orientation are also universalizable modern values.[5] Just as the former ought to be incorporated into East Asian modernity, the latter may turn out to be a critical and timely reference for the American way of life.

If Confucian modernity definitively refutes the strong claim that modernization is, in essence, westernization or Americanization, does this mean that the rise of East Asia, which augurs the advent of a Pacific century, symbolizes the replacement of an old paradigm by a new one? The answer is definitely in the negative. The idea of a kind of reverse convergence, meaning that the time is ripe for Western Europe and North America to look toward East Asia for guidance, is ill-advised. Although the need for the West, especially the United States, to transform itself into a learning as well as a teaching civilization is obvious, what East Asian modernity signifies is pluralism rather than alternative monism.

The success of Confucian East Asia in becoming fully modernized without being thoroughly westernized clearly indicates that modernization may assume different cultural forms. It is thus conceivable that Southeast Asia may become modernized in its own right, without being either westernized or East Asianized. The very fact that Confucian East Asia has provided an inspiration for Thailand, Malaysia, and Indonesia to modernize signifies that Buddhist and Islamic and, by implication, Hindu forms of modernity are not only possible but highly probable. There is no reason to doubt that Latin America, Central Asia, Africa, and indigenous traditions throughout the world all have the potential to develop their own alternatives to Western modernism.

But this neat conclusion, resulting from a commitment to pluralism, may have been reached prematurely. Any indication that this is likely to happen, a sort of historical inevitability, smacks of wishful thinking. We do not have to be tough-minded realists to recognize the likelihood of this scenario occurring. If the First World insists on its right to overdevelop, if industrial East Asia forges ahead with its accelerated growth, if the People's Republic of China immerses itself in the "four modernizations" at all costs, what shape will the world be in fifty years from now? Is East Asian modernity a promise or a nightmare? One wonders.

The current financial crisis notwithstanding, the surge in the last four decades of Confucian East Asia—the most vibrant economy the world has ever witnessed—has far-reaching geopolitical implications. Japan's transformation from an obedient student under American tutelage to the single most powerful challenger to American economic supremacy compels us to examine the global significance of this particular local knowledge. The "reform and open" policy of the People's Republic of China since 1979 has propelled it to become a gigantic development state.

Although the collapse of the Berlin Wall and the disintegration of the former Soviet Union signaled the end of international communism as a totalitarian experiment, socialist East Asia (mainland China, North Korea, and, for cultural reasons, Vietnam) seems to be in the process of reinventing itself in reality, if not in name. With thousands of political dissidents in the West and a worldwide network in support of Tibet's independence, China's radical otherness is widely perceived in the American mass media as a threat. It seems self-evident that since China has been humiliated by the imperialist West for more than a century, revenge may be China's principal motivation for restructuring world order. Memories of the Pacific theater of the Second World War and the Korean War, not to mention the Vietnam War, give credence to the myth of the Yellow Peril. The emigration of wealthy Chinese from Southeast Asia, Taiwan, and Hong Kong to North America, Australia, and New Zealand further enhances the sense of crisis that there is a Chinese conspiracy to rearrange power relationships in the global community.

The rise of "Confucian" East Asia—Japan, the four mini-dragons, mainland China, Vietnam, and possibly North Korea—suggests that despite global trends defined primarily in economic and geopolitical terms, cultural traditions continue to exert powerful influences in the modernizing process. Although modernization originated from the West, East Asian modernization has already assumed cultural forms so significantly different from those in Western Europe and North America that, empirically, we must entertain alternatives to Western modernism. However, this does not indicate that Western modernism is being eroded, let alone replaced, by East Asian modernism. The claim that Asian values, rather than Western Enlightenment values, are more congenial to current Asian conditions and, by implication, to the emergent global community in the twenty-first century is seriously flawed, if not totally mistaken. The challenge ahead is the need for global civilizational dialogue as a prerequisite for a peaceful world order. The perceived clash of civilizations makes the dialogue imperative.

The paradox, then, is our willingness and courage to understand radical otherness as a necessary step toward self-understanding. If the West takes East Asian modernity as a reference, it will begin to sharpen its vision of the strengths and weaknesses of its model for the rest of the world. The heightened self-reflexivity of the modern West will enable it to appreciate how primordial ties rooted in concrete living communities have helped to shape different configurations of the modern experience.

This is a giant step toward true communication between the West and the rest, without which basic trust and fruitful mutuality across civilizational lines can never be established. Actually, from the perspective of the global community, the dichotomy of the West and the rest is unnecessary and undesirable. It is also empirically untenable. The West, as a hegemonic power, has been trying to dominate the rest by coercion, and the rest has fully penetrated the West as a result of multiple migration: labor, capital, talent, and religion. The time is ripe for a dialogue of civilizations based on the spirit of interdependence.

part seven

PROMOTING CHANGE

20

Changing the
Mind of a Nation:
Elements in a Process for
Creating Prosperity

MICHAEL FAIRBANKS

INTRODUCTION:
BLAME THE COW FOR NO PROSPERITY

The Monitor Company worked for the government and private sector leaders of Colombia to study and provide recommendations on how the leather producers in that Andean nation could become more prosperous by exporting to the United States. We began in New York City to find the buyers of leather handbags from around the world, and we interviewed the representatives of 2,000 retail establishments across the United States. The data were complex but boiled down to one clear message: The prices of Colombian handbags were too high and the quality was too low.

We returned to Colombia to ask the manufacturers what lowered their quality and forced them to charge high prices. They told us, "No es nuestra culpa." It is not our fault. They said it was the fault of the local tanneries that supplied them with the hides. The tanneries had a 15 percent tariff protection from the Colombian government, which made the price of competing hides from Argentina too expensive.

We traveled to the rural areas to find the tannery owners. The tanneries pollute the nearby ground and water with harsh chemicals. The owners answered our questions happily. "It is not our fault," they explained, "It is the fault of the *mataderos*, the slaughterhouses. They provide a low-quality hide to the tanneries because they can sell the meat from the cow for more money with less effort. They have little concern for damaging the hides."

We went into the *campo* and found slaughterhouses with cowhands, butchers, and managers wielding stopwatches. We asked them the same questions and they explained that it was not their fault; it was the ranchers' fault. "You see," they said, "the ranchers overbrand their cows in an effort to keep the guerrillas, some of whom protect the drug lords, from stealing them." The large number of brands destroys the hides.

We finally reached the ranches, far away from the regional capital. We had reached the end of our search because there was no one left to interview. The ranchers spoke in a rapid local accent. They told us that the problems were not their fault. "No es nuestra culpa," they told us. "Es la culpa de la vaca." It's the cow's fault. The cows are stupid, they explained. They rub their hides against the barbed wire to scratch themselves and to deflect the biting flies of the region.

We had come a long way, banging our laptop computers over washboard-surfaced roads and exposing our shoes to destruction from the chemicals in the tanneries and mud. We had learned that Colombian handbag makers cannot compete for the attractive U.S. market because their cows are dumb.

Many Interpretations of the Problem

There are many different ways to consider the issues faced by our friends in Colombia. Imagine a macroeconomist's interpretation of the "blame the cow" story: He might remove the tariff and "let the market find a new equilibrium." The nongovernmental organizations (NGOs) might work to upgrade the barbed wire fence, and a business strategist might study and segment the consumer market. A sociologist might say that "the level of interpersonal trust" in the community is too low. An anthropologist might say that they are simply at "a different stage in their economic development" and should be left alone to progress naturally.

The different interpretations of our experience in Colombia shed light on the different interpretations of the impediments to creating prosperity. Prosperity, after all, is hard to define. Just as many people would view the cow story in a different light, there are many different views on what prosperity is and how to create it. To examine this further, I will break prosperity down into its broad constituents, explain why prosperity is important, and offer elements in a change process for creating prosperity.

What Is Prosperity?

Prosperity is the ability of an individual, group, or nation to provide shelter, nutrition, and other material goods that enable people to live a good life,[1] according to their own definition. Prosperity helps create space in people's hearts and minds so that they may develop a healthy emotional and spiritual life, according to their preferences, unfettered by the everyday concern of the material goods they require to survive.

We can think of prosperity as both a flow and a stock. Many economists view it as a flow of income: the ability of a person to purchase a set of goods, or capture value created by someone else. We use an upgraded notion of income called "purchasing power."[2] For example, the per capita income of Romania is about $1,350, but the purchasing power is almost $3,500 because the cost of many things is lower than the world market.

Prosperity is also the enabling environment that improves productivity. We can therefore look at prosperity as a set of stocks.[3] I list here seven kinds of stock, or capital, the last four of which constitute social capital:

1. Natural endowments such as location, subsoil assets, forests, beaches, and climate
2. Financial resources of a nation, such as savings and international reserves
3. Humanly made capital, such as buildings, bridges, roads, and telecommunications assets
4. Institutional capital, such as legal protections of tangible and intangible property, efficient government departments, and firms that maximize value to shareholders and compensate and train workers
5. Knowledge resources, such as international patents, and university and think tank capacities
6. Human capital, which represents skills, insights, capabilities
7. Culture capital, which means not only the explicit articulations of culture like music, language, and ritualistic tradition but also attitudes and values that are linked to innovation

Moving away from a conceptualization of prosperity as simply a flow of per capita income enables us to consider a broader system and the decisions for investment in an enriched and enabling "high-productive" environment.[4] Nobel laureate Amartya Sen suggests that "the advantage of a stock view would be to give us a better idea of a nation's ability to produce things in the future."[5]

Why Does Prosperity Matter?

We know that individuals around the world have vastly different purchasing power, and countries possess stocks of wealth in different proportions. According to Thomas Sowell, "We need to confront the most blatant fact that has persisted across centuries of social history—vast differences in productivity among peoples, and the economic and other consequences of such differences."[6] Recent reports by the World Bank indicate that the standard of living in many regions in Africa, Latin America, and Asia is threatened by declining productivity.

There are intimate connections between poverty and malnutrition: muscle wastage, stunting of growth, increased susceptibility to infections, and the destruction of cognitive capacity in children. Eighty-four percent of all the children in the world live in poverty, measured as less than two dollars a day in income per capita. The vast majority of all the babies in the world are born into poverty. Life expectancy, literacy, potable water, and infant mortality are correlated with the productivity and prosperity of a nation. In low-income countries, 607 women out of 100,000 died in childbirth in 1990, whereas in advanced economies only 11 out of 100,000 died.[7]

But poverty is more insidious than statistics indicate. Poverty destroys aspirations, hope, and happiness. This is the poverty you can't measure but can feel. There is a rich literature on correlation between higher incomes and productive attitudes toward authority, tolerance of others and support of civil liberties, openness toward foreigners, positive relationships with subordinates, self-esteem, sense of personal competence, the disposition to participate in community and national affairs, interpersonal trust, and satisfaction with one's own life. As an example, symposium participant Ronald Inglehart writes that higher rates of self-reporting of both objective and subjective well-being correlate with higher levels of national prosperity.[8]

How Should We Speak About Beliefs and Prosperity?

There are segments of each society that hold different beliefs about what prosperity is and how it is created. Acknowledging and understanding this is the basis for creating change. In *Plowing the Sea—Nurturing the Hidden Sources of Growth in the Developing World*, Stace Lindsay and I developed several principles related to mental models:[9]

- A mental model consists of beliefs, inferences, and goals that are first-person, concrete, and specific. It is a mental map of how the world works.[10]
- There are sets of beliefs and attitudes that are either pro-innovation and create the conditions for prosperity, or anti-innovation.[11] These beliefs form a mental model.
- A mental model can be defined, informed, and tested around a specific, well-defined objective. Nobel laureate Douglass North writes that human beings use "both . . . mental models . . . and institutions" to "shape the performance of economies."[12]
- Finally, mental models can be changed. Although culture involves the transmission of meaning from one generation to another,[13] it is unlikely that it is a genetic process.[14]

Alex Inkeles suggests that across the world there is a general convergence of actions and beliefs. He states that "there is evidence of a strong tendency for all nations to move toward increasing utilization of modes of production based on inanimate power, resting in turn on modern technology and applied science." He suggests that these "new productive arrangements" create new institutional patterns and new roles for the individual and also "*induce . . . new attitudes and values.*"[15]

Joseph Stiglitz, former chief economist for the World Bank, writes that "development represents a transformation of society, a movement from traditional relations, traditional ways of thinking, traditional ways of dealing with health and education, traditional methods of productions, to modern ways."[16]

If such prominent people are making the case, why is the action agenda of governments and international institutions so bereft of mental models research? Why are there so few formal national or regional change processes in place to change mind-sets? What positions do the world's foremost development institutions take on this? Are they constrained by lack of awareness, underdeveloped tools, poor internal consensus, political correctness with shareholders and the press, governance issues, or their own mind-set? Even Paul Krugman, one of the most influential economists in the world today, acknowledges that "economics is marked by a startling crudeness in the way it thinks about individuals and their motivations. . . . Economists are notoriously uninterested in how people actually think or feel."[17]

After five decades of, in most cases, frustratingly slow development, mental models may offer the best way to understand and attack the problem of poverty. Symposium organizer Lawrence Harrison suggests that this type of change will be hard "because it requires the capacity for objective introspection and attribution to internal factors that touch on the most sensitive questions of self-image and respect."[18] Inkeles agrees that introspection is important: "It is the mark of a modern nation that it stresses a continuous process of self-analysis. . . . [A modern nation] is self-correcting."[19]

We as practitioners constantly speculate whether prospective client nations—nations that ask for help in improving their economies—can develop a greater capacity to be self-correcting. To respond to them, we must make the first of many steps in a change process and ask, What is the nation's model for creating prosperity?

ELEMENTS OF A CHANGE PROCESS

Change is a sloppy process and will never occur in an easily described sequence. Despite this, people who want to construct their own change will have to have a schema that is shared and some sense of the components that are necessary to promote change, as well as a broad scope of skills and insights across many domains.

Leaders of nations from both private and public sectors invite us to help them improve their economies, specifically their export competitiveness. We have learned over the last decade that macroeconomic prescriptions designed in the political and intellectual capitals of North America and Europe are insufficient. Although the methodologies are complex and draw inspiration across a variety of intellectual domains, I will reduce them to ten critical elements and use illustrations from our work in several countries. I will focus more in this chapter on the first five steps, since they create the conditions for understanding steps six through ten.[20]

Decode the Current Strategy for Prosperity

Most nations that are not creating wealth at a high rate share much in common. Our evidence suggests that they are over-reliant on natural resources, including cheap labor, and that they believe in the simple advantages of climate, location, and government favor.[21] Because of this, they often do not build the capacity to produce differentiated goods and services that create greater value for demanding consumers who are willing to pay more money for these goods.

By focusing on these easily imitated advantages, on these lower forms of capital, they compete solely on the basis of price, which tends to suppress wages. Keeping wages low is competing to see which country can stay the poorest the longest. These are exports based on poverty, not on wealth creation. A nation's ability to create both price and non-price value for consumers inside and outside the country is what determines its productivity, and therefore its prosperity.[22]

Countries that are thought to be rich in natural resources are often really not rich. Venezuela is a country the size of Texas with vast forests, oil reserves, beautiful beaches, and a mix of indigenous groups and peoples from Spain, Germany, Italy, and the Middle East. Many people believe Venezuela to be potentially the richest nation in Latin America. However, the purchasing power of its average citizens has declined since the early 1970s. If you take the 1997 oil-based profits of $14 billion and divide them by its population of 21 million people, you will find that the oil income represents less than two dollars a day in income per citizen. Moreover, these profits are never distributed equitably: Venezuela possesses the highest rate of poverty increase on the continent. More than 90 percent of the country's exports consist of unprocessed natural resources. Our research suggests that the more a nation exports in natural resources, the less prosperity it creates for its average citizens.

A look at the seven forms of capital mentioned above points to the fact that Venezuela is rich in natural endowments, and when commodity prices are high, the country is temporarily cash rich. However, the country has decaying transportation and communications infrastructures that peaked in quality in the late 1970s, government institutions that are inefficient and corrupt, and university–private sector relationships that do not create knowledge capital. With respect to human capital, Venezuela suffers from some of the lowest standards for primary and secondary education on the continent. Finally, some Venezuelan values and attitudes are anti-innovation and progress resistant. For example, trust and respect for national leaders is the lowest that we have ever tested. Venezuela has been victimized by its spurious success, its overabundance of natural resources, and its failure to learn how to make tough choices and innovate.

Create a Sense of Urgency

Some nations are ready for change and others are not. What would create enormous urgency for some people does not create enough urgency for others. A sense of urgency is created when there is a gap between expectation and reality. The expectation is informed and placed in perspective by knowledge of outside events and a sense of purpose.

One African country I know is less open to change than it should be. This nation is one of the highest per capita debtors in the world. It has been given or has borrowed $8 billion since 1991, and the per capita standard of living has declined 4 percent a year over the same time span. Three out of every ten people test positive for the HIV virus. The traditional export industry lies in ruins, a victim of under-investment, declining consumer demand, and competition. Seven out of ten people live on less than one dollar a day.

When I discussed their under-funded AIDS prevention program with them and asked what they need to do about the spread of HIV, one cabinet member said, "We are telling the people to stop having sex." When I suggested that we look at some of the things that Uganda is accomplishing, they told me that they were not interested in Uganda for they, "not Uganda, had possessed the third highest standard of living in Africa" twenty-five years ago. They suggested that their cabinet had lawyers and accountants in it, and they did not have to "go back to school to learn" what other nations were doing. They criticize the World Bank and IMF in the press, blame their problems on outside events like legacy of apartheid in the region and the war in Angola. Their plan is to move into exporting maize, in which they "would have a natural advantage," and to continue borrowing from the World Bank. This year they have to use more than half their allotment of almost $400 million to repay old loans.

One might attribute their behavior to fatalism, a reverence for the past when things were better, blind pride, and an accompanying lack of openness that stands in the way of learning and innovation. One thing is certain: This country is doomed to more failure until the human crisis grows and forces them to reflect on the deep-rooted impediments to their productivity.

Understand the Range of Strategic Choices and Inform Them with Analyses

Many of the choices available to firms and governments can be reduced to the following categories:

Micro Choices. Business strategy is based on an integrated set of choices designed to achieve a specific set of objectives in an informed and timely manner. In developing nations we see few company strategies that are informed by good research, made explicit, and shared by corporate leaders. We have found seven patterns of uncompetitive behavior at the microeconomic level: over-dependence on natural resources and cheap labor; poor understanding of foreign customers' buying preferences; lack of knowledge of competitor activities; poor inter-firm cooperation; lack of forward integration into global markets; a paternalistic relationship between government and the private sector; and defensiveness in government, the private sector, the unions, and the media.

These seven patterns are the norm for companies in countries where the average citizen does not have a high and rising standard of living. The results of these seven patterns are simple exports that compete on price—and low wages—in an increasingly demanding marketplace that provides fewer returns.

To mitigate patterns of uncompetitive behavior requires a set of firm-level choices around structuring new learning and decisionmaking. Inside such patterns lies a hidden opportunity for creating prosperity.

Macro Choices.   The second choice is the extent to which government supports the private sector. Some say that government needs to do more for the private sector, and some say government needs to get out of the way. If we characterize government choices around the level of intervention in the economy, we find a broad range of choices between classic socialism and monetarism. In Cuba, the government has become over-responsible for the welfare of the average citizen, supplying housing, health care, education, jobs, food, and even entertainment and news. Ownership is by the state through collectives and is accompanied by centralized planning that uses quantitative targets and administrative prices. Income distribution tends to be even, and growth tends to be low.

The monetarist approach is a sparse but rigid social contract between government and the private sector, which in effect says that government will create a stable macroeconomic environment, and the private sector entrepreneurs will create growth. This strategy emphasizes stabilizing markets, freeing wages and currency exchange rates, and allowing markets to develop. This strategy appears to create more poverty and greater gaps in income, especially in the near term. It fails to acknowledge that the government has a role in the innovation process. It is, we believe, an overreaction to the failed policies of government intervention (e.g., the import substitution that was so popular in Africa and Latin America in the 1970s and 1980s).

Our view differs from both these national strategies. We believe that government needs to do everything it can to help the private sector succeed, except to impede competition. This means investing, or helping the private sector to invest, in the higher forms of capital. In poorer countries, government will have to do more than in richer countries. The relationship has to be specially designed, based on a nation's stage of growth and the capacities of each sector.

Create a Compelling Vision

A vision serves to create a sense of purpose that encourages people to change their actions. The following eight core elements of a good mental model emerged from our work with the leaders of Uganda.

1. A high and rising standard of living for all Ugandans.
2. An understanding that the world has changed dramatically: the costs of communications, transportation, and learning are declining rapidly.
3. An acknowledgment that Uganda is over-dependent on the basic, highly imitatable advantages of subsoil assets, climate, government favors, and cheap labor.
4. An understanding that wealth is based on insight, sophisticated human capital, and attitudes focused on competition as a force that spurs innovation and fosters human initiative, learning, interpersonal trust, and cooperation.
5. An understanding that Uganda's strategies are not a choice between economic growth and social equity, but that economic growth facilitates social equity and vice versa. The more we invest in people the better the chances for growth for a company and the nation.
6. An understanding that productivity is not just competing on the things with which Uganda is naturally endowed. Competitiveness is productivity, and productivity involves what product segments we want to compete in, where we choose to compete, and how we choose to compete.
7. An acknowledgment that the government of Uganda must do everything it can to assist the private sector, except to impede competition. It must invest in people, specialized infrastructure, learning organizations, and a non-defensive dialogue with the private sector, political opposition, unions, and other nations.
8. An understanding that the private sector in Uganda needs to invest more in learning about customer preferences, knowledge of competitor activities, new distribution channels, and investing in the improvement of its people and products.

These core elements of a vision need to be embraced by developing nations as they seek to upgrade their economies and create more prosperity for more people.

Create New Networks of Relationships

After twelve years of civil war, Salvadorans are boldly dedicating themselves to building new networks as part of a national change process between the producers and foreign consumers within the country, and between themselves and their emigrant cousins in the United States. Ornamental-plant producers have traveled to Florida and the Netherlands to meet with and learn about their distribution channels. Honey producers have undertaken surveys to learn about their German customers. Even some of the coffee growers, the oldest exporters and those most entrenched in the old ways of doing things, show signs of trying new things. They are beginning to work in eco-friendly coffee and, with other Salvadoran industries, are testing the market for such innovative products as coffee tourism.

The government has institutionalized the National Competitiveness Program and has trained facilitators to teach small and medium-sized exporters to develop business strategies. The government is investing in education networks, building an Internet program in rural areas, and providing some of their best university students with software training in India. The government and private sector are reaching out with conferences and through the Internet to the prosperous emigrant community network in the United States, inviting them to be business partners who will bring access to markets, knowledge, technology, and capital.

The leaders of El Salvador understand that communication—between rural areas and the capital, between their companies and foreign consumers, and between the nation and the emigrant community—creates more rapid flows of insight and forms the basis of their competitiveness and prosperity.

Communicate the Vision

Nations have to use all available means to change minds: electronic and print media, billboards, speeches by leaders, conferences, workshops, databases, and Web sites. The diffusion and adoption of new ways of thinking will take a predictable course.

We are mindful that the innovators are often not the principal agents of change. In fact, the early adopters often serve as role models for most of the rest of the nation. In our work, we look to champions who are highly receptive to doing things in new ways and can articulate and embody the new ideas of competitiveness, productivity, and prosperity. We have found that the people who are most effective in this part of the diffusion process are not the typical leaders with high status, but those who have internalized the ideas of competitiveness and innovation and can transmit them to domestic networks. We met and trained a coffee grower in El Salvador, who spoke to the entrenched elites in that sector. We found an imaginative taxi driver in Bermuda to work within the highly fragmented taxi community to create a new taxi-touring product. Their main objective was to demonstrate "innovativeness."

Build Productive Coalitions

Many social scientists believe that practicing change stimulates the development of a new mental model. We therefore have promoted weekly meetings to stimulate strategic thinking within clusters of related industries. We worked with the group that "blamed the cow" in workshops designed to improve interpersonal trust and seek a common strategic vision. By practicing "productive reasoning" techniques, we have created some of the conditions for group problem solving when difficult and contentious issues arose.[23]

We have encouraged hotel managers and unionized employees in a hotel industry to focus on new segments of customers to serve. We have encouraged the purchasers of state-owned enterprises and small vendors to streamline and share the former's strategy plan. And we have worked with government ministries and agricultural producers who had fought aggressively over the nation's macroeconomic agenda. These experiments in productive reasoning have led to pilot programs with specific objectives and well-thought-out metrics of success.

Develop and Communicate Short-Term Wins

People are more likely to change their attitudes and behavior when they see demonstrations of success. Politicians understand this well and are particularly attracted to this part of the process. In any change effort, we need to find examples in which good things happened because of the new vision. Some examples of success might include a new product development, a large overseas sale to new customers, or an agreement between union and management for new investment in training or improvement in working conditions. Although short-term wins do not need to be large, they need to be communicated in the context of a new way of doing things.

Institutionalize the Changes

Douglass North writes that institutions are norms.[24] Change needs to create new norms of behavior. We look not to creating new institutions but to upgrading existing institutions that have reached their functional limits due to globalization, changes in how prosperity is created, and worldwide shifts in values and attitudes. This means everything from improving the rule of law and building democracy to upgrading schools, private firms, and civic organizations.

For example, we helped an industry association change itself from a lobbying group that fights the government to an organization that does management education, fosters research and development, informs small enterprises, and supports market studies of foreign customers.

Evaluate and Affirm the Changes

Finally, we need to create the space for nations to be introspective and to self-correct. We need to create national summits and other venues with leaders of the public, private, civic, and academic sectors. These venues could allow leaders to discuss the economic and social results that the nation is experiencing, as well as the strategies, institutional mechanisms, and mental models that caused these results. Specific questions could include, What quantitative metrics can we use? What are our non-quantifiable objectives? What tools can we improve to evaluate ourselves? What kind of change can happen soon, and which kinds will be intergenerational?

Our strategy for change and creating prosperity in nations should meet the tests of actionable strategy: It should balance the past with the future, be explicit and shared, be informed with analyses, be based on an integrated set of choices, and help the people become who they want to be.

CONCLUSION

Most people believe that prosperity is a good thing. They also know that it is hard to achieve. Only a handful of the world's two hundred nations have discovered how to do it for the majority of their citizens. Even if the messages on how to create prosperity were simple and clear, it would not be for any outsider to tell nations and peoples to change. Questions of the competence, moral authority, and intentions of outsiders can justly be raised.[25] However, those of us who are interested and informed on these issues have an obligation to demonstrate to the leaders of nations that "prosperity is a choice"[26] and to clarify what those choices and trade-offs might be.

After a half century of focus on economic development, now is the time to move away from simple normative frameworks, top-down recommendations, a narrow conceptualization of prosperity, and metrics of performance based almost solely on national quantitative aggregates. Now is the time for concerted national and regional initiatives that change mental models. Now is the time to focus on the microeconomic foundations of prosperity and to diffuse "innovativeness."

Howard Gardner makes a distinction in his writing between the direct leaders of organizations and people and the indirect leaders who create learning and shape opinion.[27] In the Cultural Values and Human Progress Symposium we had a board member and a country director from the World Bank and the deputy administrator of USAID. These are leaders who allocate major resources to the problem of development. We also have among us some of the most eminent thinkers from the domains of economics, anthropology, political science, and public policy, who have opined on such diverse and relevant topics as trust, firm-level competitiveness, gender equality, and early childhood development.

We see poverty in the endless stream of social and economic indicators and other abstractions that come across our desks and pop onto our computer screens every day. Then there is the poverty that moves you when you meet a bright Indian boy from a low caste who will not attend school. There is the poverty that physically threatens you with a machete against your throat on the streets of Nairobi. And there is the poverty that sickens you when you meet an adolescent living on the streets of Bogota who lost her fingers and toes to hungry rats when she was abandoned as an infant in the ancient dank system of sewers.

Haunted by these images and inspired by the contributors to this volume, we wonder if some of the social and political problems in the Great Lakes region of East and Central Africa, or the Balkans, are linked to issues of prosperity. Instead, we must consider how the current political and military solutions in those regions can be supplemented, or even substituted, with a holistic change process.

Although every contributor shares a commitment to make lives better around the world, most of us are commenting from a point of view that is strongly guided by our professional specialty and our job description, as well as our own mental model. Our challenge is not unlike that of the experts who would attempt to fix the "blame the cow story": How to merge one set of insights with another, to begin to create a locally owned process for change in developing nations that is so thoughtfully integrated, well guided, and productively discussed that it begins to put nations and peoples on the path to high and rising prosperity. So far, the world has not seen anything like it.

21

Culture, Mental Models, and National Prosperity

STACE LINDSAY

Culture is a significant determinant of a nation's ability to prosper because culture shapes individuals' thoughts about risk, reward, and opportunity. This chapter argues that cultural values do matter in the process of human progress because they shape the way individuals think about progress. In particular, cultural values matter because they form the principles around which economic activity is organized—and without economic activity, progress is not possible.

The global economy of the twenty-first century offers both unprecedented opportunity for the creation of prosperity throughout the world and a potential threat to centuries of cultural traditions in all parts of the world, a tension that is captured in the following anecdote. After I gave a speech recently on economic competitiveness to a group of government and business leaders in Ghana, a young man approached me to ask if my speech implied that his culture had to change in order for his country to succeed in the global economy. He pointed out that in his ethnic group, tradition required a high degree of respect for the elders, and many of the elders in his village did not want the young leaders to become too involved in the affairs of national business.

His question brings to light a compelling issue: Will individuals in developing countries have to change their cultural heritage in order to participate more meaningfully in the global economy? Is it possible for a region to pre-serve its history and integrity—and to honor its local cultures—and still be globally competitive?

These are questions that many of the contributors to this volume have asked, questions to which there are no clear answers. Understanding either of the dominant themes of this volume—culture or human progress—is a diffi-cult challenge. To understand them and to integrate them is difficult in the extreme.

Contributors David Landes, Michael Porter, and Jeffrey Sachs have raised important questions about the role of other variables that affect economic development, such as government policy, geography, and disease. Others have discussed the importance of culture in shaping attitudes about work, trust, and authority—all of which influence human progress. Yet a funda-mental question remains: How can one help foster the changes necessary to create steadily rising standards of living in the developing world? Further-more, as Richard Shweder asked, would doing so threaten the integrity of the culture in question? Would it limit our ability to have other cultures illumi-nate our own?

As consultants, my colleagues at Monitor Company and I have invested considerable effort in advising business and government leaders on how to create more competitive economies. We have tried to do so in a manner that is respectful of local heritages and institutions. Time and again, we have made strong arguments for the need to change specific policies, strategies, ac-tions, or modes of communication. For the most part, the leaders with whom we have had the privilege of working have acknowledged the validity of our perspective. We have learned, however, that good answers to the pressing questions of economic development are not sufficient to engender the change needed to reverse the tides of poorly performing economies. Individuals will often accept intellectual arguments, understand their need to change, and ex-press commitment to changing, but then resort to what is familiar. This ten-dency to revert to the familiar is not a cultural trait per se, but it is indicative of some of the deeper challenges faced by those who wish to promote a dif-ferent, more prosperous vision of the future.

Economic progress depends on changing the way people think about wealth creation. This means changing the underlying attitudes, beliefs, and assumptions that have informed the decisions made by leaders that result in poor economic performance. In his remarks, Howard Gardner referred to the tendency of cognitive scientists to try to understand the mental represen-tations that individuals use to make sense of the world. This is where one must start if one wants to create lasting change. Peter Senge, among others, has called these representations "mental models," which he defines as "deeply ingrained assumptions, generalizations, or even pictures or images that influence how we understand the world and how we take action."[1]

Many contributors to this volume have pointed out that the "unit of analysis" for the question of cultural values and economic progress is not clear. Should it be groups of nations with similar religious heritage, individual nations with distinct historical and cultural values, or perhaps different communities within nations that are bound together by common beliefs? Robert Edgerton writes that there can be one economy but many cultures.

Relying on broad attributions about religious beliefs or other broad cultural characteristics to explain economic performance does not help the productive dialogue about culture. As Mariano Grondona remarked, scholars have used Confucianism to first explain Asia's failure, then its success, and then its crises. Although discussions of the impact of Catholic versus Protestant work ethics may yield interesting observations, they are too abstract to be of use for creating change. And there are always exceptions—highly productive, successful Catholics in progress-resistant cultures and highly unsuccessful Protestants in progress-prone cultures. We must develop more clarity about the unit of analysis.

Applying the filter of mental models to the task of understanding culture's influence on prosperity is a helpful exercise. Mental models are the underlying beliefs that influence the way people behave. Culture is a broader, macro-level variable. Mental models are a micro-level variable. Mental models apply to individuals and groups of individuals—and are identifiable and changeable. Culture reflects the aggregation of individual mental models and in turn influences the types of mental models that individuals have. The two are linked in a perpetually evolving system.

The real point of leverage in creating change may well be helping to change mental models at the individual level, beginning with the way individuals think about wealth creation. There is an important relationship between mental models and prosperity, one that does not necessarily force the homogenization of global culture. To understand this relationship, it will be helpful to present a brief summary of the challenges of national prosperity.

THE CHALLENGE OF NATIONAL PROSPERITY

The Engines of Growth

The broad objective of this volume is to explore the relationship between cultural values and human progress. In the following discussion, it is assumed that economic progress is fundamental to human progress. The perspectives shared relate to challenges that leaders in the developing world face to foster

economic growth and development. Economic growth is indispensable because other forms of human progress (e.g., health, education, infrastructure)
depend on productive economic activity. The question becomes one of understanding what the engines of economic growth in an economy are and how
they work, and, ultimately, of how best to encourage the productive use of a
nation's resources to create the opportunity for human progress.

This leads to a second assumption. I believe that successful businesses are
the engines of growth, for it is at the level of the individual business that
wealth creation occurs. Products are created, services are provided, productivity is enhanced, wealth is generated. Without businesses there will be no
economic progress, and without economic progress there will be no human
progress. These assumptions lead to the following syllogism:

> Human progress broadly defined is not possible without economic
>   growth.
> Successful businesses are the engines of economic growth.
> Therefore, successful businesses are a necessary precondition for
>   human progress.

Given these assumptions, the focus quickly turns to a discussion of what
makes for successful businesses and how these types of businesses can be
fostered.

Comparative Advantage and Competitive Advantage

Research by Jeffrey Sachs and by the Monitor Company into the economic
performance of nations throughout the world has revealed that nations having the greatest abundance of natural resources tend to perform more poorly
than those that do not have an abundance of natural resources.[2] Although
comparative-advantage theory would hold that countries with unique comparative advantages should specialize in their areas of strength, nations that
are rich in natural resources and focus on selling those resources in the global
marketplace tend to be the poorest on a per capita basis.

The reason for the relatively poor performance of natural resource–rich nations is that natural resources tend to be commodity products, and producers
have little control over the prices to be charged. In fact, commodity prices have
been steadily declining in real terms for the past twenty-five years. As a result,
many nations are actually exporting a greater volume of material but are earn-
ing less real money for their efforts. In today's global economy, a comparative
advantage in natural resources does not assure economic prosperity.

The same holds true for nations jockeying to take advantage of their comparative advantage in inexpensive labor. When a nation's firms develop ex-

port strategies based on low labor costs, they create a self-fulfilling cycle. In order to compete in their chosen segments, they must keep labor costs at a minimum. It therefore becomes impossible for them to increase salaries, for if they do, they will find themselves with uncompetitive products. If this happens, they will either go out of business or look to set up operations in neighboring countries that have even lower wage rates.

Both of these examples—natural resource–based strategies and inexpensive labor-based strategies—can be characterized as comparative-advantage strategies. Both have proven themselves incapable of creating high and rising standards of living.

Clearly there are many other factors that determine the ability of a nation to succeed, for example, stable macroeconomic environments, transparent and efficient government institutions, adequate infrastructure, an educated workforce, quality health care. Although these themes have received extensive analysis, research on what is necessary to create success at the firm level in the developing world is relatively sparse.

For the past twenty years, Michael Porter has written extensively about competitive advantage at the level of the firm, the region, and the nation, and his research has provoked a deeper look at the microeconomic variables that influence success. In the 1998 Global Competitiveness Report, he developed the "microeconomic competitiveness index," which measures the quality of the competitive environment in a given nation. He notes:

> There is a growing consensus that a macroeconomic policy involving prudent government finances, a moderate cost of government, a limited government role in the economy and openness to international markets promotes national prosperity. Yet a stable political context and sound macroeconomic policies are necessary but not sufficient to ensure a prosperous economy. As important—or even more so—are the microeconomic foundations of economic development, rooted in firm operating practices and strategies as well as in the business inputs, infrastructure, institutions and policies that constitute the environment in which a nation's firms compete. Unless there is appropriate improvement at the microeconomic level, political and macroeconomic reform will not bear fruit.[3]

Given the growing consensus about the foundations of macroeconomic management, and the emerging understanding of the microeconomic foundations of competitiveness, the question arises, Why is creating change so difficult in under-performing economies? Is it necessary to have a stable government, a sound economy, and a strong microeconomic foundation before a nation can experience significant gains? Clearly, that would be ideal. But economic development is often a chicken-and-egg phenomenon. Business leaders will argue that they cannot develop better strategies until the government gets its act together, and government leaders will argue that they can't take any significant steps until the business community demonstrates its willingness to compete and not seek protection from competition.

Prosperity requires that the foundations be in place but that a "competitive mind-set" that fosters innovation and productivity in the national economy also exist.

The Need for a Competitive Mind-set

Our experience advising business and government leaders has been that finding answers to the strategic problems they face is not that difficult, even in environments that are suffering from poor government policies and inadequate infrastructure. The difficulty is in changing the way that people think about their business problems. There is a legacy of comparative advantage thinking—often embedded in institutions, laws, and policies—throughout much of the developing world, a legacy that has made it very difficult for leaders to make different choices.

The following list summarizes some of the patterns of thought we have observed in business and government leaders throughout the developing world. The column on the left is a firm-level adaptation of "progress-resistant characteristics" in the typologies of Mariano Grondona and Lawrence Harrison. The column on the right represents their corresponding "progress-prone characteristics."

Comparative Advantage and Competitive Advantage

Progress-Resistant Characteristics	*Progress-Prone Characteristics*
Protected markets	Globalization and competition
Macroeconomic focus	Microeconomic focus
Access to leaders	Firm-level productivity
Focus on physical/financial capital	Focus on human/knowledge capital
Hierarchy and rigid organizations	Flexible meritocratic organizations
Economies of scale	Flexibility
Dependence on foreign partners	Migration strategies
Reactive approach	Proactive approach
Government as master strategist	Shared vision and collaboration
Redistribution of wealth	Creation of wealth
Paternalism	Innovation

To repeat, there are many real political and physical barriers to changing the way firms compete, such as poor national economic performance, poor infrastructure, and lack of skilled workers. However, business leaders no longer have the luxury of waiting for the national infrastructure to improve before changing the way they think about competition and business strategy. If they cannot begin to find innovative business solutions to their problems, there will be no improvement for the nation as a whole. Ideally, both would work together to create a dynamic system of mutual improvement.

Economic Growth and Social Equity

The current model of competition throughout much of the developing world creates a vicious cycle. Firms compete on the basis of inexpensive labor and abundant natural resources. This traps them in commodity businesses, where it is very difficult to earn high margins. Without high margins, however, they are unable to make significant investments in human capital; and without significant investments in human capital, they are unable to create deeper sources of innovation.

But there is also a virtuous cycle of economic growth and social equity on a sustainable basis. In this virtuous circle, firms take the initiative to develop more complex business products and more sophisticated business strategies. These will help create higher-margin businesses, which provide the fuel to make more investments in the workforce. A more highly educated workforce stimulates a higher rate of innovation, and higher rates of innovation yield the ability to sell increasingly complex goods and services. Seeing the world in this way makes it possible to think of developing sustainable competitive advantages and overcoming centuries of static comparative advantage.

Although this model makes intuitive sense, persuading business and government leaders to change the existing patterns of competition has proven to be quite difficult. Michael Fairbanks and I have spent much of the past decade trying to encourage government and business leaders to adopt policies and strategies that promote the creation of sustainable business growth—to move away from the illusory advantages of basic-factor thinking to competitive-advantage thinking. Our experience has led us to the conclusion that business and government leaders consistently fall into strategic and behavioral patterns that inhibit their ability to create more complex sources of advantage, and thus sustainable success in the global economy:

Strategic Patterns	*Behavioral Patterns*
Over-dependence on basic factors	Lack of cooperation
Poor understanding of customers	Defensiveness

Poor understanding of relative position	Paternalism
Lack of vertical integration	

Efforts to alter these patterns of behavior in nations throughout the world have convinced us that these microeconomic problems are rooted in the culture. Although the strategic patterns should be resolvable through the power of analysis, good business practices, and a commitment to learning, the behavioral patterns are much more difficult to see, understand, and change.

These patterns help explain why some firms are unable to become globally competitive. What is not clear is why these patterns repeat themselves in countries of widely differing political, economic, social, and cultural heritages. The macroeconomic variables that affect developing nations are quite different, but the microeconomic patterns are strikingly similar.

This observation illuminates the link between culture and economic competitiveness. The way people think about business, economics, or competition shapes the quality of the strategic choices they make.

Understanding the Way Leaders Think

One approach to understanding why business leaders organize their companies and strategies in the way they do is to understand how they think about and respond to the pressing issues they confront on a daily basis. One way to do this is to try to understand a nation by how its constituent groups think about the critical issues of the day.

National Surveys. Starting in 1992, a small team from the Monitor Company began an ongoing effort to advise business and government leaders throughout the developing world on how to improve the competitiveness of their industries. Our efforts to alter these patterns began with initiatives aimed at government policy and firm-level strategy. What we came to realize, however, was that the prevailing policy environments and the prevailing strategies-in-use were not so much the cause of the patterns we observed as the result of the way that people thought about wealth creation. This led us to develop a series of survey instruments to learn how key constituents thought about wealth creation. We began this effort in Colombia with a survey administered to approximately four hundred government and business leaders. The survey was designed to measure the way that leaders in both the public sector and private sector felt about different dimensions of the political, economic, and social problems they faced in their country. Our goal was to identify a number of the critical issues that would enable us to focus on fostering a broadly shared vision for the nation.

We began our research by simply measuring differences in attitudes about key national issues. We developed a survey instrument designed to show where there was a shared vision and where there was not. We found, for example, that there was a high degree of consensus on issues that many leaders did not consider to be very important to the nation, such as bilateral trade agreements and export promotion. We also found a very low degree of consensus on issues that the leaders felt were very important, such as exchange rates and inflation control. Although this type of research provided some insight, it did not point toward a path to change. To make this analysis more likely to facilitate change, we decided to segment our results not by national issues but by organizational affiliation, with an eye toward using the data to encourage individual organizations to change.

Since we had observed a high degree of defensiveness in government officials and business leaders, we reasoned that it would be helpful to develop explicit data that helped inform the national debate. We believed that if we could identify the critical areas of discord, we could develop a process to forge a shared vision in the private and public sectors to enable them to work together for a more competitive Colombia.

We found, for example, that contraband control was very important to the textile industry, which was fighting a surge in illegal imports, but of relatively little importance to other industries or to government leaders. Inflation control was of critical importance to the flower sector but was not as critical to the leather industry. We then promoted seminars with these individual leaders to try to get across the idea that the comparative-advantage paradigms so prevalent in their beliefs were actually a critical impediment to their becoming competitive.

This effort resulted in a better understanding of how different opinions about key issues inhibited the evolution of a shared vision. This demographic segmentation was useful, but it did not create the insights that would precipitate change. Differing opinions about political and macroeconomic issues—as important as they are—do not explain firm-level behavior.

We did discover, however, that there were striking differences between leaders in different cities, not just between leaders in industry and government. This realization led us to an in-depth investigation of the performance of five of the major cities in Colombia. We then found that each of these five cities had its own perspective, style, and work pattern, as well as level of economic success.

Geographic Surveys.   The leadership in each of the five cities that we studied—Baranquilla, Bucaramanga, Cali, Cartagena, and Medellin—held very distinct views as to what made their city competitive. The leadership of the city with the highest level of per capita wealth, Medellin, viewed that city's advantages as being grounded in assets that would now be described as social capital, relating to cultural, civic, and human resource assets. The leadership of the cities with the lowest level of per capita income, Baranquilla and Cartagena, characterized their advantages as being based on natural resources. These data suggested a strong relationship between the mind-set of a region and its degree of economic success. Each city demonstrated a high degree of variability in the way it collectively perceived its sources of competitive advantage. And it was the city with the most competitive mind-set, Medellin, that had created the highest standard of living in Colombia.

MENTAL MODELS AND CHANGE EFFORTS

The results of our work with leaders in the five cities in Colombia led us to conclude that it is not culture per se that affects the quality of choices that regions make but rather the way individual leaders think about wealth creation. It is the aggregation of individual beliefs along dimensions such as wealth creation, social capital, and action orientation. In a word, the differences we found were a function of the mental models of the leaders of these cities.

Comparative-advantage thinking is the result of deeply held assumptions about how wealth is created. It is a mental model that resists change. The challenge that most change agents face is that they are promoting solutions to problems that their constituents do not fully comprehend. The insights developed through rigorous analysis should be sufficient to motivate individuals to change. Nevertheless, what I have found is also consistent with what Peter Senge concludes:

> New insights fail to get put into practice because they conflict with deeply held internal images of how the world works, images that limit us to familiar ways of thinking and acting. That is why the discipline of managing mental models— surfacing, testing and improving our internal pictures of how the world works— promises to be a major breakthrough for building learning organizations.[4]

Changing mental models will be a major breakthrough helping leaders create nations that compete more effectively in the global economy. The primary challenge is to break through the mental models that inhibit the development of competitive companies and competitive mind-sets. Cultural change may inevitably follow, but the task is not to change culture. The task is to create the conditions that give birth to competitive companies, for these will be the engines of growth that support human progress.

Our work with public and private sector leaders at the national level helped us identify national issues that inhibit the creation of a shared national vision. Our work with leaders at the regional level helped us identify local challenges to economic prosperity. But as we began to try to change the status quo, we realized that there is a much more dynamic level of intervention with which to begin, and that is to identify groups of individuals who share similar patterns of thinking.

In order to create meaningful change, it is necessary to identify the individuals who will benefit from change. Broad attributions about "the government" or the members of a certain city are not helpful. What would be helpful is to identify people by the way they think about how wealth is created, regardless of their institutional affiliation.

While we were working in Venezuela, and in subsequent work throughout the world, we developed a survey instrument capable of doing just that. Instead of simply analyzing the divisive issues of the day, we began to study very carefully the ways in which groups of individuals thought about key issues. This approach enabled us to segment a nation not by institutional affiliation or geographic location but by belief system. In Venezuela, for example, we found five distinct segments that were distinguished by their unique views about several critical issues. The "five Venezuelas" were not defined by demographic affiliation nor by geography, but rather by beliefs about individual variables that affect the economy.

Results from another national survey of almost four hundred El Salvadoran leaders in 1997 provide evidence that perhaps the most meaningful segmentation for change agents is mental models. Kaia Miller and the Monitor team developed a survey that measured dozens of individual variables and then grouped them into eleven factors that were used to create five distinct visions of El Salvador's competitive potential.[5]

The largest group of individuals in the survey was called the "frustrateds." They can be identified primarily by their frustration with both the government and the private sector. This group has no strong opinions about what economic and development model would help El Salvador improve, yet they are the group most likely to view El Salvador as being at the point of crisis.

The second largest group was the "statists." This group believes that the only thing El Salvador needs to overcome its current challenges is a small group of governmental decisionmakers deciding all social, economic, and political issues.

Unlike the statists, the "fighters" place their faith in the average citizen. They are confident that with the right support from the government, the average citizen will lead El Salvador to a better future.

The "protectionists" were the smallest group. Although almost all groups in El Salvador demonstrate some support for government protectionism, the protectionists are the most vocal. This group openly endorses policies such as government subsidies, protective tariffs, and other forms of government protection as strategies for successful competition in the global economy.

The only group that distinguished itself noticeably from the rest of the groups was the "open economy" group. This group believes in the importance of international connections through trade, educational exchanges, and so on. It is frustrated with the quality of government support of the private sector, but it has decided to move ahead and succeed without the help of the government.

It should be noted that this survey was administered to several distinct demographic groups: business, academic, labor, and government leaders. It was also administered to several distinct geographic groups: leaders in San Salvador, Sonsonate, Santa Ana, and San Miguel. Similar to the results of the work done in Colombia five years earlier, some useful insights were gleaned from this demographic and geographic data. However, each of the five mental models described above contained a balanced mixture of each demographic and geographic group. In other words, the true divisions in the country were not a function of where people lived or what their vocation was, but of their fundamental beliefs, assumptions, and attitudes about wealth creation.

Clearly El Salvador has a national culture—one grounded in its historic role as the smallest of the Central American countries, having the highest land density and suffering through a long and bitter civil war throughout the late 1970s and 1980s. Yet our discussions with former FMLN guerrilla leaders as well as the conservative ARENA party's leaders enabled us to understand that, even in this war-torn country, shared vision is possible if the right segmentation is used. Political, economic, demographic, or geographic segmentations do not enable a sufficient understanding of how people are thinking about their reality. On the other hand, mental-model segmentation can highlight differences in attitudes and beliefs that inhibit the wealth-creation process.

In fact, after we presented the results of our mental-model work to a group of leading Venezuelans, one member of the audience raised his hand and implored us to "make them one Venezuela again." He had seen for the first time how change could occur through the creation of shared vision based on mental models.

CONCLUDING THOUGHTS

Culture matters. But engendering action at the level of culture is a Herculean task. This chapter has argued that the underlying mental models informing the choices made by individuals provide the real leverage point for creating change. To return to the question posed by the Ghanaian mentioned at the beginning of this chapter, Must culture change to accommodate the global economy? Inevitably, cultures will change. But the relevant discussion is not a discussion about culture per se; it is about the distribution of individual belief systems as they relate to the relevant dimensions of change. Marshaling efforts to identify and understand how specific mental models limit the wealth-creating process is a significant step in the right direction to ensure human progress.

I offer the following five thoughts as concluding themes for this discussion.

Successful, growth-oriented businesses are necessary preconditions for progress. They are the engines of growth. For humans to progress, they must be capable of creating rising standards of living. Although the political theorists and economists continue to deepen our understanding of how certain policy frameworks or governance influence economic success, it is becoming increasingly important to understand that, at the core, it is the individual business that is the engine of growth. More effort must be spent helping to foster more competitive business enterprises.

Some strategies are more successful than others. Some businesses are more prone to success than others. They have developed sustainable business strategies and have invested in sources of differentiation and competitive advantage. Every business has the potential to do this, but very few do.

Competitive mind-sets (mental models) shape strategy. The limiting factor of good business strategy is not education. It is not government policy. It is not macroeconomic stability. Good business strategy requires a competitive mind-set—a set of beliefs, attitudes, and assumptions that govern how one views competition and wealth creation.

Mental models are distributed across demographic/geographic segments. The absence of competitive mind-sets cannot be blamed on national policies. Nor can it be blamed on culture writ large or on specific organizations. The single most important conclusion of our research into mental models is that they are distributed widely across the population. There are certain mental models—broadly speaking, comparative-advantage mind-sets—that limit the ability of businesses to succeed.

To promote the creation of successful businesses, mental models need to be reoriented. In order to foster economic growth and human progress, it will be necessary to alter fundamental mental models that shape the way individuals think about risk, trust, competition, authority, and other critical variables.

In the end, changing mental models may cause dramatic changes in the culture of a nation or region. But efforts to change culture will not create changes in a nation's economic performance. The appropriate level of analysis must be at the level of the individual—of the firm. Efforts must be made to understand which mental models drive the strategic choices that are being made, and those mental models must then become the focus for change efforts.

22

Promoting Progressive Cultural Change

LAWRENCE E. HARRISON

Largely unnoticed in U.S. academic circles, a new paradigm—an inward-looking theory that focuses on cultural values and attitudes—is gradually filling the explanatory vacuum left by the collapse of dependency theory. Latin America has recently taken the lead in articulating this culture-centered paradigm and in contriving initiatives to translate it into actions designed not only to accelerate economic growth but to fortify democratic institutions and promote social justice. The culture paradigm also has adherents in Africa and Asia.

Of course, many analysts who have studied the East Asian economic miracles over the past three decades have concluded that "Confucian" values like emphasis on the future, work, achievement, education, merit, and frugality have played a crucial role in their development. (These Protestant ethic-like values are rooted not only in Confucianism but also in ancestor worship and Taoism, among other belief systems.) But just as the success of the East Asians in the world market—so inconsistent with dependency theory—was largely ignored by Latin American intellectuals and politicians until recent years, so was the cultural explanation for those miracles. Latin America has now for the most part accepted the economic policy lessons of East Asia and is now confronting the question, If dependency and imperialism are *not* responsible for our economic underdevelopment, authoritarian political traditions, and extreme social injustice, what *is*?

That question was posed by the Venezuelan writer Carlos Rangel in a book published in the mid-1970s in French and Spanish with titles that translate as *From the Noble Savage to the Noble Revolutionary,* and subsequently in English as *The Latin Americans—Their Love-Hate Relationship with the United States.*[1] Rangel was not the first Latin American to conclude that traditional Ibero-American values and attitudes, and the institutions that reflected and reinforced them, were the principal cause of Latin America's "failure," a word he contrasted with the "success" of the United States and Canada. Similar conclusions were recorded by, among others, Bolívar aide Francisco Miranda in the last years of the eighteenth century; by Bolívar himself three decades later; by the eminent Argentines Juan Bautista Alberdi and Domingo Faustino Sarmiento and the Chilean Francisco Bilbao in the second half of the nineteenth century; and by the Nicaraguan intellectual Salvador Mendieta early in this century.

The similar analyses of Spaniards José Ortega y Gasset, Fernando Díaz Plaja, Miguel de Unamuno, and Salvador de Madariaga, although principally focused on Spain's slow (until recent decades) modernization, also have clear relevance for Latin America.

Rangel's book, with a foreword by Jean François Revel that underscores Latin America's avoidance of self-criticism, earned him the enmity of most Latin American intellectuals and was mostly ignored by Latin American specialists in North America and Europe. Nevertheless, the book has proven to be seminal. In 1979, Nobelist Octavio Paz explained the contrast between the two Americas this way: "One, English speaking, is the daughter of the tradition that has founded the modern world: the Reformation, with its social and political consequences, democracy and capitalism. The other, Spanish and Portuguese speaking, is the daughter of the universal Catholic monarchy and the Counter-Reformation."[2]

One finds strong echoes of Rangel in Claudio Véliz's 1994 book, *The New World of the Gothic Fox,*[3] which contrasts the Anglo-Protestant and Ibero-Catholic legacies in the New World. Véliz defines the new paradigm with the words of the celebrated Peruvian writer Mario Vargas Llosa, who asserts that the economic, educational, and judicial reforms necessary to Latin America's modernization cannot be effected

> unless they are preceded or accompanied by a reform of our customs and ideas, of the whole complex system of habits, knowledge, images and forms that we understand by "culture." The culture within which we live and act today in Latin America is neither liberal nor is it altogether democratic. We have democratic governments, but our institutions, our reflexes and our mentality are very far from being democratic. They remain populist and oligarchic, or absolutist, collectivist or dogmatic, flawed by social and racial prejudices, immensely intol-

erant with respect to political adversaries, and devoted to the worst monopoly of all, that of the truth.[4]

The recent runaway best-seller in Latin America, *Guide to the Perfect Latin American Idiot*,[5] is dedicated to Rangel and Revel by its co-authors, Colombian Plinio Apuleyo Mendoza, Vargas Llosa's son Álvaro, and Cuban exile Carlos Alberto Montaner. The book criticizes the Latin American intellectuals of this century who have promoted the view that the region is a victim of imperialism. Among them are Eduardo Galeano, the Uruguayan author of the hugely popular *The Open Veins of Latin America*;[6] Fidel Castro; Che Guevara; Fernando Henrique Cardoso, the current president of Brazil; and Gustavo Gutiérrez, founder of liberation theology. Mendoza, Montaner, and Vargas Llosa strongly imply that the real causes of Latin America's underdevelopment are in the minds of the Latin Americans.

In their sequel, *Manufacturers of Misery*,[7] the authors trace the detrimental influence of traditional culture on the behavior of six elite groups: the politicians, the military, businesspeople, the clergy, the intellectuals, and the revolutionaries (see Chapter 5).

Montaner's recent book, *Let's Not Lose the Twenty-First Century, Too*,[8] underscores the costs Latin America has paid for not heeding the lessons, in cultural and policy terms, of the success of the advanced democracies. Prominent Argentine intellectual and media celebrity Mariano Grondona's 1999 book, *The Cultural Conditions of Economic Development*,[9] analyzes and contrasts development-prone (e.g., the United States and Canada) and development-resistant (e.g., Latin America) cultures.

To be sure, Latin American values and attitudes are changing, as the transition to democratic politics and market economics of the past fifteen years suggests. Several forces are modifying the region's culture, including the new intellectual current described in this chapter, globalization of communications and economics, and the surge in evangelical/Pentecostal Protestantism (Protestants now account for more than 30 percent of the population in Guatemala and about 20 percent in Brazil, Chile, and Nicaragua).[10]

The impact of the new-paradigm books and Montaner's weekly columns (he is the most widely read columnist in the Spanish language) in Latin America has been profound; in the United States, Canada, and Western Europe, on the other hand, they have gone largely unnoticed. A generation of Latin Americanists nurtured on dependency theory, or the less extreme view that the solution of Latin America's problems depends on the United States being more magnanimous in its dealings with Latin America, finds the cultural explanation indigestible. In separate seminars I have heard one prominent U.S. Latin Americanist label culture "a distraction"; another assert that culture is irrelevant to Latin America's evolution; and a third argue that culture is irrelevant to Venezuela's troubled political history. Bolívar would not have agreed.

I am particularly conscious of the seminal nature of Rangel's book because, had I not read it, I doubt that I would have written my first book, *Underdevelopment Is a State of Mind—The Latin American Case*,[11] which was published in 1985. My latest book, *The Pan-American Dream*,[12] a Spanish edition of which was published in 1999, is also dedicated to Rangel.

HOW CULTURE INFLUENCES PROGRESS

The Pan-American Dream identifies ten values, attitudes, or mind-sets that distinguish progressive cultures from static cultures. This formulation is highly relevant to Mariano Grondona's typology in Chapter 4.

1. Time orientation: Progressive cultures emphasize the future; static cultures emphasize the present or past. Future orientation implies a progressive worldview—influence over one's destiny, rewards in this life to virtue, positive-sum economics.
2. Work is central to the good life in progressive cultures but is a burden in static cultures. In the former, work structures daily life; diligence, creativity, and achievement are rewarded not only financially but also with satisfaction and self-respect.
3. Frugality is the mother of investment—and financial security—in progressive cultures but is a threat to the "egalitarian" status quo in static cultures, which often have a zero-sum worldview.
4. Education is the key to progress in progressive cultures but is of marginal importance except for the elites in static cultures.
5. Merit is central to advancement in progressive cultures; connections and family are what count in static cultures.
6. Community: In progressive cultures, the radius of identification and trust extends beyond the family to the broader society. In static cultures, the family circumscribes community. Societies with a narrow radius of identification and trust are more prone to corruption, tax evasion, and nepotism, and they are less likely to engage in philanthropy.
7. The ethical code tends to be more rigorous in progressive cultures. Every advanced democracy (except Belgium, Taiwan, Italy, and South Korea) appears among the twenty-five least corrupt countries on Transparency International's Corruption Perceptions Index. Chile

and Botswana are the only Third World countries that appear
among the top twenty-five.

8. Justice and fair play are universal impersonal expectations in
   progressive cultures. In static cultures, justice, like personal
   advancement, is often a function of who you know or how much
   you can pay.

9. Authority tends toward dispersion and horizontality in progressive
   cultures, toward concentration and verticality in static cultures.
   Robert Putnam's analysis of the differences between the north and
   the south in Italy in *Making Democracy Work* is illustrative.[13]

10. Secularism: The influence of religious institution on civic life is small
    in progressive cultures; its influence is often substantial in static
    cultures. Heterodoxy and dissent are encouraged in the former,
    orthodoxy and conformity in the latter.

These ten factors are obviously generalized and idealized, and the reality of
cultural variation is not black and white but a spectrum in which colors fuse
into one another. Few countries would be graded 10 on all the factors, just as
few countries would be graded 1. Nonetheless, virtually all of the advanced
democracies—as well as high-achieving ethnic/religious groups like the Mor-
mons, Jews, Sikhs, Basques, and East Asian immigrants in the United States
and elsewhere—would receive substantially higher scores than virtually all of
the Third World countries.

This conclusion invites the inference that what is really in play is development, not culture. The same argument could be made about Transparency
International's corruption index. There *is* a complex interplay of cause and
effect between culture and progress, but the power of culture is demonstra-
ble. It is observable in those countries where the economic achievement of
ethnic minorities far exceeds that of the majorities, as is the case of the Chinese in Thailand, Indonesia, Malaysia, and the Philippines. It can also be
seen in Costa Rica, where democratic institutions have flourished in a Third
World economy. Putnam concludes that Italy's evolution over many centuries
demonstrates that cultural values have had greater influence than economic
development. Grondona concludes in *The Cultural Conditions of Economic
Development* that culture is more powerful than economics or politics.

The ten factors I have suggested are not definitive. Grondona's typology of
development-prone and development-resistant cultures contains twenty factors, many of which overlap with my ten. But the ten factors do at least suggest what it is in the vastness of "culture" that may influence the way
societies evolve. Moreover, the new paradigm writers in Latin America (and
at least one writer in Africa) in large measure attribute the slow moderniza-

tion of their countries to just such traditional values and attitudes. Their views evoke Gunnar Myrdal's analysis of South Asia and Bernard Lewis's analysis of Islamic world, not to mention the views of such seminal culturalists as Alexis de Tocqueville, Max Weber, and Edward Banfield. *Democracy in America* is particularly relevant for those who would adduce geographic or institutional explanations for democratic development.

> Europeans exaggerate the influence of geography on the lasting powers of democratic institutions. Too much importance is attached to laws and too little to mores. . . . If in the course of this book I have not succeeded in making the reader feel the importance I attach to the practical experience of the Americans, to their habits, opinions, and, in a word, their mores, in maintaining their laws, I have failed in the main object of my work.[14]

CULTURAL INTERPRETATIONS IN OTHER REGIONS

In 1968, Gunnar Myrdal published *Asian Drama: An Inquiry into the Poverty of Nations* after ten years of study of South Asia.[15] He concluded that cultural factors, profoundly influenced by religion, are the principal obstacles to modernization. It is not just that they get in the way of entrepreneurial activity but that they permeate, rigidify, and dominate political, economic, and social behavior. Myrdal notes that the caste system "tends to make the existing inequalities particularly rigid and unyielding" and "fortifies the prevalent contempt and disgust for manual work."[16] He believes that the limited radius of identification and trust breeds corruption and nepotism.

Myrdal criticizes anthropologists and sociologists for failing "to provide the more broadly based system of theories and concepts needed for the scientific study of the problem of development" but appreciates that "attitudes, institutions, modes and levels of living, and, broadly, culture . . . are so much more difficult to grasp in systematic analysis than are the so-called economic factors."[17] He concludes with a call for cultural change with government taking the lead, particularly through the educational system.

The pace of modernization in most Islamic countries has been slow. Illiteracy, particularly among women, is still very high in many of them, as are child mortality and population growth. Its curbs on Kurdish and fundamentalist dissent notwithstanding, Turkey is the only Islamic country—secular, to be sure—that approaches modern standards of pluralistic governance. Malaysia is relatively prosperous, but its economic gains disproportionately reflect the economic creativity of its large Chinese (32 percent of the total population) minority. Oil-producing states like Saudi Arabia, the United

Arab Emirates, and Kuwait are affluent but still very traditional in many respects, as the fact that more than half of Saudi women are illiterate attests.[18]

The slow pace of progress in the Islamic world in recent centuries is in stark contrast with the progressive force that Islam was for several hundred years after it was founded by Muhammad early in the seventh century, and with the dominant power of the Ottoman Empire in the fifteenth and sixteenth centuries. Prominent among those who attribute Islam's decline to cultural factors is Bernard Lewis, who stresses the consequences for modernization of Islamic orthodoxy since the closing of the Gate of *Ijtihad* (independent analysis) by Islamic scholars between the ninth and eleventh centuries. The effect, in Lewis's view, has been to suppress enterprise, experiment, and originality and to reinforce a fatalistic worldview.[19]

Daniel Etounga-Manguelle's analysis of African culture (Chapter 6 of this volume) attributes Africa's poverty, authoritarianism, and social injustice principally to traditional cultural values and attitudes such as

- the highly centralized and vertical traditions of authority
- focus on the past and present, not the future
- rejection of "the tyranny of time"
- distaste for work ("the African works to live but doesn't live to work")[20]
- suppression of individual initiative, achievement, and saving (the corollary is jealousy of success)
- a belief in sorcery that nurtures irrationality and fatalism

For those who see "institution building" as the way to solve the problems of the Third World, particularly in the international development community, Etounga-Manguelle offers an insight that evokes Tocqueville: Culture is the mother; institutions are the children.

A decade ago, Salvatore Teresi, a founder of the European Institute of Business Administration (the French acronym is INSEAD), initiated a survey of Sicily's private and public sectors aimed, in the first instance, at a better understanding of the factors behind the island's underdevelopment. The results of the survey were strikingly similar to Edward Banfield's findings in his 1958 study of a southern Italian village, *The Moral Basis of a Backward Society*: Sicilian culture was dominated by an "exasperating" individualism, mistrust, and suspicion.[21] As in Etounga-Manguelle's analysis of African culture, the Sicilian value system suppressed cooperation, but it did not encourage competition, which was viewed as "aggression." Collusion, particularly between the public and private sectors, substituted for cooperation and competition, much as it does in the Latin American "mercantilism" described by Hernando de Soto in *The Other Path*.[22]

The survey illuminated other cultural factors that have a familiar ring: focus on the present, difficulties with strategic planning, absence of entrepreneurship, and authoritarian patron–client relationships. The survey's results, which shook the Sicilian elite, have led to a continuing program aimed at changing values and attitudes as well as strengthening management, planning, coordination, and entrepreneurship.

CHANGING THE TRADITIONAL CULTURE

In part because of the influence of the new-paradigm writers, but in some cases because of life experiences that have brought them to the same conclusions, a growing number of Latin Americans and others have initiated activities that promote progressive values and attitudes.

Octavio Mavila was for three decades the Honda distributor in Peru. A self-made man well into his seventies, Mavila has visited Japan numerous times over the years. About ten years ago, he came to the conclusion that the only really significant difference between Japan and Peru was that Japanese children learned progressive values whereas Peruvian children did not. In 1990, he established the Institute of Human Development (the Spanish acronym is INDEHU) in Lima to promote his Ten Commandments of Development: order, cleanliness, punctuality, responsibility, achievement, honesty, respect for the rights of others, respect for the law, work ethic, and frugality. In the past decade, more than 2 million Peruvian students have participated in courses sponsored by INDEHU, which has mobilized virtually all of its resources within Peru.

The Ten Commandments of Development are being preached outside of Peru too. Humberto Belli, Nicaragua's minister of education in two administrations, viewed them as central to his program of educational reform, and Ramón de la Peña, director of the Monterrey campus of Mexico's prestigious Monterrey Institute of Technology and Higher Studies (the Spanish acronym is ITESM), has promoted their use throughout the far-flung ITESM system.

The effectiveness of the evangelizing approach to cultural change needs to be evaluated. As Luis Ugalde, a Jesuit who is the rector of the Catholic University of Caracas, has observed, if children learn a progressive ethic in school and find it irrelevant to their lives outside of school, the impact may be scant. This is why Ugalde, who is convinced that values and attitudes count, is calling for anti-corruption, pro-merit campaigns in government, business, and the professions.

Corruption is in significant part a cultural phenomenon, linked, I believe, to factors such as limited radius of identification and trust, which translates into a limited sense of community, and an elastic ethical code. This conclusion is underscored by the findings of Seymour Martin Lipset and Gabriel Salman Lenz in Chapter 9. Corruption has become a high-profile issue in Latin America. On 3 March 1998, the Organization of American States adopted the Inter-American Convention Against Corruption, a fourteen-page document that by the end of that year had been ratified by thirteen countries. Few expect that the convention in and of itself is going to dramatically reduce the incidence of corruption. Among the ratifiers are four of the five Latin American countries that appear among Transparency International's ten most corrupt countries: Paraguay, Honduras, Venezuela, and Ecuador (the fifth is Colombia, which has not yet ratified). Nevertheless, it is clear that corruption is receiving far more attention than it once did, as is further attested by the growing attention paid to it by the World Bank and other development-assistance institutions.

The gender issue has also come to the fore, challenging the traditional culture of machismo, as Mala Htun makes clear in Chapter 14. Latin American women are increasingly aware of the gender democratization that has occurred in recent decades, particularly in First World countries, and they are increasingly organizing and taking initiatives to rectify the sexism that has traditionally kept them in second-class status. In several countries, laws concerning parental and property rights and divorce have been liberalized in favor of women, and nine countries have established obligatory quotas for women candidates in elections. Although these electoral laws are not uniformly effective, they are a reminder that the gender revolution, and all that it implies with respect to transformation of traditional values, is reaching Latin America.

Other organizations that have progressive cultural change as at least one of their goals have emerged spontaneously in Latin America in recent years. Examples include the following:

- ENLACE (the Spanish acronym for Encounter in the Community), a women's organization in Mexico with broad membership but few financial resources that has focused on curriculum changes in the public education system. ENLACE promotes parent, teacher, and student involvement in curricula that emphasize values and character, family stability, upward mobility, and the importance of education.
- The Regional Central Cooperative organization in Barquisimeto, Venezuela, the leaders of which are convinced that real progress in

rural Venezuela is impossible without a change in traditional campesino values and attitudes.

- Organizations in Colombia, Costa Rica, and Mexico that are promoting the idea and practice of philanthropy. Philanthropic activity has been notably absent in Latin America, reflecting the short radius of identification and trust characteristic of the traditional culture.
- Citizen Power, a group of Argentine professionals, chiefly lawyers, whose principal goals are the promotion of civic responsibility and participation and the suppression of corruption.

Other professionals are also addressing cultural change. Costa Rican psychiatrist Luis Diego Herrera is focused on personality formation and cultural transmission in childhood. A network of political scientists and sociologists linked to the World Values Survey is tracking changes in values and attitudes. Among them are Miguel Basáñez, a Mexican who is president of Marketing and Opinion Research International (MORI) USA, and Marita Carballo, director of the Gallup office in Argentina.

Many of these practitioners and several of the theorists, including Montaner, Grondona, and Ugalde, know one another, chiefly because of two symposia dedicated to the role of cultural values and attitudes in Latin America's development, the first at the Central American Business Administration Institute in Costa Rica in 1996, the second at the World Bank in Washington, D.C., in 1998. Among the panelists at the Harvard symposium on which this book is based were several people who had participated in one or both of the earlier symposia: Montaner, Grondona, Daniel Etounga-Manguelle, Michael Fairbanks, Ronald Inglehart, Stace Lindsay, and myself.

Michael Porter established the Monitor Company, a consulting organization, in Cambridge, Massachusetts, in 1983. Monitor has grown rapidly and has become an influential source of advice on competitiveness, particularly in the Third World. Monitor's Country Competitiveness Practice was founded by Michael Fairbanks and Stace Lindsay, who are the authors of chapters 20 and 21, respectively, and of the 1997 book *Plowing the Sea*.[23] Its title is drawn from Bolívar's last will and testament, written in 1830: "Whosoever works for a revolution [along the lines of the American Revolution, but in Latin America] is plowing the sea."

Both Fairbanks and Lindsay have practical experience in the Third World—Fairbanks in Africa, Lindsay in Central America and the Caribbean. In their consulting activities, they soon sensed that traditional approaches to competitiveness, which emphasize such areas as market analysis, niche identification, and productivity and management, were not enough to assure that Third World companies would compete successfully. They concluded that "invisible" factors rooted in cultural values and attitudes were the chief obstacles, and they developed a consulting approach that addresses "mental models." Their goal is to change traditional mental models that impede the creativity and efficiency necessary for competitiveness and economic growth.

Changing mental models is also Lionel Sosa's goal; his target group is Latin Americans who have migrated to the United States. In his 1998 book, *The Americano Dream*,[24] Sosa, a Mexican American, catalogues a series of values and attitudes that present obstacles to access to the upward mobility of mainstream America. They will sound familiar.

- Resignation of the poor: "To be poor is to deserve heaven. To be rich is to deserve hell. It is good to suffer in this life because in the next life you will find eternal reward."[25]
- Low priority of education: "The girls don't really need it—they'll get married anyway. And the boys? It's better that they go to work—to help the family."[26] I might mention here that the Hispanic high school dropout rate in the United States is about 30 percent, vastly higher than that of white and black Americans.
- Fatalism: "Individual initiative, achievement, self-reliance, ambition, aggressiveness—all these are useless in the face of an attitude that says, 'We must not challenge the will of God.' . . . The virtues so essential to business success in the United States are looked upon as sins by the Latino church."[27] The below-average rate of self-employment by Hispanics comes to mind.
- Mistrust of those outside the family, which contributes to the generally small size of Hispanic businesses.

Sosa goes on to present a program for success based on "the twelve traits of successful Latinos."[28] Their thrust is similar to Octavio Mavila's Ten Commandments of Development.

IN SUM

An important and promising intellectual current focused on culture and cultural changes is flowing throughout the world that has relevance for both poor countries and poor minorities in rich countries. It is not really new. Its source goes back through Banfield, Weber, and Tocqueville to at least Montesquieu. It offers an important insight into why some countries and ethnic/religious groups have done better than others, not just in economic terms but also with respect to consolidation of democratic institutions and social justice. And those lessons of experience, which are increasingly finding practical application, particularly in Latin America, may help to illuminate the path to progress for that substantial majority of the world's people for whom prosperity, democracy, and social justice have remained out of reach.

NOTES

INTRODUCTION

1. The following data are drawn from the World Bank, "Selected World Development Indicators," *World Development Report 1998/99* (New York: Oxford University Press, 1999).

2. The 1993 edition of *Social Panorama of Latin America,* by the Economic Commission for Latin America and the Caribbean, reported that "two out of every five urban residents are poor, and the ratio in rural areas is three out of every five" (p. 35). This means that 46 percent of Latin America's population was below the poverty line in 1990; 22 percent was below the *indigence* line. The 70 percent high school dropout figure is an estimate drawn from the World Bank's *World Development Report 1997,* table 7.

3. David Landes, *The Wealth and Poverty of Nations* (New York: Norton, 1998), p. 516.

4. For an early account of Basque success in what would become Venezuela, see François Depons, *Viaje a la parte oriental de la tierra firme en la América meridional* (1806; reprint, Caracas: Banco Central de Venezuela, 1960).

5. The Greenspan quotes appear in William Pfaff, "Economists Hatch a Disaster," *Boston Globe,* 30 August 1999, p. A17.

6. See Chapter 10 of this book.

7. Jared Diamond, *Guns, Germs, and Steel* (New York: Norton, 1997), p. 405.

8. Ibid., pp. 417–419.

9. Robert D. Putnam, *Making Democracy Work* (Princeton: Princeton University Press, 1993).

10. Douglass C. North, *Institutions, Institutional Change, and Economic Performance* (Cambridge: Cambridge University Press, 1990), p. 37.

11. Ibid., p. 117.

12. Quoted in the Guatemalan newspaper *La Prensa Libre,* 14 December 1999.

13. Orlando Patterson, *The Ordeal of Integration: Progress and Resentment in America's "Racial" Crisis* (Washington, D.C.: Perseus Counterpoint, 1997), p. 213.

14. Ibid., p. 109.

CHAPTER 1

This chapter is drawn from David Landes, The Wealth and Poverty of Nations *(New York: Norton, 1998).*

1. Nicholas Shumway, *The Invention of Argentina* (Berkeley: University of California Press, 1991), p. 156 n. 3.

2. Juan Bautista Alberdi, *Bases e puntos de partida para la organización política de la República Argentina* (1852), cited by Shumway, *Invention of Argentina*, p. 149.

3. Fernando Henrique Cardoso and Enzo Faletto, *Dependency and Development in Latin America* (Berkeley: University of California Press, 1979), p. 216. In all fairness, the text may read better in Spanish.

4. Matt Moffett, "Foreign Investors Help Brazil's Leader Tame Its Raging Inflation," *Wall Street Journal*, 15 December 1995, p. A1.

5. "The West and the Middle East," *Foreign Affairs,* January-February 1997, p. 121.

6. Sidney D. Brown, "Okubo Toshimichi: His Political and Economic Policies in Early Meiji Japan," *Journal of Asian Studies* 21 (1961–1962): 183–197.

7. Haruhiro Fukui, "The Japanese State and Economic Development: A Profile of a Nationalist-Paternalist Capitalist State," in *States and Development in the Asian Pacific Rim,* ed. Richard P. Applebaum and Jeffrey Henderson (Newbury Park, Calif.: Sage, 1992), p. 205

CHAPTER 2

The author is grateful to Michael Fairbanks and Kaia Miller for their thoughtful comments, as well as to the other participants of the symposium.

1. Michael E. Porter, *The Competitive Advantage of Nations* (New York: Free Press, 1990).

2. See, for example, Michael E. Porter and Mariko Sakakibara, "Competing at Home to Win Abroad: Evidence from Japanese Industry," Harvard Business School Working Paper 99–036, September 1998.

3. See, for example, Jack M. Potter, May N. Diaz, and George M. Foster, eds., *Peasant Society—A Reader* (Boston: Little, Brown, 1967).

4. A good example is the case of Chile in Anil Hira, *Ideas in Economic Policy in Latin America: Regional, National, and Organizational Case Studies* (Westport, Conn.: Praeger, 1998).

CHAPTER 4

1. Talcott Parsons, *The Social System* (New York: Free Press, 1959), chap. 1.

2. Lawrence E. Harrison, *Underdevelopment Is a State of Mind* (Cambridge: Center for International Affairs, Harvard University; Lanham, Md.: University Press of America, 1985).

3. This definition of the view of wealth in poor countries is close to the zero-sum worldview that George Foster and others have emphasized as central to "universal peasant culture."

CHAPTER 5

1. The term "mercantilist" in the sense that it is used here was popularized by Hernando de Soto in *The Other Path* (Lima: Instituto Libertad y Democracia, 1986).

2. "Neoliberalism" is the pejorative term used by critics, most of them ex-adherents of various forms of socialism, to describe free market capitalism.

3. Gutiérrez's best-known book is *Una Teología de la Liberación* (Lima: CEP, 1971).

CHAPTER 6

1. All data are from World Bank, *World Development Report 1998/99* (Oxford: Oxford University Press, 1999).

2. Hervé Bourges and Claude Wauthier, *Les 45 Afriques* (Paris: Le Seuil, 1979).

3. Frank Tenaille, *Les 50 Afriques* (Paris: Petite Collection Maspéro, 1979).

4. Cited by Alassane Ndaw, *La Pensée Africaine—Research on the Foundations of Negro-African Thought* (Paris: Nouvelles Editions Africaines, 1983), p. 233.

5. D. Bollinger and G. Hofstede, *Les différences culturelles dans le management* (Paris: Les Editions Organisation, 1987).

6. Jean-Jacques Servan-Schreiber, *L'art du temps* (Paris: Fayard, 1985).

7. Ibid.

8. Jean-François Revel, *La connaissance inutile* (Paris: Grasset, 1988), p. 99.

9. Ibid.

CHAPTER 7

This chapter draws on material from Ronald Inglehart and Wayne Baker, "Modernization, Cultural Change, and the Persistence of Traditional Values," American Sociological Review, February 2000.

CHAPTER 8

Francis Fukuyama is Omer L. and Nancy Hirst Professor of Public Policy at George Mason University. This chapter is drawn from his book The Great Disruption: Human Nature and the Reconstitution of Social Order *(New York: Free Press, 1999).*

1. Diego Gambetta, *The Sicilian Mafia: The Business of Private Protection* (Cambridge: Harvard University Press, 1993), p. 35.

2. See, for example, Edward C. Banfield, *The Moral Basis of a Backward Society* (Glencoe, Ill.: Free Press, 1958); and Robert D. Putnam, *Making Democracy Work: Civic Traditions in Modern Italy* (Princeton: Princeton University Press, 1993).

3. See the discussion of civil society in Larry Diamond, "Toward Democratic Consolidation," *Journal of Democracy* 5 (1994): 4–17.

4. Lyda Judson Hanifan, "The Rural School Community Center," *Annals of the American Academy of Political and Social Science* 67 (1916): 130–138.

5. Jane Jacobs, *The Death and Life of Great American Cities* (New York: Vintage, 1961), p. 138.

6. Glenn Loury, "A Dynamic Theory of Racial Income Differences," in *Women, Minorities, and Employment Discrimination,* ed. P. A. Wallace and A. LeMund (Lexington, Mass.: Lexington Books, 1977); Ivan H. Light, *Ethnic Enterprise in America* (Berkeley: University of California Press, 1972).

7. James S. Coleman, "Social Capital in the Creation of Human Capital," *American Journal of Sociology* supplement 94 (1988): S95–S120; Coleman, "The Creation and Destruction of Social Capital: Implications for the Law," *Journal of Law, Ethics, and Public Policy* 3 (1988): 375–404; Putnam, *Making Democracy Work,* 1993; Robert Putnam, "Bowling Alone: America's Declining Social Capital," *Journal of Democracy* 6 (1995): 65–78.

8. Everett C. Ladd, "The Data Just Don't Show Erosion of America's 'Social Capital,'" *Public Perspective* (1996): 4–22; Michael Schudson, "What If Civic Life Didn't Die?" *American Prospect* (1996): 17–20; John Clark, "Shifting Engagements: Lessons from the 'Bowling Alone' Debate," Hudson Briefing Papers, no. 196, October 1996.

9. How, then, can we get a handle on whether a given society's stock of social capital is increasing or decreasing? One solution is to rely more heavily on the second of the two data sources—survey data on trust and values.

10. Friedrich A. Hayek, *The Fatal Conceit: The Errors of Socialism* (Chicago: University of Chicago Press, 1988), p. 5; see also Hayek, *Law, Legislation, and Liberty* (Chicago: University of Chicago Press, 1976).

11. Ronald A. Heiner, "The Origin of Predictable Behavior," *American Economic Review* 73 (1983): 560–595; and Heiner, "Origin of Predictable Behavior: Further Modeling and Applications," *American Economic Review* 75 (1985): 391–396.

12. Douglass C. North, *Institutions, Institutional Change, and Economic Performance* (New York: Cambridge University Press, 1990).

13. For an overview, see Karl-Dieter Opp, "Emergence and Effects of Social Norms—Confrontation of Some Hypotheses of Sociology and Economics," *Kyklos* 32 (1979): 775—801.

14. Garrett Hardin, "The Tragedy of the Commons," *Science* 162 (1968): 1243–1248.

15. Strictly speaking, Coase himself did not postulate a "Coase theorem." Ronald H. Coase, "The Problem of Social Cost," *Journal of Law and Economics* 3 (1960): 1–44. This article is the single most commonly cited article in the legal literature today.

16. Robert Sugden, "Spontaneous Order," *Journal of Economic Perspectives* 3 (1989): 85–97; Sugden, *The Economics of Rights, Co-operation, and Welfare* (Oxford: Basil Blackwell, 1986).

17. Ellickson's own detailed field research shows that ranchers and farmers in Shasta County, California, have in fact established a series of informal norms to protect their respective interests, just as Coase predicted they would. Robert Ellickson, *Order Without Law* (Cambridge: Harvard University Press, 1991, pp. 143ff., 192.

18. Elinor Ostrom, *Governing the Commons: The Evolution of Institutions for Collective Action* (Cambridge: Cambridge University Press, 1990).

CHAPTER 9

Many thanks for the research work of Yang Zhang and Meredith Rucker. We are deeply indebted to Robert K. Merton for stimulating this chapter and offering concrete advice.

1. Arnold J. Heidenheimer, *Political Corruption: Readings in Comparative Analysis* (New Brunswick, N.J.: Transaction, 1978), p. 3.

2. Transparency International, "TI Press Release: 1998 Corruption Perceptions Index," Berlin, 22 September 1998.

3. World Values Study Group, "World Values Survey Code Book," ICPSR 6160 (Ann Arbor, Mich., August 1994).

4. Paolo Mauro, "The Effects of Corruption on Growth, Investment, and Government Expenditure: A Cross-Country Analysis," in *Corruption and the Global Economy,* ed. Kimberly Ann Elliot (Washington, D.C.: Institute for International Economics, 1997), p. 91. See also Paolo Mauro, "Corruption and Growth," *Quarterly Journal of Economics* 110, no. 3 (1995). For a more comprehensive review of the literature, see Alberto Ades and Rafael Di Tella, "The Causes and Consequences of Corruption," *IDS Bulletin* 27, no. 2 (1996): 6–10.

5. Mauro, "Effects," p. 94.

6. Andrei Shleifer and Robert W. Vishny, "Corruption," *Quarterly Journal of Economics* 109, no. 3 (1993): 599–617.

7. Sanjeev Gupta, Hamid Davoodi, Rosa Alonso-Terme, "Does Corruption Affect Income Inequality and Poverty?" IMF Working Papers 98/76 (Washington, D.C.: International Monetary Fund, 1998).

8. Daniel Treisman, *The Causes of Corruption: A Cross-National Study* (forthcoming, 1998), pp. 22–23.

9. For evidence on the relationship between democracy and economic development, see Seymour Martin Lipset, *Political Man* (Garden City, N.Y.: Doubleday, 1960); and Treisman, *Causes of Corruption.*

10. Treisman, *Causes of Corruption*, p. 6.

11. Harry Ekstein, *Division and Cohesion in Democracy: Study of Norway* (Princeton: Princeton University Press, 1966), p. 265.

12. Robert K. Merton, *Social Theory and Social Structure* (1957; reprint, New York: Free Press, 1968), pp. 246–248.

13. Edward Banfield, *The Moral Basis of a Backward Society* (Chicago: Free Press, 1958).

14. Daniel Bell, "Crime As an American Way of Life," *Antioch Review*, Summer 1953, pp. 131–154.

15. Ronald Inglehart, *The Silent Revolution: Changing Values and Political Styles Among Western Publics* (Princeton: Princeton University Press, 1977); and Inglehart, *Modernization and Postmodernization* (Princeton: Princeton University Press, 1997).

16. Plato *Republic* (trans. G. M. Grube, rev. C. D. C. Reeve [Indianapolis: Hackett, 1992], chap. 5).

17. Max Weber, *The Religion of China* (New York: Macmillan, 1951), p. 237.

18. Lawrence E. Harrison, *Underdevelopment Is a State of Mind: The Latin American Case* (Cambridge: Center for International Affairs, Harvard University; Lanham, Md.: University Press of America, 1985), p. 7.

19. Banfield, *Moral Basis*, p. 85.

20. "A Message for Europe," *Economist*, 20 March 1999, p. 15. The *Economist* expressed hope that in reform, the European Union will "exploit the Union's more northern balance and mores."

21. "Earthquake in Europe," *Financial Times*, 20 March 1999, p. 10.

22. Freedom House, *Freedom in the World: The Annual Survey of Political Rights and Civil Liberties, 1996–1997* (New York: Freedom House, 1997).

CHAPTER 11

1. Etounga-Manguelle identifies several such features (he deliberately emphasizes the negative in order to make his case): the importance of hierarchical distance in social relations; the attempt to control uncertainty through religion and immutable destiny set by nature and religion; a time orientation that does not focus on the future; a passivity in the face of power and a willingness to accept such power; subordination of the individual to the community and a rejection of "any view of the individual as an autonomous and responsible being" (Etounga-Manguelle, Chap. 6 in this volume); conviviality to excess along with rejection of open conflict and an attempt to create personal friendship rather than openly discuss differences; emphasis on current consumption rather than saving for the future; irrational beliefs (e.g., witchcraft); totalitarian polities without collective trust and goals. I have suggested others specific to childhood, such as socially distributed support and care for others; relative gender segregation; strong emphasis on achievement goals and status attainment ("having one's name known") without overt boasting; diffusion of affective ties.

CHAPTER 12

1. Among the many fascinating remarks heard at the conference were several "indigenous" testimonials from cosmopolitan intellectuals out of Africa and Latin America. These representatives from the "Third World" played the part of disgruntled "insiders," bearing witness to the impoverishment of their own native cultures, telling us how bad things can be in the home country. That role has become increasingly complex, even dubious, in our postmodern world, where the outside is in and the inside is all over the place (think of CNN, VISA, and the Big Mac). For most globe-hopping managers of the world system, including cosmopolitan intellectuals from out of the "Third World," travel plans now matter more than ancestry. Consequently, one feels inclined to raise doubts about any claims to authority based on an equation of citizenship (or national origin) with "indigenous" voice. After all, whose voice is more "indigenous"? The voice of a "Western-educated" M.B.A. or Ph.D. from Dakar or Delhi, who looks down on his or her own cultural traditions and looks up to the United States for intellectual and moral guidance and material aid? Or the voice of a

"Western" scholar who does years of fieldwork in rural villages in Africa or Asia and understands and sees value in the traditions of "others"?

One of the other noteworthy (and for me eyebrow-raising) remarks heard at the conference was the general equation of goodness and progress with Protestantism and the explicit suggestion that successful Protestant missionary efforts (the more converts the better) might enhance economic growth.

2. Many peoples in the southern world are bound by their own varieties of deep ethnocentrism, just as we are. Consequently, "others" often fail to understand us, precisely because they are ignorant of our meanings, don't know what we are up to, and find many aspects of our way of life, especially our family life practices and sexual ideals, incomprehensible from their moral point of view. They are just as blind to our moral decencies and rationality as we are to theirs.

3. This news is apparently late to arrive outside the academy, where the stereotype persists that most anthropologists are radical relativists. The "press" indulges this stereotype.

4. For an exhaustive review of medical research on the health consequences of female genital surgeries and an important critique of the advocacy literature against "female genital mutilation," see Obermeyer 1999; Obiora 1997. Obermeyer concludes that "the powerful discourse that depicts these practices as inevitably causing death and serious ill health, and as unequivocally destroying sexual pleasure, is not sufficiently supported by the evidence" (1999, 79).

5. There is also the problematic of defining a "self-monitoring group." A nationality, for example, is not necessarily a culturally relevant self-monitoring group. Nor is a civilization. The relevant communities for cultural analysis are probably not going to correspond to political or bureaucratic or census categories such as "Asian" or "Hispanic" or "black" or "Native American" or what have you. In the "law and order" context of Western liberal democracies, however, it remains an open question whether the informal norms of particular cultural communities (such as the Amish or the Satmar Hasidim) can survive without formal legal definition and protection (see for example, Stolzenberg 1997).

6. One can be a pluralist and still grant that there are true and universally binding values and undeniable moral principles, for example, "cruelty is evil" and "you should treat like cases alike and different cases differently." One of the claims of pluralism, however, is that values and principles are fully objective only to the extent they are kept quite abstract and devoid of content. A related claim is that no abstract value or principle, in and of itself, can provide definitive guidance in concrete cases of moral dispute. In other words, it is possible for morally decent and fully rational peoples to look at each other and at each other's practices and say, "Yuck!"

I call that the "mutual yuck" response. There is plenty of "mutual yucking" going on in the world today. Circumcising and non-circumcising peoples, for example, almost always have a mutual yuck response to each other. The mutual yuck response is possible because objective values cannot in and of themselves determine whether it is right or wrong to arrange a marriage; whether it is good or bad to sacrifice and/or butcher large mammals such as goats or sheep; whether it is savory or unsavory to put your parents in an old age home; whether it is vicious or virtuous to have a large family; whether it is moral or immoral to abort a fetus; whether it is commendable or contemptible to encourage girls as well as boys to enter into a covenant with God (or to become full members of their society) by means of a ritual initiation involving genital modifications. Morally decent and fully rational people can disagree about such things, even in the face of a plentitude of shared objective values.

7. It is not entirely clear to me whether this prediction presupposes only a limited form of globalization, for example, free trade at the border, or whether it allows that globalization might entail the deep penetration into other societies of Western ways of running banks, encouraging investment, enforcing contracts, and so on. Of course, if the idea of globalization is expanded beyond the economic realm (the linking of national economies) to include other realms as well (e.g., social, political, ethical, religious), then by definition globalization and westernization must go hand in hand.

COMMENTS OF DANIEL ETOUNGA-MANGUELLE,
CARLOS ALBERTO MONTANER, AND MARIANO GRONDONA ON NOTE 1,
WITH FURTHER COMMENTS BY RICHARD SHWEDER

Carlos Alberto Montaner

Richard Shweder's comment is typical of those who expect Third World reactions from Latin Americans. He simply doesn't understand that Latin America is an extension of the West. I don't understand why Shweder thinks that we ought to resign ourselves to authoritarian governments and economic models that condemn half of our people to misery when the entire world—beginning with the Japanese—believes that it was admirable when Japan copied the production techniques and social organization of the West. Perhaps the Brazilian *favelas,* with their infinite, barbaric misery, seem picturesque to him. I cannot accept those subhuman conditions. I believe that they must be eradicated and that the people living in them must have a chance for a better, more human life.

How do I know what Latin Americans want? It's very simple: by following migration trends. Surveys demonstrate that half or more of the populations of Mexico, Colombia, and Guatemala, among others, would abandon their countries for the United States. Why? Because the United States offers them what they don't find in their own countries.

What Shweder says of "these representatives from the 'Third World' play[ing] the part of disgruntled 'insiders'" could also be applied to the Americans who are concerned about improving subhuman conditions in the black and Puerto Rican ghettos. If he is to be consistently uncritical of the values and attitudes of a culture, then he should have no problem with the Sicilian *omertà.*

Daniel Etounga-Manguelle

As a "disgruntled insider" and "cosmopolitan intellectual" from Africa, I appreciate the opportunity to comment on Richard Shweder's note. I do so with some diffidence.

After all, I am responding to a Western scholar who identifies himself as more "indigenous" than I am because he "has done years of fieldwork in rural villages in . . . Asia and understands and sees value in the traditions of 'others.'"

I have to confess that I failed to receive the "intellectual and moral guidance and material aid" I expected at the Harvard symposium, so I am going to tell the truth: We Africans really enjoy living in shantytowns where there isn't enough food, health care, or education for our children. Furthermore, our corrupt chieftaincy political systems are really marvelous and have permitted countries like Mobutu's Zaire to earn us international prestige and respect.

Moreover, surely it would be terribly boring if free, democratic elections were organized all over Africa. Were that to happen, we would no longer be real Africans, and by losing our identity—and our authoritarianism, our bloody civil wars, our illiteracy, our forty-five-year life expectancy—we would be letting down not only ourselves but also those Western anthropologists who study us so sympathetically and understand that we can't be expected to behave like human beings who seek dignity on the eve of the third millennium. We are Africans, and our identity matters!

So let us fight for it with the full support of those Western scholars who have the wisdom and courage to acknowledge that Africans belong to a different world.

Mariano Grondona

There is a methodological difference between Richard Shweder and Latin Americans like Carlos Alberto Montaner and myself. Shweder's goal, were he focused on Latin America, would be to understand it. We want to change it. Anthropologists need the societies they study to remain relatively static and predictable, like an entomologist studying bees or ants. Montaner and I, on the other hand, have an existential approach to our region: It is "our" world—where we come from—which we love. Because of our commitment to it, we want it to advance to new levels of human fulfillment, closer to those in the developed world.

One must ask who represents Latin America better, Shweder and other foreign social scientists or Montaner and myself? We belong to our region. We feel it. The fact that millions of Latin Americans are "voting with their feet" as they migrate to the developed countries and that the overwhelming electoral majorities are supporting progressive governments throughout our region eloquently testifies that our views and concerns are widely shared.

To be sure, we travel back and forth between Latin America and the developed countries. But these experiences do not alienate us from Latin America. Rather, they both increase our concern about conditions, particularly for poor people, in Latin America and focus us on what needs to be done to change those conditions. Like the vast majority of our countrymen, we want our nations to have the democratic stability, justice, opportunity for advancement, and prosperity that we find in the advanced countries.

Richard A. Shweder's Reply to Montaner, Etounga-Manguelle, and Grondona

As far as I can tell nothing in note 1 (or in my chapter) recommends authoritarian rule, a life of squalor, or death at an early age. In authoritarian power orders, those in power act in such a way that only their own interests are served, and no one can stop them from doing so. I think the world would be a far better place if there were no such orders of power. And nothing suggests that we must be uncritical or accepting of the received ideas, attitudes, and practices of any cultural tradition, including our own. As I state in my chapter, "Pluralists do make critical judgments. Indeed, the 'stance of justification' is so central to my style of cultural analysis that I would define a 'genuine' culture, a culture deserving of appreciation, as a way of life that is defensible in the face of criticism from abroad."

If one truly cares to achieve some appreciation of a cultural tradition, one must usually engage in some participant observation and in a process of sympathetic understanding. One initially tries to bracket all ethnocentric reactions and discover what is good, true, beautiful, or efficient in the ideas, attitudes, and practices of "others." There is no guarantee that appreciation will be achieved. There is no guarantee that everything that is, is okay or "genuine." Ideas, attitudes, and practices that are demonstrably bad, false, ugly, or inefficient should be criticized and perhaps even changed. So much for red herrings and the bogeyman of radical relativism. My essay is in fact a critique of both radical relativism ("whatever is, is okay") and ethnocentric monism ("there is only one way to lead a morally decent, rational and fulfilling life, and it's our way"), although by my lights I did not see many radical relativists at the conference.

In a moment I will respond to one or two other points raised by Carlos Alberto Montaner, Daniel Etounga-Manguelle, and Mariano Grondona. First, however, I want to focus on what was actually said in note 1, namely, that in the postmodern world, one should be skeptical of all claims to authority based on the equation of citizenship (or national origin) with "indigenous" voice. And I want to tell you a story, which illustrates that point.

Rabindranath Tagore is modern India's most acclaimed poet. He was a recipient of the Nobel Prize for Literature in 1913, a spokesman for the India nationalist movement, and an admirer, interpreter, and literary beneficiary of the classical Sanskrit literatures of India. In 1877, Tagore visited England for the first time. He was sixteen years old. He went there to study law. In his book *India and Europe: An Essay in Understanding*, Wilhelm Halbfass quotes Tagore's impressions:

> I had thought that the island of England was so small and the inhabitants so dedicated to learning that, before I arrived there, I expected the country from one end to the other would echo and re-echo with the lyrical essays of Tennyson; and I also thought that wherever I might be in this narrow island, I would hear constantly Gladstone's oratory, the explanation of the Vedas by Max Mueller, the scientific truth of Tindall, the profound thoughts of Carlyle and the philosophy of Bain. I was under the impression that wherever I would go I would find the old and the young drunk with the pleasure of "intellectual" enjoyment. But I have been very disappointed in this.

Apparently, the young Tagore, a political and civic "outsider" to the British Isles, was culturally more English and spoke the English language far better than most Englishmen. His reference to Max Mueller is highly pertinent to note 1 because it was Max Mueller, a German philologist and "orientalist" who taught at Oxford, to whom Hindu Brahmans turned to learn about Sanskrit and their own classical literary traditions.

This situation of "outsiders" and "insiders" trading places and keeping each other's valuable cultural heritages in play is not unusual, especially in the contemporary world. We live in a world where Afro-Caribbean scholars translate ancient Greek texts, where scholars from Africa, Asia, and Europe write perceptive books about the United States, and where the Max Mueller effect is alive and well. For example, Gusii intellectuals from Kenya, some of whom are quite expert in Western philosophy and science, read Robert LeVine's work (conducted from the 1950s through 1990s) to learn about the meaning, value, and history of Gusii norms and folkways. The main point of this observation is a simple one: Statements about the pros and cons of a cultural tradition do not gain authority and should not be granted authority on the basis of claims to ancestry, membership, or national origin.

Note 1 was an aside, a parenthetical remark about my fascination with one aspect of the structural organization of the conference. The conference was choreographed in such a way that there was one session in which all the speakers from the "Third World" participated, and they spoke pretty much with one voice, supporting the idea that "Western civilization" is superior to all the rest. Now, of course, this idea is not unpopular in many capitals of Asia, Africa, and Latin America. It is especially popular among those Western, westernized, or westernizing elites who tend to view the received beliefs, attitudes, and everyday practices of non-Western peoples, even their own countrymen, as unenlightened, superstitious, magical, authoritarian, corrupt, or otherwise unworthy or embarrassing. But that type of wholesale acceptance of "Western modernity" over non-Western "traditionalisms" of various kinds has never been the only voice in town in either the "West" or the "East," the "North" or the "South," the "developed" or the "underdeveloped" world. Had there been other types of voices in the session, the voice of "Third World" intellectuals who might speak with pride and admiration about "indigenous" ideas, attitudes, and practices, the session would perhaps have been less fascinating. Perhaps I would not have been led to wonder about the use of "insider" testimonials from the "Third World" to lend authority to the idea that the Protestant "First World" really got it right.

Carlos Alberto Montaner and Mariano Grondona are impressed by migration patterns, by the fact that "millions of Latin Americans are 'voting with their feet'" in favor of the "developed" world. The first time I ever heard the "voting with your feet" argument was in the 1960s, when a famous conservative made the argument that black migration patterns into South Africa far exceeded black migration patterns out of South Africa. He interpreted this as evidence that black Africans were voting with their feet in favor of the apartheid government of South Africa over other African states! I suspect they were not voting or expressing their moral and cultural preferences at all—just going where there were higher-paying jobs.

Daniel Etounga-Manguelle seems to imply that one cannot live a dignified life and a life that is distinctively African at the same time. As I stated in my essay, I am not a fan of broad categories such as "Latin American" or "African" as ways of identifying cultural communities—Bahia is not San Paolo, the Yoruba are not the Masai. Nevertheless, I do believe, as did Edward Sapir, that "the societies in which different societies live are distinct worlds, not merely the same world with different labels attached." For a pluralist, "distinctness" or "difference" is not a term of disparagement. With complete respect for all three of my critics, whose sincerity I never doubted, whose company and conversation I much enjoyed, and whose testimonials and arguments I found fascinating, I fully confess to rejecting the idea that the only or very best way to be dignified, decent, rational, and fully human is to live the life of a North American or a northern European.

CHAPTER 14

1. Lawrence Harrison, *The Pan-American Dream* (New York: Basic, 1997), p. 18.

2. Linda Kerber, *No Constitutional Right to Be Ladies: Women and the Obligations of Citizenship* (New York: Hill & Wang, 1998), p. 307 n. 6.

3. Howard Wiarda, "Introduction: Social Change, Political Development, and the Latin American Tradition," in *Politics and Social Change in Latin America: Still a Distinct Tradition?* (Boulder: Westview, 1992), p. 14.

4. Elsa Chaney, *Supermadre: Women in Politics in Latin America* (Austin: University of Texas Press, 1979), p. 32.

5. Ronald Inglehart and Marita Carballo, "Does Latin America Exist? A Global Analysis of Cross-Cultural Differences," *PS: Political Science and Politics* 30, no. 1 (1997); see also Inglehart's chapter in this volume.

6. Data on women in government can be found at Interparliamentary Union <http://www.ipu.org/wmn-e/classif.htm>; and the U.N. WomenWatch <http://www.un.org/womenwatch>. For other aggregate data, see FLACSO, *Mujeres Latinoamericanas en Cifras* (Santiago: FLACSO, 1995); Statistical Division of the U.N. Secretariat and International Labor Organization <http://www.un.org/Depts/unsd/gender>; and the U.N. Development Program <http://www.undp.org/hdro/child.htm>. The statistics used in this chapter all come from these sources.

7. Mala Htun, "Women in Latin America: Unequal Progress Toward Equality," *Current History* 98, no. 626 (1999); Htun, "Women's Rights and Opportunities in Latin America: Problems and Prospects," in *Civil Society and the Summit of the Americas,* ed. R. E. Feinberg and R. L. Rosenberg (Miami: North-South Center Press, 1999).

8. Mary Ann Glendon, *Abortion and Divorce in Western Law* (Cambridge: Harvard University Press, 1987); Glendon, *The Transformation of Family Law: State, Law, and the Family in the United States and Western Europe* (Chicago: University of Chicago Press, 1989).

9. Jacqueline Hermann and Leila Linhares Barsted, *O Judiciário e a Violência contra a Mulher: A Ordem Legal e a (Des)ordem Familiar* (Rio de Janeiro: CEPIA, 1995), p. 63.

10. Giulia Tamayo León, "Delegaciones Policiales de Mujeres y Secciones Especializadas," *Acceso a la Justicia* (Lima: Poder Judicial, 1996); Centro Legal para Derechos Reproductivos y Políticas Públicas y Grupo de Información en Reproducción Elegida (CRLP/GIRE), *Derechos Reproductivos de la Mujer en México: Un Reporte Sombra,* December 1997; Sara Nelson, "Constructing and Negotiating Gender in Women's Police Stations in Brazil," *Latin American Perspectives* 23, no. 1 (1996); OAS/IACHR, "Report of the Inter-American Commission on Human Rights on the Status of Women in the Americas," *Annual Report 1997* (Washington, D.C.: Organization of American States.

11. U.S. Department of State, *Peru Country Report on Human Rights Practices for 1997.* Released by the Bureau of Democracy, Human Rights, and Labor, 30 January 1998.

CHAPTER 15

1. On which see James Davison Hunter, *Culture Wars: The Struggle to Define America* (New York: Basic, 1991), p. 291.

2. For recent reviews of the study of culture in the social sciences, see Diana Crane, ed., *The Sociology of Culture: Emerging Theoretical Perspectives* (Oxford: Blackwell, 1994); Jeffrey Alexander and Steven Seidman, eds., *Culture and Society: Contemporary Debates* (New York: Cambridge University Press, 1991); Richard Munch and Neil J. Smelser, eds., *Theory of Culture* (Berkeley: University of California Press, 1992), pt. 1; Robert Wuthnow and Marsha Witten, "New Directions in the Study of Culture," *Annual Review of Sociology* 14 (1988): 49–67; and Adam Kuper, *Culture: The Anthropologists' Account* (Cambridge: Harvard University Press, 1999).

3. Mabel Berezin, "Fissured Terrain: Culture and Politics," in *Sociology of Culture,* p. 94.

4. Ann Swidler, "Culture in Action: Symbols and Strategies," *American Sociological Review* 51 (1986): 273–286.

5. Orlando Patterson, *Ethnic Chauvinism: The Reactionary Impulse* (Briarcliff Manor, N.Y.: Stein & Day, 1977), pp. 177–185. Adam Kuper also emphasized this point in his *Culture,* pp. xii–xiv.

6. Walter Benn Michaels, *Our America: Nativism, Modernism, and Pluralism* (Durham, N.C.: Duke University Press, 1995), p. 15. Cited in Kuper, *Culture,* pp. 240–241.

7. Robert Blauner, "Black Culture: Myth or Reality?" in *Afro-American Anthropology: Contemporary Perspectives,* ed. Norman E. Whitten Jr. and John F. Szwed (New York: Free Press, 1970), pp. 347–366.

8. Meredith Phillips et al., "Family Background, Parenting Practices, and the Black–White Test Score Gap," in *The Black–White Test Score Gap,* ed. Christopher Jencks and Meredith Phillips (Washington, D.C.: Brookings Institution Press, 1998), chap. 4.

9. Howard Gardner, "Cracking Open the IQ Box," in *The Bell Curve Wars: Race, Intelligence, and the Future of America,* ed. Steven Fraser (New York: Basic, 1995), pp. 30–31.

10. Arthur R. Jensen, "Differential Psychology: Towards Consensus," in *Arthur Jensen: Consensus and Controversy,* ed. S. Modgil and C. Modgil (New York: Falmer, 1987), p. 376. Cited in Nathan Brody, *Intelligence* (San Diego: Academic Press, 1992), p. 297.

11. Brody, *Intelligence*, p. 309.

12. Ibid., p. 41.

13. Ibid.

14. Margaret Archer, *Culture and Agency: The Place of Culture in Social Theory* (Cambridge: Cambridge University Press, 1981), p. 1.

15. Ward Goodenough, "Culture: Concept and Phenomenon," in *The Relevance of Culture,* ed. Morris Freilich (New York Bergin & Garvey, 1989), p. 97.

16. Ibid., pp. 94–95.

17. Eugene Hunn, "Ethnoecology: The Relevance of Cognitive Anthropology for Human Ecology," in *Relevance of Culture*, p. 145.

18. Robert Boyd and Peter Richerson, *Culture and the Evolutionary Process* (Chicago: University of Chicago Press, 1985), pp. 33–37.

19. Roger Keesing, "Theories of Culture," *Annual Review of Anthropology* 3 (1974): 73–97.

20. Roy D'Andrade, *The Development of Cognitive Anthropology* (Cambridge: Cambridge University Press, 1995), p. 247.

21. Roger Keesing, "Models, 'Folk' and 'Cultural': Paradigms Regained," in *Cultural Models in Language and Thought,* ed. Dorothy Holland and Naomi Quinn (Cambridge: Cambridge University Press, 1987), pp. 369–393.

22. Ann Swidler, "Culture in Action: Symbols and Strategies," *American Sociological Review* 51 (1986): 273–288.

23. Naomi Quinn and Dorothy Holland, "Culture and Cognition," in *Cultural Models,* pp. 6–7.

24. Boyd and Richerson, *Culture*, p. 40. They admit that these models have much in common with their conception of culture, but they confine the cultural to stable social transmission because only such transmission "gives it an evolutionary dynamic different from ordinary learning and its analogs" (p. 34).

25. Ibid., p. 36. Cf. David Lewontin, S. Rose, and L. J. Kamin, *Not in Our Genes* (New York: Pantheon, 1984), chap. 5.

26. For detailed references and a review of the historiography on this subject as well as an anti-revisionist interpretation of the evidence, see Orlando Patterson, *Rituals of Blood: Consequences of Slavery in Two American Centuries* (New York: Basic Civitas, 1998), pp. 25–53.

27. Richard Sutch, "The Breeding of Slaves for Sale and the Westward Expansion of Slavery, 1850–1860," in *Race and Slavery in the Western Hemisphere: Quantitative Studies,* ed. Stanley Engerman and Eugene Genovese (Princeton: Princeton University Press, 1975), pp. 173–210.

28. Cheryll Ann Cody, "Naming, Kinship, and Estate Dispersal: Notes on Slave Family Life on a South Carolina Plantation, 1786 to 1833," *William and Mary Quarterly,* series 3, 39 (1982): 192–211.

29. Stewart Tolnay, "Black Family Formation and Tenancy in the Farm South, 1900," *American Journal of Sociology* 90 (1984): 310.

30. Anita Washington, "A Cultural and Historical Perspective on Pregnancy-Related Activity Among U.S. Teenagers," *Journal of Black Psychology* 9, no. 1 (1982): 16.

31. See, for example, Center for the Study of Social Policy, *The "Flip Side" of Black Families Headed by Women: The Economic Status of Black Men* (Washington, D.C.: Center for the Study of Social Policy, 1984); William Julius Wilson and Kathryn M. Neckerman, "Poverty and Family Structure: The Widening Gap Between Evidence and Public Policy Issues," in *Fighting Poverty: What Works and What Doesn't,* ed. S. H. Danziger and Daniel H. Weinberg (Cambridge: Harvard University Press, 1986), pp. 232–259.

32. See especially Neil G. Bennett, David Bloom, and Patricia Craig, "The Divergence of Black and White Marriage Patterns," *American Journal of Sociology* 95, no. 3 (1989): 692–722.

33. Katherine S. Newman, *No Shame in My Game: The Working Poor in the Inner City* (New York: Knopf, 1999), pp. 198–203.

34. Christopher Jencks, *Rethinking Social Policy* (Cambridge: Harvard University Press, 1992); R. G. Wood, "Marriage Rates and Marriageable Men: A Test of the Wilson Hypothesis," *Journal of Human Resources* 30 (1995): 163–193.

35. George A. Akerlof, "Men Without Children," *Economic Journal,* March 1998, pp. 287–309.

36. Lee Rainwater, "The Problem of Lower-Class Culture and Poverty–War Strategy," in *On Understanding Poverty,* ed. Daniel P. Moynihan (New York: Basic, 1969), 229–259.

37. Ibid., p. 248.

38. Ibid., p. 247.

39. See Roger Waldinger, *Still the Promised City? Afro-Americans and New Immigrants in Post-Industrial New York* (Cambridge: Harvard University Press, 1996).

40. Rainwater, "Lower-Class Culture," pp. 234–235.

41. Anderson, *Streetwise,* chap. 5. See also Richard Majors and Janet Billson, *Cool Pose* (Lexington, Mass.: Heath, 1992), chaps. 2–3; Carl Nightingale, *On the Edge: A History of Poor Black Children and Their American Dreams* (New York: Basic, 1993).

CHAPTER 16

1. John Wong, "Promoting Confucianism for Socioeconomic Development: The Case of Singapore," in *Confucian Traditions in East Asian Modernity: Moral Education and Economic Culture in Japan and the Four Mini-Dragons,* ed. Tu Wei-ming (Cambridge: Harvard University Press, 1996), p. 281.

2. John Kuo Wei Chen, "Pluralism and Hierarchy: 'Whiz Kids,' 'the Chinese Question,' and Relations of Power in New York City," in *Beyond Pluralism: The Conception of Groups and Group Identities in America,* ed. Wend F. Katkin, Ned Landsman, and Andrea Tyree (Champaign: University of Illinois Press, 1998), pp. 126–129.

CHAPTER 17

1. There are by now a great many studies of the nature and causes of the Asian financial crisis of 1997–1999. See, for example, World Bank, *Global Economic Prospects 1998–99: Beyond Financial Crisis* (Washington, D.C.: World Bank, 1998), esp. chap. 2.

2. The best-known work in the 1950s was written by the sociologist Marion Levy. See Marion J. Levy and Kuo–heng Shih, *The Rise of the Modern Chinese Business Class: Two Introductory Essays* (New York: Institute of Pacific Relations, 1949).

3. An exception is the early work of G. William Skinner on the overseas Chinese community in Thailand: *Leadership and Power in the Chinese Community in Thailand,* 2 vols. (Ithaca: Cornell University Press, 1959, 1961). Volume 2 focuses on the nature of the networks linking different business interests in the Bangkok Chinese community.

4. State Statistical Bureau, *China Statistical Yearbook 1998* (Beijing: Statistics Press, 1998), pp. 639–641.

CHAPTER 18

1. Needless to say, many other factors were important in causing the Asian economic crises, including mistakes by the IMF and the U.S. Treasury, as well as the actions of Western investors. For our purposes, however, we shall address only the cultural factor.

2. The numbers are from Nayan Chanda, "Surges of Depression," *Far Eastern Economic Review,* 31 December 1998, p. 22.

3. *Economist,* 2 January 1999, p. 56.

4. Max Weber, translated and edited by Hans H. Gerth, in *The Religion of China: Confucianism and Taoism* (Glencoe: Free Press, 1951), p. 235.

5. Ibid., p. 248. Italics added. Contrary to Weber, Robert Bellah has demonstrated that the Japanese do have some cultural traditions that match the Protestant ethic. See his *Tokugawa Religion: The Values of Pre-Industrial Japan* (Glencoe, Ill.: Free Press, 1957).

6. Francis Fukuyama suggests that a key to China's slow economic development was precisely this lack of trust for non-family members, in contrast to the Japanese, who learned that they would have to deal with non-family actors. See Fukuyama, *Trust: The Social Virtues and the Creation of Prosperity* (New York: Free Press, 1995).

7. For a comparison of the influences of family patterns on East Asian developments, see Lucian W. Pye, *Asian Power and Politics: The Cultural Dimensions of Authority* (Cambridge: Harvard University Press, 1985), chap. 3.

8. The advantages and limitations of family firms are not limited to Chinese cultural practices but were also central to the successes of the Rothschild family, with the five brothers operating at the five bases in London, Paris, Frankfurt, Vienna, and Naples. See Niall Ferguson, *The World's Banker* (London: Weidenfeld & Nicolson, 1998).

9. Danny Unger, *Building Social Capital in Thailand* (New York: Cambridge University Press, 1998), esp. chap. 1.

10. For a sophisticated examination of culture and economic development, see Peter Berger and Hsian-Huang Michael Hsiao, eds., *In Search of an East Asian Model* (New Brunswick, N.J.: Transaction, 1988).

CHAPTER 19

1. See Tu Wei-ming, ed., *Confucian Traditions in East Asian Modernity: Moral Education and Economic Culture in Japan and the Four Mini-Dragons* (Cambridge: Harvard University Press, 1996).

2. Lo Rongqu, ed., *Xihua yu xiandaihua* (Westernization and modernization) (Beijing: Beijing University Press, 1985).

3. Francis Fukuyama, *The End of History and the Last Man* (New York: Free Press, 1992).

4. Samuel Huntington, *The Clash of Civilizations and the Remaking of World Order* (New York: Simon & Schuster, 1996).

5. For a recent discussion on this issue, see William T. de Bary, *Asian Values and Human Rights: A Confucian Communitarian Perspective* (Cambridge: Harvard University Press, 1998).

CHAPTER 20

The author wishes to acknowledge the support of Abraham Sofaer and Joel Hyatt of the Hoover Institution at Stanford University. Special thanks to Jonathan Donner, Jeffrey Wetzler, Josh Ruxin, David Rabkin, Ethan Berg, and Assen Vassilev for substantive comments. The title of this chapter is also the title of a forthcoming book co-authored with Kaia Miller and Joseph Babiec.

1. Debraj Ray, *Development Economics* (Princeton: Princeton University Press, 1998), p. 9.

2. Ibid., p. 12.

3. Amartya Sen discusses the difference between a stock and flow in "The Concept of Wealth," in *The Wealth of Nations in the Twentieth Century: The Policies and Institutional Determinants of Economic Development*, ed. Ramon Myers (Stanford: Hoover Institution Press, 1996).

4. For the best practical example of this view of prosperity, look at James Wolfensohn's internal but now widely accessible memorandum on the Comprehensive Development Framework (CDF), spring 1999. The president of the World Bank has begun to implement a "holistic" approach to development around the concept of a "social balance sheet."

5. Sen, "Concept of Wealth," p. 7.

6. Thomas Sowell, *Conquests and Cultures* (New York: Basic, 1998), p. 329.

7. Alex Inkeles, *One World Emerging* (Boulder: Westview, 1998), p. 316.

8. Ronald Inglehart, *Modernization and Postmodernization: Cultural, Economic, and Political Change in Forty-Three Societies* (Princeton: Princeton University Press, 1997), chap. 1.

9. Michael Fairbanks and Stace Lindsay, *Plowing the Sea—Nurturing the Hidden Sources of Growth in the Developing World* (Boston: Harvard Business School Press, 1997).

10. We adapted this concept from the domain of cognitive psychology, first coined in 1948 by Kenneth Craik, to enrich our set of economic development tools. See also Chris Argyris, *Reasoning, Learning, and Action: Individual and Organizational* (San Francisco: Jossey-Bass, 1982); and Peter Senge, *The Fifth Discipline* (New York: Doubleday Currency, 1990), chap. 10, "Mental Models."

11. Symposium participants Mariano Grondona and Lawrence Harrison have developed this rich concept of pro- and anti-innovation value systems.

12. Douglass North, "Institutional and Economic Change," Distinguished Lecture Series 12, The Egyptian Center for Economic Studies, February 1998.

13. Clifford Geertz, *The Interpretation of Cultures* (New York: Basic, 1973), p. 89.

14. Edward O. Wilson, "From Genes to Culture," *Consilience* (New York: Knopf, 1998), chap. 7.

15. Inkeles, *One World Emerging*, p. 24; italics added.

16. Joseph Stiglitz, "Toward a New Paradigm for Development: Strategies, Policies, and Processes" (The Prebisch Lecture at UNCTAD, Geneva, 18 October 1998).

17. Paul Krugman, "Does Third World Growth Hurt First World Prosperity?" *Harvard Business Review*, June-August 1994, pp. 113–121.

18. Lawrence Harrison, *The Pan-American Dream* (New York: Basic, 1997), p. 261.

19. Inkeles, *One World Emerging,* p. 83.

20. This schema for change was inspired by the work primarily of Roger Martin, a director of Monitor Company and dean of the School of Business at the University of Toronto, and by John Kotter at the Harvard Business School. The schema has been practiced, shaped, and improved by Monitor Country competitiveness advisers Joe Babiec in Bermuda, Jim Vesterman in Colombia, Kaia Miller in El Salvador, Jeff Glueck in Venezuela, Ethan Berg in the Republic of Tatarstan, Randall Kempner in Peru, Matt Eyring in Bolivia, and Josh Ruxin in Uganda.

21. This conclusion is shared by Jeffrey Sachs and Andrew Warner. See their "Natural Resource Abundance and Economic Growth," National Bureau of Economic Research, Cambridge, Working Paper 5398, December 1995.

22. See Paul Krugman, "Does Third World Growth Hurt First World Prosperity?" *Harvard Business Review*, June-August 1994, pp. 113–121.

23. The founder and leader in this field is Chris Argyris, professor emeritus at Harvard and director of the Monitor Company. His flagship book on this subject is *Overcoming Organizational Defenses* (New York: Prentice-Hall, 1990).

24. Douglass North, *Structure and Change in Economic History* (New York: Norton, 1981), p. 201.

25. The debate on cultural relativism is outside the scope of this chapter but will be developed in detail in our book-length format. For now, look at both sides of the argument in Daniel Boorstin, *The Seekers* (New York: Random House, 1998), p. 195, and symposium participant Richard Shweder's chapter in this volume, "Moral Maps, 'First World' Conceits, and the New Evangelists."

26. The phrase "prosperity is a choice" is language shared with me by Michael Porter.

27. Howard Gardner, *Leading Minds: An Anatomy of Leadership* (New York: Basic, 1995), p. 293

CHAPTER 21

1. Peter Senge, *The Fifth Discipline* (New York: Doubleday, 1990), p. 8.

2. See Jeffrey Sachs and Andrew Warner, "Natural Resource Abundance and Economic Growth," National Bureau of Economic Research, Cambridge, Mass., Working Paper 5398, December 1995; see also Michael Fairbanks and Stace Lindsay, *Plowing the Sea: Nurturing the Hidden Sources of Growth in the Developing World* (Boston: Harvard Business School Press, 1997), chap. 1.

3. Michael Porter, "The Microeconomic Foundations of Competitiveness," in the *World Competitiveness Report* (Geneva: World Economic Forum, 1999).

4. Senge, *Fifth Discipline*, p. 174.

5. Special thanks to Jonathan Donner, who both designed the surveys and performed the analysis to generate this data. A more detailed discussion can be found in his forthcoming article, "Making Mental Models Explicit: Quantitative Techniques for Encouraging Change."

CHAPTER 22

1. Carlos Rangel, *The Latin Americans—Their Love–Hate Relationship with the United States* (New York: Harcourt Brace Jovanovich, 1977). The French edition was published in 1976 by Éditions Robert Laffont, S.A., Paris.

2. Octavio Paz, *El Ogro Filantrópico* (Mexico City: Joaquín Mortiz, 1979), p. 55.

3. Claudio Véliz, *The New World of the Gothic Fox—Culture and Economy in English and Spanish America* (Berkeley: University of California Press, 1994).

4. Ibid., pp. 190–191.

5. Plinio Apuleyo Mendoza, Carlos Alberto Montaner, and Álvaro Vargas Llosa, *Manual del Perfecto Idiota Latinoamericano* (Barcelona: Plaza y Janés Editores, 1996). Madison Books is planning to publish the English edition in 2000.

6. Eduardo Galeano, *Las Venas Abiertas de América Latina* (Mexico City: Siglo XXI Editores, 1979). This is the twenty-sixth edition. The first edition was published in 1971.

7. Plinio Apuleyo Mendoza, Carlos Alberto Montaner, and Álvaro Vargas Llosa, *Fabrixcantes de Miseria* (Barcelona: Plaza y Janés Editores, 1998).

8. Carlos Alberto Montaner, *No Perdamos También el Siglo XXI* (Barcelona: Plaza y Janés Editores, 1997).

9. Mariano Grondona, *Las Condiciones Culturales del Desarrollo Económico* (Buenos Aires: Editorial Planeta/Ariel, 1999).

10. For an analysis of the Protestantization phenomenon, see David Martin, *Tongues of Fire* (London: Basil Blackwell, 1990).

11. Lawrence E. Harrison, *Underdevelopment Is a State of Mind—The Latin American Case* (Cambridge: Center for International Affairs, Harvard University; Lanham, Md.: University Press of America, 1985).

12. Lawrence E. Harrison, *The Pan-American Dream* (New York: Basic, 1997).

13. Robert D. Putnam, *Making Democracy Work—Civic Traditions in Modern Italy* (Princeton: Princeton University Press, 1993).

14. Alexis de Tocqueville, *Democracy in America* (1966; reprint, New York: Doubleday Anchor, 1969), pp. 308–309.

15. Gunnar Myrdal, *Asian Drama—An Inquiry into the Poverty of Nations* (New York: Pantheon, 1968).

16. Ibid., p. 104.

17. Ibid., pp. 27–28.

18. World Bank, *World Development Report 1998/99: Knowledge for Development* (New York: Oxford University Press, 1999).

19. See, for example, Bernard Lewis, "The West and the Middle East," *Foreign Affairs* 76 (January-February 1997).

20. Ibid., p. 45.

21. Edward C. Banfield, *The Moral Basis of a Backward Society* (Glencoe, Ill.: Free Press, 1958).

22. Hernando de Soto, *El Otro Sendero* (Lima: Instituto Libertad y Democracia, 1986).

23. Michael Fairbanks and Stace Lindsay, *Plowing the Sea—Nurturing the Hidden Sources of Growth in the Developing World* (Cambridge: Harvard Business School Press, 1997).

24. Lionel Sosa, *The Americano Dream—How Latinos Can Achieve Success in Business and Life* (New York: Penguin, 1998).

25. Ibid., p. 2.

26. Ibid.

27. Ibid., p. 7.

28. Ibid., title of chap. 4, pp. 47–68.

BIOGRAPHICAL
SKETCHES
OF CONTRIBUTORS

Barbara Crossette is U.N. Bureau Chief for the *New York Times*. Formerly a correspondent in Southeast Asia and South Asia, she is the author of *India Facing the Twenty-First Century*; *So Close to Heaven: The Vanishing Buddhist Kingdoms of the Himalayas*; and *The Great Hill Stations of Asia*.

Robert Edgerton is professor of anthropology in the Departments of Anthropology and Psychiatry and Biobehavioral Sciences at the University of California in Los Angeles. Although his writings range across topics as diverse as mental retardation, social order, deviant behavior, and warfare, the central theme in all his work is social adaptation with a focus on the role of culture. Among his recent books is *Sick Societies*, which views human maladaptation in a cross-cultural setting.

Daniel Etounga-Manguelle, a Cameroonian, is the president and founder of the Société Africaine d'Etude, d'Exploitation et de Gestion (SADEG), which is currently involved in more than fifty development projects in west, central, and southern Africa. A former member of the World Bank's Council of African Advisors, he is the author of *L'Afrique—A-t-elle Besoin d'un Programme d'Ajustement Culturel?*

Michael Fairbanks is the leader of the Monitor Company's Country Competitiveness Practice. Over the past decade, he has advised government and private sector leaders in Africa, the Middle East, and Latin America. Co-author, with Stace Lindsay, of *Plowing the Sea: Nurturing the Hidden Sources of Growth in the Developing World*, he is a visiting scholar at the Hoover Institution at Stanford and is a member of the World Bank's Committee on Social Development.

Francis Fukuyama is Omer L. and Nancy Hirst Professor of Public Policy at the Institute of Public Policy at George Mason University and consultant to the RAND Corporation. He is the author of the prize-winning *The End of History and the Last Man*; *Trust: The Social Virtues and the Creation of Prosperity*; and *The Great Disruption: Human Nature and the Reconstitution of Social Order*. He served as deputy director of the State Department's Policy Planning Staff in 1989.

Nathan Glazer is Professor of Education and Sociology Emeritus at Harvard University and co-editor of *The Public Interest*. He has authored, among other books, *Beyond the Melting Pot* (with Daniel P. Moynihan); *Affirmative Discrimination*; *Ethnic Dilemmas*; *The Limits of Social Policy*; and most recently, *We Are All Multiculturalists Now*.

Mariano Grondona is the host of the weekly television public affairs program *Hora Clave* in Argentina. He writes a column for the Buenos Aires newspaper *La Nación* and is a professor of government at the Law Faculty of the National University of Buenos Aires. He is the author of twelve books, including the recently published *Las Condiciones Culturales del Desarrollo Económico*.

Lawrence E. Harrison directed USAID missions in five Latin American countries between 1965 and 1981. He is the author of *Underdevelopment Is a State of Mind*; *Who Prospers?* and *The Pan-American Dream*. He is currently a senior fellow at the Harvard Academy for International and Area Studies.

Mala N. Htun is assistant professor of political science at the New School University in New York. She has conducted research on state policy regarding gender issues, women's rights, and political participation in Brazil and the Southern Cone, Mexico, Peru, and Central America.

Samuel P. Huntington is Albert J. Weatherhead III University Professor as well as director of the John M. Olin Institute for Strategic Studies and chairman of the Academy for International and Area Studies at Harvard University, where he was also director of the Center for International Affairs for eleven years. He is the author of numerous books, most recently *The Clash of Civilizations and the Remaking of World Order*. During 1977–1978 he served in the Carter White House as coordinator of security planning for the National Security Council.

Ronald Inglehart is professor of political science and program director at the Institute for Social Research at the University of Michigan. He helped found the Euro-Barometer surveys and is chair of the steering committee of the World Values Survey. His most recent books are *Modernization and Postmodernization: Cultural, Economic and Political Change in Forty-Three Societies*; and, with Miguel Basáñez and Alejandro Moreno, *Human Values and Beliefs: A Cross-Cultural Sourcebook*.

David S. Landes, economic historian, is Coolidge Professor of History and Professor of Economics, Emeritus, at Harvard University. He is the author of *Bankers and*

Pashas: International Finance and Imperialism in Egypt; *The Unbound Prometheus: Technological Change, 1750 to the Present*; *Revolution in Time: Clocks and the Making of the Modern World*; and *The Wealth and Poverty of Nations: Why Some Are So Rich and Some So Poor*. He is currently working on the role and history of families in business enterprise.

Gabriel Salman Lenz is a recent graduate of Reed College in political science and is currently a researcher for Seymour Martin Lipset at George Mason University and the Woodrow Wilson International Center for Scholars.

Stace Lindsay is a founder of Monitor Company's Country Competitiveness Practice in Latin America. He is co-author with Michael Fairbanks of *Plowing the Sea: Nurturing the Hidden Sources of Growth in the Developing World* and is an adjunct professor at the Georgetown University School of Business. He is currently advising TechnoServe, a non-profit organization that works with the rural poor in Africa and Latin America, and Atlantic BioPharmaceuticals, a Cambridge-based biotechnology company.

Seymour Martin Lipset is the Hazel Professor of Public Policy at George Mason University. Previously he served as the Caroline Munro Professor of Political Science and Sociology at Stanford and as the George Markham Professor of Governmental Sociology at Harvard. He is the author of many books, including most recently *Continental Divide*; *Jews and the American Scene*; *American Exceptionalism*; and *It Didn't Happen Here: The Failure of Socialism in the United States* (forthcoming). He is a past president of the American Political Science Association and the American Sociological Association.

Carlos Alberto Montaner is the most widely read columnist in the Spanish language. Among his recent books are the best-selling *Manual del Perfecto Idiota Latinoamericano*; *Fabricantes de Miseria* (both co-authored with Plinio Apuleyo Mendoza and Álvaro Vargas Llosa); and *No Perdamos También el Siglo Veintiuno*.

Orlando Patterson, John Cowles Professor of Sociology at Harvard University, is the author of eight books, including *Freedom in the Making of Western Culture*, which won a National Book Award in 1991; *The Ordeal of Integration: Progress and Resentment in America's "Racial" Crisis*; and, most recently, *Rituals of Blood: Consequences of Slavery in Two American Centuries*. In the 1970s, he served as special adviser to Jamaican prime minister Michael Manley.

Dwight H. Perkins is the Harold Hitchings Burbank Professor of Political Economy at Harvard University. He directed the Harvard Institute for International Development from 1980 to 1995. He has authored or edited twelve books on economic history and economic development, with particular emphasis on China, Korea, Vietnam, and other nations of East and Southeast Asia.

Michael Porter is the C. Roland Christensen Professor of Business Administration at Harvard University. He is a strategic adviser to the governments of many countries, including the United States, and to major corporations. He created the Competition and Strategy Group at the Harvard Business School and is the author or editor of numerous books, including *Competitive Strategy*; *The Competitive Advantage of Nations;* and, most recently, *On Competition.*

Lucian W. Pye is Ford Professor of Political Science Emeritus at the Massachusetts Institute of Technology and a specialist in comparative politics and the political cultures and psychology of Asia. A former president of the American Political Science Association, he has edited or authored twenty-seven books, most recently *Asian Power and Politics* and *The Spirit of Chinese Politics.*

Jeffrey Sachs, Galen L. Stone Professor of International Trade at Harvard University, is the director of the Center for International Development. He serves as an economic adviser to governments in Latin America, Eastern Europe, the former Soviet Union, Africa, and Asia, and he has been instrumental in their adoption of open economic policies. His articles have appeared in several of the most widely read newspapers and journals.

Richard A. Shweder, a cultural anthropologist, is professor of human development at the University of Chicago. He is the author or editor of several books, including *Thinking Through Cultures: Expeditions in Cultural Psychology*; *Culture Theory: Essays on Mind, Self and Emotion* (with Robert A. LeVine); and *Welcome to Middle Age! (and Other Cultural Fictions).* He is a past president of the Society for Psychological Anthropology and is currently co-chair of the Social Science Research Council/Russell Sage Foundation Working Group on Ethnic Customs, Assimilation, and American Law.

Tu Wei-ming is professor of Chinese history and philosophy at Harvard University and director of the Harvard-Yenching Institute. He has also taught at Princeton and the University of California. He is the author of *Neo-Confucian Thought: Wang Yang-Ming's Youth, Centrality and Commonality, Humanity and Self-Cultivation*; *Confucian Thought: Selfhood As Creative Transformation*; and *Way, Learning, and Politics: Essays on the Confucian Intellectual.*

Thomas Weisner is professor of anthropology at UCLA. His work has focused on culture and human development, and he has done fieldwork in Kenya, in Hawaii, with countercultural families in California, and with families of children who have developmental disabilities. Recent publications include *African Families and the Crisis of Social Change* and chapters in *Ethnography and Human Development* and *Welcome to Middle Age!*

INDEX